JOURNAL FOR THE STUDY OF THE NEW TESTAMENT
SUPPLEMENT SERIES
214

Executive Editor
Stanley E. Porter

Sheffield Academic Press

Jesus, Mark and Q

The Teaching of Jesus and its Earliest Records

edited by
**Michael Labahn &
Andreas Schmidt**

Journal for the Study of the New Testament
Supplement Series 214

Copyright © 2001 Sheffield Academic Press

Published by Sheffield Academic Press Ltd
Mansion House
19 Kingfield Road
Sheffield S11 9AS
England
www.SheffieldAcademicPress.com

Typeset by Sheffield Academic Press
and
Printed on acid-free paper in Great Britain
MPG Books Ltd
Bodmin, Cornwall

British Library Cataloguing-in-Publication Data

A catalogue record for this book is available
from the British Library

ISBN 1-84127-218-3

CONTENTS

Part I
MARK AND Q

Part II
THE HISTORICAL JESUS IN NEW RESEARCH

A. RECENT TRENDS IN THE HISTORICAL AND SOCIOLOGICAL
PORTRAIT OF JESUS

PREFACE

The essays in this volume represent papers that were given at two colloquiums of the European Association for Biblical Studies. This volume assembles the papers of the first two New Testament Seminars of the European Association for Biblical Studies held during the International Meeting of the Society of Biblical Literature in Cracow in 1998 and in Helsinki/Lahti in 1999.

We are grateful to the local organizers and to the organizing board of the SBL for the splendid organization of the meetings as a whole and of our seminars within that framework. We thank the participants in our seminars who not only delivered and reworked their papers but also took part in the lively exchanges throughout the day and in the final panel discussion.

All those whose papers are printed here are grateful to Professor Stanley Porter for agreeing to publish them in the *JSNT* Supplement Series and for his helpful recommendations, to Professor Philip R. Davies for his encouragement and to the staff at Sheffield Academic Press, especially to Georgia Litherland, for their help in the production process.

Michael Labahn
Andreas Schmidt

ABBREVIATIONS

AASF	Annales Academie Scientiarum Fennicae
AB	Anchor Bible
ABRL	Anchor Bible Reference Library
ABD	David Noel Freedman (ed.), *The Anchor Bible Dictionary* (New York: Doubleday, 1992)
AELKZ	*Allgemeine evangelisch-lutherische Kirchenzeitung*
AGJU	Arbeiten zur Geschichte des antiken Judentums und des Urchristentums
AnglThr	*Anglican Theological Review*
ANRW	Hildegard Temporini and Wolfgang Haase (eds.), *Aufstieg und Niedergang der römischen Welt: Geschichte und Kultur Roms im Spiegel der neueren Forschung* (Berlin: W. de Gruyter, 1972–)
BBB	Bonner Biblische Beiträge
BBR	*Bulletin for Biblical Research*
BETL	Bibliotheca ephemeridum theologicarum lovaniensium
BEvT	Beiträge zur evangelischen Theologie
Bib	*Biblica*
BibInt	*Biblical Interpretation: A Journal of Contemporary Approaches*
BibS	Biblische Studien
BibSem	The Biblical Seminar
BIS	Biblical Interpretation Series
BJS	Brown Judaic Studies
BThSt	Biblisch-theologische Studien
BWANT	Beiträge zur Wissenschaft vom Alten und Neuen Testament
BZ	*Biblische Zeitschrift*
BZNW	Beihefte zur *ZNW*
CBQ	*Catholic Biblical Quarterly*
CIS	*Corpus inscriptionum semiticarum*
CRINT	Compendia rerum iudaicarum ad Novum Testamentum
DBI	*A Dictionary of Biblical Interpretation*
DeltBN	*Deltio biblikon meleton: Hexameniaia ekdosis ereunes Palaias kai Kaines Diathekas (Bulletin of Biblical Studies)*
DJG	J.B. Green and S. McKnight (eds.), *Dictionary of Jesus and the Gospels* (Downers Grove, IL: InterVarsity Press, 1992)

DSD	*Dead Sea Discoveries*
EHS	Europäische Hochschulschriften
EKKNT	Evangelisch-Katholischer Kommentar zum Neuen Testament
EncJud	*Encyclopaedia Judaica*
ETL	*Ephemerides theologicae lovanienses*
EuA	*Erbe und Auftrag*
EvT	*Evangelische Theologie*
ExpTim	*Expository Times*
FIOTL	Formation and Interpretation of Old Testament Literature
FRLANT	Forschungen zur Religion und Literatur des Alten und Neuen Testaments
FzB	Forschungen zur Bibel
GCS	Griechische christliche Schriftsteller
GLB	de Gruyter Lehrbücher
GNS	Good News Studies
GNT	Grundrisse zum Neuen Testament
HBS	Herders Biblische Studien
HCS	Hellenistic Culture and Society
HNT	Handbuch zum Neuen Testament
HSS	Harvard Semitic Studies
HTKNT	Herders theologischer Kommentar zum Neuen Testament
HTR	*Harvard Theological Review*
HTS	*Hervormde theologiese studies*
JBL	*Journal of Biblical Literature*
JBT	Jahrbuch für Biblische Theologie
JEH	*Journal of Ecclesiastical History*
JJS	*Journal of Jewish Studies*
JR	*Journal of Religion*
JSJ	*Journal for the Study of Judaism in the Persian, Hellenistic and Roman Period*
JSJS	Supplements to the *Journal of the Study of Judaism*
JSNT	*Journal for the Study of the New Testament*
JSNTSup	*Journal for the Study of the New Testament*, Supplement Series
JSOTSup	*Journal for the Study of the Old Testament*, Supplement Series
JSP	*Journal for the Study of the Pseudepigrapha*
JSPSup	*Journal for the Study of the Pseudepigrapha*, Supplement Series
JTh	*Journal of Theology*
JTS	*Journal of Theological Studies*
LD	Lectio divina
MTS	Marburger Theologische Studien
Neot	*Neotestamentica*
NorTT	*Norsk teologisk Tidsskrift*
NovT	*Novum Testamentum*

NovTSup	*Novum Testamentum*, Supplements
NTAbh	Neutestamentliche Abhandlungen
NTOA	Novum Testamentum et orbis antiquus
NTS	*New Testament Studies*
NTTS	New Testament Tools and Studies
OBT	Overtures to Biblical Theology
ÖTK	Ökumenischer Taschenbuch-Kommentar zum Neuen Testament
PAM	Palestine Archaeological Museum
PRE	*Pauly Real-Enzyclopädie der classischen Altertumswissenschaft*
QD	Quaestiones Disputatae
RevQ	*Revue de Qumran*
RGG	*Religion in Geschichte und Gegenwart*
RHPR	*Revue d'histoire et de philosophie religieuses*
RILP	Roehampton Institute London Papers
RM	Die Religionen der Menschheit
RNT	Regensburger Neues Testament
SBA	Stuttgarter biblische Aufsatzbände
SBB	Stuttgarter biblische Beiträge
SBEC	Studies in the Bible and Early Christianity
SBLSBS	Society of Biblical Literature Sources for Biblical Study
SBLSP	Society of Biblical Literature Seminar Papers
SBS	Stuttgarter Bibelstudien
SBT	Studies in Biblical Theology
SEAJT	*South East Asia Journal of Theology*
SJT	*Scottish Journal of Theology*
SNTSMS	Society for New Testament Studies Monograph Series
SNTU	Studien zum Neuen Testament und seiner Umwelt
SNTU.B	Studien zum Neuen Testament und seiner Umwelt B
ST	*Studia theologica*
STK	*Svensk teologisk kvartalskrift*
TANZ	Texte und Arbeiten zum neutestamentlichen Zeitalter
TBü	Theologische Bücherei
TDNT	Gerhard Kittel and Gerhard Friedrich (eds.), *Theological Dictionary of the New Testament* (trans. Geoffrey W. Bromiley; 10 vols.; Grand Rapids: Eerdmans, 1964–)
TQ	*Theologische Quartalschrift*
TRE	*Theologische Realenzyklopädie*
TRu	*Theologische Rundschau*
TSAJ	Texte und Studien zum Antiken Judentum
TTod	*Theology Today*
TTZ	*Trierer theologische Zeitschrift*
TZ	*Theologische Zeitschrift*
UTB	Uni-Taschenbücher

VTSup	*Vetus Testamentum*, Supplements
WMANT	Wissenschaftliche Monographien zum Alten und Neuen Testament
WuD	*Wort und Dienst*
WUNT	Wissenschaftliche Untersuchungen zum Neuen Testament
ZDMG	*Zeitschrift der deutschen morgenländischen Gesellschaft*
ZNW	*Zeitschrift für die neutestamentliche Wissenschaft*
ZPT	*Zeitschrift für Pädagogik und Theologie: Der Evangelische Erzieher*
ZTK	*Zeitschrift für Theologie und Kirche*

LIST OF CONTRIBUTORS

Peter Balla is Lecturer and Head of the New Testament Department of the Faculty of Theology of the Károli Gáspár Reformed University, Budapest, Hungary

F. Gerald Downing is Honorary Research Fellow, Department of Religions and Theology, University of Manchester

Craig A. Evans is Professor of Religious Studies, Trinity Western University, Langley, British Columbia, Canada

Harry T. Fleddermann is Associate Professor, Department of Religious Studies, Alverno College, Milwaukee, Wisconsin

Tom Holmén is Research Fellow of the Academy of Finland, Åbo Academy University, Department of Exegetics, Turku, Finland

Michael Labahn is a Research Assistant at Martin Luther University Halle-Wittenberg, Halle, Germany

Markus Öhler is Assistant in the Protestant Faculty, University of Vienna, Austria

Marius Reiser is Professor of New Testament, Fachbereich Katholische Theologie Johannes Gutenberg University, Mainz, Germany

Andreas Schmidt is Pastor in Dissen am Teuteburger Wald, Germany

Jens Schröter is Professor for New Testament, University of Hamburg, Hamburg, Germany

Elisabeth Schüssler Fiorenza is Krister Srendahl Professor of Scripture and Interpretation at Harvard University Divinity School, Cambridge, Massachusetts

David S. du Toit is Lecturer for New Testament Studies, Kirchliche Hochschule Bethel, Bielefeld, Germany

Part I

MARK AND Q

INTRODUCTION

Andreas Schmidt

The question of whether or not there is a direct relationship between the Gospel of Mark and 'Q', the Sayings Source, is still wide open. The thesis that Mark depended on Q, presented in different forms by, for example, David R. Catchpole,[1] Harry T. Fleddermann,[2] Jan Lambrecht,[3] Burton L. Mack[4] and Walter Schmithals,[5] has been questioned in various ways. Joachim Schüling considers that direct dependence is unlikely,[6] as does Jens Schröter in his comparitive study of Mark, Q and the *Gospel of Thomas*. These scholars concede that Mark and Q share common traditions, but they explicitly deny that there is any direct literary dependence.[7] Last, but not least, Frans Neirynck, in an

---

1. D.R. Catchpole, 'The Beginning of Q: A Proposal', *NTS* 38 (1992), pp. 205-221 (reprinted slightly revised in *idem, The Quest for Q* [Edinburgh: T. & T. Clark, 1993], pp. 60-78).

2. H.T. Fleddermann, *Mark and Q: A Study of the Overlap Texts* (BETL, 122; Leuven: Peeters, 1995).

3. Cf., e.g., J. Lambrecht, 'John the Baptist and Jesus in Mark 1.1-15: A Marcan Redaction of Q?', *NTS* 38 (1992), pp. 357-84; *idem*, 'The Great Commandment Pericope and Q', in R.A. Piper (ed.), *The Gospels behind the Gospels: Current Studies on Q* (NTTS, 75; Leiden: E.J. Brill, 1995), pp. 73-96.

4. B.L. Mack, 'Q and the Gospel of Mark: Revising Christian Origins', *Semeia* 55 (1992), pp. 15-39.

5. W. Schmithals, *Das Evangelium nach Markus* (ÖTK, 2; Gütersloh: Gerd Mohn; Würzburg: Echter Verlag, 1979); *idem, Einleitung in die drei ersten Evangelien* (GLB; Berlin: W. de Gruyter, 1985), pp. 403, 427-28.

6. J. Schüling, *Studien zum Verhältnis von Logienquelle und Markusevangelium* (FzB, 65; Würzburg: Echter Verlag, 1991), p. 215; cf. also the thorough discussion of Mk 1.1-6 and its possible relation to Q by I. Dunderberg, 'Q and the Beginning of Mark', *NTS* 41 (1995), pp. 501-511.

7. J. Schröter, *Die Erinnerung an Jesu Worte: Studien zur Rezeption der Logienüberlieferung in Markus, Q und Thomas* (WMANT, 76; Neukirchen–Vluyn: Neukirchener Verlag, 1997), pp. 1-2 n. 1, 466-67.

intensive analysis of the different possible approaches to the Synoptic problem, pleads for a simple form of the two-source hypothesis. He draws attention to a growing consensus of scholars who deny the assumed literary connection between Mark and Q. Nevertheless, in his own contribution to the commemorative volumes for Martin Hengel of 1996, in his discussion of the Baptist pericope of the same year, and in his appendix to the great monograph by Fleddermann, *Mark and Q*, in 1995, he indicates that there is still a need for further discussion.[8] We have good reason to approach the problem again. What is the state of the question? Is there any hope of some new developments?

The question of the relation between Mark and Q is unavoidable and the debate is becoming increasingly acrimonious. At the suggestion of the European Association for Biblical Studies we invited Harry T. Fleddermann and Jens Schröter to the First European New Testament Seminar, as they represent different methical approaches to the question and come to different conclusions.

Fleddermann sees a literary development, which he illustrates by Mark's use of Q in the Beelzebul controversy and the Cross saying. His comparative analysis of the texts leads him to conclude that both texts 'support the view that Mark knew and used "Q"'.

Schröter takes another path, as is obvious from the title of his essay: 'The Son of Man as the Representative of God's Kingdom: On the interpretation of Jesus in Mark and Q'. Schröter elects to approach the subject by analysing the christological development in each of the documents. After a discussion of methodology, he first draws attention to aspects of Jesus' activity and then concentrates on the Christology in Mark and Q with particular reference to Jesus as the Son of Man. He draws five conclusions. The result is that

> Q creates a Christology which is orientated mainly to the activity of the earthly Jesus and is further developed by means of the expectation of the coming Son of Man, whereas Mark integrates the Christ and Son of God title into his Son of Man concept ... The consequence of what has been

---

8.　F. Neirynck, 'The Sayings Source Q and the Gospel of Mark', in H. Cancik, H. Lichtenberger and P. Schäfer (eds.), *Geschichte–Tradition–Reflexion: Festschrift für M. Hengel zum 70. Geburtstag*. III. *Frühes Christentum* (3 vols.; Tübingen: Mohr Siebeck, 1996), pp. 125-45; *idem*, 'The First Synoptic Pericope: The Appearance of John the Baptist in Q?' *ETL* 72 (1996), pp. 40-70; *idem*, 'Assessment', in H.T. Fleddermann, *Mark and Q: A Study of the Overlap Texts* (BETL, 122; Leuven: Peeters, 1995), pp. 261-307.

presented here for the history of theology could be that the combination of the proclamation of the Kingdom with the Son of Man concept presents an independent model of early Christian thinking about Jesus, that was linked to the Antiochene model of the pre-Pauline tradition by Mark.

Harry T. Fleddermann

Mark's Use of Q: The Beelzebul Controversy and the Cross Saying

Ever since the pioneering work of Weisse the doublets, repetitions of the same material in one Gospel, have furnished one of the classic arguments for the existence of Q, for they indicate that Matthew and Luke were working with two main sources when composing their Gospels.[1] The doublets, though, also raise the issue of the relationship of Mark and Q to each other because they show that the two sources overlap. The current debate about how Mark and Q relate centers on whether or not Mark had direct access to Q. Most scholars claim that Mark and Q independently of one another drew common material from the oral tradition. Some scholars, though, maintain that Mark knew and used Q.[2]

---

1. C.H. Weisse, *Die evangelische Geschichte kritisch und philosophisch bearbeitet* (2 vols.; Leipzig: Breitkopf & Härtel, 1838), I, pp. 79-83. For the early development of the argument from the doublets, see now G. Van Oyen, 'The Doublets in 19th-Century Gospel Study', *ETL* 73 (1997), pp. 277-306.

2. For overviews of the discussion see M. Devisch, 'La relation entre l'évangile de Marc et le document Q', in M. Sabbe (ed.), *L'évangile selon Marc: Tradition et rédaction* (BETL, 34; Leuven: Leuven University Press, 2nd edn, 1988 [1974]), pp. 59-91; P. Vassiliadis, 'Prolegomena to a Discussion on the Relationship between Mark and the Q-Document', *DeltBM* 3 (1975), pp. 31-46; R. Laufen, *Die Doppelüberlieferungen der Logienquelle und des Markusevangeliums* (BBB, 54; Bonn: Hanstein, 1980), pp. 59-92; F. Neirynck, 'Recent Developments in the Study of Q', in J. Delobel (ed.), *Logia: Les paroles de Jésus—The Sayings of Jesus: Mémorial Joseph Coppens* (BETL, 59; Leuven: Leuven University Press, 1982), pp. 29-75; repr. in F. Neirynck, *Evangelica II: 1982–1991. Collected Essays* (BETL, 99; Leuven: Leuven University Press, 1991), pp. 409-464, esp. pp. 421-33, 464; F. Neirynck, 'Literary Criticism, Old and New', in C. Focant (ed.), *The Synoptic Gospels: Source Criticism and the New Literary Criticism* (BETL, 110; Leuven: Leuven University Press, 1993), pp. 13-38, esp. pp. 30-33; J. Schüling, *Studien zum Verhältnis von Logienquelle und Markusevangelium* (FzB, 65; Würzburg: Echter Verlag, 1991), pp. 167-87; C.M. Tuckett, 'Mark and Q', in C. Focant (ed.), *The Synoptic*

This is the position that I argued in my book *Mark and Q*.[3] In this essay I will revisit the argument of the book by concentrating on two texts: the Beelzebul controversy and the Cross saying.

1. *The Beelzebul Controversy*

I begin by comparing the reconstructed Q text of the Beelzebul contro-versy with Mark. Mark concludes his version with the unforgivable sin logion that appears later in Q, so I have included the unforgivable sin in this discussion.

Q 11.14-15, 17-26; 12.10	Mk 3.22-30
14 Καὶ ἐξέβαλεν δαιμόνιον κωφόν· καὶ ἐκβληθέντος τοῦ δαιμονίου ἐλάλησεν ὁ κωφὸς καὶ ἐθαύμασαν οἱ ὄχλοι.	
15 τινὲς δὲ εἶπον,	22 καὶ οἱ γραμματεῖς οἱ ἀπὸ Ἱεροσολύμων καταβάντες ἔλεγον ὅτι
ἐν Βεελζεβοὺλ τῷ ἄρχοντι τῶν δαιμονίων ἐκβάλλει τὰ δαιμόνια·	Βεελζεβοὺλ ἔχει καὶ ὅτι ἐν τῷ ἄρχοντι τῶν δαιμονίων ἐκβάλλει τὰ δαιμόνια.
17 εἰδὼς δὲ τὰ διανοήματα αὐτῶν	23 καὶ προσκαλεσάμενος αὐτοὺς ἐν παραβολαῖς
εἶπεν αὐτοῖς·	ἔλεγεν αὐτοῖς, Πῶς δύναται σατανᾶς αατανᾶν ἐκβάλλειν;
πᾶσα βασιλεία μερισθεῖσα ἐφ᾽ ἑαυτὴν ἐρημοῦται	24 καὶ ἐὰν βασιλεία ἐφ᾽ ἑαυτὴν μερισθῇ, οὐ δύναται σταθῆναι ἡ βασιλεία ἐκείνη·
καὶ οἶκος ἐπὶ οἶκον πίπτει.	25 καὶ ἐὰν οἰκία ἐφ᾽ ἑαυτὴν μερισθῇ, οὐ δυνήσεται ἡ οἰκία ἐκείνη σταθῆναι.

Gospels: Source Criticism and the New Literary Criticism (BETL, 110; Leuven: Leuven University Press, 1993), pp. 149-75; H.T. Fleddermann, *Mark and Q: A Study of the Overlap Texts* (BETL, 122; Leuven: Leuven University Press, 1995), pp. 8-16.

    3.   Fleddermann, *Mark and Q*, pp. 209-214.

Q 11.14-15, 17-26; 12.10	Mk 3.22-30
18 καὶ εἰ ὁ σατανᾶς ἐφ᾽ ἑαυτὸν ἐμερίσθη, πῶς σταθήσεται ἡ βασιλεία αὐτοῦ;	26 καὶ εἰ ὁ σατανᾶς ἀνέστη ἐφ᾽ ἑαυτὸν καὶ ἐμερίσθη, οὐ δύναται στῆναι ἀλλὰ τέλος ἔχει.
19 καὶ εἰ ἐγὼ ἐν Βεελζεβοὺλ ἐκβάλλω τὰ δαιμόνια, οἱ υἱοὶ ὑμῶν ἐν τίνι ἐκβάλλουσιν; διὰ τοῦτο αὐτοὶ κριταὶ ἔσονται ὑμῶν.	
20 εἰ δὲ ἐν πνεύματι θεοῦ ἐγὼ ἐκβάλλω τὰ δαιμόνια, ἄρα ἔφθασεν ἐφ᾽ ὑμᾶς ἡ βασιλεία τοῦ θεοῦ.	
21 ἢ πῶς δύναταί τις εἰσελθεῖν εἰς τὴν οἰκίαν τοῦ ἰσχυροῦ καὶ τὰ σκεύη αὐτοῦ ἁρπάσαι,	27 ἀλλ᾽ οὐ δύναται οὐδεὶς εἰς τὴν οἰκίαν τοῦ ἰσχυροῦ εἰσελθὼν τὰ σκεύη αὐτοῦ διαρπάσαι,
22 ἐὰν μὴ πρῶτον δήσῃ τὸν ἰσχυρόν; καὶ τότε τὴν οἰκίαν αὐτοῦ διαρπάσει.	ἐὰν μὴ πρῶτον τὸν ἰσχυρὸν δήσῃ, καὶ τότε τὴν οἰκίαν αὐτοῦ διαρπάσει.
23 ὁ μὴ ὢν μετ᾽ ἐμοῦ κατ᾽ ἐμοῦ ἐστιν, καὶ ὁ μὴ συνάγων μετ᾽ ἐμοῦ σκορπίζει.	
24 ὅταν τὸ ἀκάθαρτον πνεῦμα ἐξέλθῃ ἀπὸ τοῦ ἀνθρώπου, διέρχεται δι᾽ ἀνύδρων τόπων ζητοῦν ἀνάπαυσιν καὶ οὐχ εὑρίσκει. τότε λέγει, εἰς τὸν οἶκόν μου ἐπιστρέψω ὅθεν ἐξῆλθον.	
25 καὶ ἐλθὸν εὑρίσκει σεσαρωμένον καὶ κεκοσμημένον.	
26 τότε πορεύεται καὶ παραλαμβάνει ἑπτὰ ἕτερα πνεύματα πονηρότερα ἑαυτοῦ καὶ εἰσελθόντα κατοικεῖ ἐκεῖ· καὶ γίνεται τὰ ἔσχατα τοῦ ἀνθρώπου ἐκείνου χείρονα τῶν πρώτων.	

Q 11.14-15, 17-26; 12.10	Mk 3.22-30
	28 ἀμὴν λέγω ὑμῖν ὅτι
10 καὶ πᾶς ὃς ἐρεῖ λόγον	πάντα ἀφεθήσεται τοῖς υἱοῖς
εἰς τὸν υἱὸν τοῦ ἀνθρώπου,	τῶν ἀνθρώπων τὰ ἁμαρτήματα
ἀφεθήσεται αὐτῷ·	καὶ αἱ βλασφημίαι
	ὅσα ἐὰν βλασφημήσωσιν·
ὃς ἐρεῖ λόγον	29 ὃς δ' ἂν βλασφημήσῃ
εἰς τὸ πνεῦμα τὸ ἅγιον,	εἰς τὸ πνεῦμα τὸ ἅγιον,
οὐκ ἀφεθήσεται αὐτῷ.	οὐκ ἔχει ἄφεσιν εἰς τὸν αἰῶνα,
	ἀλλὰ ἔνοχός ἐστιν
	αἰωνίου ἁμαρτήματος.
	30 ὅτι ἔλεγον,
	πνεῦμα ἀκάθαρτον ἔχει.

The arguments for the Q reconstruction are laid out in *Mark and Q*.[4] I would like to offer further comments only on one disputed point. In my book I argued that Luke radically redacted the Parable of the Strong Man and that Matthew preserves the original Q version. Frans Neirynck maintains that the parable did not appear in Q, but rather that Matthew and Luke took it over from Mark.[5] However, this is not at all likely.

If we eliminate Luke's version as redactional, then there are only two possibilities: either Matthew's version reflects the original Q version which Mark copied from Q, or Mark's version is the original version which Matthew took over and interpolated into the Q controversy.

Neirynck claims that the main argument for including the Parable of the Strong Man in Q is its identical placement in Matthew and Luke.[6] This may be the main argument, but there are three additional arguments: the use of catchwords; the Q flavor of Matthew's text; and Matthew's redactional preferences.

4. Fleddermann, *Mark and Q*, pp. 41-58, 66-69.

5. F. Neirynck, 'Assessment', in H.T. Fleddermann, *Mark and Q: A Study of the Overlap Texts* (BETL, 122; Leuven: Leuven University Press, 1995), pp. 261-307, esp. pp. 271-73; F. Neirynck, 'The Sayings Source Q and the Gospel of Mark', in H. Cancik, H. Lichtenberger and P. Schäfer (eds.), *Geschichte–Tradition–Reflexion: Festschrift für M. Hengel zum 70. Geburtstag*. III. *Frühes Christentum* (Tübingen: Mohr Siebeck, 1996), pp. 125-45, esp. pp. 127-28.

6. According to Neirynck ('Assessment', p. 271), 'The main argument for the inclusion of this saying in Q is the placement of Matt 12,29/Luke 11,21-22 between Matt 12,27-28/Luke 11,19-20 and Matt 12,30/Luke 11,23...' Compare Neirynck, 'The Sayings Source Q', p. 127.

The first additional argument comes from Q's extensive use of catch-words. The author of Q employs catchword composition throughout the document. The catchwords fall into three categories: internal catch-words; linking catchwords; and remote catchwords. Internal catchwords bind the parts of a pericope together. Examples include 'to produce fruit' and 'fire' in John's preaching (Q 3.7-9, 16-17), and 'to follow' and 'to depart from' in the demands of discipleship (Q 9.57-60). Link-ing catchwords join consecutive pericopes. For example, 'thief', 'heart' and 'to dig' link the pericope on treasure in heaven (Q 12.33-34) to the householder and the servant left in charge (Q 12.39-40, 42b-46). Remote catchwords join more distant passages. For example, the term 'the Coming One' links John's preaching (Q 3.7-9, 16-17) and John's question (Q 7.18-19, 22-28, 31-35).[7]

To appreciate fully the use of catchwords in the Beelzebul contro-versy we need to look first at the structure of Q. The first three parts of Q deal with (1) John and Jesus, (2) the disciples, and (3) the adver-saries. The Beelzebul controversy and the demand for a sign is the first pericope in the third part of Q which contains three pericopes that center on Jesus' adversaries.[8]

III. THE ADVERSARIES

10. The Beelzebul controversy and the demand for a sign
    (Q 11.14-32)
11. Light and darkness (Q 11.33-35)
12. The woes against the Pharisees (Q 11.39-52)

7. See H.T. Fleddermann, 'The Demands of Discipleship: Matt 8,19-22 par. Luke 9,57-62', in F. Van Segbroeck, C.M. Tuckett, G. Van Belle and J. Verheyden (eds.), *The Four Gospels 1992: Festschrift F. Neirynck* (BETL, 100; 3 vols.; Leuven: Leuven University Press, 1992), I, pp. 541-61, esp. p. 553 n. 44.

8. Q's first part consists of five pericopes centering on John and Jesus:

1. John's preaching (Q 3.7-9, 16-17)
2. Jesus' temptations (Q 4.2b-13)
3. The sermon (Q 6.20-23, 27-33, 35c, 36, 37a, 38c, 41-49)
4. The centurion's servant (Q 7.1-3, 6-9)
5. John's question (Q 7.18-19, 22-28, 31-35)

Q's second part contains four pericopes on discipleship:

6. The demands of discipleship (Q 9.57-60)
7. The mission discourse (Q 10.2-16)
8. Praise of the Father and blessing of the disciples (Q 10.21-24)
9. The disciples' prayer and an exhortation to pray (Q 11.2-4, 9-13)

Internal, linking and remote catchwords all show that the Parable of the Strong Man stood in Q. The words οἶκος/οἰκία/κατοικέω ('house/ build') are both internal catchwords in the Beelzebul controversy, occuring six times (Q 11.17 [2×], 21, 22, 24, 26), linking catchwords to the sayings on light (Q 11.17 [2×], 21, 22, 24, 26, 33), and remote catchwords to the woes against the Pharisees (Q 11.17 [2×], 21, 22, 24, 26, 51).[9] In addition to οἶκος/οἰκία/κατοικέω, the remote catchwords εἰσέρχομαι ('to enter') (Q 11.21, 26, 52) and ἁρπάζω/διαρπάζω/ ἁρπαγή ('to seize/plunder') (Q 11.21, 22, 39) connect the Beelzebul controversy and the woes. These catchwords lock the Parable of the Strong Man firmly into the Q Beelzebul controversy.[10] Matthew and Luke did not take over the Parable of the Strong Man from Mark; they read it in Q.

The second additional argument for reading the Parable of the Strong Man in Q comes from the Q flavor of Matthew's text. Matthew's text contains expressions that occur elsewhere in Q. His construction ἢ πῶς δύναται ('or how can') with the infinitive has a parallel in Q 6.42 (ἢ πῶς δύνασαι λέγειν τῷ ἀδελφῷ σου) ('or how can you say to your brother'). Q 6.42 also has the combination πρῶτον...καὶ τότε ('first... and then'). and πρῶτος and τότε also occur later on in the Beelzebul controversy (Q 11.26). The verb ἁρπάζω ('to seize') is attested in Q 16.16, and as we have seen the cognate noun ἁρπαγή ('to plunder') appears in the woes (Q 11.39). In other words the sentence structure and the vocabulary of Matthew's text both reflect Q usage. The Q flavor of Matthew's text again indicates that Matthew took it over from Q and not from Mark.

The third additional argument for attributing the Parable of the Strong Man to Q comes from Matthew's redactional preferences. Granted that Matthew and Mark are close and the differences between them subtle, still it remains unlikely that Matthew here modifies Mark's text because Mark's text is more homogeneous and parallel than Matthew's. Whereas Matthew uses both ἁρπάζω and διαρπάζω (Mt. 12.29), Mark uses διαρπάζω twice (Mk 3.27). Mark also formulates the conditional and final clauses with a parallel word order. For Matthew to take the passage

---

9. Compare also οἰκοδομέω in Q 11.47.

10. Besides the catchwords that involve the Parable of the Strong Man, several other catchwords connect the first and last pericopes of the third part of Q on the adversaries: ἡ βασιλεία τοῦ θεοῦ (Q 11.20, 52), κρίσις (Q 11.31, 32, 42) and σοφία (Q 11.31, 49).

over from Mark he would have had to have disturbed the parallelism. Although such a procedure is not impossible, it is not probable because Matthew likes parallelism.[11] Furthermore, Matthew took over the preceding verses from Q unchanged, and he takes over the following verse unchanged.[12] This corresponds to a Matthean tendency to take over blocks of Q text unchanged.[13]

Once we see that Matthew and Luke did not take over the Parable of the Strong Man from Mark but derived it from Q, we can move on to compare the reconstructed Q text of the Beelzebul controversy with Mark's version. When we compare the two texts we notice numerous differences in detail and several major differences. The most noticeable difference is length. The Q text is much longer than the Markan text. The main reason Q is longer is that Q contains five sections that have nothing corresponding in Mark: (1) the exorcism of the demoniac (Q 11.14); (2) the saying about 'your sons' (Q 11.19); (3) the saying about the arrival of the kingdom (Q 11.20); (4) the saying about opposition to Jesus (Q 11.23); and (5) the return of the unclean spirit (Q 11.24-26).

Although Q is much longer than Mark, in four places Mark has a more expansive text than Q. First, instead of Q's single charge that Jesus drives out demons by Beelzebul, Mark has a double charge that Jesus is possessed and that he drives out demons by Beelzebul (Mk 3.22). Second, Mark begins Jesus' answer with a rhetorical question: 'How can Satan drive out Satan?' (Mk 3.23). Third, instead of Q's single parable of the divided kingdom, Mark has a double parable of the divided kingdom and the divided house (Mk 3.24-25). Fourth, Mark adds a version of the unforgivable sin logion to the Beelzebul controversy (Mk 3.28-30).

The sections that Q has over and above Mark all show that Mark is later than Q. Two of the sections are particularly clear. The saying about 'your sons' and the return of the unclean spirit raise dogmatic

---

11. Matthew, e.g., edits Mark's call of the disciples to make it more parallel (Mt. 4.18-22 diff. Mk 1.16-20). On Matthew's fondness for parallelism, see A. Denaux, 'Der Spruch von den zwei Wegen im Rahmen des Epilogs der Bergpredigt (Mt 7,13-14 par. Lk 13,23-24): Tradition und Redaktion', in J. Delobel (ed.), *Logia: Les paroles de Jésus—The Sayings of Jesus: Mémorial Joseph Coppens* (BETL, 59; Leuven: Leuven University Press, 1982), pp. 305-335.

12. Fleddermann, *Mark and Q*, p. 55.

13. See Mt. 3.7b-10; 6.24; 8.19-22; 12.41-42. See further Fleddermann, *Mark and Q*, p. 55.

questions that make it much easier to explain their omission than their addition. The saying about 'your sons' appears to set Jesus on the same level as his contemporaries, and the return of the unclean spirit seems to imply that Jesus' exorcisms are not definitive. It is easier to conceive of Mark omitting them than Q adding them. The other three sections that Q has over and above Mark also point in the same direction. First, Q's exorcism makes a natural introduction to the controversy. Mark's connection with Jesus' family appears secondary. Second, the saying about opposition to Jesus appeared too harsh to Mark. He replaced it later with his account of the strange exorcist (Mk 9.38-40). Third, the saying on the arrival of the kingdom forms the climax of the section and is clearly original.[14]

Of the sections that Mark has over and above Q, three also show that Mark is later than Q. First, the charge against Jesus is heightened in Mark. Not only is Jesus accused of driving out demons by Beelzebul, Mark has a further charge that Jesus is possessed (Mk 3.22). This further charge heightens the opposition against Jesus. The heightening is secondary. Second, in Q Jesus responds with a parable of the divided kingdom. One detail of the parable—one house falling against another —graphically portrays the devastation of a civil war (Q 11.17). In Mark there are two parables: the divided kingdom and the divided house (Mk 3.24-25). It is more probable that Mark developed a detail of the Q parable into a second parable than that Q collapsed a second parable into a detail of the first.[15] Third, Mark's form of the unforgivable sin logion shows signs of ongoing dogmatic reflection, for it does not contain any indication that a word spoken against the Son of Man can be forgiven and it contains technical language such as 'blasphemy'.[16]

The tradition-historical arguments show that Mark is later than Q. Can we show that Mark depends on Q? If we look carefully at Mark's text, two things become apparent. First, the text shows unmistakable signs of Mark's own hand. Second, every aspect of Mark's text reflects Q.

---

14.   Heikki Räisänen has recently demonstrated how tightly the kingdom saying fits in its context in the Beelzebul controversy. See H. Räisänen, 'Exorcisms and the Kingdom: Is Q 11:20 a Saying of the Historical Jesus?', in R. Uro (ed.), *Symbols and Strata: Essays on the Sayings Gospel Q* (Publications of the Finnish Exegetical Society, 65; Helsinki: The Finnish Exegetical Society; Göttingen: Vandenhoeck & Ruprecht, 1996), pp. 119-42.

15.   T.W. Manson, *The Sayings of Jesus* (London: SCM Press, 1949), p. 86.

16.   See further Fleddermann, *Mark and Q*, p. 69.

If we examine Mark's version of the Beelzebul controversy, we note a conscious design that bears Mark's imprint. First of all, the passage is an example of Mark's framing technique in which he splits one story and inserts a second story between the two parts of the first one.[17] In this case Mark frames the Beelzebul controversy (Mk 3.22-30) with the two parts of the pericope of Jesus' family (Mk 3.20-21, 31-35). Mark edited the Beelzebul controversy carefully to adapt it to the framing pericope of Jesus' family and to develop familiar Markan themes— Jesus' power and the evil that opposes his power.

> And the scribes coming down from Jerusalem said, 'He has Beelzebul' and 'By the leader of the demons he casts out demons'. And summoning them he said to them in parables: 'How can [πῶς δύναται] Satan cast out Satan? And if a kingdom is divided against itself, that kingdom cannot [οὐ δύναται] stand; and if a house is divided against itself, that house will not be able [οὐ δυνήσεται] to stand. And if Satan has risen up against himself and is divided, he cannot [οὐ δύναται] stand, but his end has come. But no one entering the house of a strong man can [οὐ δύναται] despoil him of his possessions, unless he first bind the strong man, and then he will despoil his house. Amen I say to you that all sins and blasphemies will be forgiven the sons of men as much as they blaspheme; but whoever blasphemes against the Holy Spirit, does not have forgiveness forever but is guilty of an eternal sin'. Because they said, 'He has an unclean spirit' (Mk 3.22-30).

Mark edits the Beelzebul controversy in the beginning, middle and end to adapt it to the new context he created by framing the controversy with the pericope of Jesus' family. At the beginning and end Mark mimics the outer frame by using the charge that Jesus is possessed as an inclusio to further frame the Beelzebul controversy (Mk 3.22, 30). This inclusio reflects the charge of Jesus' family that he is out of his mind (Mk 3.21), but significantly Mark draws the formulation of the charge that Jesus is possessed from Q where it is leveled against John the Baptist (Q 7.33). In the middle of the Beelzebul controversy Mark expands a detail of the Q parable of the divided kingdom into a second parable —the divided house—to refer to the divided house of Jesus' own family (Mk 3.25). At the end of the Beelzebul controversy Mark appends the unforgivable sin logion as a final comment on the charges leveled against Jesus (Mk 3.29-30).

---

17. See Mk 5.21-43; 6.7-30; 11.12-25; 14.1-11, 53-72. See further F. Neirynck, *Duality in Mark: Contributions to the Study of the Markan Redaction* (BETL, 31; Leuven: Leuven University Press, 1988 [1972]), p. 133.

Besides editing the Beelzebul controversy to adapt it to the framing pericope of Jesus' family, Mark also edits the Beelzebul controversy to develop the theme of Jesus' power and to brand opposition to Jesus' power as the unforgivable sin. Mark picks up the question form πῶς δύναται ('how can') with the infinitive from the Q Parable of the Strong Man (Q 11.21), and he uses it to frame a rhetorical question that announces the major theme of the section—Jesus' power (Mk 3.23). Mark then formulates three parallel sentences, each of which begins with a conditional clause and uses a form of δύναμαι ('can'; Mk 3.24, 25, 26). Throughout the Gospel Mark uses the noun δύναμις ('power') and the verb δύναμαι to show the power of God at work in Jesus, so the repetition of the Q verb δύναμαι fits Mark's theology.[18] Mark draws the logion on the unforgivable sin from the Q pericope on fearless preaching (Q 12.10), and he edits it carefully to develop the theme of blasphemy (Mk 3.28-29). Again blasphemy is a theme that appears early and late in Mark's Gospel.[19] Mark placed the unforgivable sin logion here because it helped him develop his theme, but the reference to the Holy Spirit may have suggested the move to Mark. Q contains only three references to the Holy Spirit or the Spirit of God (Q 3.16; 11.20; 12.10). Mark eliminated the reference to the Spirit from the Q Beelzebul controversy when he dropped the saying on the arrival of the kingdom (Q 11.20), because he had already used a form of the saying in Mk 1.14-15. However, he compensated for the omission by drawing the final Q reference to the Spirit forward to join it to the Beelzebul controversy.

All of Mark's redactional moves have roots in Q, and they show that Mark derived his Beelzebul controversy from Q and not from the oral tradition. First, the phenomenon of order shows that Mark depends on Q. Mark's controversy is much shorter than Q's, but the material that Mark shares with Q appears in the same order. Second, all of Mark's additions to the controversy come from Q. Mark's additional charge that Jesus is possessed or 'has Beelzebul' comes from the Q section on John's question where John's contemporaries claim that he 'has a demon' (Q 7.33). Third, Mark's rhetorical question, 'How can Satan cast out Satan?', is composed entirely of elements from the Q controversy. Fourth, the parable of the divided house develops the Q image of house falling against house. Finally, Mark joined the Q saying on the

18. For δύναμις see Mk 5.30; 6.2, 5, 14; 9.1, 39; 12.24; 13.26; 14.62. For δύναμαι see Mk 1.40; 2.7; 3.27; 5.3; 6.5; 8.4; 9.3, 22, 23, 28, 29, 39; 15.31.

19. For βλασφημέω see Mk 2.7; 15.29; for βλασφημία see Mk 7.22; 14.64.

unforgivable sin to the Beelzebul controversy. Everything in Mark comes from Q. Even the Markan expansions are based in the text of Q. The Q texts involved are scattered widely over Q, and there are no parts of Mark that do not have a Q counterpart. If Mark were drawing the Beelzebul controversy from the oral tradition, we would expect to find non-Q material mixed in. Instead everything in Mark's text comes from Q. The most obvious explanation for these facts is that Mark had the entire Q document in front of him.[20]

2. *The Cross Saying*

The Synoptic tradition contains five forms of the Cross saying. Mark places a form of the saying at the beginning of a cluster of sayings on discipleship that conclude the Caesaria Philippi pericope (Mk 8.34b), and both Matthew and Luke take over this saying in redacting Mark's pericope (Mt. 16.24; Lk. 9.23). Mark's saying begins with a conditional clause which leads into three imperatives, all positive. In addition to taking over Mark's Cross saying, Matthew and Luke have another form of the saying that begins with a relative clause and has an indicative main clause, both negative (Mt. 10.38; Lk. 14.27). Moreover, this second Cross saying in Matthew and Luke appears in a Q context in both Gospels, following the sayings on hating one's relatives (Mt. 10.37 par. Lk. 14.26). In Q the three sayings form a cluster which climaxes in the Cross saying. I proposed the following reconstruction of the sayings.[21]

> ὃς οὐ μισεῖ τὸν πατέρα αὐτοῦ καὶ τὴν μητέρα
> οὐ δύναται εἶναί μου μαθητής·
> ὃς οὐ μισεῖ τὸν υἱὸν αὐτοῦ καὶ τὴν θυγατέρα
> οὐ δύναται εἶναί μου μαθητής·
> ὃς οὐ λαμβάνει τὸν σταυρὸν αὐτοῦ
> καὶ ἀκολουθεῖ ὀπίσω μου,
> οὐ δύναται εἶναί μου μαθητής (Q 14.26a, 26b, 27).

I would like to comment only on one aspect of the reconstruction. In recent reconstructions both the International Q Project and Peter Kristen have opted for Luke's conditional clause in the sayings on hating one's

---

20. Fleddermann, *Mark and Q*, p. 61.

21. H.T. Fleddermann, 'The Cross and Discipleship in Q', in D.J. Lull (ed.), *SBL 1988 Seminar Papers* (Atlanta: Scholars Press, 1988), pp. 472-82, esp. pp. 472-79.

family.[22] However, this reconstruction does not account for Matthew's redaction of the sayings, for nowhere does Matthew turn a conditional clause introduced by εἰ ('if') into a substantival participle as he would have had to do if Q originally had a conditional clause in these sayings. Matthew does alternate between relative clauses and substantival participles, as we can see from the way he interchanges the two constructions in the sayings against oaths in Mt. 23.16-22.[23] Luke's conditional clause does not reflect Q, but stems from Luke himself. Luke introduced a similar expression (ἐρχόμενος πρός με; 'coming to me') in redacting Q 6.47 (cf. Mt. 7.24), and Luke probably changed to the conditional form in the saying on hating one's relatives under the influence of the Markan form of the Cross saying (Mk 8.34b) which he took over in Lk. 9.23. Q probably had relative clauses in the sayings on hating one's family, matching the relative clause in the Cross saying.[24]

The Cross saying is a classic overlap text. When we compare the reconstructed Q saying and the Markan saying, we notice two very different formulations of the same saying.

Q 14.27	*Mk 8.34b*
	εἴ τις θέλει ὀπίσω μου ἀκολουθεῖν,
	ἀπαρνησάσθω ἑαυτὸν
ὃς οὐ λαμβάνει τὸν σταυρὸν αὐτοῦ	καὶ ἀράτω τὸν σταυρὸν αὐτοῦ
καὶ ἀκολουθεῖ ὀπίσω μου,	καὶ ἀκολουθείτω μοι.
οὐ δύναται εἶναί μου μαθητής.	

The Markan saying is later than the Q saying. First, the Q context appears more original. As we have seen, the Q Cross saying is the climactic third saying in a cluster. The sayings are bound together thematically by the concept of discipleship and stylistically by repetition. Mark's saying introduces a series of sayings on discipleship (Mk 8.34–9.1), but it does not cohere stylistically with the following sayings. Second, the Markan saying repeats the clause on following. It appears

22. J.M. Asgiersson and J.M. Robinson, 'The International Q Project', *JBL* 111 (1992), pp. 500-508, esp. p. 507; P. Kristen, *Familie, Kreuz und Leben: Nachfolge Jesu nach Q und dem Markusevangelium* (MTS, 42; Marburg: Elwert, 1995), pp. 124-32.

23. Compare ος ἂν ὀμόσῃ … ὃς δ' ἂν ὀμόσῃ (Mt. 23.16) and ὃς ἂν ὀμόσῃ…ὃς δ' ἂν ὀμόσῃ (Mt. 23.18) with ὁ οὖν ὀμόσας (Mt. 23.20), καὶ ὁ ὀμόσας (Mt. 23.21) and καὶ ὁ ὀμόσας (Mt. 23.22).

24. See further Fleddermann, 'Cross and Discipleship', pp. 476-77.

both in the conditional clause (εἴ τις θέλει ὀπίσω μου ἀκολουθεῖν; 'if anyone wishes to follow after me'), and in the final imperative (καὶ ἀκολουθείτω μοι; 'and follow me'). This repetition is a sign of redactional reworking. Third, Mark's 'let him deny himself' seems to be an addition to the saying. It makes explicit what remains implicit in the Q saying. Clarifying additions like the one in Mark's saying show that the saying has been redactionally reworked. Fourth, Mark's saying echoes the passion narrative in the clauses on denying oneself and taking up the cross.[25] Fifth, the Q negative formulation is uncompromising; Mark's positive formulation is milder. It is more probable that an uncompromising statement was transformed into a milder statement rather than the opposite.[26]

When we examine the differences between Mark and Q, it becomes apparent that we can trace them back to the Markan redaction of the Q saying. The most significant difference between Mark's saying and the Q saying is Mark's positive formulation. Mark's context makes it probable that the shift comes from Mark. In his introductory verse (Mk 8.34a), Mark has Jesus address both the disciples and the crowd. The crowd in Mark is basically friendly toward Jesus, and they are potential disciples. For this reason, the positive formulation which aims to win acceptance fits Mark's context better than the uncompromising negative formulation of Q, so it is likely that Mark is responsible for the positive form of the saying. Elsewhere in the overlap texts Mark tones down and modifies uncompromising Q statements.[27] Mark's new context is also responsible for the repetition of 'following' in the saying. Since the saying introduces a group of sayings on discipleship, Mark draws the clause on following forward and places it in a conditional clause. The form of the clause (εἴ τις θέλει; 'if anyone wishes' plus an infinitive) corresponds to the form of another programmatic saying in Mk 9.35 that also introduces teaching on discipleship. The first imperative, 'let him deny

---

25. The verbs ἀρνέομαι and ἀπαρνέομαι dominate the accounts that deal with Peter's denial (see Mk 14.30, 31, 68, 70, 72), and the verb αἴρω with τὸν σταυρὸν αὐτοῦ surfaces in the account of Simon of Cyrene (Mk 15.21).

26. See further Fleddermann, *Mark and Q*, pp. 138-39.

27. Above we saw that Mark eliminates Q's exaggeration in calling the mustard a 'tree' (cf. Mk 4.30-32 with Q 13.18-19). Mark tones down the Q equipment rule by introducing some exceptions (cf. Mk 6.8 with Q 10.4). Mark also shifts away from Q's harsh view of outsiders (cf. Mk 9.40 with Q 11.23). See Fleddermann, *Mark and Q*, p. 209.

himself', is an interpretive addition that Mark uses to connect the saying with the passion narrative. The term 'deny' comes from the story of Peter's denial in Mark's passion narrative (Mk 14.30, 31, 68, 70, 72). Mark introduces the clause 'let him deny himself' to develop further his understanding of discipleship. For Mark, the disciple must either deny himself or, like Peter, he ends up denying Jesus. The second imperative clause, 'let him take up his cross', reflects the first condition in the Q relative clause, but again Mark has let the passion narrative influence the wording by substituting ἀράτω ('take up') instead of using Q's λαμβάνω ('take up'; cf. Mk 15.21). Mark's third imperative, 'and follow me', reflects the second Q condition, but in Mark's redaction it echoes the initial conditional clause and forms the climax of the three imperatives. We can explain the shift from the Q saying to Mark's saying by appealing to known Markan redactional concerns.[28]

I would like to address the alternate position that Mark and Q drew the Cross saying independently of one another from the oral tradition. First, I will offer some considerations to show that it is unlikely that any form of the Cross saying circulated in the oral tradition. Then I will show why it is more likely that the author of Q created the Cross saying.

First of all, it remains unlikely that any form of the Cross saying circulated in the oral tradition. The five forms of the Cross saying in the Gospels all go back to Q and Mark. The saying in *Gos. Thom.* 55 reflects redactional changes that Matthew and Luke introduced into the saying, so Thomas depends on the Synoptic forms of the Cross saying and does not provide an independent witness that the saying circulated in the oral tradition.[29] Outside of the Gospels the saying appears nowhere in the New Testament. The silence of Paul is particularly significant. The cross forms a major theme in Paul's theology, and Paul returns to it again and again. The cross is God's power and weakness, God's wisdom and folly (1 Cor. 1.18-25). Paul talks about being crucified with Christ (Gal. 2.19), and he can talk about enemies of the cross of Christ (Phil. 3.18), but nowhere does Paul say that the Christians should take up the cross or

28. See further Fleddermann, *Mark and Q*, pp. 139-41.

29. *Gos. Thom.* 55 reads: 'Jesus said, "Whoever does not hate his father and mother cannot be a disciple to me, and whoever does not hate his brothers and sisters, and take up the cross in my way, will not be worthy of me".' *Gos. Thom.* 55 reflects redactional Matthew in the phrase 'will not be worthy of me' and redactional Luke in the phrase 'brothers and sisters'. See further Fleddermann, *Mark and Q*, pp. 141-42.

carry the cross. Nor does a form of the Cross saying surface anywhere else in the writings of the New Testament outside of the Synoptics. There is no evidence that the Cross saying circulated in the oral tradition prior to Q. Furthermore, there is evidence that the author of Q formulated the Cross saying.

As we have seen, the Q saying lies in a cluster of sayings on discipleship:

ὃς οὐ μισεῖ τὸν πατέρα αὐτοῦ καὶ τὴν μητέρα
οὐ δύναται εἶναί μου μαθητής·
ὃς οὐ μισεῖ τὸν υἱὸν αὐτοῦ καὶ τὴν θυγατέρα
οὐ δύναται εἶναί μου μαθητής·
ὃς οὐ λαμβάνει τὸν σταυρὸν αὐτοῦ
καὶ ἀκολουθεῖ ὀπίσω μου·
οὐ δύναται εἶναί μου μαθητής (Q 14.26a, 26b, 27).

The three sayings form a tight rhetorical and conceptual unit. Repetition dominates the rhetoric. The main clause is identical in all three sayings. This end repetition, called epiphora or epistrophe, appears quite commonly in biblical and Hellenistic rhetoric. Besides end repetition, the sayings also have initial repetition with similar negative relative clauses (ὃς οὐ ['whoever'] with the present indicative). Initial repetition, called anaphora or epanaphora, also appears commonly in ancient rhetoric. The combination of initial and end repetition, called symploche, does not appear often, and it is an initial signal that the Q cluster is a tight rhetorical unit.[30] But even the combination of initial and end repetition does not exhaust the rhetorical features of the cluster. Within the three relative clauses repetition also crops up. The initial objects echo one another with an identical masculine article at the beginning and an identical masculine genitive pronoun at the end (τὸν πατέρα αὐτοῦ ... τὸν υἱὸν αὐτοῦ ... τὸν σταυρὸν αὐτοῦ). The cluster climaxes in the third saying on taking up the cross. The Cross saying is longer than the first two sayings, for it contains two predicates joined by καί (λαμβάνει τὸν σταυρὸν αὐτοῦ καὶ ἀκολουθεῖ ὀπίσω μου). However, the first two sentences prepare for the third by having two objects joined by καί (τὸν πατέρα αὐτοῦ καὶ τὴν μητέρα...τὸν υἱὸν αὐτοῦ καὶ τὴν θυγατέρα). These extraordinarily dense rhetorical features prove that the sayings form an original unit and were not at one time separate sayings that were secondarily adapted to one another.

30. See Fleddermann, *Mark and Q*, p. 138.

Furthermore, the vocabulary and the rhetorical features of the Q Cross saying have parallels in other parts of Q. Except for the word 'cross' which appears only here in Q, the rest of the vocabulary appears elsewhere in Q, and some of the words are common. The verb 'hate' recurs in Q 16.13; δύναμαι ('can') and λαμβάνω ('take up') are common in Q.[31] The nouns 'father', 'mother', 'son', 'daughter' and 'disciple' all have Q parallels, and again some appear often in Q.[32] The constant repetition of αὐτοῦ ('his') also has Q parallels (see, e.g., Q 3.16-17). Furthermore, the threefold repetition of the main clause has a parallel in the apocalyptic discourse where the author of Q three times repeats a main clause, 'thus will be the day of the Son of Man' (Q 17.24, 26, 30). The vocabulary and rhetorical features show that the cluster was composed by the author of Q. A study of the theme of the cluster will confirm this linguistic analysis.

The cluster of sayings draws together two lines of thought that run through the Q document. The first two sayings draw to a close Q's treatment of the relationship of the disciple to his or her family. In the demands of discipleship (Q 9.57-60) Q shows that discipleship must override every human bond, even the sacred bond that ties families together. In the enigma of Jesus' mission (Q 12.51-53) Jesus' coming splits families into hostile camps. The two sayings on hating father and son, mother and daughter, draw this line of thought to its climax. The disciple must hate his or her family. The Cross saying completes a separate Q theme—the identity of Jesus and the disciple. In the persecution beatitude (Q 6.22-23) the disciple is identified with Jesus in suffering and persecution. Q returns to the theme in the demands of discipleship (Q 9.57-60) where the disciple shares Jesus' homelessness, and this theme is continued in the equipment rule of the mission discourse (Q 10.4) where the disciples are not to take provisions for their journey. The Cross saying brings this theme to a climax by demanding that the disciple take up the cross. Because the cluster of sayings in

31. For δύναμαι see Q 3.8; 6.39, 42, 43; 12.5, 25; 14.20; 16.13 (2×). For λαμβάνω see Q 10.4; 11.10; 13.19, 21; QMt. 25.16, 18, 20, 24.

32. For πατήρ see Q 3.8; 6.35, 36; 9.59; 10.21 (2×), 22 (3×); 11.2, 11, 13, 47, 48; 12.30, 53. For μητήρ see Q 12.53. The noun υἱός occurs 11 times in the expression ὁ υἱὸς τοῦ ἀνθρώπου (Q 6.22; 7.34; 9.58; 11.30; 12.8, 9, 10, 40; 17.24, 26, 30), and it is common elsewhere in Q (see Q 4.3, 9; 6.35; 10.6, 22 [3×]; 11.11, 19, 48; 12.53; 13.28). For θυγάτηρ see Q 12.53. For μαθητής see Q 6.40 (2×); 7.18; 10.2.

Q 14.26-27 draws together two separate lines of thought in the Q document, it comes from the hand of the author of Q, so Mark in using the Cross saying depends on redactional Q.

3. *Conclusion*

Two positions confront one another in the present debate on the relationship of Mark and Q. The majority of scholars maintain that Mark and Q independently of each other drew the material they have in common from the oral tradition. A minority view holds that Mark depends directly on Q for the common material, and I argued for this position in my book *Mark and Q*. In this essay I have highlighted the argument of the book by revisiting two texts that illustrate the difficulties of trying to explain the overlap texts by appealing to the oral tradition. Mark's Beelzebul controversy is a complex composition, but every part of the composition has a Q parallel. If Mark were drawing the material from the oral tradition we would expect to find some non-Q material in his composition. Instead everything comes from Q. The most natural conclusion we can draw from this composition is that Mark had the entire Q document in front of him. The Cross saying provides further evidence that the oral tradition cannot explain the overlap texts. Attempts to explain Mark's Cross saying from the oral tradition falter on two facts: (1) we have no evidence that a form of the Cross saying ever circulated in the oral tradition; and (2) quite a bit of evidence exists that the author of Q first formulated the Cross saying as part of the conditions of discipleship (Q 14.26-27). Both the Beelzebul controversy and the Cross saying support the view that Mark knew and used Q.

THE SON OF MAN AS THE REPRESENTATIVE OF GOD'S KINGDOM: ON THE INTERPRETATION OF JESUS IN MARK AND Q*

Jens Schröter

1. *Methodological Considerations*

The term 'Christology' with regard to early Christian literature applies to the process within which diverse Jewish expectations of figures, appearing as God's representatives at the end of time, were linked to the historical person Jesus of Nazareth.[1] Within this wider usage the way the term χριστός ('Christ' = the anointed one) is used in early Christian writings must be delineated. This has first to be pointed out in order to bring into sharper focus the question of whether the application of the title 'Christ' to Jesus in the early Christian writings is used in a preferred way. In particular, an investigation focused on the narrative presentations of his activity and fate cannot proceed from the presupposition that the specific characteristics of those narratives may be understood on the basis of the belief that Jesus is Christ, as though the term Christ was already qualified in a particular way.[2] Rather, a look at the beginnings of the reception of Jesus' preaching in relation to the Christ-title

---

* A shorter version of this article was delivered in the European 'Mark and Q' Seminar at the International Meeting of SBL, 18–22 July 1998 in Krakow. I wish to thank Professor Alan Mitchell for his help in preparing the English translation.

1. Cf. J.D.G. Dunn, 'Christology', *ABD*, I, pp. 979-91, esp. pp. 980-82.

2. According to J. Gnilka, behind Mark's Gospel lies a proto-passion, in which the death of Jesus, according to the model of the Suffering Just One, has been linked to the confession of him as Messiah. Moreover, this proto-passion, according to Gnilka, may have been imbedded in the kerygma of the cross and resurrection, which the author had taken from a creedal formulation such as 1 Cor. 15.3-5 (cf. J. Gnilka, *Theologie des Neuen Testaments* [HTKNT, 5; Freiburg: Herder, 1994], pp. 143-51). Such a correspondence between an alleged narrative behind the Markan passion narrative and a text such as 1 Cor. 15.3-5 can, of course, only be maintained if the decisive elements of the latter, namely ἀπέθανεν ὑπὲρ τῶν ἁμαρτιῶν ἡμῶν,

allows important differentiations to emerge. Above all, in view of the oft-represented thesis that the already present kerygma of the cross and resurrection may play a decisive role in Mark's Christology, these differentiations might be important for the apprehension of Mark's christological thinking—and therefore for the beginnings of the narrative explanation of the Jesus tradition in general.[3]

as well as the appearance to the disciples, are ignored. Although Gnilka is of the opinion that with the Gospel of Mark 'something new appears' (*Theologie des Neuen Testaments*, p. 151), this judgment is nevertheless qualified by the view that this new element cannot be understood from the Gospel's content, but only from the connection of the Jesus tradition with the kerygma of the cross and resurrection. Similarly K. Backhaus, ' "Lösepreis für viele" (Mk 10.45): Zur Heilsbedeutung des Todes Jesu bei Markus', in T. Söding (ed.), *Der Evangelist als Theologe: Studien zum Markusevangelium* (SBB, 163; Stuttgart: Katholisches Bibelwerk, 1995), pp. 91-118, esp. p. 91. The view of the origin of the literary form 'Gospel' out of the connection of the kerygma about the passion and the likewise 'kerygmatic' biographic tradition does not contribute, however, in a decisive way to the understanding of the Markan narrative, because the final text is assumed to be intelligible only as a combination of antecedent sources. This is not fundamentally different, if one assesses with G. Strecker that 'die Verbindung von θεῖος ἀνήρ-Vorstellung und dem Menschensohnbegriff' was 'vormarkinisch und offenbar auf hellenistischem Boden entstanden', and regards the basic structure of the Markan Christology therefore as already embedded in the pre-Markan tradition (cf. G. Strecker, *Theologie des Neuen Testaments* [ed. F.W. Horn; Berlin: W. de Gruyter, 1996], p. 374). For a criticism of the premises that lay behind these approaches see N. Petersen, *Literary Criticism for New Testament Critics* (Philadelphia: Fortress Press, 1978), esp. pp. 17-23. Such theories about the origin of the Gospel of Mark do not only suffer from methodological deficiencies of the form- and redaction-critical approach, but furthermore do not take into account sufficiently the insight that the Gospel of Mark must be seen as a coherent literary work with a narrative structure (cf., e.g., D.E. Aune, *The New Testament in its Literary Environment* [Philadelphia: Westminster Press, 1987], pp. 24, 46-66; T. Onuki, *Sammelbericht als Kommunikation: Studien zur Erzählkunst der Evangelien* [WMANT, 73; Neukirchen–Vluyn: Neukirchener Verlag, 1997]).

3. The views of J. Schniewind ('Zur Synoptiker-Exegese', *TRu* 2 [1930], pp. 129-89, esp. p. 183), and more recently of H. Frankemölle (*Evangelium—Begriff und Gattung: Ein Forschungsbericht* [SBB, 15; Stuttgart: Katholisches Bibelwerk, 1988], p. 210), that a kerygmatic meaning and a historical explanation must be kept in view when interpreting the Gospels, remains undisputed. The assessment of Frankemölle, 'Wer diese grundsätzliche Einheit in den neutestamentlichen Traditionen auflöst, arbeitet mit falschen Alternativen...' (*Evangelium*, p. 210), without a doubt has to be agreed with. However, the question has not yet been answered as to how the term 'kerygma' with regard to the Gospels has to be understood. The

Particularly important is the perception of this double use of the term 'Christology' with regard to Q. In Q, according to unanimous opinion, the designation χριστός does not occur, but the term 'Christology' (in the wider sense, to be sure) is nevertheless applied to it in scholarship.[4] In Mark, as will be shown below, the designation χριστός describes only one, albeit important, aspect of his interpretation of Jesus' appearance.[5] Moreover, since the designation χριστός (respectively מָשִׁיחַ = the anointed one) is a particular qualified part of expectations about the end of time in Second Temple Judaism,[6] exegetical language must pay attention to the precise meaning of those terms. This means that the terms 'Christ', (respectively 'Messiah') and 'christological' (or 'messianic') should be restricted to those concepts which are related to them.[7] This is true regardless of the fact that χριστός has become a proper name for Jesus already at an early stage[8] and that, according to Acts 11.26,

somewhat wholesale reference to the 'kerygma of the cross and resurrection' as well as the biographical Jesus tradition is hardly specific enough as an answer because it does not grasp precisely the location of Mark and Q within the history of early Christianity. Cf. G. Dautzenberg, 'Der Wandel der Reich-Gottes-Verkündigung in der urchristlichen Mission', in G. Dautzenberg, H. Merklein and K. Müller (eds.), *Zur Geschichte des Urchristentums* (QD, 87; Freiburg: Herder, 1979), pp. 11-32.

4. Cf. A. Polag, *Die Christologie der Logienquelle* (WMANT, 45; Neukirchen–Vluyn: Neukirchener Verlag, 1977); C. Tuckett, *Q and the History of Early Christianity* (Edinburgh: T. & T. Clark, 1996), chap. 7, 'Q's Christology' and many others.

5. M. de Jonge, 'The Earliest Use of Christos: Some Suggestions', *NTS* 32 (1986), pp. 321-43, esp. pp. 324-29; C. Breytenbach, 'Grundzüge markinischer Gottessohn-Christologie', in C. Breytenbach and H. Paulsen (eds.), *Die Anfänge der Christologie* (Festschrift F. Hahn; Göttingen: Vandenhoeck & Ruprecht, 1991), pp. 169-84.

6. These expectations should be regarded as diverse and not as fixed concepts. Cf. J.J. Collins, *The Scepter and the Star: The Messiahs of the Dead Sea Scrolls and other Ancient Literature* (New York: Doubleday, 1995); J.H. Charlesworth, *The Concept of the Messiah in the Pseudepigrapha* (ANRW II, 19.1; Berlin: W. de Gruyter, 1979), pp. 188-218; J. Neusner, W.S. Green and E. Fredrichs (eds.), *Judaisms and their Messiahs at the Turn of the Christian Era* (Cambridge: Cambridge University Press, 1987).

7. Cf., e.g., O. Hofius, 'Ist Jesus der Messias? Thesen', in W. Breuning (ed.), *Der Messias* (JBT, 8; Neukirchen–Vluyn: Neukirchener Verlag, 1993), pp. 103-29 esp. p. 104.

8. This arises primarily from usage already established in the pre-Pauline tradition (cf. the formulations Ἰησοῦς χριστός and, respectively, the inversion

the followers of Jesus in Antioch were designated as χριστιανοί ('Christians').

Approaches to New Testament Christology, principally since Wilhelm Bousset's influential work,[9] have given much attention to the use of christological titles.[10] In more recent scholarship, that approach has been criticized in three ways. First, it was pointed out that the uses of these titles[11] in Jewish texts have to be distinguished from the way they are applied to Jesus.[12] Those aspects from among a range of meanings for each particular expression, which were invoked to interpret the activity of Jesus, can only be drawn from the actual usage of each expression and not, therefore, from a history of religions analysis that is detached

---

Χριστὸς Ἰησοῦς, as well as the stereotypical uses ἐν Χριστῷ and εὐαγγέλιον τοῦ Χριστοῦ). Cf. M. Hengel, 'Erwägungen zum Sprachgebrauch von χριστός bei Paulus und in der vorpaulinischen Überlieferung', in M.D. Hooker (ed.), *Paul and Paulinism: Essays in Honour of C.K. Barrett* (London: SPCK, 1982), pp. 135-59. In relation to this one can also mention the misunderstanding of Suetonius, *Claudius* 25.11, *idem*, *Caesar* 5.25 and Tacitus, *Annals* 15.44, who confuse the designation 'Christ' with the proper name 'Chrestus'. The use of χριστός as a *cognomen* is also reflected in Mk 1.1.

9. W. Bousset, *Kyrios Christos: Geschichte des Christusglaubens von den Anfängen des Christentums bis Irenaeus* (Göttingen: Vandenhoeck & Ruprecht, 5th edn, 1965).

10. M. Hengel, 'Christological Titles in Early Christianity', in *idem*, *Studies in Early Christianity* (Edinburgh: T. & T. Clark, 1995), pp. 359-89; F. Hahn, *Christologische Hoheitstitel: Ihre Geschichte im frühen Christentum* (FRLANT, 83 [= UTB, 1873]; Göttingen: Vandenhoeck & Ruprecht, 5th edn, 1995); R.H. Fuller, *The Foundations of New Testament Christology* (New York: Charles Scribner's Sons, 1965); O. Cullmann, *Die Christologie des Neuen Testaments* (Tübingen: J.C.B. Mohr [Paul Siebeck], 3rd edn, 1963).

11. The use of the word 'title' may be somewhat misleading in that the impression might be given that concepts were transferred to Jesus which could be established by means of a history of traditions investigation. In view of the more recent discussion about designations which are of central importance here, such as especially ὁ υἱὸς τοῦ ἀνθρώπου, χριστός, υἱὸς θεοῦ and κύριος, the existence of such concepts has become more and more questionable. It seems therefore advisable to refrain from such an assumption. Instead, the question of which aspects of meaning were actually realized in the concrete usages must be pursued by investigating these uses individually.

12. L. Chouinard, 'Gospel Christology: A Study of Methodology', *JSNT* 30 (1987), pp. 21-37, esp. pp. 23, 28.

from it.[13] In the application of these designations to the concrete historical person of Jesus, transformations of their use in contemporary
Judaism were necessary, resulting in new semantic aspects.[14] Moreover,
as will be shown below, it may sometimes be misleading to interpret
the designations κύριος ('Lord') or υἱὸς θεοῦ ('Son of God') against
their titular use in other writings without considering the possibility of
a non-titular usage. Second, orienting an investigation solely towards
'titles' allows only certain aspects of an interpretation to be seen and
neglects the possibility that the meaning of Jesus could also derive from
other parts of a text.[15] This could prove important above all for those
approaches that describe the importance of Jesus in a narrative manner.
Third, there is no strict historical correspondence between an interpretation of Jesus and an early Christian 'group' behind it. If, for example, in
Q, we have a concept in which Jesus' death and resurrection play no
outstanding role, that does not automatically lead to the conclusion of a
group without any interest in these subjects, that is, whose christological thought is comprehensively represented through that approach. We
cannot know from Q (or other early Christian approaches) what its addressees had thought. What we can know, instead, is only what its
author thought was essential to pass on to them.[16] Without arguing for
uniformity in the christological thinking of early Christianity, it should

13. This results from the semantic consideration, that, whereas the lexical meaning arises from the use of an expression in different contexts and thereby a spectrum
of possible meanings can be described, the actual meaning in a concrete instance
cannot be fixed in that way. For this, further aspects—e.g. grammatical, syntactical
as well as co-textual considerations—have to be included.

14. N.A. Dahl, 'The Messiahship of Jesus in Paul', in *idem*, *Jesus the Christ:
The Historical Origins of Christological Doctrine* (Minneapolis: Fortress Press,
1991), pp. 15-25, esp. p. 17.

15. L.E. Keck, 'Toward the Renewal of New Testament Christology', *NTS* 32
(1986), pp. 362-77, esp. p. 369; and already P. Vielhauer, 'Ein Weg zur neutestamentlichen Christologie? Prüfung der Thesen Ferdinand Hahns', in *idem*, *Aufsätze
zum Neuen Testament* (TBü, 31; Munich: Chr. Kaiser Verlag, 1965), pp. 141-98,
esp. pp. 143, 196. Cf. now also the approach taken by M. Karrer, *Jesus Christus im
Neuen Testament* (GNT, 11; Göttingen: Vandenhoeck & Ruprecht, 1998).

16. Drawing immediate conclusions from texts about communities or groups
whose existence might be reflected in those texts is a carry over from form criticism, which needs a fundamental revision. Here it might be noticed that the use of
the category *Sitz im Leben* resulted in a dramatic disregard for the rhetorical
function of the Gospels. Cf. also I.H. Henderson, *Jesus, Rhetoric and Law* (BIS, 20;
Leiden: E.J. Brill, 1996).

be stressed that it is not possible to draw immediate conclusions from a text—or even a certain designation—as to the historical situation which may lie behind it.[17] The assumption of certain groups with opposing Christologies at the beginning of Christianity, whose existence could be detected from sources allegedly utilized in the early Christian scriptures,[18] seems to be questionable. A closer look at the designations and ideas used to interpret the historical person Jesus of Nazareth shows, instead, that these terms influenced each other and, as a result, their meanings often overlap. Therefore they should not be strictly delimited from one another.[19]

In the discussion of Mark's Christology it was assumed that in his own approach Mark may be correcting an older understanding, in which the miracles of Jesus played a decisive role, and which interpreted the title υἱὸς θεοῦ ('Son of God') in terms of a Hellenistic θεῖος ἀνήρ ('Divine Man') notion.[20] Consequently, this approach studies the development of Christology in Mark's Gospel as a reaction to older traditions.[21] With

17. Cf. N.A. Dahl, 'Sources of Christological Language', in *idem, Jesus the Christ*, pp. 113-35, esp. pp. 125-26.

18. Thus H. Koester, *Ancient Christian Gospels: Their History and Development* (London: SCM Press, 1990). Cf. earlier J.M. Robinson and H. Köster, *Entwicklungslinien durch die Welt des frühen Christentums* (Tübingen: J.C.B. Mohr [Paul Siebeck], 1971).

19. Cf. de Jonge, 'Earliest Use', p. 322.

20. Cf., e.g., T.J. Weeden, *Mark: Traditions in Conflict* (Philadelphia: Fortress Press, 1971), among others. D.S. du Toit has demonstrated the questionableness of the presupposed notion of a θεῖος ἀνήρ concept in early Christianity in general. Cf. D.S. du Toit, *Theios Anthropos: Zur Verwendung von* θεῖος ἄνθρωπος *und sinnverwandten Ausdrücken in der Literatur der Kaiserzeit* (WUNT, 2.91; Tübingen: J.C.B. Mohr [Paul Siebeck], 1997). The postulation of such a christological view, which was assumed also for Paul's opponents in 2 Corinthians (cf. D. Georgi, *Die Gegner des Paulus im 2. Korintherbrief: Studien zur religiösen Propaganda in der Spätantike* [WMANT, 11; Neukirchen–Vluyn: Neukirchener Verlag, 1964]), might, therefore, require at least a new foundation.

21. Taken to the extreme this position was pursued to the point that one can deny a consistent Christology for Mark's Gospel at all and, instead, regard his work as a synthesis of previous perspectives. Cf. E. Trocmé, 'Is there a Markan Christology?', in B. Lindars and S.S. Smalley (eds.), *Christ and Spirit in the New Testament* (Festschrift C.F.D. Moule; Cambridge: Cambridge University Press, 1973), pp. 3-13. Here it becomes obvious that a redaction-critical view remains unsatisfying, when it is designed as a continuation of 'form-critical' beginnings.

regard to Q, analogous ideas have been maintained. The temptation story in Q 4 is, for example, thought to be a text that entered the Q document only at a later stage in its history of composition and interpreted older traditions from a distinct christological perspective.[22] Similarly, some have argued that Q 10.21-22 would reflect a view of Jesus that is foreign to the rest of Q and should be regarded, therefore, as a later intrusion. The view of Jesus as υἱός ('Son'), who stands in an exclusive relationship with God as πατήρ ('Father'), is thought to express an already developed christological stage, which one could not presuppose for the older traditions of Q.[23] According to yet another view, the bulk of the Son of Man sayings in Q are attributed to a later stage of the literary development of the Q document. It is assumed that the prophetic-apocalyptic intensification of the message of Jesus was caused by a situation in which the messengers of Q met with opposition from their fellow Jews and reacted with the proclamation of Jesus as the Son of Man, returning in judgment.[24]

---

22. S. Schulz, *Q: Die Spruchquelle der Evangelisten* (Zürich: Theologischer Verlag, 1972), pp. 177-90; J.S. Kloppenborg, *The Formation of Q: Trajectories in Ancient Wisdom Collections* (Philadelphia: Fortress Press, 1987), pp. 247-48; A.D. Jacobson, *The First Gospel: An Introduction to Q* (Sonoma, CA: Polebridge Press, 1992), pp. 86-95, among others.

23. R. Uro, *Sheep among the Wolves: A Study on the Mission Instructions of Q* (AASF, 47; Helsinki: Suomalainen Tiedeakatemia, 1987), pp. 114, 200-40; Jacobson, *The First Gospel*, p. 147, among others.

24. The discussion about the Son of Man sayings in Q varies quite widely and is marked by a number of hypotheses about different layers in Q. The details cannot be documented here. One might refer, however, to H. Koester, 'The Sayings of Q and their Image of Jesus', in W.L. Petersen, J.S. Vos and H.J. de Jonge (eds.), *Sayings of Jesus: Canonical and Non-Canonical. Essays in Honour of Tjitze Baarda* (NovTSup, 89; Leiden: E.J. Brill, 1997), pp. 137-54. Koester undertakes a critical re-examination of the schematic separation, wisdom–apocalyptic, which has played a central role in parts of recent Q research. He expresses the alternative view that the redaction of Q, which was directed towards judgment and responsible for the intrusion of the apocalyptic Son of Man sayings, may be linked to a tendency which was already present in the older layers. There Jesus is presented as an eschatological prophet, but not as a social reformer or a Cynic philosopher. This view is an important and necessary correction to a particular tendency in American Q research and, in addition, does more justice to what John S. Kloppenborg intended in his comprehensive work on Q. For the argument followed here it may suffice to indicate that also among those who plead for several layers of composition in Q, the tendency can be observed not to play out one layer against the other.

The following remarks leave aside differentiations such as those. I do not deny, thereby, the importance of the quest for the history of traditions. However, the following interpretation is based on three considerations, which make it advisable to refrain from the above-mentioned ways of proceeding.[25] First, according to the methodological basis for this study, it is not plausible to assume a difference between tradition and redaction, which would allow the recovery of the main idea of a text only from the latter. The adoption of a tradition is a conscious decision by itself, which has to be considered on a par with the changes that an author made to it. Moreover, in the case of Mark and Q such changes are difficult to demonstrate.[26] Secondly, it is difficult to prove that particular traditions were picked up principally from a critical perspective with the result that two opposing perspectives would be reflected within one and the same work. With regard to Mark today the insufficiency of such a model is widely acknowledged, but for Q it should be taken into account as well. The methodological conclusion should be that a quest for traditions behind a text must be closely tied to a literary analysis of that text itself. Thirdly, it can be demonstrated exegetically that the Christology of Mark cannot adequately be understood on the basis of a conflict model[27] and that the Q texts mentioned above do not introduce a view which is foreign to the older traditions

25. For the following remarks I should like to refer particularly to C. Tuckett's important monograph on Q: *Q and the History of Early Christianity: Studies on Q* (Edinburgh: T. & T. Clark, 1996).

26. Cf. C. Tuckett, 'On the Stratification of Q', in J.S. Kloppenborg and L.E. Vaage (eds.), *Early Christianity, Q and Jesus* (Semeia, 55; Atlanta: Scholars Press, 1992), pp. 213-22; C. Breytenbach, 'Das Markusevangelium als traditionsgebundene Erzählung? Anfragen an die Markusforschung der achtziger Jahre', in C. Focant (ed.), *The Synoptic Gospels: Source Criticism and the New Literary Criticism* (BETL, 110; Leuven: Peeters, 1993), pp. 77-110, esp. pp. 98-101.

27. The perspective on the function of the δυνάμεις Jesus in Mark has changed essentially since the time of the studies of Weeden, Schreiber and others. Hence, we can refrain here from further substantiation. Cf., e.g., A. Lindemann, 'Die Erzählung der Machttaten Jesu in Markus 4,35–6,6a: Erwägungen zum formgeschichtlichen und zum hermeneutischen Problem', in C. Breytenbach and H. Paulsen (eds.), *Die Anfänge der Christologie* (Festschrift F. Hahn; Göttingen: Vandenhoeck & Ruprecht, 1991), pp. 185-207, esp. pp. 206-207; R. Schmücker, 'Zur Funktion der Wundergeschichten im Markusevangelium', *ZNW* 84 (1993), pp. 1-26.

and therefore would have to be separated from these.[28] A quest for older traditions may allow a look into the early phase of the Jesus tradition and, in addition, sharpen the view of the character of the texts in question.[29] It is difficult in this way, however, to grasp the profile of Mark and Q themselves.

On the basis of these assumptions I will ask how the activity and destiny of Jesus in Mark and Q were interpreted. As opposed to the pre-Pauline and Pauline stream of tradition, the earthly activity of Jesus in Mark and Q becomes an essential element which shapes the particular narrative content in a way that is relevant to the genre. Thus, the character of those approaches can be seen in the emphasis of the enduring meaning of Jesus within a perspective which transcends the time of his earthly activity. For an appropriate approach to both concepts I will, therefore, ask—according to the conviction that Mark's Gospel is a biographical narrative and Q a sayings-biography[30]—how the activity

28. On the temptation narrative, cf. C. Tuckett, 'The Temptation Narrative in Q', in F. van Segbroeck *et al.* (eds.), *The Four Gospels* (Festschrift F. Neirynck; BETL, 100; Leuven: Peeters, 1992), pp. 479-507; on the Son of Man sayings see C. Tucket, 'The Son of Man in Q', in M.C. de Boer (ed.), *From Jesus to John: Essays on New Testament Christology in Honour of Marinus de Jonge* (JSNTSup, 84; Sheffield: JSOT Press, 1993), pp. 196-215; on 10.21-22 see Tuckett, *Q and the History of Early Christianity*, pp. 276-81. Form-analytical arguments (thus M. Sato, *Q und Prophetie: Studien zur Gattungs- und Traditionsgeschichte der Quelle Q* [WUNT, 2.29; Tübingen: J.C.B. Mohr (Paul Siebeck), 1988], p. 36 in reference to the temptation narrative) are often based on the circular argument that at a first stage of composition Q may have been characterized by sayings of Jesus, which then leads to the removal of other genres (as e.g. Q 4.1-13 or 7.1-10) from this postulated layer.

29. It is, e.g., probable that Mark and Q felt obliged to preserve and to pass on the proclamation of Jesus. By comparison, neither the assumption of an ideological opposite of the oral and the written traditions, nor that of early Christian prophets who spoke in the name of the exalted one, are actually plausible.

30. D. Dormeyer, *Das Neue Testament im Rahmen der antiken Literaturgeschichte: Eine Einführung* (Darmstadt: Wissenschaftliche Buchgesellschaft, 1993), pp. 214-25; C. Breytenbach, 'Das Markusevangelium als episodische Erzählung', in F. Hahn (ed.), *Der Erzähler des Evangeliums: Methodische Neuansätze in der Markusforschung* (SBS, 118/119; Stuttgart: Katholisches Bibelwerk, 1985), pp. 137-69; J. Schröter, *Erinnerung an Jesu Worte: Studien zur Rezeption der Logienüberlieferung in Markus, Q und Thomas* (WMANT, 76: Neukirchen–Vluyn: Neukirchener Verlag, 1997), pp. 459-61.

of Jesus is shaped in these writings and interpret the designations (or titles) used for Jesus within their respective frameworks. This seems to be a plausible way of proceeding because essential elements of the presentations of Jesus are expressed in narratives about Jesus or in speeches by him.[31] Thereby, two aspects will emerge as particularly important, namely the proclamation of the Kingdom and the self-designation of Jesus as ὁ υἱὸς τοῦ ἀνθρώπου ('the Son of Man'). It is just these points that manifest the connection of Jesus' preaching with the meaning of his person. Therefore, the approaches which are based on a rather strict separation of both aspects[32] must be called into question. Other designations can be analysed only in light of this perspective. These shall be addressed in the third part of the essay. Finally, some consequences for the origins of early Christology shall be drawn.

2. *Aspects of Jesus' Activity*

With regard to the concepts of Mark and Q it can be stated in principle that the beginning of the βασιλεία ('Kingdom') is the central issue of Jesus' appearance. In Mark this event is closely bound up with Jesus' performing of healings, exorcisms and other miracles, whereas in Q the same event is expressed in the first place in his speeches.[33] Moreover, it is of central importance for Mark's narrative that Jesus is introduced already at the beginning as χριστός and (if one follows the variant from

31. R.C. Tannehill, 'The Gospel of Mark as Narrative Christology', in N.R. Petersen (ed.), *Perspectives on Mark's Gospel* (Semeia, 16; Atlanta: Scholars Press, 1980), pp. 57-95; M.E. Boring, 'The Christology of Mark: Hermeneutical Issues for Systematic Theology', in R. Jewett (ed.), *Christology and Exegesis: New Approaches* (Semeia, 30; Atlanta: Scholars Press, 1985), pp. 125-53. In Q, by comparison, the interpretation is worked out implicitly rather than explicitly (cf. Polag, *Christologie*, p. 127).

32. Cf., e.g., P. Vielhauer, 'Gottesreich und Menschensohn in der Verkündigung Jesu', in *idem, Aufsätze zum Neuen Testament*, pp. 55-91, whose thesis was taken up by J.M. Robinson, 'The Q Trajectory: Between John and Matthew via Jesus', in B. Pearson (ed.), *The Future of Early Christianity: Essays in Honor of Helmut Koester* (Minneapolis: Fortress Press, 1991), pp. 173-94.

33. The διδάσκειν of Jesus, mentioned for the first time in Mk 1.21, is illustrated in 1.23-26 by an exorcism, which therefore functions as proof of the διδαχὴ καινή, (1.27). In Q, on the other hand, the opening speech stands at the beginning at 6.20-49, and is, therefore, deliberately put before the healing of the centurion's servant, which follows it.

א¹ B D L W 2427) as υἱὸς θεοῦ. An analogous statement for Q cannot be made, since its beginning is lost. It should be noted, however, that in Q Jesus is also introduced as υἱὸς θεοῦ before his first activity, namely in the temptation narrative.[34] In order to ascertain what is expressed about Jesus with the help of these designations, one has first to pay attention to their use within Mark and Q themselves, before one can broaden the investigation by looking at aspects of their meaning in other Jewish texts.[35] In Mark and Q it is the beginning of God's Kingdom which forms the basis for the application of the designations χριστός and υἱὸς θεοῦ to Jesus, although a difference in meaning with regard to the latter will emerge below. Hence, the readers have information about Jesus' identity from the beginning, although the concrete meaning of those designations can only be grasped by following the narrative outline. In addition, both approaches have to deal with the historical fact that the

34. Q 4.3, 9. Whether this was preceded by a report on the appointment of Jesus as Son of God—perhaps in analogy to the Markan baptism narrative—must remain hypothetical.

35. Cf. Boring, 'The Christology of Mark', p. 131, on Mark. It will be shown that the assumption of a Son of God Christology in Mark is not without problems. It is likewise questionable for an explanation of the Son of God texts in Mark to refer back to a pre-Markan mission Christology (see J. Ernst, *Das Evangelium nach Markus* [RNT, 2; Regensburg: Pustet, 1981], pp. 42-44) or to regard with U.B. Müller 'das jüdische Denkmodell vom leidenden Gerechten, den Gott ins Recht setzt' as the presupposition for the application of these designations to Jesus in Rom. 1.3-4 as well in Mark (cf. U.B. Müller, '"Sohn Gottes": Ein messianischer Hoheitstitel Jesu', *ZNW* 87 [1996], pp. 1-32, esp. p. 12). Similarly D. Lührmann, Biographie des Gerechten als Evangelium: Vorstellungen zu einem Markus-Kommentar', *WuD* 14 (1977), pp. 25-50. The basic text on the Suffering Righteous One from Wis. 2.12-20 is referred to by Kloppenborg, in order to clarify the meaning of Jesus' death in Q. Cf. Kloppenborg, ' "Easter Faith" and the Sayings Gospel Q', in R. Cameron (ed.), *The Apocryphal Jesus and Christian Origins* (Semeia, 49; Atlanta: Scholars Press, 1990), pp. 71-99. Kloppenborg, by picking up a thesis of G.W.E. Nickelsburg, even assumes the existence of a particular form, the wisdom tale, in which the motif of the persecution and subsequent justification of the Just One may be a constitutive element. This scheme is assumed to be the basis of narratives such as the story of Joseph, Ahikar, and Esther among others, and may be presupposed also for the Markan passion narrative and for Q. Whether the mentioned texts really belong to a common genre, might be questioned. It is even more difficult to demonstrate the existence of a pre-Markan passion narrative on the basis of such an assumed genre and also to presuppose such a narrative as the formative component of Q's story of Jesus.

one so described was killed. This factor was integrated into the interpretation of his activity, as was also the use of these designations for him. It is necessary, therefore, to put the interpretation of Jesus' activity and destiny into sharper focus.

Both Mark and Q establish a chronological and geographical framework for the appearance of Jesus.[36] John the Baptist marks a decisive event in the history of Israel;[37] the wilderness and the region around the River Jordan are the places of his activity.[38] Moreover, both Mark and Q presuppose the absence of Jesus in their own time and understand the present as a time for the preaching of the Kingdom of God, respectively the gospel, until his return (Q 10.9; Mk 13.10). The activity of Jesus is mainly located in Galilee,[39] whereas Jerusalem appears as a hostile place.[40] The narrative world is comprised further of a circle of persons,

36. For further substantiation see J. Schröter, 'Markus, Q und der historische Jesus. Methodische und exegetische Erwägungen zu den Anfängen der Rezeption der Verkündigung Jesu', *ZNW* 89 (1998), pp. 173-200.

37. This becomes clear in the scriptural quotation in Mk 1.2/Q 7.27, which explains the appearance of John, as well as in Q 16.16 (Matthaean reading, see Mt. 11.12-13), where the time of John and Jesus is qualified as the time of the βασιλεία, as opposed to that of the law and the prophets (for further substantiation for the latter see J. Schröter, 'Erwägungen zum Gesetzesverständnis in Q anhand von Q 16.16-18', in C. Tuckett [ed.], *The Scriptures in the Gospels* [BETL, 131; Leuven: Peeters, 1997], pp. 441-58, esp. pp. 443-50).

38. The expression ἐν τῇ ἐρήμῳ in Mk 1.4 falls back on the previously cited text of Isaiah and applies to John, who is portrayed as a prophet. For Q, the phrase πᾶσα ἡ περίχωρος τοῦ Ἰορδάνου (Mt. 3.5/Lk. 3.3) can be assumed with certainty. It describes the area of the Baptist's activity. If thereby an allusion to Gen. 13.10-11 (cf. *1 Clem.* 11.1) is intended, the Baptist's preaching of repentance would be compared to the judgment of Sodom and Gomorrah. This could find further support in 10.12, where an even harsher penalty is threatened against the cities that reject the Q-messengers. Cf. J.S. Kloppenborg, 'City and Wasteland: Narrative World and the Beginning of Sayings Gospel (Q)', in D.E. Smith (ed.), *How Gospels Begin* (Semeia, 52; Atlanta: Scholars Press, 1990), pp. 145-60, esp. pp. 151-52. In any case, with the localization of John a programmatic scene is described, which is important for what follows.

39. Nazareth (in Q: Ναζαρά), Capernaum as well as Bethsaida are mentioned by both. In Q, in addition, the name of Chorazin is mentioned. In Mark the Sea of Genesareth belongs to the scenery of the narrative world.

40. See already Mk 3.22; 7.1 where Jesus' opponents come from Jerusalem to Galilee. From ch. 11 onwards Jerusalem is permanently designed as a place of hostility against Jesus. In Q 13.34 Jerusalem is related to the killing of the prophets.

who are either in a friendly or an unfriendly relationship with the main character, Jesus.[41] It is obvious, therefore, that in both concepts the activity of a concrete person within a particular narrative world is designated.[42] This must be kept in view, because it leads to the consequence that designations applied to the main character Jesus have to be interpreted in connection with the narrated events.

The use of a narrative means of presentation by Mark is incomparably more detailed than what we find in Q.[43] This becomes immediately obvious by looking at Mark's extensive use of the *chreia* form, which plays only a marginal role in Q. This form-analytical observation is important for the classification of both writings, because it links Mark's Gospel with Hellenistic rhetoric.[44] Thereby, it is striking that the Markan *chreiai* are closely linked to each other by the account and in this way contribute to a larger biographical framework.[45] This can be shown, for

41. To the former group belong the disciples and John; to the latter the Pharisees and the scribes (Mark), Jesus' family (Mark), Satan as well as the demons.

42. It should be noted, by the way, that this is one of the important differences that distinguishes Q from the *Gospel of Thomas*. In recent scholarship comparing Q and the *Gospel of Thomas* the similarities are often stressed. This should not lead, however, to results which are based on neglecting differences which are of (at least) equal importance.

43. Cf. E. Best, 'Mark's Narrative Technique', *JSNT* 37 (1989), pp. 43-58.

44. For research on *chreia* from a rhetorical perspective cf. V.K. Robbins, 'The Creia', in D.E. Aune (ed.), *Greco-Roman Literature and the New Testament* (SBLSBS, 21; Atlanta: Scholars Press, 1988), pp. 1-23; R.F. Hock, 'Cynics and Rhetoric', in S.E. Porter (ed.), *Handbook of Classical Rhetoric in the Hellenistic Period 330 B.C.—A.D. 400* (Leiden: E.J. Brill, 1997), pp. 755-73; R.F. Hock and E.N. O'Neil, *The Chreia in Ancient Rhetoric. I. The Progymnasmata* (Atlanta: Scholars Press, 1986). The Claremont Chreia Project, as well as the Pronouncement Stories Group of the SBL, have, however, developed a perspective that has not principally distanced itself from the form-critical paradigm. Cf. B.L. Mack and V.K. Robbins, *Patterns of Persuasion in the Gospels* (Sonoma, CA: Polebridge Press, 1989); V.K. Robbins, 'Progymnastic Rhetorical Composition and Pre-Gospel Traditions: A New Approach', in C. Focant (ed.), *The Synoptic Gospels: Source Criticism and the New Literary Criticism* (BETL, 110; Leuven: Peeters, 1993), pp. 111-47. The problems related to that will have to be discussed in another place.

45. Temporal and geographical expressions, which connect the narrated scenes to one another are, e.g., εὐθύς, πάλιν, ὀψίας γενομένης, ἐξῆλθεν ἐκεῖθεν, among others.

example, by the explicit connections between individual scenes.[46] With regard to Q, it is significant, by analogy, that an image of Jesus is shaped by means of the composition of larger speeches out of individual sayings. This is accomplished in the portrayal of Jesus—which is to some extent also created by the use of *chreiai*—and in the already mentioned composition of a temporal and spatial world. Moreover, the treatment of the sayings and parables by connecting them to larger speeches is paralleled in Mark to a certain extent.[47] This phenomenon could be taken as evidence for the fact that both Mark and Q partially depend on a common basis for their image of Jesus.

As I have pointed out already, the activity of Jesus in Mark and Q is dominated by the announcement of the present βασιλεία τοῦ θεοῦ. From the time of the Babylonian exile, this notion of the reign of God had not been formulated any longer as something perceived to be an earthly experience,[48] but rather was seen to be the hope that had yet to be realized in future events.[49] Thus, a notion which usually was used to design a future event became the central idea for understanding the

46. Cf., e.g., the reference back in 8.18c-21, referring to 6.41-44, as well as the reference back in 16.7, referring to 14.28.

47. Cf. my *Erinnerung an Jesu Worte*.

48. Research on the subject of God's βασιλεία has relativized the often maintained singularity of this central concept of Jesus' preaching by referring to the early Jewish horizon of expectations, which was dominated in particular by the situation of the Diaspora, the oppression by Gentile peoples, and by the corresponding expectations of a gathering of his people by God himself. Cf., e.g., A.M. Schwemer, 'Gott als König und seine Königsherrschaft in den Sabbatliedern aus Qumran', in M. Hengel and A.M. Schwemer (eds.), *Königsherrschaft Gottes und himmlischer Kult im Judentum, Urchristentum und in der hellenistischen Welt* (WUNT, 55; Tübingen: J.C.B. Mohr [Paul Siebeck], 1991), pp. 45-118; J. Becker, *Jesus von Nazaret* (Berlin: W. de Gruyter, 1996), pp. 100-21; J.P. Meier, *A Marginal Jew: Rethinking the Historical Jesus*. II. *Mentor, Message, and Miracles* (ABRL; 2 vols.; New York: Doubleday, 1994), pp. 237-88; M. Wolter, ' "Reich Gottes" bei Lukas', *NTS* 41 (1995), pp. 541-63, esp. pp. 545-47; M. Welker and M. Wolter, 'Die Unscheinbarkeit des Reiches Gottes', in W. Härle and R. Preul (eds.), *Reich Gottes* (Marburger Jahrbuch Theologie, 11; MTS, 53; Marburg: Elwert, 1999), pp. 103-16. On the background in Old Testament writings cf. E. Zenger, 'Herrschaft/Reich Gottes II: Altes Testament', *TRE* 15 (1986), pp. 176-89.

49. There are good reasons to assume that this has its origin in the activity of Jesus itself, although this question is not of central importance for the argument followed here.

activity of Jesus. Jesus' first public appearance in Mk 1.15 and Q 6.20 is clearly linked to the βασιλεία ('Kingdoms') theme. For Mark it concerns the call to μετάνοια ('repentance') and πιστεύειν ('believe') in the face of the βασιλεία, which is now breaking in, whereas in Q the βασιλεία is promised to the poor. A difference between Mark and Q is that Mark situates the preaching about the βασιλεία by use of a term that only appears in Hellenistic literature, εὐαγγέλιον ('gospel'). According to Mk 13.10 the εὐαγγέλιον is to be announced to all peoples in the time prior to the return of the Son of Man. Q, on the other hand, uses the verb εὐαγγελίζειν ('proclaiming good news'; 7.22), picked up from Isa. 61.1. This verb has a close link to the βασιλεία-theme as well because it occurs within the sketch of Jesus' activity, which answers John the Baptist's question of whether Jesus is ὁ ἐρχόμενος ('the Coming One').[50] The description of Jesus' activity in Q 7.22[51] alludes to several passages from Isaiah, and thereby forms an inclusio with 6.20, insofar as the πτωχοί ('poor'), who are pronounced blessed there, appear again as the recipients of Jesus' εὐαγγελίζειν.[52] To understand the βασιλεία-theme more clearly one has to look at the presentation of Jesus' activity and at the relationship of the beginning of God's reign to its completion. Both aspects lead to the question of Jesus' identity and, therefore, to the question of the image of Jesus, as that has been designed in Mark and Q.

A comparison of the healings and exorcisms reported in Mark and Q is striking. This stream of the Jesus tradition is only marginally represented in Q.[53] That does not mean, however, that it is not important for Q's

50. Luke connected both terms directly with one another and speaks of the εὐαγγελίζειν τὴν βασιλείαν τοῦ θεοῦ (Lk. 4.43; 8.1; 16.16). In Acts, Jesus himself becomes the content of εὐαγγελίζειν (Acts 5.42; 8.35; 11.20). Both are connected in Acts 8.12 where Philip is εὐαγγελιζόμενος περὶ τῆς βασιλείας τοῦ θεοῦ καὶ τοῦ ὀνόματος Ἰησοῦ Χριστοῦ.

51. F. Neirynck, 'Q 6.20b-21; 7.22 and Isaiah 61', in C. Tuckett (ed.), *The Scriptures in the Gospels* (BETL, 131; Leuven: Peeters, 1997), pp. 27-64, csp. pp. 45-51.

52. J.M. Robinson, 'The Sayings Gospel Q', in F. van Segbroeck *et al.* (eds.), *The Four Gospels* (Festschrift F. Neirynck; BETL, 100; Leuven: Peeters, 1992), pp. 361-88, esp. p. 366; J.M. Robinson, 'The Incipit of the Sayings Gospel Q', *RHPR* 75 (1995), pp. 9-33, esp. p. 32.

53. One has to recognize a phenomenon analogous to the *chreiai*. The healing stories occur frequently in Mark and Luke. Matthew and Q take them up only sparingly, pushing to the fore instead the teaching of Jesus.

image of Jesus. Rather, it contributes to a more comprehensive picure of events which manifest the reign of God. The poor, the hungry and the weeping are promised satisfaction in their need as something that takes place at the end of time, whereas the beginning of this satisfaction is already experienced by the eyewitnesses to Jesus.[54] From that a particular establishment of priorities emerges: care for daily needs is a behaviour which characterizes Gentiles, but which, for the Jesus movement, should be replaced by striving after the βασιλεία.[55] Because God now establishes his reign, cooperation is the highest command. The addressees of Q are asked to announce the nearness of the βασιλεία (10.9), and to realize its appearance symbolically through the renunciation of the usual outfitting for the journey (10.4), as well as through the ethic of love of enemies, of renunciation of revenge, and of not judging (6.27-42).

Jesus' δυνάμεις ('mighty works') have to be understood against this background as tokens of proof of the established reign of God. The reported cure in 7.1-10 serves as a symbolic realization of the βασιλεία, announced by Jesus in his opening speech in 6.20-49. Likewise, the δυνάμεις in 10.13-15 are mentioned as the reason the inhabitants of Chorazin and Bethsaida should change their minds in view of the beginning reign of God. Finally, in 11.14-20 an exorcism is the cause of a dispute over the origin of Jesus' power, which culminates in the statement that the decisive difference between Jesus' exorcisms and those of other Jewish exorcists consists in the fact that the activity of Jesus signifies the appearance of the βασιλεία τοῦ θεοῦ ('Kingdom of God').

Q 7.22 is again of importance in relation to this phenomenon. At the end of the first part of Q the activity of Jesus is summarily described by referring to prophecies from Isaiah about God's activity at the end of time. The events mentioned there are only partly explicitly reported in Q. This demonstrates that Jesus' activity as a whole was regarded as the fulfilment of the expectations for the end of time and was interpreted in this light. Such an understanding of Q 7.22 is supported by additional evidence from 4Q521 2.ii, where healing the blind, raising the dead and

---

54. It is not accidental then that in 10.23 another beatitude occurs, which thematically is closely related to 6.20-21: μακάριοι οἱ ὀφθαλμοὶ οἱ βλέποντες ἃ βλέπετε.

55. Q 12.29-31. Cf. further 11.3 as well as 4.4. These texts show that Q demands leaving the care of daily need to God, as well as asking him for the establishment of his reign.

preaching the good news to the poor are presented as events of the end-time.[56] For the question discussed here it is of particular interest to note that neither in Qumran nor in any other Jewish text of the Second Temple period are such activities presented as works of God's Messiah(s). Rather they are expected of God himself.[57] Q 7.22 has to be regarded, therefore, as an astounding culmination of the events of the end-time, which are not explained by the conviction that Jesus is God's Messiah, especially since this designation is absent from Q. Instead, that Jesus' activity was interpreted in such a way can only be explained by referring to his claim to be God's decisive envoy and to the use of the designation 'Son of Man'. Before I return to this question I shall first look at an analogous phenomenon in Mark.

In Mark 7.37 one finds a reference to Isa. 35.5 which reflects on the miracles of Jesus in Gentile regions and which, in its summarizing character, is comparable to Q 7.22. The healings and exorcisms of Jesus are interpreted, as well, as proofs of the time of salvation now breaking in. Mark, however, places greater weight on the description of these δυνάμεις, exercised by Jesus, than Q does. The concerned reports are

---

56. The edition and discussion of the text was done by E. Puech, 'Une apocalypse messianique (4Q521)', *RevQ* 15 (1992), pp. 475-522, esp. p. 485.

57. Controversial in the discussion of this fragment from Qumran is whether one should read in l. 1 the singular משיחו or the plural משיחיו. From this decision the question depends on whether the texts treat the activity of God through his Messiah at all. If the text says that the Messiah heals the lame, restores the dead to life, preaches the good news to the poor, satisfies the lowly, leads the lost and fills the hungry it would be a remarkable analogy to Q 7.22 (and Lk. 4.18-19), which would prove the mentioned activities as works of the (a?) Messiah already in pre-Christian times. (J.J. Collins interprets it this way [*Scepter*, pp. 205-206].) The possibility of a singular variant cannot be excluded—although on the basis of קדושים in l. 2, it is at least ambiguous (cf. Puech, 'Une apocalypse messianique', p.486). For the skeptical position cf. J. Maier, *Die Qumran-Essener: Die Texte vom Toten Meer*, II (UTB, 1863; Munich: Reinhardt, 1995), p. 683 n. 651. In any case, it might not b plausible to refer the deeds mentioned in the text to the Messiah because from l. 5 onwards the text speaks explicitly about the activity of God himself (cf. אדני in line 5 and 11). Also the reference to Isa. 61.1 which is cited in Q 7.22 and 11QMelch 2.18 cannot solve this problem. On the one hand Q—as opposed to 11QMelch —does not speak about the anointed one. On the other hand, in 11QMelch the deeds from Q 7.22 and 4Q521 are not mentioned. It is, of course, instructive that in 11QMelch there is also a connection between the end-time messenger and the εὐαγγελ- terminology—here by referring to the εὐαγγελιζόμενος from Isa. 52.7 (ll. 15-16).

concentrated in the first part of the narrative and therefore present the basis for the christologically pivotal text 8.27-33, where Peter answers Jesus' question of his identity with σὺ εἶ ὁ χριστός ('you are the Christ'). In this text the activity of Jesus, which was already depicted as the appearance of the βασιλεία (1.15), is interpreted for the first time in the narrative by using the designation χριστός. Even if the following command to silence indicates the incompleteness of this understanding, it is nevertheless clear that the presentation of the actual occurrence of the βασιλεία is given incomparably more room than is the case in Q. The reason for this has to be sought in the opposite direction to those approaches that assume a more or less fortunate attempt at integration with another Christology. Since the appearance of the reign of God announced by Jesus is—for the recipients of Mark's Gospel—ambivalent, unclear and, at best, perceived as a contradictory truth, the actuality of its occurrence must be described.[58] Since the reign of God manifests itself only in secrecy, Jesus' disciples have to be explicitly instructed about the μυστήριον τῆς βασιλείας ('secret of the Kingdom'), which exists in the connection of the inconspicuous beginning, in the present, to the powerful completion, by God himself, in the (near) future.

This phenomenon calls attention to the fact that the miracle stories are immediately concerned with the problem of Jesus' identity, which on the narrative level is controversial and whose final resolution will take place only in the future. The occasional command to silence thereby links Jesus' mighty acts to Peter's confession of Jesus as the Christ. Consequently, a closer connection between the appearance of the reign of God and Jesus, as its decisive representative, is established. This connection, however, should not be interpreted in such a way that Jesus himself is claimed to be the μυστήριον ('secret') mentioned in ch. 4.[59] Rather, the μυστήριον τῆς βασιλείας consists of the relationship of its present hiddenness with its future fulfilment by God and the coming

---

58. Schmücker correctly observes that without the miracle stories '[d]ie βασιλεία-Verkündigung...innerhalb der markinischen Jesus-Erzählung eigentümlich uneingelöst [bliebe]', because '[e]rst durch die Wundergeschichten...sichtbar [wird], was das Nahesein der βασιλεία τοῦ θεοῦ bedeutet' ('Zur Funktion der Wundergeschichten', p. 21).

59. See M. Theobald, 'Gottessohn und Menschensohn: Zur polaren Struktur der Christologie im Markusevangelium', *SNTU* 13 (1988), pp. 37-97, esp. p. 46 n. 31.

of the Son of Man.[60] Therefore, the concept of the reign of God, starting in secrecy in the present, and that of the controversial identity of Jesus, sometimes expressed by the prohibition against making that identity known, prove to be two corresponding lines, which in 8.38–9.1 are explicitly brought together. There the announcement of coming of the Son of Man is immediately continued by referring to the imminent in-breaking of God's reign. Consequently, the miracles of Jesus are the beginning of God's reign; they do not, however, reveal Jesus' identity.[61]

From these observations we may derive several fundamental conclusions.

1. The decisive event of Jesus' coming has to be seen in the appearance of the reign of God that is inseparably linked to it. An analysis of the depiction of Jesus in Mark and Q (and perhaps in the Synoptics in general) has to start, therefore, with the assumption that Jesus is the decisive representative of the establishment of God's reign. The designations that are applied to him become accessible in their specific meaning only from this perspective. It follows further that the concepts of Mark and Q can only be grasped as a consequence of the presentation of the activity and destiny of Jesus. It seems unlikely in the face of this conclusion that for early Christians there was ever an 'unmessianic

60. The oft-discussed question of the connection of the βασιλεία theme to Christology, according to the view presented here, cannot be answered in accordance with Wrede's interpretation, who, along with many others, linked both directly with one another and therefore identified the Messianic secret with the μυστήριον τῆς βασιλείας of 4.11. But the parables are not about the question of Jesus' identity, but about the beginning and the completion of God's kingdom. The question of Jesus' identity has to be differentiated from this aspect.

61. Theobald, 'Gottessohn und Menschensohn', p. 70, therefore correctly remarks that the miracles of Jesus 'nicht isoliert zu betrachten, sondern einzuordnen [sind] in die übergreifende Dynamik der anbrechenden Gottesherrschaft'. However, from my perspective it is not convincing to argue that according to Mark 'nicht die Heilungen und Exorzismen *heilsbegründend* waren, sondern allein die Ereignisse um den "Menschensohn": sein Tod am Kreuz sowie sein erhofftes Eintreten als Auferstandener für die an ihn Glaubenden beim nahen Gericht' ('Gottessohn und Menschensohn', p. 70; author's emphasis). The death on the cross in Mark's narrative is hardly 'the reason for salvation', but rather part of the divine plan for the Son of Man, Jesus, whose goal is the completion of the reign of God. The βασιλεία, which breaks in by means of the miracles, cannot therefore be subordinated to the death of the Son of Man with regard to its relevance for salvation.

character for the life and activity of Jesus'.[62] The decisive difference to (pre-)Pauline Christology lies, accordingly, in the fact that in the Synoptics 'Christology' has to be understood from the outset as a function of the importance of Jesus' appearance, and it can be asked, along with Gerhard Dautzenberg, whether from a historical point of view this does not speak for a priority of the concepts reflected in Mark and Q.[63]

2. In Mark, as well as in Q, the question of the relationship of the beginning of the reign of God to its fulfilment arises against this background. In Mark, this is a problem in particular, presumably because of the historical background of the rejection of Jesus' message by some of his Jewish contemporaries, and the historical background of the Jewish war and its consequences for Jesus' followers. These two background issues lead to the specific Markan theory of the 'secret of the Kingdom', which must be realized in order to belong to those whom the Son of Man will gather at his coming (13.27). In Q the small beginning and the great completion are opposed to one another,[64] whereby the stress lies on the warning to watchfulness in the face of the unexpected coming of the Son of Man.

3. The meaning of Jesus' death has to be determined against this horizon. It is no accident that this death is brought into connection with the forgiveness of sins only marginally in Mark and not at all in Q.[65] More important in this regard is the claim that God confirms his envoy

---

62. See W. Schmithals, 'Vom Ursprung der synoptischen Tradition', *ZTK* 94 (1997), pp. 288-316, esp. p. 305.

63. Cf. *idem*, 'Der Wandel der Reich-Gottes Verkündigung', pp. 23-24.

64. Instructive in this regard is a comparison of the versions of the Parable of the Mustard Seed in Mark and Q. Within Mk 4 it forms the conclusion to the instruction ἐν παραβολαῖς, which began in v. 3. It concludes therefore the account of the ambivalence of the present reception of the βασιλεία, which was begun in the Parable of the Sower with a view towards the end. In Q, on the other hand, by coupling it with the Parable of the Leaven, the accent is placed on the successive converting effect that the βασιλεία, once 'sown', produces.

65. To connect the expressions δοῦναι τὴν ψυχὴν αὐτοῦ λύτρον ἀντὶ πολλῶν in 10.45 and αἷμα τῆς διαθήκης τὸ ἐκχυννόμενον ὑπὲρ πολλῶν in 14.24 with the forgiveness of sins is, in any case, not compelling. Even if one does this, the texts cannot be put together into a coherent model of interpretation of the death of Jesus. Rather they remain as isolated expressions. The emphasis rather lies on the concept of the divine δεῖ of the passion predictions, which should be regarded as apologetic and orientated towards a history of salvation.

despite his apparent failure. This is expressed by Mark by the announcement of the resurrection as well as by the verification of it in the report of the discovery of the empty tomb. Moreover, in both Mark and Q the exaltation of Jesus is presupposed and constitutes the basis for the conviction that he himself will appear as the judging Son of Man and therefore complete his earthly activity.[66]

4. The approach to 'Christology' in Mark and Q has to be developed in a close connection with the description of the beginning reign of God. In what follows it will be shown that the decisive designation with which the claim that Jesus is the representative of the βασιλεία is expressed is ὁ υἱὸς τοῦ ἀνθρώπου. This remarkable agreement of Mark and Q leads to the question of whether the 'Christology' of Mark and Q is designed on the basis of the parallelism between the βασιλεία concept and the Son of Man expression.[67]

3. *Jesus, the Son of Man: On the Concept of 'Christology' in Mark and Q*

The question of Jesus' identity in Mark and Q arises out of his claim that his activity inaugurates the beginning of the reign of God. On the narrative level this is brought to expression by the questions posed as reaction to his powerful activity: τί ἐστιν τοῦτο ('What is this?'; Mk 1.27); τίς ἄρα οὗτός ἐστιν ('Who then is this?'; Mk 4.41); πόθεν τούτῳ ταῦτα, καὶ τίς ἡ σοφία ἡ δοθεῖσα τούτῳ, καὶ αἱ δυνάμεις τοιαῦται διὰ τῶν χειρῶν αὐτοῦ γινόμεναι ('Where did this man get all this? What mighty works are wrought by his hands?'; Mk 6.2); respectively σὺ εἶ ὁ ἐρχόμενος ('Are you the Coming One?' [or: 'the One who is to come']; Q 7.19). Moreover, according to Mk 6.14-16 and 8.28, irritations originate about who Jesus might be. What follows develops the thesis that the answer to the problem should emerge from an analysis of the use of the expression 'Son of Man', whereas υἱὸς θεοῦ is a category

66. Mk 8.38; 13.26-27; 14.62; Q 11.30; 12.8-9, 39-40; 17.23-24.

67. This approach has been hindered by the division of the Son of Man sayings into three distinct groups since R. Bultmann, and the subsequent discussion about which one of them could be reclaimed for Jesus himself. It has also been hindered by P. Vielhauer's dictum that the reign of God and the Son of Man would be incompatible ideas. In Q research these premises continue to have a lasting effect to the most recent discussion.

subordinated to it.[68] The use of χριστός by Mark, on the other hand, is interpreted, as well, by the expression 'Son of Man'. Other designations achieve no comparable weight of their own, but are arranged in relation to the Son of Man concept.[69]

One should begin with the often noticed observation that the term ὁ υἱὸς τοῦ ἀνθρώπου manifests the peculiarity that it is only used as a self-designation of Jesus.[70] However, Jesus (almost) never calls himself χριστός[71] or υἱὸς θεοῦ. These designations, on the contrary, are applied to him by others.[72] In addition to that, the Son of Man sayings show the

68. G. Dautzenberg formulated correctly: 'Wenn es einen Titel gibt, der im Markusevangelium alle Aspekte und Stadien der Geschichte Jesu von seinem Auftreten in Galiläa bis zu seiner Parusie integriert, dann ist es der Titel "Menschensohn" und nicht der Titel "Sohn Gottes" ' (cf. ' "Sohn Gottes" im Evangelium nach Markus', in *idem, Studien zur Theologie der Jesustradition* [SBA, 19; Stuttgart: Katholisches Bibelwerk, 1995], pp. 98-105, esp. p. 102). This applies to Q analogously. Cf. P. Hoffmann, *Studien zur Theologie der Logienquelle* (NTAbh NS 8; Münster: Aschendorff, 3rd edn, 1982), pp. 142-58 and earlier H.E. Tödt, *Der Menschensohn in der synoptischen Überlieferung* (Gütersloh: Gerd Mohn, 2nd edn, 1963), pp. 224-45. It is, therefore, hardly plausible when Theobald, 'Gottessohn und Menschensohn', p. 46, speaks about the 'für ihn [sc.: Markus, J.S.] bzw. seine Gemeinde christologisch maßgebenden Gottessohn-Titel', which according to him interprets the Christ-title.

69. This approach, therefore, goes against that of J.D. Kingsbury, *The Christology of Mark's Gospel* (Philadelphia: Fortress Press, 1983). According to Kingsbury, the expression 'Son of Man' is not used by Mark to clarify the identity of Jesus for his readers, but has to be understood anyway as a 'title of majesty' (*Christology*, pp. 159-73). Decisive for this view is Kingsbury's argument that the secret of the identity of Jesus is not revealed by the Son of Man expression (*Christology*, p. 171). This has to be grasped instead by the expressions 'Messiah', 'Son of David', 'King of the Jews' and 'Son of God'. In my opinion this confuses the evidence. Who Jesus is, is expressed with the help of the Son of Man expressions, which present therefore the basis for the interpretation of the Christ and Son of God expressions and qualify them in a particular manner. How that happens, has yet to be explained.

70. The exceptions of Jn 12.34 and Acts 7.56, which do not fundamentally change this finding, can be left aside.

71. Mk 9.41 is an exception, reflecting the post-Easter Christian creed, which therefore penetrates the narrative level. The inconsistency that Jesus designates himself as the Christ here, was already noticed by Matthew and changed in εἰς ὄνομα μαθητοῦ.

72. From that, one has to differentiate the self-designation of Jesus as ὁ υἱός in Mk 13.32 and Q 10.22. The mentioned result is supported by both texts, because in

peculiarity that a predication is linked to them, by means of which the identity of Jesus is described. He is presented, for example, as the one vested with power to forgive sins, as the suffering one, or as the one returning for final judgment.[73] This marks a characteristic difference with regard to the expressions χριστός and υἱὸς θεοῦ. The Christ-title is nowhere linked to predication, which would explain it further. That is true apart from the double combination with the designation υἱὸς θεοῦ (respectively υἱὸς τοῦ εὐλογητοῦ; 'Son of the Blessed') in Mk 1.1 and 14.61, which is of course itself in need of explanation. By means of the designation Son of God in two texts, the acceptance of Jesus as Son by God is anticipated or confirmed (1.11 and 9.7). The concrete meaning of this designation, however, likewise arises only out of its relation to the expression 'Son of Man'. Moreover, the expression 'Son of Man' serves to link Jesus' earthly power and lowliness with his function as a judge at the end of time. Finally, the remarkable positioning of the Son of Man expressions has to be noticed, which point to their particular interpretative meaning within Mark and Q. They occur in all three parts of Mark's Gospel and indicate how the expressions Christ and Son of God have to be understood. In Q, they frame the first complex 6.20–7.35 and then open the second (9.58), which is concluded by the saying of Jesus as the Son (10.22). In the later part, the relationship of earthly

both of them the Son of Man expressions are explained with the help of the relation υἱός–πατήρ. Mk 13.32 occurs in the context of a speech about apocalyptic events and speaks of angels, a son and a father. The scene is like the one in 8.38, where the theme is the arrival of the Son of Man ἐν τῇ δόξῃ τοῦ πατρὸς αὐτοῦ μετὰ τῶν ἀγγέλων τῶν ἁγίων. There the Son of Man is also seen as the Son of the Father. (Cf. also B. Lindars, *Jesus Son of Man: A Fresh Examination of the Son of Man Sayings in the Gospels in the Light of Recent Research* [London: SPCK, 1983], pp. 112-13) With regard to Q 10.22 it has to be pointed out first that the saying, together with 9.58, creates a frame for the second part of Q, and thus corresponds with a Son of Man saying. Furthermore, it is probable from its content that the exclusive position of Jesus as the Son to God as the Father corresponds to those expressions which speak of the appearance of the Son of Man in the end-time judgment (cf. 11.30; 12.8-9). Jesus as the one to whom the Father has handed everything over is, for Q, Jesus the Son of Man, who, in judgment, acknowledges those who have acknowledged him and denies those who have denied him. Cf. also Hoffmann, *Studien zur Theologie der Logienquelle*, pp. 121-22.

73. It is therefore somewhat incomprehensible, why Theobald ('Gottessohn und Menschensohn', pp. 42-43) speaks of the 'verhüllenden' or 'esoterischen' character of the Son of Man expressions. At any rate no other expression says so much about Jesus as this one.

authority and eschatological power (12.8-9), as well as the return at the end of time (11.30; 12.40; 17.24), are the main subjects of interest.

A particularity of the Markan use of Son of Man comprises the way the earthly power of Jesus is presented by means of this expression. Within the complex 2.1–3.6 in the Son of Man sayings in 2.10 and 28, the ἐξουσία ('authority') for the forgiveness of sins, which is actually held by God (cf. v. 7c), is reclaimed by Jesus himself, and on the other hand, his status as κύριος regarding the Sabbath is maintained. It is important here that the first text, where Jesus is designated 'Son of Man', occurs in the context of a charge of βλασφημία ('blasphemy') and therefore marks the beginning of the conflict with the Jewish authorities. This is relevant from the standpoint of composition, as the last Son of Man saying in 14.62 occurs again in a similar frame of reference (cf. 14.64).[74] Therefore, it becomes obvious that it is Jesus' claim to be the Son of Man which led to his rejection and killing. Q, on the other hand, is readily able to identify the earthly one with the coming one and therefore to speak in the words of the earthly Jesus while simultaneously speaking in the words of the coming Judge.[75]

A second perspective, which links Mark and Q, is the view of the lowliness of the Son of Man. For Mark it has to be stressed that the Son of Man saying in 8.31, which interprets the Petrine confession in 8.29, represents a revised view of God's anointed one.[77] Leaving aside the occurrence in 1.1, which lies on another level of the narrative, 8.29 is

---

74. Theobald, 'Gottessohn und Menschensohn', p. 47, also calls attention to this inclusio.

75. One might also say that for Q there is no reason for a separate emphasis on the authority of the earthly Jesus. That one who calls the disciples to follow him and is rejected by 'this generation' is at the same time Jesus the Son of Man, who will return in authority. Only if this identity becomes a problem, must it be substantiated further how this takes place in Mark.

76. Regardless of how one thinks of the question of history of traditions, it may have become clear that Mark carries out his revision of the χριστός-concept in view of the activity and destiny of Jesus that modifies the concept of a royal messianology, as witnessed, e.g., by *Pss. Sol.* 17, 18; 4QpGen[a] 1.5 as well as by *4 Ezra* and *2 Baruch* Cf. perhaps also 1QSa 2.12, 14, 20. Only under this presupposition do Pilate's question σὺ εἶ ὁ βασιλεὺς τῶν Ἰουδαίωνυ (15.2), the inscription on the cross, as well as the mocking invitation ὁ χριστὸς ὁ βασιλεὺς Ἰσραὴλ καταβάτω

the first occurrence of the designation Christ, which is used with an article and, therefore, has a titular meaning. It is of particular importance for the Markan narrative that this verse is continued by a Son of Man expression, which is already qualified in a particular way. In view of Markan reports it is in no way self-evident that Jesus is designated by the title ὁ χριστός. Rather, Mark connects two lines of early Christian christological thinking by interpreting the Christ-confession with the Jesus tradition, in which the Son of Man expression was much more important.[77]

That the Christ-title is not found in Q is, therefore, not surprising. For Q there is no need to interpret this title, since by means of the Son of Man expression the essential aspects of Jesus' meaning could be expressed.[78] Analogous to the Markan sayings on the lowliness and suffering of the Son of Man in Q are those on the rejection by 'this

---

νῦν ἀπὸ τοῦ σταυροῦ in 15.32 make sense. For the line of argumentation followed here we can, therefore, leave aside the discussion about the origin of the Christ-designation which was taken up anew by M. Karrer, *Der Gesalbte: Die Grundlagen des Christustitels* (FRLANT, 151; Göttingen: Vandenhoeck & Ruprecht, 1991). Cf., however, the critical remarks of D. Zeller, 'Zur Transformation des χριστός bei Paulus', in *Der Messias*, pp. 155-67, esp. pp. 155-62.

77. This recalls, in a certain way, Bultmann's thesis that Mark's Gospel combined the hellenistic Christ kerygma with the Jesus tradition. The decisive distinction, however, lies in the fact that Bultmann did not reckon with a distinct concept of Mark's narrative but rather had postulated simply the acceptance of a kerygma that came from the Hellenistic sphere. Against that view is the opinion given here, that Mark's Gospel offers a profound reflection of the Christ-confession and puts it on a new theological basis. That is where the specific theological contribution of Mark can be seen. Along this line lies the contribution of Theobald ('Gottessohn und Menschensohn', p. 47) who, in opposition to Bultmann, moves in a different direction, claiming that Mark's professed Christology 'nicht ohne weiteres in die vorpaulinische Traditionslinie eingezeichnet werden darf' ('Gottessohn und Menschensohn', p. 57). It remains questionable, however, whether a pre-Markan 'Kerygma von [Jesu] Sterben, Auferstehen und Kommen zum Gericht' should be assumed, that would have been transposed by Mark into the passion narrative ('Gottessohn und Menschensohn', p. 57).

78. The historical question of whether Jesus was crucified as a Messiah (see, e.g., N.A. Dahl, 'The Crucified Messiah', in *idem, Jesus the Christ*, pp. 27-47, esp. p. 37), cannot be pursued further here. Accepting this, the meaning of the death of Jesus in Q would not be considered so relevant that it would have resulted in a new theological interpretation of the Christ-title.

generation' (7.34), as well as those on his homelessness (9.58). In some respect 6.22 and 12.10 can also be understood in that way, because here the rejection of the Son of Man and of his followers are closely related to each other. Hence, Q reflects the rejection of and enmity to Jesus in these Son of Man sayings, even if his death is not explicitly mentioned.

A last aspect concerns the linking of the present with the future Son of Man. The double tradition in Mark 8.38/Q12.8-9 can serve here as a point of departure. In that saying the attitude towards the Son of Man is placed in direct relation to the final judgment.[79] This pivotal text explicitly expresses the identity of the earthly Jesus with the coming Son of Man. Moreover, it becomes obvious that in both Mark and Q a close connection between discipleship and the Son of Man coming to the final judgment is produced, although with the distinction that Mark demands only not being ashamed whereas Q cautions against the open confession.

In the further development of his thought, Mark links the perspective of the coming Son of Man explicitly with Dan. 7.13-14 (13.26-27; 14.62). The question of Jesus' identity, which emerged in view of his powerful activity and became critical by the announcement of his suffering is now answered: the connection of power and suffering is understood by means of the insight that Jesus is the Son of Man who is returning at the end of time, as it was already announced in the scriptures.[80] In Q, where the reference to Daniel 7 does not occur explicitly, a connection between Jesus, as one of the messengers sent by Wisdom (7.35), or as one of the prophets (11.49), and his judging role at the end of time is made.

Against this background the question of the meaning of the expression Son of Man has to be raised. In more recent times (out of a rejection of the thesis of an apocalyptic Son of Man idea common in Second

---

79. Despite the view formulated several times by Hoffmann, that the Son of Man expression in Q 12.8-9 may have been first inserted by Luke, I follow here the majority view of scholarship, namely that Matthew changed the Q text. The Son of Man expression can therefore be presupposed for Q. On the conversation with Hoffmann cf. Schröter, *Erinnerung an Jesu Worte*, pp. 362-65.

80. In my opinion it contradicts the logic of the narrative, when Theobald ('Gottessohn und Menschensohn', p. 44) argues against it, that the reader or listener of Mark's Gospel in 2.28 is already 'reminded' of 12.36-37.

Temple Judaism[81]) it has been argued that the expression should be explained against its Aramaic background.[82] The problem, however, remains whether this explanation is really helpful for the interpretation of the use of this expression in the Gospels.[83] The Aramaic expression (א)שׁנ(א) בר ('Son of Man') categorizes the speaker, using it as a self-designation, in a group, to which he adds himself. It means, then, 'someone like me'. From the Son of Man sayings in Mark and Q it becomes clear that what Jesus does with these sayings goes against Aramaic usage, since there is no evidence for the use of (א)שׁנא בר as a substitute for the exclusively understood personal pronoun.[84] That the expression points to the humanity of Jesus and transcends it at the same time, showing a polarity of Son of Man and Son of God in Markan Christology,[85] can hardly be demonstrated. Rather, the expression stresses the particularity of Jesus by means of determined predications, without stressing his humanity.[86]

---

81. Cf. N. Perrin, *A Modern Pilgrimage in New Testament Christology* (Philadelphia: Fortress Press, 1974), pp. 23-36.

82. From the extensive literature the following may be cited: G. Vermes, 'The Use of שׁנ בר נשׁא/בר in Jewish Aramaic', in M. Black (ed.), *An Aramaic Approach to the Gospels and Acts* (Oxford: Clarendon Press, 3rd edn, 1967), pp. 310-30; P.M. Casey, 'General, Generic and Indefinite: The Use of the Term "Son of Man" in Aramaic Sources and in the Teaching of Jesus', *JSNT* 29 (1987), pp. 21-56; *idem*, 'Idiom and Translation: Some Aspects of the Son of Man Problem', *NTS* 41 (1995), pp. 164-82; J.M. Robinson, 'The Son of Man in the Sayings Gospel Q', in C. Elsas *et al.* (eds.), *Tradition und Translation: Zum Problem der interkulturellen Übersetzbarkeit religiöser Phänomene* (Festschrift C. Colpe; Berlin: W. de Gruyter, 1994), pp. 315-35.

83. Cf. already the objections of J.A. Fitzmyer, 'The New Testament Title "Son of Man" Philologically Considered', in *idem*, *A Wandering Aramean*, in *idem*, *The Semitic Background of the New Testament* (Grand Rapids: Eerdmans, 1997), pp. 143-60.

84. This is no different than if one regards some of them as authentic words of Jesus. What meaning the expression possesses in Mark and Q is not clarified in that way.

85. This is Theobald's argument. Thereby Son of God or Christ should refer to the earthly Jesus as the messenger of the reign of God, coming near. Son of Man, on the other hand, should refer to the death, resurrection and return (cf. 'Gottessohn und Menschensohn', p. 41).

86. This applies also to the sequence in 2.27-28. The Son of Man expression in v. 28 can hardly be understood as picking up the term ἄνθρωπος from v. 27 (leaving aside that in this case the omission of v. 27 and not v. 28 by Matthew and

An interpretation of the expression 'Son of Man' in Mark and Q has, therefore, to take its starting point from the sayings in the Gospels themselves. Here the expression 'Son of Man' explains the particular claim of Jesus, describes his rejection linked to that claim, and finally expresses his power, which is not falsified by his death, shifting the final revelation of his power to the future. In this way, the expression Son of Man in Mark and Q becomes a title of honour, by means of which the reign of God and the person of Jesus are linked with one another in one concept. With regard to the background of the designation the following can be said: even if it is undisputed that one cannot speak of a fixed concept of the Son of Man that served as the background of the early Christian use of the term, it becomes clear that the expression ὁ υἱὸς τοῦ ἀνθρώπου could be used in Mark and Q to depict a representative of God's final judgment at the end of time. The fact that Mark explicitly refers back to Daniel 7 shows that he was aware of such a possibility of using the expression. This is further supported by the use of the expression to designate a figure at the end of time, who is also empowered by God in *1 Enoch* 46, 48, 69, 71 and *4 Ezra* 13.[87] Even if one wanted to ignore these sources,[88] the fact remains that the expression ὁ υἱὸς τοῦ ἀνθρώπου could be used to describe the appearance of Jesus at the end of time by referring to Daniel 7. In this regard, the early Christian texts themselves are evidence for the use of this expression as a description of God's final envoy. The use in Mark and Q thereby demonstrates that it had already entered the Jesus tradition at an early stage. In view of what was said above about the Son of Man sayings it becomes clear that a fixed concept was not transferred to him. Rather, the expression was interpreted anew in view of his activity and destiny.

Luke would be scarcely plausible). Rather this verse presents the conclusion of the entire episode vv. 23-28 and forms moreover an inclusio with v. 10. The particularity, therefore, lies in the claim of Jesus, whereas his humanity is not emphasized here.

87. J.J. Collins, 'The Son of Man in First-Century Judaism', *NTS* 38 (1992), pp. 448-66.

88. Because of the problem of dating, the value of these texts for an analysis of the Gospels is controversial, as is well known. Nevertheless, even if both texts came from the end of the first century (or later), it is not possible to identify any clear Christian influence in them. For a reflection on the influence of Dan. 7 in Jewish literature both texts are without a doubt important witnesses.

To sum up: in both Mark and Q, Jesus, as the powerful ambassador of the reign of God, is interpreted by means of the designation Son of Man, which is used to depict his activity and destiny. At the same time this expression in Mark serves to interpret the expectation of God's kingly anointed one anew. Moreover, from the description of the activity of Jesus, interpreted with the help of quotations from Scripture in Q 7.22, and by analogy by means of the narration of his miracles in Mark, it becomes obvious that the meaning of Jesus is not described by the expectation linked to the kingly anointed one. Rather, Mark latches on to χριστός, which already existed as the *cognomen* for Jesus, and reshapes it as a title by integrating it into his Jesus narrative. Therefore, it cannot be demonstrated that he is looking back to a tradition in which the Christ-title was already linked to Jesus' death as a saving event because such a link does not occur directly in Mark. Apparently, then, Mark has situated this title in a way that retains it for Jesus and links it with the Son of Man Christology that arises out of the Jesus tradition. Q, on the other hand, shows no interest in using the designation Christ or relating it to the Son of Man concept.

In addition, something should be said about the expression Son of God. In Mark, this designation is interpreted in 9.9 and in 14.62 by means of the Son of Man concept. In this way, the meaning of this expression is not yet exhausted. Rather it also occurs in the baptism narrative, in a saying of the unclean spirit in 5.7, and in the centurion's confession in 15.39. In Q, it occurs in the temptation narrative as an address by the διάβολος ('devil') to Jesus. Mark uses this designation to depict Jesus as the bearer of God's Spirit. In light of the first passion prediction the special relationship between God and Jesus is confirmed again. This still does not answer the question of whether a specific concept of a Son of God lies in the background.

From a history of traditions perspective it is not immediately apparent why Jesus is designated Son of God. Certainly, a similarity of meaning has to be noted for 'Son of God' and 'Christ' (cf. 1.1; 14.62). However, the χριστός is never designated in Jewish texts as Son of God. The fragment 4Q246 ii,[89] which is at times pulled into the discussion here, can hardly be claimed as a workable basis for such an understanding, because the 'Son of God' and 'Son of the Most High' (די אל ברה, respectively בר עליון) mentioned there are not unambiguous as

---

89. Cf. Collins, *Scepter*, pp. 154-64.

designations for the anointed one.[90] Furthermore, it should be noted that the expression is never used in Q in relation to those texts, which were disposed towards such a use, and were also received in other places, such as 2 Sam. 7.1 or Ps. 2.7 (LXX),[91] whereas in Mark there is a reference to Ps. 2.7 (LXX) in the baptism narrative.

Wisdom 2–5 was also referred to, where the suffering righteous one is designated as Son of God. The analogies to Mark and Q exist in the fact that in both cases immortality (Wis. 3.4: ἀθανασία ['immortality'], 5.15; δίκαιοι δὲ εἰς τὸν αἰῶνα ζῶσιν ['the righteous live forever']), resurrection (Mk 8.31; 9.31; 10.34; 14.28; 16.6), or exaltation (Q 13.35; 11.30)[92] are placed over against the present suffering, by means of which a justification of the sufferings in the present by God occurs. It has to be noted, however, that a reference to this text occurs nowhere in Mark or Q. Furthermore, it deals with the exemplary righteous one and not with a concrete individual, not to mention God's final envoy.[93] The Son of God designation, moreover, never occurs in Mark and Q in the sayings on suffering. [94]

It follows, therefore, that the use of the designation Son of God in Q can be understood analogously to how it is used in Wisdom 2–5 (or also *Jos. Asen.* 6.3, 5; 21.3, where Joseph as the obedient one of God is designated as a Son of God). In the programmatic temptation story Jesus demonstrates his true divine sonship, which exists in his obedi-

---

90. For discussion and evaluation of the text cf. Fitzmyer, 'A Wandering Aramean', pp. 90-93 and pp. 102-107; cf. also *idem*, 'The Palestinian Background of "Son of God" as a Title for Jesus', in T. Fornberg and D. Hellholm (eds.), *Texts and Contexts: Essays in Honor of Lars Hartman* (Oslo: Scandinavian University Press, 1995), pp. 567-77 and Müller, ' "Sohn Gottes" ', pp. 2-4.

91. On the reception of both texts in early Christianity cf., e.g., Heb. 1.5. As is well known, Ps. 2.7 (LXX) probably also lies behind the voice from heaven in the baptism of Jesus in Mk 1.11. 2 Sam. 7.14 is received as well in 4QMidrEschat[a] 3.1, where it deals with the fulfilment of the prophecy of the coming offspring of David and not with the description of that figure as a Son of God.

92. On this cf. D. Zeller, 'Entrückung zur Ankunft als Menschensohn (Lk 13.34f.; 11.29f.)', in *A cause de l'évangile: Etudes sur les Synoptiques et les Actes offertes au P. Jacques Dupont, O.S.B. à l'occasion de son 70ᵉ anniversaire* (LD, 123; Paris: Publications de Saint André, 1985), pp. 513-30.

93. Cf. the plural in Wis. 3.1-9.

94. An exception is Mk 15.39 where the centurion confesses the divine sonship of Jesus in view of his death. Cf. the remarks on this text below.

ence to God by his rejection of the temptations of the διάβολος. Consequently the story in the first place proves that he belongs to God. Moreover, the exceptional temptations distinguish him in a special way and move him into God's proximity. The expression Son of God is used here, then, as a description of Jesus' relationship to God, without mentioning his lowliness or his function as saviour at the end of time. In Q, it is only the designation Son of Man which functions in such a way.

In Mark this is different. Only the centurion's confession can be interpreted in the sense just described. In view of the crucifixion, he understands that Jesus' obedience is based on his relationship to God, and therefore he designates him as υἱὸς θεοῦ (without the article as in Q 4.3, 9). For the other texts, however, such an interpretation does not suffice. In the baptism narrative, the bestowing of the Spirit is linked with sonship, which Jesus has as the authorized representative of God, who then possesses power over the demons, who must acknowledge him. Different from what one finds in Q, Mark's Jesus is the adopted Son of God from the beginning, which means that he has power to battle the reign of Satan with God's Spirit and to bring on the reign of God (3.23-27). Different from the temptation narrative in Q, the designation υἱὸς θεοῦ in Mark gains weight insofar as he expands the expression in a titular sense, comparable to its use in Rom. 1.3. In this text Jesus is depicted as the appointed Son of God from the moment of his resurrection, whereas in Mark his earthly activity is characterized as taking place by means of God's Spirit. On the other hand, the centurion's confession in 15.39 shows that Mark knew the ambiguity of the designation υἱὸς θεοῦ. The centurion designates Jesus in view of his death on the cross as someone(!) who was (!) a υἱὸς θεοῦ. This statement, therefore, can be understood against the background of Wis. 2–5.[95] Mark's reader understands, however, the 'actual' meaning of this saying, which contains what was explained earlier in the narrative.

Regarding the designation of Jesus as κύριος, it can be shown that this characterization does not relate to the exalted Jesus, as is the case in Phil. 2.11, Rom. 10.9 and 1 Cor. 12.4. Rather Jesus as κύριος remains on the level of an earthly authority. The presentation of Jesus as the exalted κύριος, essentially influenced by Ps. 109.1 (LXX) (i.e. Ps. 110.1),

---

95. It is not accidental that Luke changed the Markan formulation of this text to δίκαιος ἦν.

does not directly occur in Mark and Q.[96] In 12.35-36 Mark places the reception of this scriptural text under the question of whether the Christ is the Son of David (which from the scriptural argument is answered in the negative). This constitutes a clear difference from Acts 2.34; Rom. 8.34; 1 Cor. 15.25; Col. 3.1; Eph. 1.20; and Heb. 1.3, 13; 8.1; 10.12-13, where the already accomplished exaltation of Jesus is expressed with the help of these verses from the Psalm. Also, the call to prayer which occurs in its Aramaic form in 1 Cor. 16.22 and *Did.* 10.6 and its Greek form in Rev. 22.20, μαράνα θά, respectively ἔρχου κύριε Ἰησοῦ ('Come, Lord Jesus'), does not correspond to anything in the early Jesus tradition. On the contrary, the Markan use of the psalm can only be apprehended from his use of the Christ-title, which is interpreted by the reference to the coming Son of Man. In Mark and Q, therefore,[97] κύριος is only used to express the earthly authority of Jesus.

In sum, it can be stated that the centre of the christological thought in Mark and Q can be seen in the placement of the authority of the earthly Jesus against the horizon of his return as judge at the end of time. The Son of Man designations thereby served as a foundation which was then elaborated on. The presentation of the exalted, presently reigning κύριος remains foreign to the stream of the Jesus tradition at this stage. Matthew and Luke will be the first to change this.[98]

96. The question cannot be discussed here of how the application of the κύριος-title to Jesus might have come about. The discussion has been influenced, as is well known, by the fact that the rendering of the name Yahweh by κύριος does not occur in the pre-Christian LXX manuscripts (PapFouad 266: יהוה respectively a lacuna; 4Q24: ΙΑΩ; 8HevXIIgr: יהוה). This finding is supported further by fragments from Aquila as well as the Hexapla. Nevertheless, it can be shown that Jews could have designated God by means of 'lord' (מרה, κύριος) (cf. 11Q10 24.6; 4Q202 4.5; Josephus, *Ant.* 13.68; 20.90; *T. Levi* 18.2; *1 En.* (Gr.) 10.9). Furthermore, the question remains as to what was pronounced instead of the lacunae which occur in the LXX texts, i.e. instead of the tetragrammaton, ΙΑΩ or ΠΙΠΙ (cf. Fitzmyer, *A Wandering Aramean*, pp. 115-42, esp. pp. 122-23).

97. Cf. Q 6.46; 7.6; 9.59 (in parables 12.42-43, 45-46; 13.25; 16.13 as well as 19.6, 18), as a designation for God in 4.8, 12; 10.2, 21; 13.25; Mk 2.28; 7.28 and 11.3.

98. Bousset's thesis of the opposition of a Son of Man Christology to a Kyrios Christology in the oldest period of Christianity is agreed with, to a certain extent, in my considerations. His view of the history of religions backgrounds as well as of an opposition of a Hellenistic and Palestinian sphere of early Christianity would, of course, have to be modified.

In conclusion, it can be argued that the presentation of Jesus in Mark and Q is orientated towards the designation Son of Man, which serves to integrate the different aspects of his activity and destiny, whereas the other designations are interpreted by their integration in this concept. Moreover, in Q a 'mission-Christology' can be detected, according to which Jesus is presented in confrontation with this generation and designated as τέκνον τῆς σοφίας ('child of wisdom'; 7.35). This tradition is connected to that of the violent destiny of prophets (cf. also 11.49-50; 13.34). The appearance of Jesus is interpreted here against the horizon of the rejection by Israel and, in the face of this rejection, is defended. The problem of the discrepancy of the claim of Jesus on the one hand, his rejection and death on the other, is resolved therefore in Q by referring to the tradition of wisdom, who finds no place on earth, as well as to the violent destiny of prophets. In Mark this problem is solved by means of the hidden identity of Jesus,[99] which makes it possible to retain the belief that he is God's final envoy also in view of his death. Finally, both concepts characterize the present time as an interim time until the fulfilment of the reign of God. In place of this gap in the Pauline Christology there is the concept of the present reign of Κύριος Ἰησοῦς ('Lord Jesus'), whereas in Matthew it is resolved by the presence of the exalted one in his community, in Luke by the concept of the ἅγιον πνεῦμα ('Holy Spirit'), and in John by the παράκλητος, ('Counselor Paraclete') whom Jesus sends in his place.

4. *Conclusions*

The reflections presented here lead to the following conclusions:

1. The oft-mentioned view that at the beginning of christological thinking there existed the confession of the resurrected one as the Christ and the exalted Son of God, into which, then, the Son of Man sayings had been inserted,[100] can be modified by means of an analysis of the

---

99. Perhaps this formulation is more correct than the common expression 'messianic secret'. This is to some extent not completely precise, since actually what is held in secret is not the messiahship of Jesus (it must rather be understood in the correct way), but his true identity as the condemned, killed and nevertheless returning authoritative Son of Man.

100. See H. Merklein, 'Die Auferweckung Jesu und die Anfänge der Christologie (Messias bzw. Sohn Gottes und Menschensohn)', in *idem*, *Studien zu Jesus und Paulus* (WUNT, 43; Tübingen: J.C.B. Mohr [Paul Siebeck], 1987), pp. 221-46.

narratives about the activity and destiny of Jesus. Such a model must presuppose that the confession of Jesus as the Christ and Son of God lies also behind Q, although it is not made explicit here.[101] Such an argument from silence cannot be excluded in principle, although it moves perhaps too quickly from the view developed in the stream of the early Jesus tradition into the creedal tradition developed in the pre-Pauline/Pauline stream. The remarks presented here could, instead, point in a different direction.

2. In the (Galilean) stream of the Jesus tradition an independent perspective could have emerged, which was orientated to Jesus' proclamation of the Kingdom as well as to the Son of Man designation. These aspects were then expanded, in view of the death of Jesus as well as in view of the experience of his resurrection or exaltation, to the expectation of the fulfilment of the reign of God by God himself, and to the conviction that Jesus will play a decisive role in it. The latter was made clear by Mark by referring to Dan. 7.13-14. This view is supported by the observation that the designations χριστός as well as υἱὸς θεοῦ are not used in Q (or not in a titular manner), and that in Mark they are interpreted by the designation Son of Man.[102]

3. By their subordination to the designation Son of Man the titles Christ and Son of God in Mark get a distinct eschatological orientation. This applies also to the absolute ὁ υἱός in Q 10.22 and Mk 13.32, which has to be interpreted here by the Son of Man concept—similarly as υἱὸς αὐτοῦ in 1 Thess. 1.10.[103] The Christology of Mark and Q is therefore oriented to the expectation of the return of the presently absent Son of Man, Jesus, who obligates his disciples to continue his activity in the time until this return. In Mark this can be expressed also as κηρύσσειν τὸ εὐαγγέλιον εἰς πάντα τὰ ἔθνη ('proclaiming the gospel to all

---

101. Merklein, 'Die Auferweckung Jesu', p. 245.

102. In my estimation, Hahn's thesis, that the designations 'Messiah' and 'Son of God' may have been originally applied to the function of Jesus at the end of time and only secondarily to his resurrection and exaltation (cf. *idem, Hoheitstitel*, pp. 180, 288), succeeds in plausibility regarding development in the stream of the Jesus tradition. I differ from Hahn with regard to the pagan-hellenistic influence on the υἱὸς θεοῦ concept, as well as with regard to the development of the Son of Man concept.

103. Also without assuming an ὁ υἱὸς τοῦ ἀνθρώπου in the formula behind 1 Thess. 1.9-10, it is obvious that the use of the designation Son in a functional perspective concurs with the view on the coming Son of Man in Mark and Q.

nations'), pointing to the Gentile missionary orientation of the Gospel of Mark.

4. Q creates a Christology which is orientated mainly to the activity of the earthly Jesus and is further developed by means of the expectation of the coming Son of Man, whereas Mark integrates the Christ and Son of God title into his Son of Man concept. Hence, one can recognize distinctive theological perspectives: Q rests completely on the basis of the Jesus tradition and interprets this in a post-Easter time. Mark, on the conversly, creates a link to the confession Ἰησοῦς Χριστός, that is, to the concept of Jesus as the one who is appointed by God to be his son. The latter happens however not by referring to the exalted κύριος, but in the perspective of the returning Son of Man.

5. The consequence of what has been presented here for the history of theology could be that the combination of the proclamation of the Kingdom with the Son of Man concept presents an independent model of early Christian thinking about Jesus, that was linked to the Antiochene model of the pre-Pauline tradition by Mark. One can ask whether this should not lead to a more balanced description of the christological development by weighting the approach more strongly, which was orientated to the narrative re-working of the Jesus tradition. That a fixed kerygma was presupposed in that stream cannot be demonstrated, in any case, by an investigation of Mark and Q. The development in the stream of the Jesus tradition could rather have occurred the other way around.

Part II

THE HISTORICAL JESUS IN NEW RESEARCH

INTRODUCTION

Michael Labahn

In his introduction to recent research David S. du Toit says that it 'is today generally accepted that the last 20 years of research into the life of Jesus constitute a new phase in the history of Jesus research'. The leading characteristic of this new phase is the emphasis on the Jewishness of Jesus. The absolute 'criterion of dissimilarity' has been criticized[1] and has recently been displaced in favour of the 'criterion of plausibility of context' ('Kontextplausibilität') and the 'criterion of plausibility of effect' ('Wirkungsplausibilität').[2] This has led to a new willingness to take the historical information about Jesus to be found in the Gospels at face value. The Dead Sea Scrolls have helped us to see Judaism no longer primarily in terms of the later rabbinic texts. We now have direct access to Judaism at the time of Jesus. We now also take more notice of the early Christian non-canonical texts. Therefore, we have chosen to tackle 'The Historical Jesus in New Research', building on the first European New Testament Seminar which dealt with the literary relationship of the earliest New Testament documents of the life[3] and teaching of Jesus, Q[4] and Mark.

---

1. Cf. also T. Holmén, 'Doubts about Double Dissimilarity. Restructuring the Main Criterion of Jesus-of-History Research', in B. Chilton and C.A. Evans (eds.), *Authenticating the Words of Jesus* (NTTS, 28.1; Leiden: E.J. Brill: 1999), pp. 47-80, and A. Puig i Tàrrech, 'La recherche du Jésus historique', *Bib* 81 (2000), pp. 179-201 (185-94).

2. G. Theissen and D. Winter, *Die Kriterienfrage in der Jesusforschung: Vom Differenzkriterium zum Plausibilitätskriterium* (NTOA, 34; Freiburg: Universitätsverlag; Göttingen: Vandenhoeck & Ruprecht: 1997); ET *Criteria in Jesus Research: From Dissimilarity to Plausibility* (Tools for Biblical Studies, 4; Leiderdorp: Deo, 2000).

3. I don't want to get into discussion here about the question of how deeply the Sayings Source was influenced by biographical genres in comparison with Mark (cf., e.g., J. Schröter, *Die Erinnerung an Jesu Worte: Studien zur Rezeption der*

This part of the volume contributes to the newly raised discussion focusing on some of these burning issues. The articles of this volume, initially papers presented at the second European New Testament Seminar, have been revised. The aim of the second European New Testament Seminar held on 20 July 1999 at the Lahti Research and Training Centre during the International Meeting of the Society of Biblical Literature (18–21 July, organized by the University of Helsinki) was to examine new scholarly approaches and to survey particular fields of study. Rather than have a general discussion of the many different interpretations of Jesus,[5] many of them incompatible, we thought it best to discuss special issues that are important whatever the general approach to the problem. For that purpose we asked scholars belonging to different schools and different traditions for contributions. We selected the following themes which held out promise of being fruitful: the social

Logienüberlieferung in Markus, Q und Thomas [WMANT, 76; Neukirchen–Vluyn: Neukirchener Verlag, 1997], p. 120 [with a reference to Lukian, Demonax], p. 460: 'biographische Erzählung'). Nevertheless, in the final form of Q there are biographical strands, as has been shown by J.S. Kloppenborg, *The Formation of Q: Trajectories in Ancient Wisdom Collections* (Studies in Antiquity and Christianity; Philadelphia: Fortress Press, 1987). Cf. now M. Frenschkowski, 'Welche biographischen Kenntnisse von Jesus setzt die Logienquelle voraus? Beobachtungen zur Gattung von Q im Kontext antiker Spruchsammlungen', in J.M. Asgeirsson, K. de Troyer and M.W. Meyer (eds.), *From Quest to Q: Festschrift J.M. Robinson* (BETL, 146; Leuven: Peeters, 2000), pp. 3-42.

4. Of course we have to recognize that there is some strong criticism from a number of different points of view of the two-document hypothesis in English-speaking scholarship; cf. now, e.g., the critical survey of D.L. Dungan, *A History of the Synoptic Problem: The Canon, the Text, the Composition, and the Interpretation of the Gospel* (ABRL; New York: Doubleday, 1999).

5. For an overview of recent general interpretations of Jesus see, e.g., the presentation of B. Witherington, III, *The Jesus Quest: The Third Search for the Jew of Nazareth* (Downers Grove, IL: InterVarsity Press, 1995). See also the surveys of W.G. Kümmel, *Vierzig Jahre Jesusforschung (1950–1990)* (ed. H. Merklein; BBB, 91; Bonn: Beltz Athenäeum, 1994), and *idem*, 'Jesusforschung seit 1981', in *TRu* 56 (1991), pp. 27-53, 391-420; W.R. Telford, 'Major Trends and Interpretive Issues in the Study of Jesus', in B. Chilton and C.A. Evans (eds.), *Studying the Historical Jesus: Evaluations of the State of Research* (NTTS, 19; Leiden: E.J. Brill, 2nd edn, 1994), pp. 33-74; M.J. Borg, *Jesus in Contemporary Scholarship* (Valley Forge, PA: Trinity Press International, 1994). See also the essay of D.S. du Toit in this book and the bibliography of C.A. Evans, *Life of Jesus Research: An Annotated Bibliography* (NTTS, 24; Leiden: E.J. Brill, 1996).

classification of Jesus as prophet; Jesus' Jewishness; the effect of the discovery and publication of the Dead Sea Scrolls for research into the historical Jesus; the question of a Cynic philosophical background in the life and teaching of Jesus and his earliest followers; and the much disputed role of eschatology in the preaching of Jesus. There was also room to discuss the theological meaning of different aspects of the research into the historical Jesus and for the issue of the hermeneutic presuppositions of those who were researching. The opening essay in this collection gives an introduction to recent research which sets the other essays in the context of the larger debate. Of course this collection represents only a small sample of the possible historical, methodological, sociological, archaeological and theological issues that might have been discussed in the context of the Third Quest, but we hope it will prove useful and fruitful.

The recent trends have by no means led to a standard picture. As David S. du Toit points out in his article, 'Redefining Jesus: Current Trends in Jesus Research', the portraits of Jesus presented by M.J. Borg, R.A. Horsley, J.D. Crossan, E.P. Sanders, and J. Becker are all significantly different. But there are common trends. They all draw on the scholarly methods and the exegetical presuppositions of the Second Quest. They all try to understand Jesus in the context of first-century Palestine. In abandoning the criterion of double dissimilarity, they all place Jesus in the setting of contemporary Judaism: his social identity and the narrative tradition about him. Du Toit emphasizes that the Third Quest is resolutely historical in its investigation, in contrast to the dogmatic and theological obsessions of the older Quest.[6]

---

6.   The older Jesus research tried, with the help of the criterion of double dissimilarity, to work out what was distinctive about Jesus. However, recent investigation into the historical Jesus is also not completely free of theological, social or political presuppositions, which determine their picture of Jesus. For example, the non-eschatological picture of Jesus given by B.L. Mack and J.D. Crossan is criticized by G. Theissen and A. Merz, *Der Historische Jesus: Ein Lehrbuch* (Göttingen: Vandenhoeck & Ruprecht, 1996), p. 29, as having 'mehr kalifornisches als galiläisches Lokalkolorit'. The old and famous résumé of the liberal German Jesus research of Albert Schweitzer is still valid for today's investigations. The authors of the different portraits of Jesus often project their own theological and ethical ideas back onto Jesus (A. Schweitzer, *Geschichte der Leben-Jesu Forschung* [UTB, 1302; Tübingen: Mohr Siebeck, 9th edn, 1984). Any research should have a clear insight into its own sociological, historical, theological and biographical

The baseline may be agreed, but du Toit draws attention to significant differences: an eschatological Jesus or a non-eschatological Jesus; Jesus as prophet or teacher of wisdom; a political Jesus or a non-political Jesus. On Jesus as prophet or teacher of wisdom, du Toit combines this with a discussion of the layers of tradition within the sources and with a discussion of the Cynic hypothesis. Du Toit concludes by pointing out that the criticism of the older form-critical approach has not produced a new agreed paradigm for handling the history of the transmission of the Jesus traditions.[7]

The other contributions confirm du Toit's sketch of the complex and divergent portraits of Jesus within the Third Quest, differing both in content and in method. For example, to portray Jesus as a 'prophet' integrates him clearly with the Judaism of his day. Not only is there difference in detail about Jesus as prophet but there is also—as Markus Öhler points out—a remarkable vagueness about the definition of a prophet. Vagueness infects not only the classical definition of a prophet but also infects the modern attempts to define a prophet in the sociology of religion.

In his essay 'Jesus as Prophet: Remarks on Terminology', Öhler examines the underlying concept of prophetism implicit in the new general portraits of Jesus' character and teaching by E.P. Sanders, G. Theissen and A. Merz, J.D. Crossan and J. Becker. He asks, first, who is called a prophet and what are the characteristics of anyone who is called a prophet. He then asks whether Jesus was called a prophet and what were his prophetic characteristics. He draws attention to the different understanding of the phenomenon of prophetism within the Third Quest and deplores the failure to consider prophets in the Hellenistic context. He sees problems in the simple application of the term 'prophet' to Jesus. He calls for a comparative approach that also includes present-day uses of the term. Either these considerations will lead to a more exact definition of the concept of 'prophet' or the phenomenological justification for the use of the term will have to be regarded as problematic.

presuppositions of research, and should provide others with free access to these assumptions.

7. Cf., e.g., my own remarks concerning the transmission of the Jesus traditions in discussion with the old form-historical approach and with new investigations into the oral transmission of tradition: M. Labahn, *Jesus als Lebensspender: Untersuchungen zu einer Geschichte der johanneischen Tradition anhand ihrer Wundergeschichten* (BZNW, 98; Berlin: W. de Gruyter, 1999), pp. 89-99.

Another important feature of the Third Quest is to emphasize the Jewishness of Jesus. What is gained from this? Tom Holmén, in his article 'The Jewishness of Jesus in the "Third Quest"', points out that the emphasis is not new at all, being important for Albert Schweitzer and the history of religion school, for example. However, whereas the New Quest or the Second Quest aimed to show Jesus' distinctiveness within Judaism, the Third Quest seeks to set him within the Judaism of his time. Classical Judaism in now seen as a complex phenomenon, marked by deep differences. In the light of this, Holmén argues that it is no longer sufficient simply to emphasize Jesus' Jewishness. We have to face the question of what Jewishness means, and then we have to ask what is the distinctive Jewishness of Jesus. Holmén proposes an 'essentialist' strategy for defining Jewishness, 'in terms of core belief and foundational metaphor', without abandoning the basic insight of the diversity of Judaism in Jesus' time.

If the modern picture of Judaism is now far different from the picture of Judaism in the older quest of the historical Jesus as, for example, in the writings of Rudolf Bultmann,[8] that is largely due to research into the Dead Sea Scrolls.[9] Craig A. Evans, in his essay 'The New Quest for Jesus and the New Research on the Dead Sea Scrolls', argues that not only do the Scrolls illuminate the Jewish context of the preaching of Jesus, but they also provide a basis for criticizing some recent interpretations of Jesus, especially the findings of the Jesus Seminar in the United States. Nevertheless, the Scrolls are only one source for reconstructing the historical context of Jesus' ministry—Evans sets Jesus' preaching in a wider context of Jewish traditions—and they are not able

---

8.   The 'New Quest' or 'Second Quest' that came after Bultmann and began a more intensive quest of the historical Jesus started to use these sources for New Testament interpretation (cf. the handbook of H. Braun, *Qumran und das Neue Testament* [2 vols.; Tübingen: Mohr Siebeck, 1966]), but only a small portion of the texts was available and the direction of research was still restricted by the methodological criterion of double dissimilarity.

9.   From the enormous volume of recent work on the Qumran Scrolls I merely draw attention to some works which provide a recent general orientation on research into the Scrolls. Cf., e.g., S.E. Porter and C.A. Evans (eds.), *The Scrolls and the Scriptures: Qumran Fifty Years After* (JSPSup 26; RILP, 3; Sheffield: Sheffield Academic Press, 1997); P.W. Flint and J.C. VanderKam (eds.), *The Dead Sea Scrolls after Fifty Years: A Comprehensive Assessment* (2 vols.; Leiden: E.J. Brill, 1999); L.H. Schiffman and J. VanderKam (eds.), *The Encyclopedia of the Dead Sea Scrolls* (2 vols.; Oxford: Oxford University Press, 2000).

to solve all the questions about the Jewish background of Jesus. He argues that when comparing Jesus with the Judaism of his day what is decisive are 'patterns or collocations of themes and concepts'. He discusses three patterns: first, the proclamation of the kingdom of God, drawing not only on the War Scroll and the Rule of Blessing but also on the Songs of the Sabbath; secondly, the Jubilee Proclamation, drawing on 4Q521, 11QMelch and 1QMyst 1.i.5-8; and thirdly, the criticism of the Temple Establishment. The three patterns are closely related and they together form an eschatological paradigm which makes Jesus not a member of the Qumran community but working in parallel to it.

In his paper 'The Jewish Cynic Jesus', F. Gerald Downing assumes that the Gospels contain adequate reliable information about the activities of Jesus. He draws on the work of the Oxford philosopher J.L. Austin on Speech Acts to overcome the common dichotomy between traditions about Jesus' sayings and deeds. He argues that since we have scarcely any independent information about Galilee, the Synoptic Gospels are to be regarded as primary sources and the criterion for judging the reliability of our other sources, at this point taking issue with Sean Freyne, R.A. Horsley, R. Riesner, and G. Theissen and A. Merz in particular. The result is that Jesus is a Jew, but nevertheless the Jewish traditions of salvation do not completely comprehend the 'langue' of Jesus. Downing reckons that other Jewish traditions, as for example that of apocalyptic or wisdom, are only partially significant, and he seeks for a more comprehensive context. He concludes that 'Cynic influences could provide *some* of the context', but the influence of 'popular contemporary Cynism' does not make Jesus any less of a Jew than a Philo or a Josephus. Downing meets criticisms of his position by drawing attention to the diverse nature of classical Cynicism. He also draws on his own work and in controversy with his critics notes the coincidences between Cynic philosophy and the teaching of Jesus on matters that are not met in the cultural context of Galilee nor in Jewish sources, for example the lack of anxiety for food, clothing and possessions, the lack of respect for parents, the use of parables, the eating of Jesus' flesh and blood, love of enemies, and avoidance of judging. All these have close Cynic parallels. By reference to Menippus, Meleagar and Oenoaus from Gadara, he argues that Cynic influence in Galilee was possible and that this is supported by reports in the Gospels as well as by the writings of Paul, who made use of traces of Cynicism in the early Christian movement.

In his contribution on 'Eschatology in the Proclamation of Jesus' Marius Reiser turns to the basic features of the proclamation of Jesus. He is strongly critical of the methodological doubt and the hermeneutic of suspicion that governs much modern work. On the question of the historical possibility of the reported sayings of Jesus about judgment, he argues that we have no other access to his thought than the Gospels. These sources have to be read with sympathy and with an effort to understand them in their own terms. The starting point must be an analysis of the oldest form of the text, and any additions and editorial remarks are not *eo ipso* to be rejected. We can assume authenticity so long as there are no convincing counter-arguments. He would restrict the weight given to the criterion of dissimilarity but, in contrast with G. Theissen and D. Winter, he would not abandon it. There must be in the process of analysis a dynamic hermeneutical circle between our presuppositions and the detailed exegesis. Consequently Reiser rejects the non-eschatological interpretation of Jesus offered by M.J. Borg and M. Ebner and he develops a view of the eschatological preaching of Jesus which shows itself in the central theme of the βασιλεία τοῦ θεοῦ understood as a spatial kingdom which is powerfully effective. He argues that Jesus understood himself in the light of Isa. 52.7 and 61.1-2 as a messenger of joy in whose ministry the βασιλεία τοῦ θεοῦ realized itself. Since present and future form a 'paradoxical unity', the proclamation of judgment belongs to the eschatological preaching of Jesus, despite the doubts of some scholars engaged in the Third Quest.

The quest for the historical Jesus forms part of the problems dealt with by theology and hermeneutics. The contributions of Peter Balla and Elisabeth Schüssler Fiorenza touch on these issues.

Peter Balla's essay, 'What Did Jesus Think about his Approaching Death?', begins from the observation that what Jesus himself thought about his own death must be taken notice of in assessing the theological value of speech about the salvific death of Jesus. In practice, however, scarcely any mention is made in the literature of the Third Quest of the sayings concerning Jesus' expectation of death or sayings in explanation of why he had to die—perhaps because there is so much emphasis placed on the humanity of Jesus. He pleads for a re-opening of the question and offers an analysis of three complexes: the passion predictions, which he regards as older traditions not made up by the evangelists which 'may ... be regarded as—at least in some parts—authentic sayings of Jesus'; the entry into Jerusalem and the cleansing of the Temple, where he argues that Jesus expected his possible death; and Jesus' words at the last supper. (Balla works at a certain critical distance from the two-document hypothesis.) In his interpretation of the words at the last supper, he finds not only the expression of Jesus' expectation of a violent death but also the interpretation of this death as a 'life sacrificed for others'.

Elisabeth Schüssler Fiorenza puts herself forward as 'a feminist reconstructive historical model of egalitarian possibility' and asks us to enter into her perspective on the quest for the historical Jesus. What possible hermeneutical presuppositions, she asks, can have produced such a broad and conformist stream of research as the Third Quest. She suggests an answer to her own question in her essay, 'The Rhetorics and Politics of Jesus Research: A Critical Feminist Perspective'. She begins with the observation that no full-scale treatment of the *historical* Jesus has yet appeared from a feminist theological perspective. (She will not allow her own classical work *In Memory of Her*[10] to count as such.) In her search for the reason for this, and for the consequent failure in dialogue of the Third Quest with feministic approaches, she finds the causes in the social location and rhetorical situation of these quests which she positions in the conservative political movement with its tendency to exclude women's and minorities' interests. She does not think that the 'Historical-Jesus and Women Research' marks a step forward, above all because of its positivistic view of history. Although she accepts that this movement rightly locates Jesus in the Judaism of his time, she mounts a critique of their method of posing historical questions, in place of which she sets up her own feminist hermeneutic. The criteria of plausibility and the locating of Jesus in his Jewish context do not work for Jesus because he was in conflict with the hegemony of patriarchal and kyriarchal structures. The result of the employment of these criteria is that Jesus is bound into the hegemony of this framework. Schüssler Fiorenza proposes virtually a Fourth Quest for the historical Jesus which would employ a reconstructive historical model that takes account of the rhetorical function of the research activity of the person who is doing the research. With the aid of a 'criterion of possibility' the egalitarian tendencies of the early Jesus Movement would be stressed, and research would win through to 'an emancipatory

---

10. E. Schüssler Fiorenza, *In Memory of Her: A Feminist Theological Reconstruction of Christian Origins* (New York: Crossroad, 1983); cf. also *idem, Jesus: Miriam's Child, Sophia's Prophet* (New York: Continuum, 1994).

reconstructive model of early Christian beginnings'. This model would disclose a struggle between the egalitarian vision and the kyriarchal reality that is present in other cultural and historical contexts and not just in Christianity.

The individual contributions show that the current attack on the quest for the historical Jesus has not led to any final results. We need to be more precise in our use of the terminology of social identity and to bestow more care on the definition of the terms. The same goes for our analysis of social context. The discussion of method is by no means settled. The problem of how to secure the historical basis for reconstructing the history of Jesus is still unresolved because of linguistic theories on the one hand and criticism of the older form-critical approaches on the other hand. Theories that ascribe only one simple cause for the distinctive proclamation of Jesus no longer convince.

There was some agreement that the 'criterion of double dissimilarity', when mechanically applied, led to incomplete and unhistorical results. But there was also some criticism of attempts being made in recent works to abandon this criterion in favour of the criterion of plausibility. There is continuing interest in new methods of research into the Jesus of history which introduce new approaches and new methods, often drawing on other disciplines. There is no doubt of the need to keep the discussion open.

The point of departure remains the New Testament Gospels, chiefly the Synoptic Gospels, and other data and other sources have to be brought into critical dialogue with these texts. Within the Synoptics the Sayings Source Q—if its existence can be accepted as I would propose —plays a central role, although the significance of the other early Christian traditions about Jesus cannot be disputed. In contemporary research attention has been given above all to the extra-canonical early Christian literature,[11] and the Fourth Gospel is not neglected.[12]

---

11. Cf., e.g., J.D. Crossan, *The Historical Jesus: The Life of a Mediterranean Peasant* (San Francisco: HarperSanFrancisco, 1991); S.J. Patterson, *The Gospel of Thomas and Jesus* (Sonoma, CA: Polebridge Press, 1993).

12. In recent research there is again some willingness to use the Gospel of John as a source for reconstructing the historical Jesus; cf. the careful remarks by D.M. Smith, 'Historical Issues and the Problem of John and the Synoptics', in M.C. de Boer (ed.), *From Jesus to John: Essays on New Testament Christology in Honour of Marinus de Jonge* (JSNTSup, 84; Sheffield: JSOT Press, 1993), pp. 252-67. Cf. most recently, e.g., F.J. Moloney, 'The Fourth Gospel and the Jesus of History',

It is now well recognized as a basic step that the tradition about the deeds of Jesus as well as the tradition about the words of Jesus offers noteworthy material for the reconstruction of the historical Jesus. For example, the exorcisms and the healings of Jesus[13] are significant, as well as the cleansing of the Temple, which is not just an important element in explaining the crucifixion of Jesus. A comprehensive picture of the proclamation of the historical Jesus will only emerge when the traditions about both his words and his deeds are combined.

Contemporary research under the banner of the Third Quest has produced some helpful results concerning the life, the deeds and the teaching of the historical Jesus which provides us with a basic picture of Jesus and his extraordinary trust in God. This trust in God—surprising and rather shocking to modern ears—provides an important centre of discussion. The Third Quest helps us to understand Jesus better against the background of the Judaism of his day to which he belonged. It also helps to break down the isolation of the historical Jesus from later developments within early Christianity. Clearly, the quest must continue and not rest on its laurels. The numerous open questions summon us to further discussion, and more exact definitions and better methods are called for in many areas of investigation. And we cannot avoid the responsibility of thinking about the significance of the historical Jesus and his teaching for our present age, with its implications for church, society and politics. Yet neither the canonical Gospels nor the extra-canonical sources generate a unified picture of Jesus and his own context, especially in Galilee, the centre of his activity. Consequently critical research remains an urgent need. We cannot expect to reach a simple and unified result because the picture of Jesus itself from the very beginning was not unified.[14]

NTS 46 (2000), pp. 42-58, with some interesting and challenging observations. Nevertheless, I still think that the use of the Gospel of John in searching for the historical Jesus is only at the best of supplementary value, and that the Fourth Gospel will not play a major role in this research.

13. Cf. on this problem the work of J. Frey, e.g., 'Zum Verständnis der Wunder Jesu in der neueren Exegese', *ZPT* 51 (1999), pp. 3-14; also the work of J.P. Meier, although I think that he is too positive in his estimate of the healing miracles: *A Marginal Jew: Rethinking the Historical Jesus*. II. *Mentor, Message, and Miracles* (ABRL; 2 vols.; New York: Doubleday, 1994): 'Part Three: Miracles'.

14. Cf. F. Mussner, *Jesus von Nazareth im Umfeld Israels und der Urkirche: Gesammelte Aufsätze* (ed. M. Theobald; WUNT, 111; Tübingen: Mohr Siebeck, 1999), pp. 119-20, 154-62.

A

RECENT TRENDS IN THE HISTORICAL AND SOCIOLOGICAL PORTRAIT OF JESUS

REDEFINING JESUS: CURRENT TRENDS IN JESUS RESEARCH

David S. du Toit

1. *Introduction*

It is today generally accepted that the last 20 years of research into the
life of Jesus constitute a new phase in the history of Jesus research.[1]
This new surge of interest in the historical figure of Jesus was inaugu-
rated at the end of the 1970s by a number of studies which were
concerned with questions on historical method and its application to the
historical problems posed by the critical quest for Jesus.[2] A superficial
survey of the large number of publications spawned by this revival of
Jesus research[3] suffices to indicate to the observer that this new phase is

---

1.   See, among others, S. Neill and T. Wright, *The Interpretation of the New
Testament 1861–1986* (Oxford: Oxford University Press, 1987), pp. 379-403, esp.
p. 379, where he coins the term 'Third Quest' for the new phase of research;
J. Riches, *A Century of New Testament Study* (London: Lutterworth, 1993), pp. 89-
124, esp. pp. 121-24; M. Borg, 'A Renaissance in Jesus Studies', *TTod* 55 (1988),
pp. 280-92; J.H. Charlesworth, *Jesus within Judaism* (London: SPCK, 1988), p. 2,
who considers the new phase to reflect 'a paradigm shift in Jesus-research'. See
also W.R. Telford, 'Major Trends and Interpretive Issues in the Study of Jesus', in
B. Chilton and C.A. Evans (eds.), *Studying the Historical Jesus: Evaluations of the
State of Research* (NTTS, 19; Leiden: E.J. Brill, 1994), pp. 33-74, esp. pp. 33-34,
57-61.
2.   See, e.g., the contributions of B.F. Meyer, *The Aims of Jesus* (London: SCM
Press, 1979); J. Riches, *Jesus and the Transformation of Judaism* (London: Darton,
Longman & Todd, 1980); A.E. Harvey, *Jesus and the Constraints of History*
(Philadelphia: Westminster Press, 1982).
3.   See C.A. Evans, *Life of Jesus Research: An Annotated Bibliography* (NTTS,
24; Leiden: E.J. Brill, 1996). See also W.G. Kümmel's surveys in the *TRu* NS 53–
56 (1988–91), compiled in W.G. Kümmel, *Vierzig Jahre Jesusforschung (1950–
1990)* (BBB, 91; Bonn: Beltz Athenäum, 1994), pp. 535-690. Already several
monographs deal with the period, of which I name two: M. Borg, *Jesus in Contemporary Scholarship* (Valley Forge, PA: Trinity International Press, 1994) and

characterized by its diversity rather than the congruency of its results. In this it differs significantly from the preceding phase of Jesus research which was conducted within a set of clearly defined and widely accepted parameters and consequently produced results which differed in detail but not with respect to the general contours of the image constructed of Jesus.[4] In this essay I intend to demonstrate this extraordinary variety of positions by presenting a selection of monographs on Jesus which represent some of the most influential positions in current Jesus research. In a second step I shall point out some trends common to these very diverse attempts at solving the historical question posed by Jesus' life and work, and shall explain them against the background of other developments in New Testament research during the later part of the twentieth century. Conversely I shall also discuss several of the major divergent trends in current research and shall advance some explanations for their emergence.

2. Influential Recent Images of Jesus

a. Marcus Borg: Jesus as Charismatic

One of the most influential voices in the current debate on Jesus is certainly that of Marcus Borg. His portrait of Jesus is documented in two books published in the 1980s, namely in the edited version of his doctoral thesis,[5] of which the main theses were developed further in an extremely influential popular monograph on Jesus.[6] Borg portraits Jesus as an example of the phenomenological category of the charismatic holy man, that mediates the numenous to others, that is, of a person vividly in touch with another, spiritual reality who typically performs as healer, lawmaker, diviner, prophet, and so on. Accordingly Jesus is

B. Witherington, III, *The Jesus Quest: The Third Search for the Jew of Nazareth* (Downers Grove, IL: InterVarsity Press, 1995).

   4.   Of course there had been exceptions to the rule, e.g. S.G.F Brandon, *Jesus and the Zealots* (New York: Charles Scribner's Sons, 1967), arguing that Jesus' views were not incompatible with those of the Zealots; furthermore C.H. Dodd, *The Founder of Christianity* (New York: Macmillan, 1970). For the studies by Geza Vermes and Morton Smith see below.

   5.   M. Borg, *Conflict, Holiness and Politics in the Teachings of Jesus* (Lewiston, NY: Edwin Mellen Press, 1983)

   6.   M. Borg, *Jesus: A New Vision* (San Francisco: Harper & Row, 1987). See also M. Borg, *Meeting Jesus Again for the First Time* (San Francisco: HarperCollins, 1994).

seen as a healer,[7] furthermore as social prophet, initiator of a revitaliza-
tion movement and sage.[8]

Central to this image of Jesus is a specific understanding of the social
world of first-century Palestine: it was a time of conflict between rich
and poor, Jews and Romans. According to Borg, Jews in this situation
rallied under the banners of the Torah and the Temple and considered
holiness as divine obligation in the face of the Gentile pollution of
Israel. Therefore holiness, understood as purity, was the core value,
determining the identity of Israel; consequently all conflicts about
purity were essentially political.

Borg draws his picture of Jesus on this background: the Gospel narratives concerned with table fellowship, Sabbath conflicts, purity, tithing
and temple controversies indicate that Jesus radically criticized holiness
as the core value which structures society. Postulating as the central
premise that Jesus, engaged in an intra-Jewish conflict concerning the
correct understanding of the tradition,[9] replaced the dictum 'Be holy as
God is holy' (Lev. 19.2) with 'Be compassionate as God is compassionate' (Lk. 6.36), Borg argues that Jesus advocated compassion as
an alternative, inclusive paradigm for the transformation of Israel. Jesus
emerges as a *teacher of wisdom* who criticizes and undermines the
conventional wisdom undergirding society, as a *founder* of a revitaliza-
tion movement, that visibly and radically challenged the norms of his
contemporaries in order to revitalize Israel, and furthermore as a *social
prophet* who confronts contemporary Israel with the threat of a historical catastrophy because of its insistence to live according to the norms
of ethical purity and not according to the ideal of compassion.

For an adequate understanding of Borg's portrait of Jesus it is important to register his specific understanding of Jesus as prophet. Borg
rejects the notion of Jesus as eschatological prophet announcing the
imminent end of the world.[10] Rather he was a social critic in the vein of

---

7.   Borg, *Conflict*, pp. 260-65; Borg, *Jesus*, pp. 39-75. In Borg's earlier monograph the category of the holy man is only mentioned in passing (*Conflict*, p. 88), in
Jesus it is a structuring principle pivotal for the understanding of Jesus as a
spiritual, charismatic person: Jesus' relationship to the spiritual sphere serves as
source of his healing powers and of his mission as prophet and sage.

8.   Borg, *Jesus*, pp. 76-90.

9.   Borg considers the Gospels' presentation of Jesus' conflict with the Pharisees as authentic.

10.   His case rests on four points: (1) all sayings about the future Son of Man are

Israel's classical prophets, dealing with the current political ambitions and direction of Israel. In the face of an impending historical catastrophe he calls on Israel to revise its course and return to a new life according to the will of God, exchanging the principles of purity and exclusiveness for those of compassion and inclusiveness, that is, social convention for a life in the Spirit. This conflict between Jesus and the social elite is a conflict between different modes of existence which in the end caused his death,[11] for Jesus questioned the fundamental principles and ethos of his contemporaries and thereby became a threat to society.

b. *Richard Horsley: Jesus as Popular Prophet Mediating a Social Revolution*

In some respects a very different image of Jesus is drawn by Richard Horsley, a prolific writer on issues concerning the shape of first-century Palestine and the world of Jesus and the early Christian movement. Horsley's portrait of Jesus is presented in his *Jesus and the Spiral of Violence*,[12] a monograph flanked by two other important books from his pen concerned with related issues.[13] On the basis of a novel sociological

not authentic; (2) belief in an imminent end of the world arose with the belief in the second coming of Jesus; (3) the atmosphere of crisis in the gospels is a reflection of a social crisis on which Jesus acted, not of a crisis caused by the expectation of the impending end of the world; (4) consequently the notion of the kingdom of God should be understood in a non-eschatological sense. See especially M. Borg, 'A Temperate Case for a Non-Eschatological Jesus', *SBLSP* 25 (1986), pp. 521-35 (reprinted in *Foundations and Facets Forum* 2.3 [1986], pp. 81-102).

11. Borg considers the Gospel narratives of the entrance into Jerusalem, the conflict in the temple and the conflict with the authorities as historical: they are provocative prophetic acts and utterances of Jesus, confronting Jerusalem with its imminent destruction and a calling for a change of course towards the alternative of peace offered by Jesus.

12. R.A. Horsley, *Jesus and the Spiral of Violence: Popular Jewish Resistance in Roman Palestine* (San Francisco: Harper & Row, 1987).

13. R.A. Horsley and J.S. Hanson, *Bandits, Prophets, and Messiahs: Popular Movements at the Time of Jesus* (Minneapolis: Winston, 1985); R.A. Horsley, *Sociology and the Jesus Movement* (New York: Crossroad, 1989). The first work is concerned with the structure of resistance in first-century Palestine and paves the way for *Jesus and the Spiral of Violence*; in the latter Horsley describes early Palestinian Christianity, i.e. the so-called Jesus Movement, and provides the reader with some theoretical background on the sociological model which he applies to structure the available data on Jesus and the Jesus Movement. See also R.A.

analysis of the available data Horsley draws a picture of Jesus as a popular prophet mediating a social revolution among the peasant population of Palestine.

For Horsley a proper understanding of Jesus could only be attained through locating him firmly in the concrete social situation of first-century Palestine. Fundamental to his portrait of Jesus is the notion of the 'imperial situation', that is, his perception of first-century Palestine as a subject country of the Roman Empire which through the means of power and retainer agents is dominated, exploited and pacified in the interests of the imperial society.[14] It was a situation of oppression and latent and explicit conflict between economically oppressive urban ruling elites (Jewish aristocrats, Herodian and Roman officials) and economically oppressed rural peasants who had to carry a heavy burden of tribute, taxes and tithings to support the ruling elites. Increasing indebtedness to wealthy creditors caused various forms of social hardship to them, for example, poverty, land loss, hunger, and so on. Inherant to this imperial situation is a spiral of violence: structural violence or institutionalized injustice leads to protest and resistance met by ever-increasing repression, which in the end effects social revolt.[15]

According to Horsley, popular resistance was supported by a long-standing tradition asserting God's decisive and liberative action to restore independence and justice to Israel. A distinct variant of this tradition was apocalypticism, which in the context of an imperial situation exercises three functions: it keeps the remembrance of God's previous acts of deliverance alive by reaffirming the traditional symbolic universe; it envisions a radically better life, expecting the restoration of social structures according to God's revealed will; and it critically demystifies the powers of the established order by stripping it of divine authority and exposing it as permeated with demonic forces.[16]

Horsley, *Archaeology, History, and Society in Galilee: The Social Context of Jesus and the Rabbis* (Valley Forge, PA: Trinity Press International, 1996).

14. Cf. Horsley, *Jesus*, pp. 3-19 and Horsley, *Sociology*, pp. 71-72. Horsley applies a sociological model based on cross-cultural analysis of the 'colonial situation' to the available data on first-century Palestine; see Horsley, *Jesus*, pp. 328-29 n. 2.

15. Cf. Horsley, *Jesus*, pp. 20-145, esp. pp. 116-20, where he draws a vivid picture of the many-faceted popular peasant resistance in first-century Palestine.

16. Cf. Horsley, *Jesus*, pp. 121-45, 157-60. Horsley emphasizes that apocalyptic texts do not manifest an alienation from concrete history, but are thoroughly historically orientated. Furthermore they do not reflect a conflict between conventicles or

Against this background Horsley draws his portrait of Jesus. Drawing on contemporary apocalypticism for his proclamation of the kingdom of God, 'Jesus' overall perspective was that God was bringing an end to the demonic and political powers dominating his society so that renewal of individual and social life would be possible'.[17] In proclaiming God's kingdom Jesus shared with most of his contemporaries the expectation that God will renew Israel through vindication of the righteous and judgment of the unrighteous. Assuming the role of a traditional Israelite prophet Jesus calls for repentance in the face of God's imminent judgment and spells out the dire consequences to his intransigent contemporaries.[18] The principal thrust of Jesus' ministry, though, was to manifest and mediate God's kingdom—through healings, exorcisms, acts of forgiveness, festive banqueting with friends[19] and through symbolizing the restoration of Israel by calling the Twelve.[20] Jesus believed that God was presently and imminently effecting a historical transformation of the contemporary world. Thus Jesus was engaged in the renewal of the sociopolitical form of traditional peasant life, that is, of local communities, exchanging oppressive, patriarchal structures for egalitarian, familial structures.[21] The radical, ethical sayings of Jesus concerning the cancellation of debts, lending without regard to repayment, giving up of possessions, avoidance of the courts, and so on, are therefore not

sects opposed to the dominant society, but rather of the people generally opposed to the ruling elites.

17. Cf. Horsley, *Jesus*, p. 157. He stresses the fact that the symbol of the kingdom of God does not refer to the end of time, i.e. to the *eschaton*, but is a political metaphor referring to concrete history.

18. Cf. Horsley, *Jesus*, pp. 193-98. He considers the woes on Chorazin, Bethsaida and Capernaum to be authentic, cf. also his comments on Lk. 10.10-12 par. and 11.31-32 par. in this context.

19. Cf. Horsley, *Jesus*, pp. 167-92.

20. Cf. Horsley, *Jesus*, pp. 201-206.

21. Cf. Horsley, *Jesus*, pp. 209-245. After having analysed the relevant texts, Horsley concludes that there is no evidence that Jesus recruited or specially welcomed social outcasts such as tax collectors, sinners, prostitutes, beggars, cripples and the poor: these traditions he ascribes to the early Christian communities. Rather, the evidence of the healing narratives indicate that Jesus restored the healed to normal social interaction in their communities. In a similar vein he claims that Jesus did not call a movement of wandering charismatics into being, who would themselves constitute a social group. Rather, the disciples were commissioned as catalysts of a broad popular movement.

interpreted as being intended for itinerant charismatics, but are considered as guidelines for local communities. Similarly the command to love one's enemy does not generally refer to radical pacifism, but to relations of solidarity in the community in the face of structural oppression.[22]

A central aspect of Jesus' ministry was his conflict with the ruling institutions of his society. Jesus saw no role for these institutions in the coming kingdom. Taking the traditions about Jesus' prophecies of the imminent destruction of the temple and of his demonstration against the temple, of his lament over Jerusalem and the prophetic parable against the priestly aristocracy (Mk 12.1-12) as authentic, Horsley concludes that Jesus rejected these institutions through which the priestly aristocracy controlled society. He concludes that Jesus was engaged in catalysing a social revolution in anticipation of a political revolution to be effected by God.[23] This conflict with the political institutions of the day therefore also accounts for his death on the cross.[24]

c. *John Dominic Crossan: Jesus as Peasant Jewish Cynic*
J.D. Crossan presented the scholarly and general public his understanding of Jesus in his *The Historical Jesus*, a masterfully written book which not only impresses with well-informed historical arguments and rigorous methodology but also as an astounding piece of literary prose.[25] In the face of a large number of variant scholarly pictures of Jesus, Crossan insists that only proper and lucid methodology could lead out of the existing quagmire of scholarly eclecticism. He proposes a complex procedure in which cross-cultural and cross-temporal social anthropology, Graeco-Roman history and the analysis of the literary traditions about Jesus are combined in a reciprocal investment of different but supplementary information in order to produce an effective

22. Cf. Horsley, *Jesus*, pp. 209-284.
23. Cf. Horsley, *Jesus*, pp. 285-317, see also p. 325.
24. Cf. Horsley, *Jesus*, pp. 160-64.
25. J.D. Crossan, *The Historical Jesus: The Life of a Mediterranean Peasant* (San Francisco: HarperSanFrancisco, 1991). It was published in a popular format as *Jesus: A Revolutionary Biography* (San Francisco: HarperSanFrancisco, 1994); cf. also his *The Essential Jesus. Original Sayings and Earliest Images* (San Francisco: HarperSanFrancisco, 1998). In the following all references apply to *The Historical Jesus* (1991).

hypothesis on the question of the historical Jesus.[26] On the level of analysis of the tradition, this presupposes a sophisticated procedure to determine the relevance of the transmitted material: all the relevant sources, both intra- and extra-canonical, are determined and then sorted in order to arrive at a stratification of the data in chronological order and in terms of independent attestation.[27] Crossan now insists that in order to establish an informed and controlled hypothesis on the historical Jesus the traditions of the first stratum must be given priority, and among them, priority should be given to those traditions which have the highest count of independent attestation.[28] All traditions of singular attestation are bracketed and not taken into account for the framing of a basic hypothesis of the historical Jesus. The hypothesis, formulated on the basis of the multiple attested traditions of the first stratum, provides a framework which can be used to establish the relevance of the remaining traditions for a reconstruction of a picture of the historical Jesus.[29]

Crossan situates Jesus firmly within first-century Mediterranean society, pictured as a hierarchically stratified agrarian society which was characterized by marked social inequality. Power, prestige and privilege were concentrated on a small number of people adhering to the privileged classes (i.e. the governing-, retainer-, merchant- and priestly classes) which dominated the vast majority of peasants and artisans, the unclean, and the expendable outcasts. Society was predominately structured by patron–client relationships with honour and shame as core values: access to power and privilege is brokered by patrons, a fact which also applies to the sphere of religion.[30]

26. Crossan, *Historical Jesus*, pp. xxvii-xxxiv.

27. Crossan identifies 522 traditional complexes, of which 342 are attested only once, and 180 have multiple independent attestation, cf. Appendix 1, pp. 427-50.

28. According to Crossan the first stratum (30–60 CE) contains, apart from the Pauline Letters and Q, a miracle collection used by both Mark and John, an apocalyptic source behind Mt. 24 and *Did.* 16, the earliest layer of the *Gospel of Thomas (Gos. Thom.* 1), the Egerton Gospel, the *Gospel of the Hebrews*, an extract from the *Gospel of Peter*, the so-called Cross Gospel, furthermore two papyrus fragments *P. Vienna G.* 2325 and *P. Oxy.* 1224. This stratum contains 186 traditional complexes, of which 55 meet the criterion of multiple attestation.

29. Cf. Crossan, *Historical Jesus*, p. xxxii. In an 'Overture', pp. xiii-xxvi, Crossan lists the words of Jesus he regards as authentic, also indicated in the inventory of traditions (pp. 434-50).

30. Cf. esp. Crossan, *Historical Jesus*, pp. 9-15, 43-71.

Against this background Crossan depicts the situation in first-century Palestine as a situation of structural inequality and accompanying peasant hardship—including physical and mental illness, that is, (demonic) possession[31]—which naturally enough invoked widespread social unrest. He distinguishes various types of peasant resistance that correspond with the social types of protesters, millennial and oracular prophets, bandits, messiahs and magicians.[32] The last category refers to holy men radically challenging the established religio-political system's institutionalized and ritualized access to and control over divine power.[33] Crossan distinguishes another category of protest, the response of Cynicism against the core values of patronism and honour and shame in Graeco-Roman culture. Cynicism presents 'a deliberate, counter-cultural activity, a calculated repudiation of hierarchical social values' and a drive for social egalitarianism.[34] The main thesis of Crossan's book is that Jesus belonged to these two categories of peasant protest: he was a Jewish peasant Cynic, acting as healer and exorcist, that is, as magician.

Jesus began his career as a follower of John the Baptist, but broke with him and his apocalyptic teaching as is indicated by the saying of Jesus that states that the least in the kingdom of God is greater than John (Q 7.28/11.11; *Gos. Thom.* 46), and furthermore by those traditions which posit conflicting lifestyles for John and Jesus: John was an apocalyptic ascete, Jesus was accused of being a glutton and a drunkard because of his open commensality, widely attested in the first stratum.[35] In full correspondence with the fact that Jesus parted with John was his understanding of the kingdom of God as a non-eschatological, sapiential kingdom, as attested by a number of first-stratum sayings and parables.[36] It was a radically egalitarian mode of life in the present world which rendered sexual, social, political, familial and religious distinctions irrelevant and anachronistic.[37] Radical egalitarianism in Jesus'

---

31. For the connection of illness and possession with the colonial condition cf. Crossan, *Historical Jesus*, pp. 313-17, 324.

32. Cf. Crossan, *Historical Jesus*, pp. 103-124.

33. Cf. Crossan, *Historical Jesus*, pp. 137-58, 303-310.

34. Cf. Crossan, *Historical Jesus*, pp. 72-90, 332-53.

35. Cf. Crossan, *Historical Jesus*, pp. 227-64 and Appendix 3, p. 453.

36. Cf. Crossan, *Historical Jesus*, Appendix 3, pp. 459-60.

37. Cf. Crossan, *Historical Jesus*, pp. 265-302, esp. p. 298. Crossan undergirds his construct of a non-apocalyptic Jesus by arguing that the multiple attested future

teaching was matched by his Cynic-like lifestyle of itinerancy coupled with open commensality, thus a lifestyle repudiating the basic values of his society, patronism and honour and shame.[38] Completing the picture of Jesus is the fact that he was a healer and exorcist and therefore challenged the religious monopoly of the official religion of his time by bypassing the institutions of priests and temple in his mediating of forgiveness and health.[39] In order not to create new dependencies and hierarchies Jesus committed himself and his followers to radical itinerancy, thereby avoiding any form of patronage by moving around and coming to the people instead of them supplicating to him from a position of inferiority.[40]

According to Crossan, Jesus' ministry of open commensality and free healing in conjunction with radical itinerancy set him in a functional opposition to the temple in Jerusalem. Accepting the authenticity of an action by Jesus symbolically destroying the temple (possibly at Passover) in conjunction with a saying by him threatening the destruction (but not a future rebuilding!) of the temple, and concluding with an analysis of the passion traditions as to their inauthenticity, Crossan proposes that Jesus was swiftly arrested and then unspectacularly trialed by Pilate and sentenced to be crucified.[41]

d. *E.P. Sanders: Jesus as Eschatological Prophet of Israel's Restoration*
One of the most discussed depictions of Jesus in recent research is that presented by E.P. Sanders, best known for his many contributions on first-century Palestinian Judaism.[42] Sanders proposed his view of Jesus in his controversial monograph *Jesus and Judaism*, which was followed by a more popularized version *The Historical Figure of Jesus*.[43] Using

---

Son of Man sayings in the first stratum (cf. Appendix 4, pp. 454-56) are not authentic, but products of later Christology (pp. 238-55).

38. Cf. Crossan, *Historical Jesus*, pp. 261-64, 332-48, 421-22.

39. Cf. Crossan, *Historical Jesus*, pp. 303-338, 344, 346-47.

40. Cf. Crossan, *Historical Jesus*, pp. 345-48.

41. Cf. Crossan, *Historical Jesus*, pp. 354-94.

42. See, e.g., E.P. Sanders, *Paul and Palestinian Judaism* (London: SCM Press; Valley Forge, PA: Trinity Press International, 1977); *idem*, *Jewish Law from Jesus to the Mishna: Five Studies* (London: SCM Press; Valley Forge, PA: Trinity Press International, 1990); E.P. Sanders, *Judaism: Practice and Belief, 63 BCE–66 CE* (London: SCM Press; Valley Forge, PA: Trinity Press International, 1992).

43. E.P. Sanders, *Jesus and Judaism* (London: SCM Press; Valley Forge, PA:

a method of controlled hypothesis-building,[44] Sanders developed an image of Jesus as an autonomous charismatic prophet[45] of Israel's eschatological restoration.

Sanders's main thesis is that certain unassailable facts about Jesus' life[46] situate him firmly on a trajectory between John the Baptist, an eschatological prophet calling for redemption, and the early Christians, a messianical movement expecting the imminent end—that is, he fits the category of a prophet of Jewish eschatological restoration.[47] Therefore Jewish eschatology, and more specifically Jewish restoration eschatology,[48] provides the most plausible framework for a historical interpretation of the available data on Jesus, particularly of his announcement of the coming kingdom of God. According to Sanders, Jesus saw himself as the last messenger of God before the establishment of the kingdom and expected a new order which would imminently be created by a mighty act of God. The coming kingdom would not be the absolute end of the world, but neither would it be perfectly continuous with the present order: it would be otherworldly with analogies to the present order as is illustrated by the fact that Jesus expected for the kingdom a new temple and the re-establishment of the 12 tribes with a leading role for him and his followers.[49] These traditions also point to a strong

Trinity Press International, 1985); *idem, The Historical Figure of Jesus* (Harmondsworth: Penguin Books, 1993).

44. Cf. Sanders, *Jesus and Judaism*, pp. 1-22. Sanders suggests a method which is based on the construction of sensible historical hypotheses, which could explain causes and effects. He takes his point of departure in the fact that historical persons and events are constrained by their historical context, so that it is crucial to establish a secure context or a framework of interpretation into which the data of Jesus' life could be fitted.

45. On the religious type of Jesus cf. Sanders, *Jesus and Judaism*, pp. 170-73, 237-40; *idem, Historical Figure*, chap. 15.

46. Cf. Sanders, *Jesus and Judaism*, p. 11: Jesus was baptized by John; he was a Galilean who preached and healed; he called disciples and spoke of them as being the Twelve; he confined his activity to Israel; he engaged in a controversy about the temple; his followers continued after his death as an identifiable movement; some Jews persecuted parts of the new movement.

47. Cf., e.g., Sanders, *Jesus and Judaism*, pp. 8-13, 323-24, 334-35.

48. For the structure of 'restoration eschatology', see Sanders, *Jesus and Judaism*, pp. 77-119; cf. also *idem, Judaism: Practice and Belief*, pp. 279-303.

49. Cf. particularly Sanders, *Jesus and Judaism*, pp. 228-37.

implicit self-claim of Jesus: he probably saw himself as God's viceroy in the coming kingdom.[50]

Central to Sanders's portrait of Jesus is his claim that Jesus' adherence to Jewish restoration eschatology implies his acceptance of the very basis of Jewish religion (called 'covenantal nomism' by Sanders). Analysing the traditions concerning Jesus and the law, Sanders concludes that Jesus was indeed—with one exception[51]—in full compliance with the law. The Gospel narratives depicting Jesus in conflict with the Pharisees over purity laws and the Sabbath reflect concerns of the early Christian communities and should therefore not be ascribed to Jesus; neither should the conflict between Jesus and Pharisees in the Gospel tradition be considered historical. The traditions of the moral exhortations of Jesus suggest that he expected of his followers a high level of morality in basic accordance with Jewish law.[52] Although Jesus did not abrogate the law there is on the other hand clear evidence that Jesus did not consider the Mosaic dispensation to be absolutely binding: his expectance of the destruction of the old temple and especially the fact that he admitted unrepentant sinners to the kingdom seem to indicate that he considered the law not to be final, but expected that in the new age God would go beyond the law.[53] This correlates with other aspects of Jesus' ministry, namely with his parables teaching that God in his capacity as a compassionate God will effect a surprising reversal of values in the coming kingdom, admitting 'good and bad alike' (Mt. 22.10); furthermore it correlates with his ideal of moral perfection based on compassion which he himself proved in his attitude of love and unconditional acceptance towards sinners.[54]

If Jesus fits well into a Jewish framework, the question of the cause of his death becomes acute. Sanders argues that certainly Jesus' activities as healer could have met with some suspicion by some, and that his teaching of a reversal of values must have been disturbing to some Jews, but nothing of this could account for his crucifixion. His commandment

---

50. Cf., e.g., Sanders, *Jesus and Judaism*, pp. 306-308, 321-22, 324; *idem, Historical Figure*, chap. 15.

51. Mt 8.21-22 par.; cf. Sanders, *Jesus and Judaism*, pp. 252-54.

52. Cf. Sanders, *Historical Figure*, chap. 13.

53. On Jesus' relationship to the law and the representatives of Israel, esp. the Pharisees, cf. Sanders, *Jesus and Judaism*, pp. 245-89 and the excellent chap. 14 in *idem, Historical Figure*.

54. Cf. Sanders, *Historical Figure*, chap. 13.

to a would be-follower to 'let the dead bury the dead' must, though, have been blatantly offensive to a great many Jews and points in the direction of the crucial factor ultimately causing his death: on some points Jesus blatantly challenged the adequacy of the Mosaic dispensation. This he did particularly in two instances: claiming to speak for God, he promised the wicked access to the kingdom of God if they accepted him, therefore bypassing restitution and/or sacrifice as required by the law; and furthermore he ostentatiously (at Passover and in Jerusalem) announced the destruction of the temple. This renunciation of the adequacy of the Mosaic dispensation was highly offensive to broad stratums of Jewish society and accounts for the opposition he met in Jerusalem. After his symbolic entry and his explicit demonstration in the temple he was arrested by the Jewish authorities and on their behest trialed and executed by Pilate for sedition or treason, namely, for claiming to be a potential king.

e. *Jürgen Becker: Jesus as Eschatological Prophet Mediating God's Presence*

As a last image of Jesus I shall consider Jürgen Becker's *Jesus von Nazaret*,[55] one of the few recent Jesus monographs by a German scholar.[56] Becker develops his image of Jesus on the basis of an analysis of the Jesus traditions of the Synoptic Gospels.[57] Taking the criterion of

---

55. J. Becker, *Jesus von Nazaret* (Berlin: W. de Gruyter, 1996); ET *Jesus of Nazareth* (Berlin: W. de Gruyter, 1998).

56. The wave of interest in Jesus research since the early 1980s initially made hardly any impact on German scholarship. An exception was G. Theissen, whose Jesus novel, *Der Schatten des Galiläers* (Munich: Chr. Kaiser Verlag, 1986); ET *The Shadow of the Galilean* (1987) was recently followed by an informative textbook on the historical Jesus: G. Theissen and A. Merz, *Der historische Jesus: Ein Lehrbuch* (Göttingen: Vandenhoeck & Ruprecht, 1996); ET *The Historical Jesus: A Comprehensive Guide* (Minneapolis: Augsburg–Fortress, 1998). Cf. also J. Gnilka, *Jesus von Nazareth: Botschaft und Geschichte* (HTKNT, 3; Freiburg: Herder, 1990) of which W. Telford said, 'Gnilka's book...is disappointing, in...that it fails to take account of developments in the eighties (especially in North American scholarship) and hence witnesses to the sad gulf that exists between Continental and North American scholarship' (Telford, 'Major Trends', p. 41 n. 27).

57. Cf. Becker, *Jesus von Nazaret*, pp. 10-13 (ET pp. 8-10). He does accept that the Gospel of John could be used to decide some of the biographical issues, but is of the opinion that all other extra- and intra-Christian sources (esp. *T. Flav.*; *Gos. Thom.*) do not substantially add to our knowledge of Jesus.

dissimilarity as a methodological starting point, he tries to ascertain those essential elements of the life and teaching of Jesus which establish his individuality *within* the context of early Judaism, that is, his individuality is strictly understood in the general sense of human individuality as a historical variant of its historical context.[58] Becker develops a picture of Jesus as a first-century Jewish prophet mediating eschatological salvation to Israel.[59]

He commences by analysing the Baptist traditions and pictures John as a prophet announcing God's imminent judgment over *all* Israel: Israel has forfeited the covenantal promise of salvation and receives in John's baptism one last chance to escape God's wrath. Otherwise destruction by God's representative, carefully argued by Becker to be the Son of Man, is unavoidable.[60] Since John offers the remission of sins through baptism and therefore sets up an alternative to cultic practice, he stands, at least indirectly, in conflict with the temple cult. Jesus, so much is certain, was baptized by John. He thus identified himself with John's message and became his follower and probably baptized alongside him.[61] Becker argues that Jesus was also the theological heir of John: he adopted John's verdict that in face of God's imminent judgment all Israel was lost. He did not assume, though, as John did, that this is God's last word to Israel, but thought it his task to announce God as the ultimate saviour of Israel, a God who rejoices at finding a lost member of Israel. He therefore situated John's prophecy of judgment in another context, namely that of God's benevolence, that is, of God's rule.[62]

Becker situates Jesus and his proclamation of God's rule in the context of conceptions of divine kingship in early Judaism. In line with widespread belief in early Judaism, Jesus expected a new age under God's exclusive rule, a new dispensation in basic continuity with the

58. Becker, *Jesus von Nazaret*, pp. 17-18 (ET pp. 13-14). Becker furthermore emphasizes the complexity of the (dis-)continuity of Jesus and earliest Christianity and demands that the historian should demonstrate to what extent the history of Jesus relates to the genesis and development of early Christianity, cf. *Jesus von Nazaret*, pp. 4-5, 17-18 (ET pp. 4-5, 13-14).

59. Cf. Becker, *Jesus von Nazaret*, pp. 267-75 (ET pp. 211-17) for a discussion of the social type Jesus represented.

60. Cf. Becker, *Jesus von Nazaret*, pp. 37-58 (ET pp. 33-48).

61. Cf. Becker, *Jesus von Nazaret*, pp. 59-63 (ET pp. 49-53).

62. Cf. Becker, *Jesus von Nazaret*, pp. 63-99 (there esp. 98-99), 168-76 (ET pp. 53-83 [78-80], 135-41).

present creation, qualified by the Creator God's everlasting presence and gifts.[63] Becker argues that Jesus understood his own time as already partaking of this future dispensation of God's coming rule: Jesus interprets his own time to be the turning point between the old and the new dispensation, because the process of the installment of God's eschatological rule had already commenced through his own activities.[64] Jesus' ministry therefore consists in mediating divine proximity[65] through narrating parables, holding festive banquets with friends, disciples and outcasts,[66] healing the ill and exorcising demons.[67] Becker can formulate pointedly that Jesus thus *realizes* God's rule.[68] Therefore the decision for or against Jesus and his proclamation of God's approaching rule will be decisive[69] in the coming judgment by the Son of Man.[70]

63. Cf. Becker, *Jesus von Nazaret*, pp. 100-21, 155-68 (ET pp. 85-99, 125-35).

64. Cf. Becker, *Jesus von Nazaret*, pp. 124-54 (ET pp. 100-25).

65. Cf. Becker, *Jesus von Nazaret*, pp. 176-233 (ET pp. 141-86).

66. Becker situates Jesus' festive banqueting not only against the background of the apocalyptic expectation of the eschatological banquet (Isa. 25.6), but particularly against the sapiential tradition of the Creator God as nourisher of the hungry and poor: God the Creator personally nourishes them as part of the introduction of the final dispensation. The banquets are concrete realizations of the approaching reign of God in which unjust sinners and the destitute are integrated into the community. This abolition of the discrimination between just and unjust, pure and impure must have been highly offensive and thus provoked confrontation with those devoted to the law, cf. Becker, *Jesus von Nazaret*, pp. 194-211 (ET pp. 155-69).

67. Becker's analysis of the miracle traditions results in ascribing to Jesus the interpretation of his healings and exorcisms as expressions of the immediate proximity of God's eschatological rule, which integrate the sick, frequently considered as sinners and outcasts, in the eschatological dispensation, which is understood to be God's restitution of his creation, cf. Becker, *Jesus von Nazaret*, pp. 212-33 (ET pp. 169-86).

68. Cf. Becker, *Jesus von Nazaret*, p. 134: 'Jesus läßt also Gott selbst zum Herrschen kommen' (ET p. 109: 'When Jesus acts it is God's kingdom itself that happens'); elsewhere he formulates: '[Jesus] versteht sich als Bewirker endzeitlicher Vollendung' (*Jesus von Nazaret*, p. 271) (ET p. 215: '...he also understood himself as one commissioned to usher in the final age'). This, however, does not imply that Jesus expected to bring about God's reign in its fullness, he rather thought of the rule of God as approaching over time (see pp. 128-29; ET pp. 105-106) and to be completed by God in a final act (including the gathering of the nations).

69. Cf. Becker, *Jesus von Nazaret*, pp. 73-91, 137-39, 261-67 (ET pp. 60-73, 111-13, 206-211), furthermore the discussion of Jesus' call for uncompromised discipleship, *Jesus von Nazaret*, pp. 289-337 (ET pp. 235-71).

70. Becker considers Jesus to have expected the Son of Man figure as God's

Against the background of this eschatological horizon of the dynamic process of the realization of God's rule in Israel Jesus addresses his ethical commands to all Israel. Its main thrust is that human conduct should be in correspondence with God's approaching rule. God's rule, that is, God's benevolence towards the lost, is the sole ethical criterion which Jesus considers as the measure for everything else. Taking this as his point of departure, Jesus assumes for himself the prophetical authority to proclaim the will of God, resulting in an intensification of the Torah on some points and his willingness to contradict it particularly on cultic issues and questions of purity.[71]

Against, the background of this picture of Jesus, Becker argues that Jesus' death should be considered to have been a consequence of his conduct and proclamation as a whole: by denying Israel its history of salvation, by identifying his work with the realization of God's rule and by repeatedly offending the divisions between pure and impure, just and unjust, Jesus must have isolated himself completely in the Jewish society, so that it saw fit to act against him as a false prophet who deceives Israel (Deut. 13.1-6; 18.9-22).[72] The priestly aristocracy arrested Jesus during Passover and after interrogation handed him over to Pilate who convicted him of attempting to usurp power.

f. *Concluding Remarks*

Although a number of other studies could surely be added,[73] the above-mentioned monographs provide us with a relatively representative cross-

---

representative in the eschatological judgment (*Jesus von Nazaret*, pp. 234-67 [ET pp. 186-211]).

71. Cf. Becker, *Jesus von Nazaret*, pp. 210-11, 358-87 (ET pp. 168-69, 287-308). Becker considers Jesus to have been part of an internal debate in Second Temple Judaism on the interpretation of the Torah. According to him, Jesus represented a novel position in this debate, cf. Becker, *Jesus von Nazaret*, pp. 288, 339-58 (ET pp. 234, 271-87).

72. Becker considers neither the sayings on the destruction of temple nor the narratives of Jesus' action in the temple to be of historical value (*Jesus von Nazareth*, pp. 400-13 [ET pp. 325-26]). Assuming that Jesus was isolated and the target of widespread hostility, he argues on the basis of Lk. 13.31-33 and Mk 14.25 par. that Jesus knew of the danger to his life and therefore reckoned with his approaching death, see Becker, *Jesus von Nazaret*, pp. 413-21 (ET pp. 336-42).

73. E.g. E. Schüssler Fiorenza, *In Memory of Her: A Feminist Theological Reconstruction of Christian Origins* (New York: Crossroad, 1983), pp. 105-159; *eadem*, *Jesus: Miriam's Child, Sophia's Prophet* (New York: Continuum, 1994);

section of positions taken in the current debate on Jesus and clearly
demonstrate the state of current research. Although the accounts of
Jesus' life and work do overlap at many points, the respective 'complete pictures' drawn by these scholars seem to be at variance with each
other to the point of being mutually exclusive. Alternatively a close
scrutiny of the highly diverse images of Jesus suggests that notwithstanding the obvious and profound differences among them there is
substantial common ground shared by all of them which transcends the
occasional agreement on some disputed points. An analysis of the current trends in Jesus research should account for both of these tendencies
reflected by the studies discussed here.

3. *Common Trends in Current Jesus Research*

Although current Jesus research is characterized by a vast spectrum of
different and even mutually exclusive pictures of Jesus, it reflects a
number of common assumptions which guarantee a certain measure of
unity in the Jesus debate and account for the common trends which
could be identified. In the following I identify a number of such common trends and their underlying assumptions, and suggest that these
common trends result from both continuity and discontinuity vis-à-vis
previous research.

a. *Continuity with the Second Quest*
First of all it is necessary to point out that the so-called 'Third Quest'[74]
cannot be viewed in isolation from the general history of the life-of-

D.C. Allison, *Jesus of Nazareth: Millenarian Prophet* (Minneapolis: Augsburg–
Fortress, 1998); D.E. Oakman, *Jesus and the Economic Questions of his Day*
(SBEC, 8; Lewiston, NY: Edwin Mellen Press, 1986); S. Freyne, *Galilee, Jesus and
the Gospels: Literary Approaches and Historical Investigations* (Dublin: Gill &
Macmillan, 1988); J.P. Meier, *A Marginal Jew: Rethinking the Historical Jesus*
(2 vols.; New York: Doubleday, 1991, 1994); B. Witherington III, *The Christology
of Jesus* (Philadelphia: Fortress Press, 1990); *idem, Jesus the Seer: The Progress
of Prophecy* (Peabody, MA: Hendrickson, 1999); N.T. Wright, *Who Was Jesus?*
(Grand Rapids: Eerdmans, 1993); *idem, Jesus and the Victory of God* (Christian
Origins and the Question of God, 2; Minneapolis: Fortress Press, 1996); *idem, The
Challenge of Jesus: Rediscovering Who Jesus Was and Is* (Downers Grove, IL:
InterVarsity Press, 1999).

74. I use the term 'Third Quest' for the current phase of Jesus research. Although the term 'New Quest' is usually employed for the phase in research intro-

Jesus research in the twentieth century. It should (and has been) argued that the recent developments in Jesus research are broadly in continuity with previous research on Jesus.[75] The Third Quest shares with the Second Quest most of its basic critical presuppositions: the quest for Jesus is conducted within the framework of modern historical criticism, assuming that the Jesus tradition should be subjected to historical analysis in order to reveal the Jesus of history covered by many layers of Christian tradition and dogma. As part of this process it holds a number of theoretical and methodological presuppositions in common with its predecessors. Jesus research since 1980 shares with the Second Quest the two-source hypothesis as a broad framework of the search for Jesus, furthermore the assumption of the arbitrary, that is, non-biographical arrangement of the Gospel material in Mark (and consequently also in the other Synoptics) and John, it similarly presupposes the kerygmatic nature of the Gospel tradition and the consequent stratified nature of the tradition. The list of shared presuppositions marking the common ground between the phases of research before and after 1980, between the Second and Third Quests, can effortlessly be extended.[76] Notwithstanding the characteristic diversity of present Jesus research it should therefore be maintained that it is nevertheless conducted within a framework of common assumptions which it shares with the so-called 'Second Quest' and is therefore broadly in continuity with it.[77]

duced by E. Käsemann's famous essay, I designate this period of Jesus research (approximately 1950–80/90) for the sake of clarity as the 'Second Quest' (the New Quest in the meantime has become an old quest!). The Jesus research of the nineteenth century up to A. Schweitzer's well-known book is called the 'First Quest'. The phase between First and Second Quest dominated by R. Bultmann's indifference towards the historical Jesus is called the 'No Quest phase'.

75. See Telford, 'Major Trends', pp. 57-61, who is cautious of overestimating the differences of the new phase of Jesus research vis-à-vis the so-called Second Quest. See also A. van Aarde, 'Tracking the Pathways of Willem Vorster in Historical Jesus Research', *Neot* 28 (1994), pp. 235-51, esp. pp. 240-46.

76. See van Aarde, 'Pathways', pp. 240-46, who quotes from an unpublished research report by W.S. Vorster 32 assumptions common to both phases. In my opinion almost a third of the 26 assumptions identified by him as typical of the Third Quest should also be counted as shared assumptions of both periods.

77. Rightly Telford, 'Major Trends', p. 61, warns against hailing a New Age in Jesus research and van Aarde, 'Pathways', p. 246 cautions against premature talk of a paradigm shift.

b. *The Quest for a Contextual Jesus*
Notwithstanding some basic and broad continuity with the Jesus research of the Second Quest, current Jesus research indeed has distinct
features which clearly distinguish it from previous research and should
be considered as characteristic traits of current work on Jesus. The first
and foremost feature of the so-called Third Quest is the generally shared
presupposition of its participants that a proper historical understanding
of Jesus demands understanding him within (not: against the background
of!) the social, cultural, economic, political and religious context of
first-century Palestine. In this the new phase of Jesus research
distinguishes itself on some crucial points from the preceding Second
Quest. In the first instance it is characterized by a common concern to
present a comprehensive picture of Jesus, thereby breaking with the
Second Quest which characteristically occupied itself almost exclusively with the teachings or sayings of Jesus. Common to studies of the
new phase is an understanding of Jesus within the context of his life as
a whole (see pp. 101-105). Secondly: had it been the expressed goal of
the Second Quest to identify those elements in Jesus' life and teaching
which distinguish him from others, therefore emphasizing his *singularity*, the Third Quest emphasizes the *continuity* between Jesus and his
environment, assuming him to be an integral part of it, without which a
comprehensive picture of the person and life of the man could not be
attained (see paragraphs 1 and 2 below).

1. *Aspects of Jesus' Life as Context for his Teaching.* One of the hall-
marks of the Second Quest was its concentration on the sayings tradition
as a source for reliable knowledge about Jesus.[78] With this concentrated
focus on Jesus' teaching corresponds a neglect of the significance of
other traditions for a historical portrait of Jesus. This one-sidedness was
among others informed by the results of form criticism.[79] After William
Wrede's discovery of a theological concept as organizing principle in

---

78. Already Bultmann limited the enterprise to a presentation of the teaching of
Jesus; see R. Bultmann, *Jesus* (Tübingen: J.C.B. Mohr [Paul Siebeck], 1926), pp.
10-11: 'Man kann dies [i.e. Jesus' work] ... nur als seine Lehre erfassen.' The
Second Quest, which developed within the Bultmann school, continued this view
and it consequently determined the character of Jesus portrayals of this period.

79. Other crucial influences could be discerned, e.g. the fact that the Second
Quest developed and was conducted in circles which were closely connected to the
movement of dialectical theology. Behind the focus of the Second Quest on the

Mark's Gospel had discredited the biographical traditions in the Gospel as key to a biography of Jesus, form critics demonstrated that the passion narratives are for the most part the product of theological and scriptural reflection and therefore as source material for the life of Jesus only of very limited value.[80] They furthermore considered the miracle narratives to be for the most part legendary compositions of early Hellenistic Christianity, which are said to have the function of epiphany narratives, projecting the Son of God Christology back into the life of Jesus.[81] The result of this devaluation of the historical value of the narrative traditions in the Gospels (especially the miracle tradition) is well known: Jesus portrayals of the Second Phase are portrayals of the *teachings* of Jesus; other aspects of his life play only a subordinate role and serve at best as a foil for the presentation of his teaching.[82]

Recent Jesus research, on the contrary, features a renewed interest in other aspects of Jesus' life than his teaching: one can clearly discern a movement away from the sole concentration on the teachings and sayings of Jesus towards an endeavour to relate Jesus' teaching with other

sayings traditions an ideological motif can be discerned, i.e. the theological bias towards the (spoken) word in dialectical theology.

80. M. Dibelius, *Die Formgeschichte des Evangeliums* (Tübingen: J.C.B. Mohr [Paul Siebeck], 3rd edn, 1959), pp. 178-218; R. Bultmann, *Geschichte der synoptischen Tradition* (Göttingen: Vandenhoeck & Ruprecht, 3rd edn, 1957), pp. 282-308.

81. Bultmann, *Geschichte*, pp. 223-60; Dibelius, *Formgeschichte*, pp. 66-100. In form criticism the development of the miracle tradition was explained with reference to the Hellenistic concept of the *theios aner*, which is said to have been adopted by the Hellenistic church in order to portray the earthly Jesus as divine man (see Bultmann, *Geschichte*, p. 256; H.D. Betz, 'Jesus as Divine Man', in F.T. Trotter [ed.], *Jesus and the Historian* [Festschrift E.C. Colwell; Philadelphia: Fortress Press, 1968], pp. 114-33, esp. pp. 116-17) In this fashion the divine man hypothesis situated the miracle tradition in the context of the history of early Christianity and consequently reduced its relevance for the understanding of Jesus' person to a minimum.

82. Norman Perrin and Günther Bornkamm may serve as typical examples for this tendency in the New Quest. Significant is the title of Perrin's book, *Rediscovering the Teaching of Jesus* (London: SPCK, 1967). In Bornkamm's influential monograph the miracle tradition plays only an insignificant role, since he concentrates solely on the teaching of Jesus (see G. Bornkamm, *Jesus von Nazareth* [Stuttgart: W. Kohlhammer, 15th edn, 1995], passing references to Jesus' deeds only on pp. 54-55 and 120). In Kümmel's survey of the Jesus research of 1950–90 only approximately 25 of 700 pages are dedicated to the miracle question, see Kümmel, *Vierzig Jahre*, pp. 277-96, 516-19.

aspects of his life. This, in the first instance, is reflected by the trend in recent Jesus studies to grant more weight to the miracle or healing traditions to inform the picture of the historical Jesus.[83] It is generally accepted that Jesus was a healer and/or exorcist, that his healing activities formed an integral part of his mission in Galilee and that no adequate picture of Jesus could be drawn without considering his healing activity and its meaning within the context of his social world.[84]

A second indication of the movement away from the one-sided preoccupation with the teaching of Jesus is the ever-increasing attention which is now being paid to Jesus' social relationships. This is a consequence of the application of sociological methods to the Jesus tradition.[85] Particularly Jesus' behaviour towards women, impure and social outcasts and his dining practice within the context of a hierarchically structured and patriarchal society receive a lot of attention and are considered to be central to an adequate understanding of Jesus.[86] It should, however, be noted that the Third Quest is not concerned with the factuality or authenticity of certain incidents but attempts to relate typical activities of Jesus to each other, to his teaching and to the social

83. See esp. Crossan, *Historical Jesus*, pp. 303-353; Borg, *Jesus*, pp. 39-75; Sanders, *Historical Figure*, chap. 10, but also Becker, *Jesus von Nazaret*, pp. 211-33 (ET pp. 169-85). An exhaustive treatment is found in Meier, *Marginal Jew*, II, pp. 509-1038. For a critical review of the trends in modern research on the miracle traditions, cf. B.L. Blackburn, 'The Miracles of Jesus', in B. Chilton and C.A. Evans (eds.), *Studying the Historical Jesus: Evaluations of the State of Research* (NTTS, 19; Leiden: E.J. Brill, 1994), pp. 353-94.

84. Morton Smith's provocative book *Jesus the Magician* (London: Harper & Row, 1978) played an important part in reversing the bias against the narrative and especially the miracle tradition. Smith heavily criticized Jesus research conducted within the context of the form-critical approach as prejudiced in favour of a portrait of Jesus as a teacher. Although his own handling of the tradition rightly was severely criticized, his demand for a closer scrutiny of the miracle narratives as source material for an understanding of the historical Jesus was heeded especially by American scholars and is consequently now reflected by current Jesus research.

85. A sociological approach to the history of early Christianity was introduced into New Testament scholarship by G. Theissen, W. Meeks, B. Malina, E. Schüssler Fiorenza, R. Horsley and many others. Using sociological models they try to reveal social structures implicitly reflected by the texts and use these to reconstruct the social and communicative contexts in which the texts attain meaning.

86. How central these aspects could be in the Third Quest is indicated by Crossan in the preface of his book on Jesus (see Crossan, *Historical Jesus*, p. xxix), where he designates the chapter on 'Magic and Meal' as the key chapter of the book.

structures of his time in order to attain a perception of his place within society and his communicative effect on that society.

Another aspect to be considered in this respect is the fact that in recent research the so-called 'facts' of Jesus' life are accorded a lot more weight than in previous research.[87] Historical facts such as the baptism by John, the crucifixion by the Romans, the role played by Jewish leaders in the death of Jesus, and so on, are no longer considered to be incidents of only little interest for the understanding of the historical Jesus, but are now viewed as important indicators of what kind of person Jesus might have been. These facts (especially the events surrounding his death)[88] constitute set points in the life of Jesus which require the historian to relate them to other aspects of his life (e.g. his teaching, healings, social conduct) and to correlate them with his social context, that is, to fit them into the cultural matrix of first-century Palestinian Judaism. They therefore serve as important beacons which take on the function of directing the process of constructing a plausible historical hypothesis on the life of Jesus.[89]

2. *The Quest for Contextual Continuity*. Characteristic of current Jesus research is its endeavour to situate Jesus firmly *within* his historical context. The underlying assumption at the basis of the whole enterprise is that every individual person stands in a network of diachronic and synchronic continuities to the surrounding world.[90] Applied to Jesus this implies that his historical context is not relevant in the sense that it provides a background which could merely serve as a foil against which he could be presented. Rather the context is seen as a crucial source that informs our knowledge about Jesus.[91] In essence this means that as

---

87. See esp. Sanders, *Jesus and Judaism*, pp. 3-22; also Harvey, *Constraints*, pp. 5-6.

88. Cf. R.A. Horsley, 'The Death of Jesus', in B. Chilton and C.A. Evans (eds.), *Studying the Historical Jesus: Evaluations of the State of Research* (NTTS, 19; Leiden: E.J. Brill, 1994), pp. 395-422.

89. Cf. Sanders, *Jesus and Judaism*, pp. 18-22.

90. The issue of the constraints by the historical context was introduced into Jesus research by A.E. Harvey in his Bampton Lectures of 1980, published as *Jesus and the Constraints of History* (1982). In a narrower sense of linguistic conventions the same problem was discussed by Riches, *Jesus and the Transformation of Judaism*. These works can therefore be considered to have initiated current Jesus research.

91. 'The social world of Jesus is not studied for the sake of supplying back-

Jesus was a man of his time his behaviour was constrained by cultural, social and linguistic conventions of his time, which could serve as crucial elements in building a profile of what kind of historical person he might have been.[92]

In its search for continuity between Jesus and his context current Jesus research clearly distinguishes itself from the preceding phase of the Second Quest. For during the Second Quest Jesus research did not focus on the possible continuities that could have determined the life of Jesus but in a quest for Jesus' exceptionality or singularity it rather concentrated on the ways in which Jesus differed from his context.[93] It is a common trend in current Jesus research that this occupation with singularity is viewed as an inadequate historical approach which should be replaced by an approach seeking to draw a portrait of Jesus which is historically plausible.[94] Such a pursuit for historical plausibility reckons with substantial overlapping of an individual subject with his historical context and assumes that individuality is a function of the combination of several contextual factors rather than decontextualized singularity.[95] This quest for historical plausibility can rightly be said to be one of the distinctive features of current Jesus research.

c. *The Demise of the Criterion of Dissimilarity*
The development of the Third Quest as a pursuit for a Jesus which stands in general continuity with his historical social context reflects a departure from the basic tenet of the second phase of Jesus research,

ground material, but in order to supply contexts of interpretation of texts of a different nature' (van Aarde, 'Pathways', p. 243); see also H. Boers, 'Context in the Interpretation of the Jesus Tradition', *Neot* 28 (1994), pp. 159-79.

92. This explains the prominent role that social history plays in the current debate. Social analyses by means of sociological methods are viewed as essential instruments to construct as complete as possible a plausible historical context of Jesus which could inform our picture of Jesus himself.

93. For a good review of the positions held in this regard, see Dagmar Winter's analysis of the Second Quest in G. Theissen and D. Winter, *Die Kriterienfrage in der Jesusforschung: Vom Differenzkriterium zum Plausibilitätskriterium* (Göttingen: Vandenhoeck & Ruprecht, 1997), pp. 117-45; ET *Criteria in Jesus Research: From Dissimilarity to Plausibility* (Tools for Biblical Studies, 4; Leiderdorp: Deo, 2000).

94. Theissen and Winter, *Kriterienfrage*, pp. 175-217.

95. On the problem of contextual individuality, see Theissen and Winter, *Kriterienfrage*, pp. 188-91.

namely the criterion of (double) discontinuity or dissimilarity.[96] The Second Quest can be characterized as a protracted scholarly debate on the refinement and the application of this basic principle.[97] It is therefore highly significant that W.G. Kümmel, summarizing his impressions of 30 years of Jesus research from 1950 until 1980, formulates as a result of this debate that the criterion of double dissimilarity is untenable, since it isolates Jesus from his Jewish context, eliminates the connection between him and early Christianity and therefore falsifies the image of Jesus to the extent of becoming an ahistorical abstraction.[98]

The failure of the criterion of discontinuity was furthermore the result of developments in other disciplines. Especially the research on Second Temple Judaism demonstrated that the concept of a normative, rather monolithic Judaism predominant in the Second Quest is inadequate and does not reflect the complexities and diversity of Judaism in the days of Jesus.[99] The diversity of Judaism contemporary to Jesus effectively reduces the value of the criterion of discontinuity with respect to

96. The criterion was initially formulated by Ernst Käsemann in his famous essay which reopened the quest for the historical Jesus, 'Das Problem des historischen Jesus', *ZTK* 51 (1954), pp. 125-53 (144) = *idem, Exegetische Versuche und Besinnungen* (Göttingen: Vandenhoeck & Ruprecht, 1961), pp. 187-213 (205).

97. See Theissen and Winter, *Kriterienfrage*, pp. 117-44.

98. 'Und bei der unerläßlichen Diskussion der Kriterien für die Ausscheidung der zum Verständnis des Jesus der Geschichte brauchbaren ältesten Überlieferung hat sich doch wohl die Anschauung durchgesetzt, daß die immer wieder vertretene Vorherrschaft oder gar Alleingültigkeit des Kriteriums der Abweichung Jesu vom Judentum und frühen Christentum unhaltbar ist, weil von dieser Voraussetzung aus Jesu selbstverständlichem Zusammenhang mit der konkreten Wirklichkeit seiner jüdischen Umwelt ebenso wie der Zusammenhang des frühen Christentums mit Jesus beseitigt und die Person und Lehre Jesu zu einer ungeschichtlichen Abstraktion verfälscht werden', W.G. Kümmel, 'Nachwort', in *idem, Dreissig Jahre Jesusforschung (1950–1980)* (BBB, 60; Bonn: Beltz Athenäum, 1985), pp. 535-41 (537) = *idem, Vierzig Jahre*, pp. 691-95 (693). Kümmel obviously did not realize that this insight necessarily implies the failure of the whole endeavour of the New Quest because of the pivotal role the criterion of dissimilarity played in the Second Quest. But as those words were written, the decisive studies, which initialized the Third Quest (Vermes, Smith, Meyer, Riches, Harvey), were already making their mark on the scholarly debate on the historical Jesus.

99. I only refer to some of the major developments in this field: vast research on the Old Testament Apocrypha (Charlesworth *et al.*) and Jewish apocalypticism, the publication of and research on the documents from Qumran (Vermes *et al.*), research on Hellenistic Judaism (Hengel *et al.*) and the development of rabbinic

Judaism to the question of discontinuity with respect to particular Judaisms, that is, to the search of Jesus' position on the broad spectrum covered by contemporary Judaism. In a similar vein the awareness of the complexity and diversity of earliest Christianity advanced rapidly in New Testament research.[100] This led to a sharp increase in the range of possible continuities and discontinuities between Jesus and the many forms of early Christianity which effectively reduces the relevance of the discontinuity criterion vis-à-vis early Christianity.

The endeavour of the Third Quest firmly stands in the tradition of those who had rejected the criterion of double dissimilarity. After 20 years of Jesus research under reversed premises it is clear that the criterion of dissimilarity with respect to Judaism generally had been discarded. It was replaced by a procedure which allows the criterion of discontinuity to function only within a framework of basic continuity: only those traditions, which can be demonstrated to derive from first-century Palestinian Judaism, are considered as authentic Jesus traditions. Contextual continuity vis-à-vis first-century Palestinian Judaism is considered to be a necessary though not sufficient criterion of authentic Jesus tradition. It is complemented by the quest for an individual profile of Jesus within his Jewish context, that is, the specific combination of contextual elements which account for the historical individuality of Jesus.[101]

Whereas the criterion of contextual continuity with respect to Judaism can be considered broadly accepted in current Jesus research, such a clear-cut consensus on the role of the criterion of dissimilarity vis-à-vis early Christianity had not yet been reached. Generally accepted is the

Judaism (esp. the work of J. Neusner, E.P. Sanders) since 1945 completely changed our perception of Judaism before the destruction of the Temple.

100. Cf. among others J.M. Robinson and H. Koester, *Trajectories through Early Christianity* (Philadelphia: Fortress Press, 1971); B. Mack, *A Myth of Innocence: Mark and Christian Origins* (Philadelphia: Fortress Press, 1988); K. Berger, *Theologiegeschichte des Urchristentums* (Tübingen: Francke, 1994).

101. On the criterion of contextual continuity see Theissen and Winter, *Kriterien-frage*, pp. 183-94, 209-212, 215-17. They speak of 'Kontextplausibilität', 'Kontextentsprechung' and 'kontextuelle Individualität'. Theissen and Winter suggest that an analysis of the methodological praxis of the Third Quest indicates that current Jesus research is directed by a 'criterion of historical plausibility', which could be differentiated into several interrelated subcriteria. They thus do not propose a new criterion, but aim at systematizing the methods practised by Jesus scholars since 1980 (*Kriterienfrage*, p. ix).

methodological premise that Jesus traditions which are at odds with the interests of the early church are authentic.[102] On the other hand a substantial measure of continuity between Jesus and the earliest church should be assumed as highly probable, and consequently a historical plausible picture of Jesus demands consideration of this fact.[103] The pursuit for historical plausibility therefore calls for an application of the criterion of dissimilarity in such a fashion that the resulting portrayal of Jesus is compatible with the ensuing emergence and development of early Christianity.[104]

d. *Jesus within Judaism*

It could be said to be a trend common to practically all recent research on Jesus, that it sets Jesus firmly within Judaism. This development should be considered the logical consequence of the quest for a contextual Jesus. The aim is to map Jesus onto Second Temple Judaism, to blend an image of Jesus into the general picture of Judaism. This is reflected by countless studies which stress the Jewishness of Jesus and explore the significance of this theme.[105] This trend in Jesus research

---

102. Cf. Theissen and Winter, *Kriterienfrage*, pp. 176-80.

103. In some Third Quest studies on Jesus the criterion of dissimilarity is applied with its full force with respect to early Christianity. This tends to isolate Jesus fully from ancient Christianity, thereby assuming a position similar to that taken by R. Bultmann earlier in the century who set Jesus firmly within the context of Judaism (cf. Theissen and Winter, *Kriterienfrage*, pp. 107-116, on Bultmann's picture of Jesus). Whereas the Second Quest, under the influence of its concern to determine the relationship between the Jesus of history and kerygmatic Christ, subtlety tended towards stressing the elements of continuity with early Christianity as well as the discontinuity with Judaism, some Third Quest studies tend towards emphasizing the discontinuity of Jesus with Christianity.

104. On the application of the criterion of historical plausibility with respect to early Christianity cf. Theissen and Winter, *Kriterienfrage*, pp. 206-209, 212-17. Becker, *Jesus von Nazaret*, pp. 4-5, 17-19 (ET pp. 4-5, 13-15) demands that a portrayal of Jesus must be embedded in a history of early Christianity and its reception of Jesus and should explain in what sense Jesus is to be considered the starting point of this history.

105. This trend is reflected by many of the titles of recent studies on Jesus: 'Jesus the Jew' (Vermes); 'Jesus and Judaism' (Sanders); 'Jesus within Judaism' (Charlesworth), 'The Life of a Mediterranean Jewish Peasant' (Crossan); 'A Marginal Jew' (Meier), etc. For literature on the issue of the Jewishness of Jesus cf. Telford, 'Major Trends', pp. 70-71. See esp. D.A. Hagner, *The Jewish Reclamation of Jesus* (Grand Rapids: Zondervan, 1984). A marked exception in this respect is Mack,

was paved by a number of Jewish scholars who, unfettered by typical Christian theological issues, constructed alternative pictures of Jesus which stressed the proximity of Jesus and Judaism.[106] In this respect the contributions of Geza Vermes stand out as having exerted an important influence on recent Jesus research.[107]

The endeavour of situating Jesus within his contemporary Jewish context has many facets, but one can distinguish two strains among the studies occupied with setting Jesus within the context of Judaism. One trend is to situate Jesus within the matrix of the world of ideas of first-century Judaism, that is, to determine his place within a Jewish history of ideas or a history of Jewish religion. Such studies are largely concerned with determining Jesus' relationship to positions held by his contemporaries on issues like the Law, the Temple, the Messiah, eschatology and apocalypticism.[108] The other trend is represented by studies which rather fit Jesus into a context of first-century Palestinian Judaism in materialist terms and not in terms of a set of ideas. Such studies are above all concerned with determining Jesus' role in the concrete social situation of his time, that is, with his place within the social structure of Palestinian Judaism and his impact on these structures and the corresponding social conditions.[109] Of course, both trends are not mutually exclusive and influence each other respectively.

e. *Giving Jesus Names: The Quest for Jesus' Social Type*
A further characteristic trait of current Jesus research is the widespread concern to determine Jesus' social type. At stake is the social identity of

---

Myth of Innocence, who draws a rather unJewish picture of Jesus as a Cynic teacher that is more Hellenistic than Jewish.

106. A long list of such scholars could be named since the beginning of the twentieth century: T. Klausner, L. Baeck, S. Sandmel, S. Ben-Chorin, D. Flusser, H. Falk. Cf. Theissen and Winter, *Kriterienfrage*, pp. 148-51.

107. G. Vermes, *Jesus the Jew: A Historian's Reading of the Gospels* (London: Collins, 1973); *idem, Jesus and the World of Judaism* (London: SCM Press, 1983); *idem, The Religion of Jesus the Jew* (London: SCM Press, 1993).

108. Of the above discussed authors Sanders and Becker clearly belong to this category. Cf. also Vermes, *Jesus the Jew*, and *idem, Religion*; Meyer, *Aims*, Harvey, *Constraints*, Charlesworth, *Jesus within Judaism*.

109. Crossan, Horsley and to some extent Borg are representatives of this approach, see also Mack, *Myth of Innocence*, pp. 25-132 and Schüssler Fiorenza, *Memory*, pp. 105-159.

Jesus, that is, his role in society.[110] The quest for the social identity in current research is determined by the fact that the tradition presents Jesus as teacher, prophet and miracle-worker or healer. The problem of determining his social identity consists in determining the relative weight of these traditions with respect to each other and vis-à-vis other contextual factors. Although the endeavour to determine Jesus' social type can be said to be one of the common features of the Third Quest, the same cannot be said of the results. Depending on whether one attributes more weight to the one or the other aspect of the tradition or context Jesus emerges as teacher of wisdom (Vermes, Downing), as subversive sage (Borg, Crossan), Rabbi (Flusser, Chilton) or Pharisee (Falk), as magician (Smith) or charismatic holy man (Vermes, Borg, Freyne), as social prophet (Horsley, Borg, Oakman) or eschatological prophet (Sanders, Charlesworth, Becker). This large spectrum of diverse social types reflects a characteristic feature of the whole enterprise: current Jesus research is notwithstanding some common trends characterized by some major divergent trends which account for the diverse pictures presented of Jesus.

f. *Concluding Remarks*

In conclusion I want to draw attention to another characteristic feature of current Jesus research, namely the tendency to consider the quest for Jesus strictly in terms of history, that is, devoid of any dogmatic or theological interests.[111] It should be observed that this trend results not so much from material considerations than from a number of sociological factors of which two should be mentioned here: first, the fact that the centre of gravity in Jesus research had in recent years shifted from Germany towards North America[112] had the effect that theological

110. The notion of the social type was introduced into modern Jesus research by M. Smith. In his book *Jesus the Magician* he claims that it is the task of the historian to determine the social identity of Jesus, i.e. to characterize him with social categories of his time, which were applied by society to make sense of such an outsider-career. Smith suggests the social type of the magician *(magos/theios aner)*.

111. This trend is also reflected by titles such as 'A Historian's Reading of the Gospels' (Vermes), 'The Historical Jesus' (Crossan), 'The Historical Figure of Jesus' (Sanders), to name a few.

112. Contributing factors to this shift were the rapid acceleration of the emancipation of America from theological developments in Europe since 1960, the resulting establishment of American dominated scientific forums (AAR, SBL, the Jesus Seminar) and an enormous market for theological and religious books in North

faculties (especially the Protestant faculties in Germany) do not determine the agenda of Jesus research anymore[113] as had been the case previously.[114] Secondly, corresponding with this development is the growing involvement of Jewish scholars in Jesus research who are less interested in typical Christian theological issues.[115]

4. *Diverging Trends in Current Jesus Research*

Even a cursory comparison of the various Jesus pictures constructed during the phase of the Third Quest necessarily leads to the impression that the enterprise lacks unity. Despite some common assumptions which account for a certain measure of homogenity, the Third Quest is characterized by a number of diverse developments which seem to reflect some irreconcilable differences on a number of fundamental issues. In the following I draw attention to some of the major divergent trends in current Jesus research.

a. *An Eschatological or a Non-Eschatological Jesus?*
Probably the most striking difference of opinion in current Jesus research applies to the question as to whether Jesus' message was thoroughly eschatological or not.[116] Had Jesus research since the beginning

America, a factor of which the influence on the scientific process should not be underestimated.

113. Jesus research is now rather determined by typical North American factors. Jesus is, e.g., a subject of teaching not only within theological faculties and church seminaries but also in other university faculties and institutions devoid of theological concerns. To a certain extent its programme is also dictated by general public interest for an important figure of Western cultural history and his significance for ethical issues.

114. All three previous phases of Jesus research were decisively informed by theological issues: the First Quest with its pictures of Jesus as teacher of moral values clearly reflected the inclination of liberal protestant theology towards historism and its concern for morality as the uppermost religious category; the No-Quest Phase resulted from the emphasis on the kerygma and the kerygmatic Christ over and against the historical Jesus in dialectical theology and particularly in the thought of R. Bultmann; the Second Quest was dominated by the concern to determine the extent of the continuity between the historical Jesus and the kerygma of early Christianity as it was programmatically formulated by E. Käsemann in 1954.

115. Cf. the above-mentioned influential studies of M. Smith and G. Vermes.

116. The meaning of the term 'eschatological' became blurred in New Testament

of the twentieth century been underpinned by the common conviction that Jesus proclaimed a thoroughly eschatological message, a large number of scholars now have broken with this consensus and no longer think that Jesus expected the imminent end of the world brought about by God through the apocalyptical coming of his kingdom. This view is widely held especially among scholars in North America associated with the influential Jesus Seminar and the Historical Jesus Section of the Society of Biblical Literature.[117] The fundamental importance of this difference in opinion is immediately obvious: it concerns the framework of reference of Jesus' proclamation of the kingdom of God and therefore affects the understanding of the essence of his teaching.

At the very basis of the disagreement on the (non-)eschatological nature of Jesus' message lie a number of longstanding controversies on some important *unsolved* problems presented by the Jesus tradition. Central to the debate is the highly complex problem presented by the Son of Man sayings.[118] A large number of scholars consider the so-called eschatological sayings on the imminent coming of the Son of

research: it is applied in a narrow sense to refer to the 'last things' and corresponds largely with apocalypticism. However, it is also used in a broader sense to refer metaphorically to a fundamental negation of the world or the existing order without implying an objective change in the world whatsoever. Used in this broad sense there would be consensus among most scholars that Jesus was a figure with an eschatological message, used in the narrow sense; a large number of scholars will dissent. On the dual use, see M. Borg, 'Reflections on a Discipline: A North American Perspective', in B. Chilton and C.A. Evans (eds.), *Studying the Historical Jesus: Evaluations of the State of Research* (NTTS, 19; Leiden: E.J. Brill, 1994), pp. 9-31 (19-20). In this essay I use the term only in its narrow sense.

117. See Borg, 'Reflections', pp. 19-21 and M. Borg, 'A Temperate Case for a Non-Eschatological Jesus', *SBLSP* 25 (1986), pp. 521-35, also H. Weder, *Gegenwart und Gottesherrschaft* (BThSt, 20; Neukirchen–Vluyn: Neukirchener Verlag, 1993). Some of the counter-arguments are summarized by D.C. Allison, 'A Plea for Thoroughgoing Eschatology', *JBL* 113 (1994), pp. 651-68. Of the above-discussed pictures of Jesus, Borg and Crossan represent the non-eschatological current in recent research, Sanders and Becker the eschatological current. Horsley occupies a position somewhere in-between. For a discussion of his view of an imminent, non-transcendental eschatology see above, pp. 85-88.

118. The Son of Man debate of the past four decades produced a consensus about the fact that there had never existed a Jewish titular usage of the Son of Man designation and that the Greek expression reflects an original Aramaic expression. With respect to the origin and development of the Son of Man tradition the debate was inconclusive. For a short but accurate review of the current state of the Son

Man not to be authentic Jesus tradition but rather to be post-Easter creations of early Christianity.[119] Recently, though, it was argued anew that the Son of Man tradition has its origin in Jesus' references to the Son of Man as an eschatological figure.[120] Fiercely disputed, furthermore, is the (non-)eschatological nature of the so-called kingdom sayings: whereas a large number of scholars currently argue that the authentic kingdom sayings do not reflect an imminent eschatology but rather refer to a present mode of (social and/or moral) renewal,[121] others argue in favour of interpreting them eschatologically.[122]

of Man research, see J. Schröter, *Die Erinnerung an Jesu Worte: Studien zur Rezeption der Logienüberlieferung in Markus, Q und Thomas* (WMANT, 76; Neukirchen–Vluyn: Neukirchener Verlag, 1997), pp. 451-55.

119. This position was introduced by P. Vielhauer, 'Gottessohn und Menschensohn in der Verkündigung Jesu', in *idem, Aufsätze zum Neuen Testament* (TBü, 31; Munich: Chr. Kaiser Verlag, 1965), pp. 51-79. N. Perrin, *A Modern Pilgrimage in New Testament Christology* (Philadelphia: Fortress Press, 1974), pp. 23-40, 57-83, argued in a similar fashion. In current Jesus research this position was introduced by M. Borg (see, e.g., Borg, 'A Temperate Case', pp. 525-27) and is carefully argued by Crossan within the framework of his stratification model (*Historical Jesus*, pp. 238-59). This position is often complemented by the notion that the Son of Man tradition originated in Jesus' use of a generic Aramaic expression ('anybody, somebody') that could have been used to refer indirectly to the speaker ('somebody like myself'), see, e.g., Crossan, *Historical Jesus*, pp. 255-59.

120. A. Yarbro Collins, 'The Origin of the Designation of Jesus as "Son of Man"', *HTR* 80 (1987), pp. 391-408; *idem*, 'Daniel 7 and Jesus', *JTh* 93 (1989), pp. 5-19. In a similar vein argues Becker, *Jesus von Nazaret*, pp. 112-17, 249-67 (ET pp. 93-96, 197-211). The question is inextricably entangled with research on the use of the Son of Man expression in the Ethiopian *Apocalypse of Enoch*. Here it seems that a consensus is emerging regarding its Jewish provenance and its origin in several stages between 100 BCE and 70 CE (see the contributions of Borsch, Black and VanderKam in J.H. Charlesworth [ed.], *The Messiah* [Minneapolis: Augsburg–Fortress, 1992]).

121. On this cf. Borg, 'A Temperate Case', pp. 525-27, where he summarizes the arguments presented in his book *Conflict, Holiness and Politics in the Teachings of Jesus*. See also Crossan, *Historical Jesus*, pp. 265-302, who by means of his stratification model reduces the kingdom sayings said to be relevant for a reconstruction of Jesus' message to 12 non-eschatological sayings (see Appendix 5, pp. 459-60), which consequently render a Jesus proclaiming a sapiential kingdom. It should be noted that regarding the understanding of Jesus' proclamation of God's kingdom in a non-eschatological sense the views of N. Perrin had a large impact on North American scholarship.

122. Some of the counter-arguments are summarized by Allison, 'Thoroughgoing

It should be noted that these controversies concern unsolved issues in current research and that a consensus is not in sight. Both the traditions of the Son of Man and the kingdom of God present us with complexities which could hardly be solved in an unequivocal manner. The ambiguity inherent in the tradition can only be resolved by complementing the traditions with other less ambiguous data from the tradition (criterion of coherence). To prevent total circularity and uncontrollable arbitrariness, the above-mentioned criterion of historical plausibility should at this point be considered as an important corrective against full-scale relativity.[123] This means that in this particular case the construction of a non-eschatological or eschatological Jesus can only be considered a historically plausible hypothesis if it can be set in the context of a comprehensive explanation of the historical developments along a trajectory from an eschatologically orientated Baptist movement to an eschatologically orientated early Christianity.[124]

b. *Prophet or Sage?*

Closely related to the question of the eschatological nature of Jesus' proclamation is another characteristic aspect of current Jesus research. A growing number of scholars are quitting the traditional consensus

Eschatology', pp. 659-63. Allison aptly notices that some of the relevant kingdom sayings (e.g. Mk 1.15; 9.1; 14.25; Lk. 10.9/Mt. 10.7) could reasonably be given a temporal sense (although not necessarily so): the tradition can therefore be interpreted differently. This implies that a verdict on the (non-)eschatological nature of the kingdom sayings can hardly be reached without a complementary context of interpretation. An eschatological interpretation of the kingdom of God is among others proposed by Sanders, *Jesus and Judaism*, pp. 123-56; Becker, *Jesus von Nazaret*, pp. 100-275 (ET pp. 85-224); and Meier, *Marginal Jew*, II, pp. 237-507.

123. Cf. Theissen and Winter, *Kriterienfrage*, pp. 206-214, esp. p. 208. Since the pictures of a non-eschatological Jesus isolate Jesus from the ensuing Christian movement, they are confronted with the reproach that they draw a historically implausible picture of Jesus. This is the essence of the critique of Allison, 'Thoroughgoing Eschatology'; see also H. Koester, 'Jesus the Victim', *JBL* 111 (1992), pp. 3-15, esp. pp. 7-8, 13-15.

124. Traditionally the continuity between Jesus and ensuing Christianity on this point is assumed, not argued. J. Becker attempts to argue for an eschatological Jesus on the basis of contextual continuity to John the Baptist and on grounds of historical plausibility with respect to cause and effect vis-à-vis early Christianity ('Wirkungsplausibilität'). Of the proponents of a non-eschatological Jesus, B. Mack does relate his Jesus to a corresponding view of the origins of Christianity, cf. his *Myth of Innocence* and *idem, The Lost Gospel: The Book of Q and Christian*

that Jesus had been an eschatological prophet. They suggest that Jesus was rather a teacher of wisdom. According to this position Jesus was a sage, an aphorist who created sapiential sayings and taught a form of subversive wisdom.[125] It is characteristic of this trend that wisdom or sapiential teaching and apocalyptical or eschatological teaching are considered to be mutually exclusive. This assumption conflicts with the traditional hypothesis that the sapiential aspects of Jesus' teaching should be subordinated to or at least be considered as a complement of his eschatological proclamation of the kingdom.[126] We are therefore at this point again confronted with diverging trends in the scientific community. Apart from the differences in opinion about the authenticity of the eschatological traditions in the Gospels, several reasons can be advanced for this development. I want to focus on two fundamental issues which lie at the very basis of this rift in current research.

1. *The Problem of Stratification: Early Sapiential Layers in the Tradition.* One of the main factors that contributed to the notion of Jesus being a teacher of wisdom rather than an eschatological prophet is the contention that a stratification of the Jesus tradition indicates that the earliest Jesus tradition was devoid of eschatological themes. It is argued that the earliest layers of the Jesus tradition are sapiential in character and that only secondary layers reflect an interest for eschatology which is judged to be an indication of the sapiential nature of Jesus' teaching.[127]

Origins (San Francisco: HarperCollins, 1993). It remains, however, to be seen if this view will assert itself as a historically plausible construction of Christian origins.

125. Again this position is dominating in circles affiliated to the Jesus Seminar in the USA. Some of the prominent proponents are D. Crossan, B. Mack, L. Vaage and E. Schüssler Fiorenza.

126. For a review of the different models in recent research correlating apocalypticism and wisdom in Jesus' teaching see M. Ebner, *Jesus—ein Weisheitslehrer? Synoptische Weisheitslogien im Traditionsprozess* (HBS, 15; Freiburg: Herder, 1998), pp. 1-18. Ebner proposes a solution according to which Jesus' teaching should be seen as mainly sapiential, however framed by certain apocalyptic presuppositions (*Jesus*, pp. 373-430). See also W.S. Vorster, 'Jesus: Eschatological Prophet and/or Wisdom Teacher?', *HTS* 47 (1991), pp. 526-42, who also questions the usefulness of a strict division of the two categories.

127. To name some prominent examples: Mack, *Myth of Innocence*, pp. 57-62, and in several other of his publications; L. Vaage, 'Q[1] and the Historical Jesus', *Foundations and Facets Forum* 5 (1989), pp. 159-76 (in later publications more

For an adequate understanding of this development in current research it is important to relate it to other developments in New Testament research. Especially in North America (but increasingly elsewhere) the trajectory hypothesis of H. Koester and J. Robinson[128] had in recent years taken the place of traditional form criticism as a scientific paradigm that serves as a framework for the debate on the development of the Jesus tradition.[129] This model proposes on the basis of genre analyses sever l genre-orientated, collections which are said to have preceded the canonical Gospels. Of special importance is the notion of an early Gattung of sayings collections (the *logoi sophon*) of which Q and the *Gospel of Thomas* (and/or a common source) are said to be examples. This theory was developed further by J. Kloppenborg with his proposal of a collection of sapiential speeches as the first layer in the history of the formation of Q.[130] Because of its chronological proximity to Jesus the early sapiential strata of the tradition (especially of Q) is in many circles currently judged to be proof of the sapiential character of Jesus' teaching.[131]

cautious). As can be expected, protest followed suit, e.g. Koester, 'Jesus the Victim', p. 7; Allison, 'Thoroughgoing Eschatology', pp. 661-62. See also R. Horsley, 'Q and Jesus: Assumptions, Approaches and Analyses', *Semeia* 55 (1991), pp. 175-209, esp. 196-209.

128. Robinson and Koester, *Trajectories*; H. Koester, *Ancient Christian Gospels: Their History and Development* (Valley Forge, PA: Trinity Press International, 1990).

129. See Schröter, *Erinnerung*, pp. 31-40, 72-78, 93-100, 132-36 for an excellent analysis of the history of this development and its underlying assumptions. It is important to take note of the fact that the Robinson–Koester hypothesis does not break with form criticism but rather develops its fundamental assumptions in another direction.

130. J.S. Kloppenborg, *The Formation of Q* (Philadelphia: Fortress Press, 1987). Kloppenborg himself emphasizes that his conception of an early sapiential layer in Q may not be misused to argue for a non-eschatological Jesus on the basis of the (false) assumption that priority in the chronological development of Q reflects priority in the history of tradition; see J.S. Kloppenborg, 'The Sayings Gospel Q and the Quest of the Historical Jesus', *HTR* 89 (1996), pp. 307-344, and already in Kloppenborg, *Formation*, pp. 244-45. For a similar argument, cf. Koester, 'Jesus the Victim', pp. 3-15, esp. p. 7.

131. D. Crossan is one of the most influential exponents of this trend. However, he reaches his conclusion by means of a complex method of analysis of individual traditional units which are regarded as relevant for the construction of a picture of Jesus if belonging to the earliest stratum of tradition and/or if multiply attested in the tradition. On the basis of this stratigraphical procedure with unequivocal

2. *The Problem of Sources.* A second important factor causing a shift towards understanding Jesus as a sage in opposition to the notion of him having been an eschatological or apocalyptical prophet is the tendency in some quarters to consider an *a priori* decision in favour of the canonical sources as a basis for Jesus research as (theologically) biased and therefore detrimental to an objective quest for the historical Jesus.[132] This development coincides with a revival of interest in the apocryphal literature in North America[133] and is dependent on hypotheses about the relative antiquity and independence of the apocryphal literature and/or (parts of) the Jesus traditions contained in them.[134] Of special importance is the *Gospel of Thomas* in this respect, which is

preference for early layers in the tradition he attains his image of a sapiential Jesus; see esp. Crossan, *Historical Jesus*, pp. 227-302.

132. In his introduction to the Semeia volume issued on the topic C.W. Hedrick speaks of 'the tyranny of the synoptic Jesus' (*Semeia* 44 [1988], pp. 1-8) and claims that the canonical literature 'controls both how the past is reconstructed, as well as the very substance of the reconstruction itself' (p. 2).

133. This is reflected by a flood of publications on the apocryphal literature and related topics. Cf., e.g., R. Cameron (ed.), *The Other Gospels: Non-Canonical Gospel Texts* (Philadelphia: Westminster Press, 1982); P. Beskow, *Strange Tales about Jesus: A Survey of Unfamiliar Gospels* (Philadelphia: Fortress Press, 1983); J.D. Crossan, *Four Other Gospels: Shadows on the Contours of Canon* (Minneapolis: Winston, 1985); J.D. Crossan, *The Cross that Spoke: The Origins of the Passion Narrative* (San Francisco: Harper & Row, 1988); Koester, *Ancient Gospels.* Two *Semeia* volumes are dedicated to the question of the apocryphal literature and its implications for the study of the historical Jesus and Christian origins (*Semeia* 44 [1988] and 49 [1990]). See also the critical treatments of these tendencies by J.H. Charlesworth and C. Evans, 'Jesus in the Agrapha and Apocryphal Gospels', in B.D. Chilton and C.A. Evans (eds.), *Studying the Historical Jesus: Evaluation of the State of Research* (NTTS, 19; Leiden: E.J. Brill, 1994), pp. 479-533 and Meier, *Marginal Jew*, I, pp. 112-66.

134. This can be illustrated with reference to Crossan's methodological praxis. To his earliest stratum of tradition are reckoned an apocalyptic source behind Mt. 24 and *Did.* 16, the earliest layer of the *Gospel of Thomas (Gos. Thom.* 1), the Egerton Gospel, the *Gospel of the Hebrews*, the so-called Cross Gospel and two papyrus fragments *P. Vienna G.* 2325 and *P. Oxy.* 1224; to the second stratum belong the *Gospel of the Egyptians*, the *Secret Gospel of Mark*, the second layer of the *Gospel of Thomas (Gos. Thom.* 2), parts of the Dialogue of the Saviour and *P. Oxy.* 840. Cf. the criticism of Charlesworth and Evans and Meier (see previous note).

considered by many to date in substance from the first century[135] and is ranked as a first-class source for research on the historical Jesus.[136]

3. The Problem of Applicability: Jesus and the Cynics. This is perhaps the best place to call attention to another trend characteristic of recent Jesus research: namely, the depiction of Jesus by some scholars not only as sage or wisdom teacher but more specifically as a Cynic sage. The Cynic hypothesis—a variant of the hypothesis of a sapiential Jesus —proposes that the earliest layer of tradition (especially Q) presents Jesus (and the earliest Jesus movement) as Cynic(s),[137] and that this is a true reflection of the real Jesus. The Cynic hypothesis has been vigorously propagated by Gerald Downing[138] and apparently independently from him by Burton Mack.[139] The extremely controversial Cynic hypothesis[140] hinges on a number of problems relating to the applicability

135. On the history of research of the *Gospel of Thomas* and its place in the history of early Christianity, see Schröter, *Erinnerung*, pp. 122-40. S.J. Patterson disputes in several publications the dependence of the *Gospel of Thomas* on the Synoptic Gospels, e.g. S.J. Patterson, 'The Gospel of Thomas and the Synoptic Tradition: A *Forschungsbericht* and Critique', *Foundations and Facets Forum* 8 (1992), pp. 45-97.

136. A driving force behind this trend is S.J. Patterson, cf. 'The Gospel of Thomas and Jesus: Retrospectus and Prospectus', *SBLSP* 29 (1990), pp. 614-36; *idem, The Gospel of Thomas and Jesus* (Sonoma, CA: Polebridge Press, 1993).

137. Already G. Theissen had drawn attention to the proximity of the social form of wandering charismatics in the Christian community behind Q to that of Cynic parallels in antiquity, see also Kloppenborg, 'Formation', pp. 306-316; F.G. Downing, 'Quite like Q. A Genre for Q: The "Lives" of Cynic Philosophers', *Bib* 69 (1988), pp. 196-225; and three recent dissertations by J. Tashjian, R. Uro and L. Vaage, conveniently summarized by J. Tashjian, 'The Social Setting of the Q Mission: Three Dissertations', *SBLSP* 27 (1988), pp. 636-44.

138. See F.G. Downing, 'Cynics and Christians', *NTS* 30 (1984), pp. 584-93; *idem*, 'The Social Contexts of Jesus the Teacher: Construction or Reconstruction', *NTS* 33 (1987), pp. 439-51; *idem, Jesus and the Treat of Freedom* (London: SCM Press, 1987); *idem, Christ and the Cynics* (Manuals, 4; Sheffield: JSOT Press, 1988); *idem, Cynics and Christian Origins* (Edinburgh: T. & T. Clark, 1992), pp. 143-68.

139. Mack, *Myth of Innocence; idem, Lost Gospel.* Also proposing Cynicism as a model for understanding Jesus is Crossan, *Historical Jesus*, pp. 72-90, 332-53.

140. Cf. H.D. Betz, 'Jesus and the Cynics: Survey and Analysis of a Hypothesis,' *JR* 74 (1994), pp. 453-75 and the ensuing debate: P.R. Eddy, 'Jesus as Diogenes? Reflections on the Cynic Jesus Thesis', *JBL* 115 (1996), pp. 449-69; D. Seeley, 'Jesus and the Cynics Revisited', *JBL* 116 (1997), pp. 704-712; G. Downing, 'Deeper Reflections on the Jewish Cynic Jesus', *JBL* 117 (1998), pp. 97-104.

of the parallel Cynic material to the Jesus tradition. Disputed is whether the large catalogue of parallels between the Jesus and Cynic traditions provided by Downing and others are merely referring to superficial and accidental parallels or if they are supported by a common (philosophical) deep structure.[141] Disputed furthermore is if the Cynic hypothesis can stand up to a form-critical examination,[142] if there had been any Cynic presence in Galilee at all[143] and whether the social structures (e.g. itinerancy) reflected by the traditions on Jesus and Cynics are overlapping enough to substantiate the claim that Cynicism can serve as a framework of interpretation for the historical Jesus and his followers.[144]

c. *Jesus as an Agent of Social Change?*

Another much disputed issue in current Jesus research concerns the question of Jesus' relation to the sociopolitical issues of his day. A clear trend can be discerned of scholars who attribute a political role to Jesus or consider him primarily as an agent of sociopolitical change.[145] He is characterized as a social prophet (Borg, Kaylor, Schüssler Fiorenza), a social reformer (in very different ways Theissen, Horsley, Freyne), or a

141. Betz, 'Cynics', pp. 470-72; and Ebner, *Weisheitslehrer?*, pp. 399-416.

142. C. Tuckett, 'A Cynic Q?', *Bib* 70 (1989), pp. 349-76, demonstrated that Q does not correspond with the genre of a Cynic *Bios* (however cf. Schröter, *Erinnerung*, pp. 436-61 on the biographical nature of Q). Ebner, *Weisheitslehrer?*, see esp. pp. 395-99, demonstrated that the wisdom sayings of Jesus are (particularly in Q) not transported by means of apophthegms, as is the case in the Cynic traditions; furthermore, the aphoristic rejoinders of Cynics are demonstrated to be different in character from the proverbial wisdom of Jesus.

143. Cf. Betz, 'Cynics', pp. 471-72 ('fanciful conjecture'!). The question about a Cynic presence in Galilee is closely connected to questions concerned with the degree of Hellenization Galilee was subjected to during the first century and with the character of Sepphoris and its relevance for a picture of Jesus and his followers (cf. R. Batey, *Jesus and the Forgotten City: New Light on Sepphoris and the Urban World of Jesus* [Grand Rapids: Eerdmans, 1991]); cf. Freyne, *Galilee*, and E.P. Sanders's challenge to the construct of a thoroughgoing Hellenized and Romanized Galilee ('Jesus in Historical Context', *TTod* 50 [1993–94], pp. 429-48).

144. Horsley, *Sociology*, pp. 116-21; *idem*, *Jesus*, pp. 228-31; Freyne, 'The Geography, Politics, and Economics of Galilee and the Quest for the Historical Jesus', in B. Chilton and C.A. Evans (eds.), *Studying the Historical Jesus: Evaluations of the State of Research* (NTTS, 19; Leiden: E.J. Brill, 1994), pp. 75-121, particularly pp. 116-21.

145. This is a new trend in Jesus research typical of the Third Quest: the Second Quest was characterized by a tendency to view Jesus as apolitical, non-revolu-

peasant protester (Crossan). Again this question is intrinsically intertwined with the problem of Jesus' attitude towards eschatology and
apocalypticism: those who consider Jesus primarily to be an eschatological prophet tend to refrain from attributing to him a prominent
sociopolitical role in society, whereas those who lay the emphasis on
Jesus' sapiential teaching render prominent the subversive character of
his wisdom and point out its social and political implications.[146] However, within the broad current of those who consider Jesus to have been
active in propagating and effecting socio-political change, there exists a
large spectrum of different and partially conflicting opinions on the
exact nature of Jesus' role as such an agent of social change.

The reasons for the very many different answers given to the question
concerning Jesus' sociopolitical role are many and complex, but at the
very basis of the startling variety of hypotheses lies the fact that an
answer entails bringing together two extremely complex sets of data.
For the formulation of a hypothesis on Jesus' sociopolitical role in society requires that one relates the Jesus tradition to a hypothetical reconstruction of the social context with all its complexities and variables.
The results of such an enterprise is therefore very much dependent on
the construction of the social world of Jesus as a context for his words
and deeds.[147]

---

tionary and non-violent (e.g. O. Cullmann, *Jesus und die Revolutionäre* [Tübingen:
J.C.B. Mohr [Paul Siebeck], 2nd edn, 1970]; M. Hengel, *War Jesus revolutionär?*
[Stuttgart: Calwer Verlag, 1970]), with the outsider position of Brandon, of Jesus as
a revolutionary Zealot (S.G.F. Brandon, *Jesus and the Zealots* [Manchester: Man-
chester University Press, 1967]). Pioneer of the current development was G. Theis-
sen with his *Soziologie der Jesusbewegung* (Munich: Chr. Kaiser Verlag, 1977) =
Sociology of Early Palestinian Christianity (Philadelphia: Fortress Press, 1978), and
G. Theissen, *Studien zur Soziologie des Urchristentums* (WUNT, 19; Tübingen:
J.C.B. Mohr, 1979).

146. This can only be a rule of thumb. Although proponents of a thoroughly
eschatological Jesus such as Sanders and Becker generally draw a rather apolitical
Jesus (but see Becker, *Jesus von Nazaret*, pp. 194-211 [ET pp. 155-69]), some
proponents of an eschatological Jesus do consider him as politically highly active
(Theissen, in another sense also R. Horsley and R.D. Kaylor). Whereas proponents
of a non-eschatological sapiential Jesus normally tend to ascribe to him an active
subversive role in the society of his day (Borg, Crossan, Downing, Schüssler
Fiorenza), B. Mack proposes that his subversive wisdom, although containing social
critique, was addressed at individuals and did not intend a renewal of social or
communal structures.

147. Seán Freyne's *dictum* that the quest for the historical Jesus is in danger of

Almost all current efforts to picture Jesus as an agent of social change depend on identifying and reconstructing *oppressive structures* or *structural conflict* in Jesus' social context and on relating the Jesus tradition to them. Two (partially overlapping) models of structural oppression and conflict are proposed by scholars to function as context for the interpretation of the Jesus traditions. A number of scholars propose ancient patriarchalism as the context against which an appropriate and socially relevant reading of the Jesus tradition becomes possible.[148] They suggest that relating the Jesus tradition to patriarchal inequality and oppression implies that Jesus confronted and criticized such social structures and introduced a renewal movement with an inclusive, egalitarian and non-hierarchical ethos as an alternative to the traditional patriarchal values and hierarchical structures in society. Such an inclusive and egalitarian ethos rendered sexual, social, familial and religious distinctions irrelevant.[149]

The second proposal suggests that the Jesus tradition should be set in the context of political oppression and ensuing economic hardship. According to this model the Roman Empire was a hierarchically structured agrarian society, characterized by its highly unequal distribution of power, privilege and wealth.[150] The Galilean peasantry which constituted Jesus' primary context figured at the very bottom of the pyramid of power and was subjected to oppression. Various axes of oppression could be distinguished: (1) political oppression exerted by the Roman Empire[151] and mediated by the house of Herod and its retainers which

becoming the quest for the historical Galilee is well taken; see Freyne, *Geography*, p. 76.

148. Pioneering this model was E. Schüssler Fiorenza with her feminist analysis of Christian origins, see esp. Schüssler Fiorenza, *Memory*, pp. 1-95 (on fundamentals of a feminist approach), 97-159 (on the Jesus Movement).

149. Prominent representatives of this model are Schüssler Fiorenza, Borg, Crossan, and Witherington, who all lay heavy emphasis on the liberational character of Jesus' words and deeds and on the corresponding egalitarian structures within the Jesus movement; see, e.g., Schüssler Fiorenza, *Memory*, pp. 140-54 ('Liberation from Patriarchal Structures and the Discipleship of Equals'), and Crossan, *Historical Jesus*, pp. 261-82, 341-45.

150. See the very influential descriptions of the so-called 'imperial situation' presented by Horsley, *Sociology*, pp. 65-101; cf. also *idem, Jesus*, pp. 3-19; and Crossan, *Jesus*, pp. 43-71.

151. The exact nature of Roman presence in Galilee is disputed: some scholars

manifested itself in a heavy tax burden and economic exploitation;[152] (2) religious oppression exercised by the Jerusalem temple aristocracy and its retainers through cultic domination and by means of tithes and taxes[153] resulting in cultic marginalization and further economic hardship;[154] (3) cultural dominance exerted by the urban Roman-Greek culture resulting in conflict between flourishing (Hellenistic) cities and the impoverished surrounding countryside.[155] In addition to these, other structural factors such as the lack of resources (particularly land), overpopulation and other economic hazards (crop failure, war) compounded the effects of structural oppression, leading to mass impoverishment

reckon with heavy Roman presence and influence in Galilee, particularly in urban areas, cf. Batey, *Forgotten City*, also R.D. Kaylor, *Jesus the Prophet: His Vision of the Kingdom on Earth* (Louisville, KY: Westminster/John Knox Press, 1994), but see the more cautious approach of Freyne, *Galilee*, esp. pp. 136-43; Sanders, *Historical Context*, esp. pp. 438-41.

152. Cf. Horsley, *Sociology*, pp. 88-90; *idem, Jesus*, pp. 279-84, 286-88.

153. See S. Applebaum, 'Economic Life in Palestine', in S. Safrai and M. Stern (eds.), *The Jewish People in the First Century* (CRINT, 1.2; Philadelphia: Fortress Press, 1976), pp. 631-700. Sanders, *Judaism: Practice and Belief*, pp. 157-69, promotes a less dramatic view of the tax burden.

154. Cf. Horsley, *Sociology*, pp. 72-75; *idem, Jesus*, pp. 28-33, for sketches of overt structural oppression exerted by the temple aristocracy and its retainers on Galilean peasants, provoking general dissatisfaction and conflict with the cult and its representatives. See also Crossan, *Historical Jesus*, pp. 304-326, who suggests that the Palestinian peasants were caught in a 'perfect circle of victimization' by the temple system (p. 324). Freyne, however, challenges this view and suggests that Galilean peasants generally supported the cult in Jerusalem and therefore did not provide a proper setting for a peasants based protest movement against the temple cult and its representatives (*Galilee*, pp. 178-190, 224-39); see also S. Freyne, 'Galilee–Jerusalem Relations in the Light of Josephus' *Life*', *NTS* 33 (1987), pp. 600-609.

155. For tensions between urban and rural areas and between the non-Jewish and Jewish populations of particular Galilean cities, see Freyne, *Galilee*, pp. 143-75. Some scholars emphasize the cultural and economic continuity between the Hellenized Galilean cities such as Tiberias and Sepphoris and the surrounding rural areas; see, e.g., Batey, *Forgotten City*, and T. Longstaff, 'Nazareth and Sepphoris: Insights into Christian Origins', *AnglThR* 11 (1990), pp. 8-15. Latent economic urban–rural tensions could also be assumed between Jerusalem and rural Galilee, although these tensions were probably mitigated by the common culture and world view; cf. Freyne, *Galilee*, pp. 150-52.

through indebtedness and land-loss, to banditry and pillage,[156] and generally to a condition of social unrest and a revolutionary climate.[157]

The various pictures of Jesus as an agent of social change which result from such a reconstructed social context are contingent on the various combinations of the above-mentioned factors and the proposed mode of interaction of Jesus with these factors. Again two general patterns emerge: Jesus is either viewed as the founder of a renewal movement which functions as an *alternative community*, that is, as an alternative to a society fraught with oppressive structures;[158] or he is seen as a (radical) reformer who founded a *renewal movement within society* concerned with reforming society itself and its institutions in face of structural oppression.[159]

5. *Concluding Remarks*

I conclude this essay with a few remarks on probably the most central problem behind the diversity that can be observed in current Jesus research. The Second Quest was conducted within a relatively stable methodological paradigm, namely form criticism and its corollary, redaction criticism. The theoretical presuppositions of form criticism had been heavily criticized by several scholars with the effect that the confidence in form criticism as a tool for historical analysis had been

156. Horsley especially promoted the view that banditry was rife in Galilee at the time of Jesus, see Horsley and Hanson, *Bandits*, pp. 48-87, but cf. the very different assessment of the data by Freyne, *Galilee*, pp. 163-67.

157. See the description by Horsley, *Sociology*, pp. 83-101; *idem, Jesus*, pp. 3-58, depicting Galilee as caught in a spiral of debt and violence, hovering on the brink of social conflict and revolution. The situation was less volatile according to Freyne, *Galilee*, pp. 161-67.

158. This position was introduced by G. Theissen in his pioneering work *Sociology of Early Palestinian Christianity*. The studies of Schüssler Fiorenza, Crossan and to some extent Borg represent variants of Theissen's original hypothesis.

159. The most prominent advocate of this position is R. Horsley, who considers Jesus to have been a social reformer engaged in the renewal of the sociopolitical form of traditional peasant life in anticipation of a political revolution to be effected by God. R.D. Kaylor makes a similar proposal, suggesting that Jesus addressed his social criticism at the powerful in order to effect social change. To a certain extent S. Freyne's proposal of Jesus as a social prophet engaged in the universalizing of peasant land and property values (Freyne, *Galilee*, pp. 239-47) also belongs to this category.

severely eroded.[160] During the last two decades the Third Quest developed and gained momentum, notwithstanding this methodological crisis in the discipline. It is therefore not surprising that it bears traces of it in the form of a complete lack of consensus on one of the most fundamental questions of the whole enterprise, namely on the question of the process of transmission of the Jesus traditions.[161] Current reconstructions of the historical Jesus are either based on antiquated form-critical principles[162] or they are constructed without being at all set within the framework of a theory about the processes and the modalities of transmission in early Christianity.[163] The extreme diversity in current Jesus research could therefore be an indication of the urgent need to develop a comprehensive theory of the process of transmission of tradition in

160. Cf. E. Güttgemanns, *Offene Fragen zur Formgeschichte des Evangeliums* (BEvT, 54; Munich: Chr. Kaiser Verlag, 1970); G. Stanton, 'Form Criticism Revisited', in M. Hooker and C. Hickling (eds.), *What about the New Testament? Essays in Honour of Christopher Evans* (London: SCM Press, 1975), pp. 13-27; W. Kelber, *The Oral and the Written Gospel* (Philadelphia: Fortress Press, 1983), pp. 1-43; K. Berger, *Einführung in die Formgeschichte* (Tübingen: Mohr Siebeck, 1987); Schröter, *Erinnerung*, pp. 1-65. In the light of the results of research on orality particularly the form-critical claim that it is possible to reconstruct the sayings of Jesus, is not tenable anymore.

161. This is among others acutely reflected by the dispute over the relevant textual basis for a reconstruction of a picture of the historical Jesus referred to above. The scholars involved in answering this question argue from very different frameworks of interpretation, which all presuppose certain more or less explicitly articulated theoretical assumptions on the modalities and processes of transmission of tradition in early Christianity.

162. This verdict also applies to those who are committed to the trajectory concept of Koester and Robinson, as Schröter, *Erinnerung*, pp. 31-40 aptly demonstrates.

163. E.g. Sanders, *Jesus and Judaism*, pp. 1-58, esp. pp. 14-16, who is generally sceptical about form-critical methodology, proposes a method of controlled hypothesis building which largely dispenses with reconstructing the sayings tradition. In the face of the crisis of form criticism and the lack of an alternative coherent theory of transmission of tradition in early Christianity, Crossan (*Historical Jesus*, pp. xxx-xxxiv, 427-52) tries to bypass the problem by implementing a rigid statistical procedure based on multiple attestation. Of the many critical responses to Crossan's proposal see esp. W. Kelber, 'Jesus and Tradition: Words in Time, Words in Space', *Semeia* 65 (1995), pp. 139-67, who criticizes the assumptions on the modalities of tradition tacitly inherent in the procedure advanced by Crossan.

early Christianity,[164] which could serve as an alternative to form criticism and provide new analytical tools for the quest for the historical origins of Christianity.[165]

164. Explicitly formulated by Crossan, *Historical Jesus*, pp. xxvii-iii, who suggests stringent and objective method as an avenue to escape from the quagmire of 'acute scholarly subjectivity', which led to such diversity in Jesus research ('an academic embarrassment'!).

165. See, e.g., the proposal of Schröter, *Erinnerung*, esp. pp. 1-5, 462-66, 482-86, who, by taking up developments in research on orality, memory and cultural remembrance, suggests that the quest for the historical Jesus should be conducted within the framework of a theory of cultural remembrance applied to the Jesus tradition, in which the history of Jesus' proclamation is conceived as the history of its reception and/or remembrance in early Christianity.

JESUS AS PROPHET: REMARKS ON TERMINOLOGY

Markus Öhler

'προφήτης κτλ. is a group which is marked both by solemnity and also by lack of content; it simply expresses the formal function of declaring, proclaiming, making known.'[1] With these words Helmut Krämer puts forward the case I want to discuss in this essay. Krämer came to this solution after studying the usage of προφήτης and its derivatives and as far as I know he has not been disproved.[2] What I want to do in this essay is to ask some recent contributors to the Third Quest about their thoughts when they call Jesus a prophet. Did they think of the Old Testament prophets, and if so which ones? Did they put Jesus in the same category as those figures who were regarded as prophets in early Judaism? Is Jesus called a prophet because of his function as a messenger of God or because of his mighty deeds? Or was it, to name another possibility, because he had a perception of future things to come? But before I can dedicate myself to the Third Quest I will have to make a short glimpse at the term 'prophet' itself.

---

1. H. Krämer, 'προφήτμς κτλ. A: The Word Group in Profane Greek', *TDNT*, VI, pp. 783-96 (795). Krämer takes the position from E. Fascher, Προφήτης: *Eine sprach- und religionsgeschichtliche Untersuchung* (Giessen: Alfred Töpelmann, 1927), p. 51: 'Προφήτης allein ist ein "Rahmenwort" ohne konkreten Inhalt.'

2. On the contrary this view is also held, e.g., by J. Ernst, *Johannes der Täufer: Interpretation–Geschichte–Wirkungsgeschichte* (BZNW, 53; Berlin: W. de Gruyter, 1989), p. 290: 'Die Kennzeichnung eines Menschen als Prophet ist eine Worthülse, die mit Inhalt gefüllt werden muß'. See also M. Tilly, *Johannes der Täufer und die Biographie der Propheten: Die synoptische Täuferüberlieferung und das jüdische Prophetenbild zur Zeit des Täufers* (BWANT, 137; Stuttgart: W. Kohlhammer, 1994), p. 13. The judgment of D.E. Aune, *Prophecy in Early Christianity and the Ancient Mediterranean World* (Grand Rapids: Eerdmans, 1983), p. 4, that Krämer's conclusion is 'semantic nonsense', misses the point that 'prophet' is defined through its context.

1. *Terminology*

In studies on the history of Religion, two paradigms are used to describe a prophet: the biblical picture of a prophet; and the prophet in a socio-religious perspective.[3] From the latter viewpoint—not in overall contrast to the biblical description—several significant signs have been reconstructed that prophets have in common. For example, they are announcers of God's will, sometimes predictors of the future. They receive their messages in visions or aurally, even in ecstatic experiences, and prophets are sent by the godhead. Normally they are called out of their daily life and they represent the godhead in opposition to or in representation of a certain group. In many instances it is very hard to determine who should be considered a prophet and who not, because many religious leaders share some of the features of prophets, but only a few share all. Even those who regarded themselves as prophets, such as Mohammed and Zarathustra, could lose this title depending on socio-religious typology.[4] One must also be aware that most of our definitions of 'prophet' draw their elements from the biblical figures. David Potter recently pointed to this and stated:

> The stress in these definitions on 'speech', and the concurrent image of the prophet as a person, almost always male (often with a long white beard and a staff), who delivers a prophecy at divine initiative simply fails to account for much of the activity that was regarded as 'prophetic' in the ancient world.[5]

3. See G.T. Sheppard and W.E. Herbrechtsmeier, 'Prophecy: An Overview', in M. Eliade (ed.), *The Encyclopedia of Religion*, XII (New York: Macmillan, 1987), pp. 8-14; W. Klein, 'Propheten/Prophetie: I. Religionsgeschichtlich', *TRE* 27 (Berlin: W. de Gruyter, 1987), pp. 473-76; J. Ebach, 'Prophetismus', in H. Cancik, B. Gladigow and K.-H. Kohl (eds.), *Handbuch religionswissenschaftlicher Grundbegriffe* (Stuttgart: W. Kohlhammer, 1998), IV, pp. 347-59. For a comparison of the Old Testament prophets with similar religious figures see R.R. Wilson, *Prophecy and Society in Ancient Israel* (Philadelphia: Fortress Press, 1980); T.W. Overholt, *Prophecy in Cross-Cultural Perspective: A Sourcebook for Biblical Researchers* (SBLSBS, 17; Atlanta: Scholars Press, 1986). For a phenomenological approach see G. van der Leeuw, *Phänomenologie der Religion* (Neue theologische Grundrisse; Tübingen: J.C.B. Mohr, 4th edn, 1977), pp. 244-50; F. Heiler, *Erscheinungsformen und Wesen der Religion* (RM, 1; Stuttgart: W. Kohlhammer, 1961), pp. 395-402.

4. See, e.g., J. Wach, *Religionssoziologie* (Tübingen: J.C.B. Mohr [Paul Siebeck], 4th edn, 1951), p. 394, who denies that Mohammed or Zarathustra were prophets.

5. David Potter, *Prophets and Emperors: Human and Divine Authority from*

In antiquity almost everyone could call himself a prophet, and many different religious figures were depicted with this title. The simple word προφήτης causes some problems, since it is not clear whether προ- stands for the emphasis of the speech (φημί) or for the forward-looking character of a prophet's words.[6] Though 'speaker, spokesman' is the general sense of the word, meaning differs according to the context. Prophets could be bearers and exegetes of oracles, poets, messengers, priests and so on. This title has to be filled with content.

In early Judaism there was no common definition either: the LXX translates the Hebrew נביא, the classical term denoting the Old Testament prophets, consistently with προφήτης, but in contrast προφήτης was also used to translate ראה (1 Chron. 26.28; 2 Chron. 16.7, 10; Isa. 30.10) and הוזה (2 Chron. 19.2; 29.30; 35.15), both actually meaning 'seer'. Josephus reports that several figures of his time who lead crowds against the Romans, called themselves 'prophets'.[7] A historian named Kleodemos Malchas is also regarded as a prophet by Josephus.[8] Far from using the title exactly, Josephus should make us careful to restrict the meaning to a specific sense. Thus by way of summarizing, Rebecca Gray closes her inquiry on Josephus's use of the word field προφήτης: 'All these figures... are recognizably prophetic from the modern-critical point of view. This study of the evidence from Josephus has shown, however, that his definition of prophecy was considerably broader than the modern one.'[9]

Augustus to Theodosius (Revealing Antiquity, 7; Cambridge, MA: Harvard University Press, 1994), p. 10. A comprehensive view of prophecy in the ancient world is provided by Fascher, Προφήτης, pp. 11-224; Aune, *Prophecy*, pp. 23-79.

6.   Although this question seems to be solved in favour of the first possibility (see Fascher, Προφήτης, p. 6; M.C. van der Kolf, 'Prophetes', *PRE* 23.1 (1957), cols. 797-814 [797-98]).

7.   Theudas (*Ant.* 20.97-98), the Egyptian (*War* 2.261-63; *Ant.* 20.169-72) and anonymous prophets (*War* 6.286-87). Accordingly he uses the term ψευδοπροφήτης for the Egyptian (*War* 2.261) and an anonymous prophet (*War* 6.285). In *Apion* 2.91 Josephus accuses Apion of acting as a (false) prophet.

8.   Κλεόδημος δέ φησιν ὁ προφήτης ὁ καὶ Μάλχος ἱστορῶν τὰ περὶ Ἰουδαίων (*Ant.* 1.240). Josephus uses a notice of Alexander Polyhistor and it is not entirely clear whether ὁ προφήτης is part of the citation or used here in a different sense; see D.E. Aune, 'The Use of προφήτης in Josephus', *JBL* 101 (1982), pp. 419-21; L.H. Feldman, 'Prophets and Prophecy in Josephus', *JTS* 41 (1990), pp. 386-422 (400-401). See also Tit. 1.12: A Crete prophet says about his compatriots: They are always liars, vicious brutes, lazy gluttons.

9.   Rebecca Gray, *Prophetic Figures in Late Second Temple Jewish Palestine: The Evidence from Josephus* (New York: Oxford University Press, 1993), p. 165.

In the New Testament Jesus is called a prophet several times.[10] In Mk 6.15 and 8.28 this is never accounted as a positive possibility, but as one of the popular views held on Jesus. The formulation ὡς εἷς τῶν προφητῶν ('as one of the prophets') is not clear at all: does it mean that Jesus reminded some people of the classic prophets like Isaiah or Jeremiah?[11] Or was he regarded as one of the prophets of his time?[12] Obviously Matthew thought of the former possibility, because he even provided an example for an Old Testament prophet Jesus could have been compared to: Jeremiah (16.14). Luke on the other hand leads his audience in another direction, because he gives the information that people thought of the resurrection of one of the prophets of old (9.8, 19).[13] From these alterations of the Markan text, one can conclude that Luke and Matthew were somewhat uncertain about the term 'prophet'.

10. Mk 6.4 par.; 6.15 par.; 8.28 par.; Mt. 14.5; 21.11, 46; Lk. 7.16, 39; 11.49; 13.33; 20.6; 24.19; see also Jn 4.19; 6.14; 7.40, 52; 9.17; Acts 3.22; 7.37.

11. For an eschatological understanding of this text see, e.g., O. Cullmann, *Die Christologie des Neuen Testaments* (Tübingen: J.C.B. Mohr [Paul Siebeck], 4th edn, 1966), pp. 33-34; F. Hahn, *Christologische Hoheitstitel: Ihre Geschichte im frühen Christentum* (Göttingen: Vandenhoeck & Ruprecht, 5th enlarged edn, 1995), p. 222 n. 3.

12. And if that should be the case, were prophetical figures such as Theudas, John the Baptist or Jesus ben Hananias counted under this category because of similarities with Old Testament prophets? See, e.g., G. Friedrich, 'προφήτης κτλ. D: Prophets and Prophetism in the New Testament', *TDNT*, VI, pp. 828-61 (842); J. Gnilka, *Das Evangelium nach Markus (Mk 1-8,26)* (EKKNT, 2.1; Zürich: Benzinger Verlag; Neukirchen–Vluyn: Neukirchener Verlag, 3rd edn, 1989), p. 249; D. Lührmann, *Das Markusevangelium* (HNT, 3; Tübingen: J.C.B. Mohr [Paul Siebeck], 1987), p. 116. R.A. Horsley, ' "Like One of the Prophets of Old": Two Types of Popular Prophets at the Time of Jesus', *CBQ* 47 (1985), pp. 435-63, put his finger on a deficiency when he demanded more focus on concrete social phenomena such as the appearance of prophecy (p. 436).

13. Obviously he does that because of the parallel formulation of the resurrection of John the Baptist (9.7, 19), although he uses ἀνίστημι instead of ἐγείρω, both meaning 'raise up'. In Acts 3.22-23 (cf. 7.37) Peter refers to Jesus as the (eschatological) prophet like Moses (Deut. 18.15, 18): Προφήτην ὑμῖν ἀναστήσει κύριος ὁ θεὸς ὑμῶν. It seems possible that the term ἀνίστημι in Lk. 9.8, 19 could give a first hint on that. On Luke's prophetical picture of Jesus see esp. G. Nebe, *Prophetische Züge im Bilde Jesu bei Lukas* (BWANT, 127; Stuttgart: W. Kohlhammer, 1989). On the expectation of the eschatological prophet like Moses, which is also a prominent christological feature in the Gospel of John (6.14; 7.40), see D.C. Allison, Jr, *The New Moses: A Matthean Typology* (Minneapolis: Fortress Press, 1993), pp. 73-84.

This uncertainty is also demonstrated in the development of Christology in the early church.[14]

Including Justin, this title is never again assigned to Jesus until the end of the second century. Following Acts 3.22-23, it later becomes one minor title among others and is mostly interpreted in an exaggerating way. Jesus was not only prophet, but his pre-eminence lay in his being the Son of God and First-born of all creation.[15] Augustine comments: 'Sic autem propheta Christus, Dominus prophetarum.'[16] Only in the Pseudo-Clementines does the true prophet play a very prominent role: Jesus was not only the absolute prophet, but he was the final incarnation of the prophet, who was in the beginning of the world (*Hom.* 3.20.2).[17] As the prophet he proclaims the νομιμὸς γνῶσις ('legitimate knowledge') which shows the way to salvation (*Hom.* 11.19.3).

What we can draw from this short glimpse on terminology is first that there was no clear definition of προφήτης in antiquity even as it is today. Equally it was never quite clear to early Christian authors in which respect Jesus was a prophet or could be understood as one. And my question now is whether this has changed in the debate over the historical Jesus in the last few years. Far from claiming to be an intimate authority on the Third Quest, I have chosen five prominent scholars who have provided important contributions to this debate: E.P. Sanders, Gerd Theissen and Annette Merz, John Dominic Crossan and Jürgen Becker. I will continue with the help of a schema, which will follow two steps: First, who is called a prophet and what are his characteristics?

14. See esp. A. Grillmeier, *Jesus der Christus im Glauben der Kirche. I. Von der Apostolischen Zeit bis zum Konzil von Chalcedon (451)* (Freiburg: Herder, 1979), pp. 32-40.

15. Origen, *Commentary on Matthew* 17.14 on Mt. 21.45-46: πλὴν οὐχ ἡ ὑπεροχὴ αὐτοῦ ἐν τῷ προφήτην αὐτὸν εἶναι ἦν ἀλλ᾽ ἐν τῷ υἱὸν Θεοῦ πρωτότοκον πάσης κτίσεως.

16. 'If Christ is a prophet, then as Lord of the prophets' (*Tractates on the Gospel of John* 24.7).

17. On that see G. Strecker, 'Die Pseudoklementinen: Einleitung', in W. Schneemelcher (ed.), *Neutestamentliche Apokryphen. II. Apostolisches, Apokalypsen und Verwandtes* (Tübingen: J.C.B. Mohr [Paul Siebeck], 5th edn, 1989), pp. 439-47 (444-45); H.J.W. Drijvers, 'Adam and the True Prophet in the Pseudo-Clementines', in *idem, History and Religion in Late Antique Syria* (Variorum Collected Studies Series, 464; Aldershot: Variorum, 1994), pp. 314-23; C.A. Gieschen, 'The Seven Pillars of the World: Ideal Figure Lists in the Christology of the Pseudo-Clementines', *JSP* 12 (1994), pp. 47-82.

Secondly, Is Jesus called a prophet and what prophetical characteristics does he have?

2. E.P. Sanders

a. *Who Is Called a Prophet and What Are his Characteristics?*
In his book *The Historical Figure of Jesus* E.P. Sanders bases his contribution to the Third Quest on his studies on Jesus and Judaism.[18] Thus he presents a Jesus whose primary—or more correctly only—context is first-century Judaism. In his earlier *Jesus and Judaism* Sanders already shows some awareness of the ambiguity of the title 'prophet': 'We have, then, fairly wide agreement on a general category, but it is a category which contains people who differed from one another in substantial ways' (p. 239). It is not surprising that Sanders's only interest in his later monograph on Jesus is in Israelite and Jewish prophets, as there are Old Testament prophets, John the Baptist, Honi the Circle-drawer and the sign prophets. Old Testament prophets are—together with Moses and the priests—spokesmen of God (Figure, p. 47). They perform symbolic actions (p. 253) and miracles (p. 149: Elijah and Elisha) and wait for God's intervention through a foreign army (p. 259). John the Baptist is—not surprisingly—the first person to be called a prophet in Sanders's book.[19] This is connected with John's criticism of Antipas's marriage and the Baptist's popularity. He was a preacher of repentance (p. 233), knowing that God's final judgment was at hand. John the Baptist might actually have dressed like Elijah the prophet (Mk 1.6).[20] According to Sanders the main characteristics of the sign prophets[21] such as Theudas and the Egyptian were that they 'gathered

18. *The Historical Figure of Jesus* (Harmondsworth: Penguin Books, 1993); *Jesus and Judaism* (London: SCM Press, 1985). References in this essay are—if not otherwise noted—to *The Historical Figure of Jesus*, of which a German translation appeared under the misleading title *Sohn Gottes: Eine historische Biographie Jesu* (trans. U. Enderwitz; Stuttgart: Klett-Cotta, 1996).

19. Figure, p. 22: 'John was widely believed to be a prophet'. See Mk 11.32 par.; Lk. 7.26 par. Q; Lk. 1.76; Jn 1.21.

20. On that see my *Elia im Neuen Testament: Untersuchungen zur Bedeutung des alttestamentlichen Propheten im frühen Christentum* (BZNW, 88; Berlin: W. de Gruyter, 1997), pp. 35-36 (with literature).

21. Sanders uses this term only in his *Jesus and Judaism* (p. 303). On that terminology see P.W. Barnett, 'The Jewish Sign Prophets—A.D. 40–70: Their Intentions and Origin', *NTS* 27 (1981), pp. 679-97; see also C.A. Evans, *Jesus and*

followers and promised "deliverance"' (p. 30). Some of them 'intentionally modelled their own actions on those of biblical figures' (p. 84): Theudas and the prophet from Egypt both recall, among other Old Testament stories, especially the Exodus traditions. The sign prophets promised miracles (p. 139) and were possibly regarded as the last prophets before God's day (p. 163).[22] Generally, prophets to some extent were a centre of fear and a threat for authorities (p. 260). They directed their intention to poor and weak people and outsiders (p. 107). Prophets are 'charismatics' insofar as they are believed to have a 'special ability to influence God' (p. 140). They are autonomous, because they are not part of a special group.

b. *Is Jesus Called a Prophet and what Prophetical Characteristics Does He Have?*

In Sanders's view Jesus is clearly a prophet: 'I continue to regard "prophet" as the best single category' (p. 153). Sanders gives this clear statement in debate with Morton Smith's designation of Jesus as magician.[23] He does that during the discussion of Jesus' miracles, although he admits that Jesus was an exorcist as well. Exorcism was definitely not a characteristic feature of prophets, as Sanders states explicitly (p. 149). But it is interesting that Sanders mainly discusses the question whether Jesus was a prophet or not in the pages which deal with his miracles. The background is probably the sign prophets who promised eschatological miracles. Jesus did not do anything like this, says Sanders, and on account of that he was not regarded as an eschatological prophet (p. 164). What his audience could see from his healing

---

his Contemporaries: Comparative Studies (AGJU, 25; Leiden: E.J. Brill, 1995), p. 73 ('messianic prophets', but to Evans 'sign prophets' also seems appropriate); M.D. Hooker, *The Signs of a Prophet: The Prophetic Actions of Jesus* (Harrisburg, PA: Trinity Press International; London: SCM Press, 1997), pp. 13-15. Aune, *Prophecy*, pp. 127-29, regards them as eschatological prophets within a millennarian movement. J. Becker, *Johannes der Täufer und Jesus von Nazareth* (BibS, 63; Neukirchen–Vluyn: Neukirchener Verlag, 1972), pp. 47-48, describes them as eschatological prophets claiming to perform miracles as typological repetition of the Exodus. For a sociological perspective see Horsley, 'Prophets', p. 454: 'prophets who led movements'; R.L. Webb, *John the Baptizer and Prophet: A Socio-Historical Study* (JSNTSup, 62; Sheffield: JSOT Press, 1991), p. 333: 'leadership popular prophets'.

22. For critics on this view see Gray, *Figures*, pp. 140-43.

23. M. Smith, *Jesus the Magician* (London: Gollancz, 1978).

miracles and exorcism was that he was on intimate terms with God; he was accredited as a spokesman of God. The category 'spokesman', which was earlier assigned to Moses, the priests and the prophets, is here used for Jesus. 'He regarded himself as God's true messenger' (p. 167), as 'the agent of the Spirit of God' (p. 168). He was 'a *charismatic and autonomous prophet*' (p. 238), which means that he got his authority directly from God. To God, Jesus had a very close relationship, just like other charismatic prophets.[24] But again, as in the case of exorcism, the title prophet is not sufficient. Sanders thinks of Jesus as a 'viceroy: at the head of the judges of Israel, subordinate only to God himself' (p. 239).

One of the most important points in Sanders's reconstruction of Jesus' life is the event in the temple. Like the Old Testament prophets Jesus used symbolic actions (p. 253) and this was his most important one. With his 'prophetic threat' (p. 260) against the temple in deed and word Jesus acted 'as a radical first-century eschatologist' (p. 259), waiting for God's intervention and the new age. Jesus learned this feature of his preaching from John the Baptist. Very important for Sanders in this respect is that Jesus did not promise an eschatological miracle, but performed a symbolic action announcing an eschatological event. Sanders calls this 'a distinction in Jesus' *style*'.[25]

To summarize: Sanders regards Jesus as a radical eschatological prophet. He draws parallels mainly from contemporary figures, although there are structural similarities also to Old Testament prophets. These parallels gather around certain deeds, to a much lesser extent around words. However, for Sanders 'prophet' alone is not enough to describe Jesus in a proper way.

3. *Gerd Theissen and Annette Merz*

Gerd Theissen and Annette Merz present a comprehensive work on the historical Jesus, which is based on many socio-historical studies.[26]

---

24. Citing G. Vermes, Sanders (p. 239) apparently thinks of Honi and Hanina ben Dosa; see G. Vermes, *Jesus der Jude: Ein Historiker liest die Evangelien* (Neukirchen–Vluyn: Neukirchener Verlag, 1993), p. 55.

25. *Jesus and Judaism*, p. 235. All references in the text are to the German edition.

26. *Der historische Jesus: Ein Lehrbuch* (Göttingen: Vandenhoeck & Ruprecht, 1996); ET *The Historical Jesus: A Comprehensive Guide* (London: SCM Press, 1998).

a. *Who Is Called a Prophet and What Are his Characteristics?*

The first prophets, with whom Theissen and Merz deal in detail, are the sign prophets (pp. 141-42). Their characteristics are the promise of miracles, the gathering of followers, and the change of location. They—like John the Baptist and Jesus—reactivate eschatological hopes, and they do this by recalling the Israelite history (Exodus, conquest of Canaan). Most of them directed their message and deeds against the occupational forces, and only a few against their own people (Jesus ben Hananias—a prophet of doom, John the Baptist, Jesus of Nazareth).

The Old Testament prophets are mentioned very often in Theissen's and Merz's book. As spokesmen of God they use prophetical genres of speech. With 'Thus says the Lord...' they identify their message as stemming from the mouth of God himself (p. 456). They use symbolic actions (p. 170) and base their authority on calling experiences (p. 196). In early Judaism they were sometimes regarded as anointed (pp. 453, 463). Some prophets like Elijah even called successors and many stood in opposition to the city of Jerusalem and the temple (Uriah, Jeremiah; also the Samaritan prophet;[27] p. 170). Jewish prophets including John the Baptist often suffered a violent fate (p. 378).

According to Theissen and Merz, John himself unquestionably had a prophetical self-image (p. 192). John was a preacher of repentance, who warned of the coming judgment and offered the last possibility to escape God's wrath. He saw himself as the last messenger of God, maybe even as Elijah.[28] John's prophetical role should—according to Theissen and Merz with reference to Tilly[29]—be defined in comparison with contemporary figures (p. 192 n. 17).

27. See Josephus, *Ant.* 18.85-87, although one must see that opposition against the temple in Jerusalem was a typical feature of Samaritan religion itself and not only of this particular prophet. Josephus does not—by the way—call the Samaritan a 'prophet'. Cf. J. Zangenberg, *Frühes Christentum in Samarien: Topographische und traditionsgeschichtliche Studien zu den Samariatexten im Johannesevangelium* (TANZ, 27; Tübingen: Francke, 1998), pp. 140-48.

28. On this thesis see my *Elia*, pp. 103-110: John's self-image as prophet stems from the fact that he took Elijah as his personal model and functioned as the eschatological Elijah according to Mal. 3.23-24. Could it be possible that Jesus also modelled his life according to an Old Testament prophet, e.g. Elijah (cf. J.P. Meier, *A Marginal Jew: Rethinking the Historical Jesus.* II. *Mentor, Message, and Miracles* [ABRL; 2 vols.; New York: Doubleday, 1994], pp. 1044-45)?

29. Tilly, *Johannes*, pp. 13-30.

b. Is Jesus Called a Prophet and What Prophetical Characteristics Does He Have?

Theissen and Merz title one chapter of their book: 'Jesus als Prophet: Die Eschatologie Jesu' (pp. 221-55). This already demonstrates that, with reference to Jesus, they define the title prophet according to his speech. From this one can also assume that Theissen and Merz think of prophetism in terms of 'announcing future things'. According to them, Jesus on the one hand represents an apocalyptic message regarding its content, but on the other hand this message is presented in a prophetic way. His preaching is revival of apocalypticism in a prophetic form (p. 229).[30] This prophetic presentation, however, is only one aspect of Jesus' overall characterization as a Jewish charismatic.[31] The other aspects are his being a performer of miracles and a teacher of wisdom (pp. 216-18). In discussion with Morton Smith and his picture of Jesus as magician, Theissen and Merz point to Jesus' prophetic self-image, which evidently should help to interpret Jesus' miracles (p. 276). Jesus possibly experienced a prophetic call, assumedly in the fall of Satan (Lk. 10.18)—so Theissen and Merz (p. 196), less in his baptism. Jesus shares the opposition against the temple with some Old Testament prophets. This is not only a cultic, but also a social protest. He announced the destruction of the temple using a symbolic act (pp. 170, 380-81). Another symbolic act was the last supper, which should inaugurate the new cult replacing the temple cult until the coming of the βασιλεία (p. 380). Instead of 'Thus speaks the Lord...' Jesus uses 'Amen!' In this Theissen and Merz see the claim that even more than a prophet is speaking here (p. 456).[32] Just like Elijah, Jesus calls people to follow him (p. 199), and he also has some similarities with the sign-prophets: with his announcement of a new temple he takes up a theme of the Israelite history, he gathers followers, he proceeds to the place of the

---

30. 'Jesus vertritt *inhaltlich* eine Variante apokalyptischer Erwartung, *formal* aber begegnet sie als Prophetie—nicht in Form einer esoterischen Geheimschrift aus grauer Vorzeit, sondern als an seine Person gebundene Proklamation (in mündlicher Form). *Seine Verkündigung ist Revitalisierung von Apokalyptik in prophetischer Form*' (italics original).

31. On the discussion on this terminology see also B.J. Malina, *The Social World of Jesus and the Gospels* (London: Routledge, 1996), pp. 123-42.

32. 'Hier spricht ein Prophet—ja vielleicht mehr als ein Prophet!' Theissen and Merz choose this formulation, although they certainly know that it is depicted by Jesus to John the Baptist (Lk. 7.28 par. Q). Maybe they were also inspired by Lk. 11.32 par. Q: '... something greater than Jonah is here!'

expected miracle and he dies by the hands of the Romans. With this fate he counted himself in a line with other persecuted Jewish prophets (p. 378).

Altogether the prophetic activity of Jesus plays an important role in Theissen's and Merz' reconstruction, even if it is only one part of his charismatic personality. To define this prophetic part, they mainly draw on the Old Testament prophets for his preaching activity, but also on contemporary prophets for his deeds.

4. *John Dominic Crossan*

John Dominic Crossan's books on the historical Jesus[33] received so much resonance and comments that I can keep my exposition short.

a. *Who is Called a Prophet and What Are his Characteristics?*
Crossan uses more than 100 pages before he tells us of the first histor-ical person who acted like a prophet: Josephus (p. 111). His prediction, that Vespasian was going to become emperor (*War* 3.399-402), was not only an oracle, but 'an application of Jewish messianism' (p. 112) to the victorious general. In his chapter 'Magician and Prophet' (pp. 137-67) Crossan deals with the question of terminology only concerning 'magician', whereas 'prophet' seems to be clear to him. The first prophets in this part of the book are Elijah and Elisha (pp. 138-41), and Crossan is more interested in their miraculous power, than in their prophetical work. 'They combine magic and prophecy, and, as prophetic magicians or magical prophets, they continue ... the Mosaic model' (p. 141). Another group of prophets is made up of peasants (pp. 158-67), such as Theudas, the Egyptian and others. Crossan calls this 'mil-lennial prophecy' (p. 158), which seeks 'to seduce or invoke, initiate or create a transcendental violence' (pp. 158-59), although it regarded itself as peaceful.[34] These prophets tried to re-enact the Exodus with

---

33. To name only three: *The Historical Jesus: The Life of a Mediterranean Jewish Peasant* (San Francisco: HarperSanFrancisco, 1991); *Jesus: A Revolutionary Biography* (San Francisco: HarperSanFrancisco, 1994); *The Essential Jesus: What Jesus Really Taught* (San Francisco: HarperSanFrancisco, 1996). References in this essay are to the first one, *The Historical Jesus*.

34. Appendix 2B (p. 451) counts 10 prophets between c. 30 CE and 73 CE: John the Baptist, the Samaritan Prophet, Theudas, the Egyptian Prophet, Jesus ben Hana-nias, Jonathan the Weaver, and several unnamed prophets.

their crossing through the Jordan into the desert, because they wanted to flee from slavery like their fathers from Egypt (p. 196). John the Baptist finally was a prophet too, and even Jesus confirmed this initially (Lk. 7.26 par. Q; p. 237).[35] John was a preacher of apocalypticism and thus he also was a political prophet in some way (p. 235). Generally prophets are just one group of brokers among others. For Crossan, prophets seem to be people who announce coming things. Unfortunately he does not use his cross-cultural competence to bring new features into the discussion on prophetism—he on the contrary has a very narrow comprehension of this title.

b. *Is Jesus Called a Prophet and What Prophetical Characteristics Does He Have?*
The short answer is 'no'. Jesus cannot be a prophet, since this is a title for a broker. Instead, Crossan's Jesus was a Jewish Cynic, who 'proclaimed and sought to institute a brokerless and egalitarian kingdom, a kingdom without any mediators between individuals and God, not even Jesus himself'.[36]

5. *Jürgen Becker*

Jürgen Becker with his book on the historical Jesus offered the fruits of his many studies on certain aspects of this topic.[37] Again I will apply two questions to this book.

a. *Who Is Called a Prophet and What Are his Characteristics?*
The first prophet appearing in Becker's book is John the Baptist (pp. 37-58). He is a prophet of judgment in the tradition of the Old Testament

35. From the following verse Lk. 7.28 Q 'I tell you, among those born of women no one is greater than John; yet the least in the kingdom of God is greater than he' (cf. *Gos. Thom.* 46), Crossan detects a reversal of Jesus' opinion on John and his message: 'John's vision of awaiting the apocalyptic God, the Coming One, as a repentant sinner, which Jesus had originally accepted and even defended in the crisis of John's death, was no longer deemed adequate. It was now a question of being in the Kingdom' (pp. 237-38). I doubt that this can be shown with these two verses, since Lk. 7.28 is certainly not a word of the historical Jesus.

36. B. Witherington, III, *The Jesus Quest: The Third Search for the Jew of Nazareth* (Downers Grove, IL: InterVarsity Press, 1995), p. 64.

37. *Jesus von Nazaret* (Berlin: W. de Gruyter, 1996); ET *Jesus of Nazareth* (Berlin: W. de Gruyter, 1998). All references in the text are to the German edition.

and early Judaism. Although he did not call himself a prophet, he speaks in prophetical genres (p. 268). A similar figure is Jesus ben Hananias (pp. 42, 57 n. 21, 270).[38] The so-called 'prophets of Exodus'[39] like Theudas or the Egyptian try to inaugurate the last days by means of repeating the miracles of Moses and Joshua (p. 269). This eschatological prophetism is somehow also connected with messianic claims (p. 402).[40] Another prophet, one who bases his words on Scripture, was the Teacher of Righteousness, and Becker additionally calls him a prophet of salvation (p. 270). Old Testament prophets are frequently mentioned in Becker's book, very often in connection with genres of speech: prophetical threat of judgment (p. 47), prophetical words of discussion (p. 64), typical ironical imperative, frequent in prophecy (p. 403), and so on. To question a prophet's legitimization stood to reason for Old Testament prophets as well as for Jesus (p. 229). However, there was an inflation of prophets, since this title was depicted to all great figures of Israelite history such as Abraham, Aaron and Moses. The notion of the imminent end of this world is already a feature of Old Testament prophecy (Amos, Deutero–Isaiah), which is shared by different circles in early Judaism including the Exodus prophets. Generally prophets speak and act with immediate authority from God and proclaim their experience of God and their authorization (p. 268). People recognize them as prophets, though they do not call themselves by this name.[41] With their specific authority prophets can predict single events (p. 270).

b. *Is Jesus Called a Prophet and What Prophetical Characteristics Does He Have?*

According to Becker, Jesus was an 'apocalyptical prophet of the Kingdom of God, mediating solution' (p. 234), a prophet, who not only *predicts* coming things and raises hope, but also *realizes* the coming things

---

38. Josephus, *War* 6.300-309. In Becker's book on John (*Johannes*, p. 46), Jesus ben Hananias is ranked among political prophets without an eschatological alignment, whereas Aune, *Prophecy*, pp. 135-37, regards him as an 'isolated eschatological prophet'.

39. See above n. 21.

40. This seems to be an alteration compared to other comments of Becker on these figures. According to Becker, *Johannes*, pp. 49-50, one has to be cautious to connect eschatological prophets with the idea of messianism.

41. See also the report of Lucian on Alexander of Abonuteichos: Lucian is almost beaten by the audience because he calls Alexander by his name and not by his title προφήτης (*Alex.* 55).

and executes the completion of the kingdom of God (p. 274). With his prophetical appearance Jesus was part of the Israelite tradition, though Becker refuses the thesis that Jesus stands in direct continuation of Old Testament prophecy (p. 268 n. 142).[42] Becker rejects this, because Jesus primarily has to be seen in the light of contemporary Jewish prophets, who generally stand in a certain relationship to their Old Testament ancestors. This is demonstrated in the genres Jesus chooses to proclaim the βασιλεία τοῦ θεοῦ, his prominent theme: words of discussion, judgment and scolding all have a prophetical sound. From this one can see that Becker defines 'prophet' mainly in terms of Old Testament figures. Like them and like his prophetical colleagues, Jesus stands outside of culture and society (pp. 57, 62). Although Jesus took the prophetical role from John the Baptist (p. 270), he not only warned of the near judgment, but also was a prophet of salvation (p. 272). He shares this role with the Teacher of Righteousness, but Jesus' authority is not based on Scripture. Instead, Jesus takes his authority directly from God, although he does not mention a vocation.[43] Also, he did not predict single events, as prophets often do. Especially the word against the temple has no historical background, says Becker (p. 406). But the main difference between all other prophets and Jesus is that he executes the kingdom of God, instead of talking about it (p. 274). He performs that through words (parables) and deeds (table fellowship and miracles).[44] As 'the one who causes the apocalyptic completion' (p. 271) he takes the role of an eschatological prophet like the returned Elijah or the prophet like Moses, although he does not identify himself with one of them. Finally, Becker also tries to apply Jesus' prophetical role in his discussion on Jesus' trial. Jesus was accused of being a false prophet and condemned by his Jewish opponents according to Deut. 13.1-6; 18.9-22 (p. 412).[45]

42. See, e.g., C.G. Montefiore, *The Synoptic Gospels Edited with an Introduction and a Commentary* (repr.; 2 vols.; New York: Ktav, 1968), I, pp. cxvii-cxx.

43. For this aspect Becker does not point to the baptism of Jesus, which is sometimes regarded as a parallel to Old Testament prophets. See on that discussion, e.g., Aune, *Prophecy*, p. 161.

44. From that it becomes clear why it is not enough for Becker to call Jesus an exorcist and healer, or charismatic, teacher or rabbi (p. 272). The category 'eschatological prophet who executes the salvation he announces' summarizes all this and exceeds it.

45. These texts and their Jewish exegesis, by the way, are directed against seducers to other Gods or against prophets, whose predictions fail, and this was certainly not the case with Jesus.

To summarize: Becker offers a very distinct definition of the prophetical role of Jesus, which has to be greatly appreciated. He draws the main characteristics from Old Testament prophets, not without noticing the differences between the first century CE and their times. But he also overtakes himself in a certain way: the prophet Jesus takes a role which goes far beyond that of all other prophets. The prophet himself executes the eschatological salvation which he proclaims. But isn't that true for the sign prophets as well? If I understand Becker rightly, I suppose he sees the discrepancy to Theudas and the Egyptian therein, that Jesus did not want to accelerate the coming of the time of salvation, but already acted *in it* as its performer. As a consequence, belief in him became the criterion for receiving a place in the kingdom of God. All these elements really are a new quality, but is it still prophecy?[46]

6. *Conclusion*

With the following concluding remarks I will try to formulate some points on the state of the Third Quest in regard to the prophetical role of Jesus, and add some demands for future work.

First, the quality of a prophet does not seem to be quite clear-cut. This was as true for antiquity as it is for the Third Quest.[47] I have detected very different forms of reconstructing prophetical features: some that are based on speech (Theissen and Merz, Becker) and others that are orientated on deeds (Sanders, Crossan). Features which for one scholar are strictly prophetic are sapiental for the other, and this is without any discussion of definitions.

A second important point is the question about the parallels that are gathered together to reconstruct the prophetical role of a person. In most cases this is still the Old Testament tradition, even if this is mediated via the false prophets in Josephus. This stems from the fact that the

---

46. One could point to Alexander of Abonuteichos for an example of a prophet, who also exceeds all connotations of this title; see U. Victor, *Lukian von Samosata: Alexandros oder der Lügenprophet* (Religions in the Graeco-Roman World, 132; Leiden: E.J. Brill, 1997).

47. M.E. Boring ('Early Christian Prophecy', *ABD*, V, pp. 495-502, esp. p. 496) points to an SBL Seminar paper from 1973, which presented a definition of early Christian prophets, but not generally of prophetism. D.C. Allison does also not deal with the question of definition (*Jesus of Nazareth: Millenarian Prophet* [Minneapolis: Fortress Press, 1998]).

Jewish context is the dominant factor in reconstructing the historical Jesus. However, Hellenistic manifestations of prophetism are left out, although the authors of the New Testament and Josephus and their audiences must have had contact with different prophets than the Israelite and early Jewish ones. One cannot ignore the fact that the New Testament is a Hellenistic book, even if it recounts events in Galilee and Judah.

Thirdly, let us suppose that an SBL Seminar sometime in this millennium agrees on a definition of 'prophet'. I 'prophesy' that scholars will still disagree over which characteristics are true for Jesus. If, for example, only his preaching will be enough to call him a prophet, every priest who preaches every Sunday should be called a prophet as well. Maybe it is possible to solve this question, if we consider preaching about the future to be the main characteristic of a prophet. But here the problem arises as to whether we will only note clear predictions of coming events, or whether the message of the kingdom of God will be enough. Are there any typical acts that could definitely be called 'prophetic' without characterizing every symbolic action as such? Did Jesus have a personal call, a vision or audition? Did he take a prophet such as Elijah or John the Baptist as his model?

Fourthly, I think that our work must not be directed only at historical forms of prophetism, but also at today's discussion on these religious manifestations. Concerning the question of Jesus' prophetical role we could get some stimulation from a comparative theological point of view.[48] For example, if it is true that prophets are almost always connected to a specific group, 'whose position in society is outside the normal channels of power and influence',[49] we could all the more ask which groups that could be in Jesus' case. The peasants, oppressed by the Roman army, or people who desired for a religious revolution? What about ecstatic behaviour, which is often regarded as a regular feature of a prophet? All this could even lead to the conclusion that we should give up the definition of Jesus as a prophet (like Crossan did, though without considering contemporary religious studies). I must admit that with these thoughts I touch a crucial question. We—all being

48. However, we must bear in mind that we will probably not get any clear definition from this side either: 'Comparative theorists working with modern evidence have not yet established a single dominant interpretation of prophecy' (Scheppard and Herbrechtsmeier, 'Prophecy', p. 13).

49. Scheppard and Herbrechtsmeier, 'Prophecy', p. 13.

historians—have the problem of deciding whether we take our categories from antiquity (as it is often done, e.g., regarding Jesus' miracles) or from modern scholarship.

Irrespective of which possibility we choose, we also have to consider an additional complication: the term 'prophet' is not only defined varyingly in scholarly discussions, but all the more so in cultural and religious communities. Islam, Judaism, Christianity and other religions, and all in their various forms, have their own views on prophetism.[50] And if we look at the secular meaning of the word, we must conclude that it is possibly not correct to call Jesus a prophet, because in my environment people think of a prophet as an announcer of coming events (and nothing more).[51] Moreover, this is an aspect which, for example, plays no role in Becker's reconstruction, although he subsumes all aspects of Jesus under the category 'prophet'. How many misunderstandings will develop if we use such categories without asking for today's meaning? Couldn't this be avoided with clear definitions?

By contrast, one must concede that the definition of Jesus as a prophet —whatever this may mean—will cause less offence than other titles, such as Son of God or Messiah. Even other faiths such as Islam or Judaism can cope with that designation.[52] Additionally the advantage of the category 'prophet' lies in its broadness, which makes it possible to include many characteristics of Jesus that would not be able to be reckoned with narrower titles such as 'Messiah'. One must, however, consider that the title 'prophet' was very rarely applied to Jesus in early

50. For the Islamic view on prophetism see T. Fahd, 'Nubuwwa', in C.E. Bosworth, E. van Donzel, W.P. Heinrichs and G. Lecomte (eds.), *The Encyclopaedia of Islam: New Edition* (Leiden: E.J. Brill, 1995), VIII, pp. 93-97; for Judaism see W.S. Wurzburger, 'Prophets and Prophecy: Modern Jewish Thought', *EncJud*, XIII, cols. 1179-81.

51. See Ebach, 'Prophetismus', pp. 347-48. Looking for commercial use of 'prophet' on the Internet I found two sites demonstrating this use without a long search. One software package is called 'Power Prophet' (http://www.siemens.at/pse/PProphet/de/Inhalt.htm), a tool to predict the development of share indices and rates of exchange; the other one is 'Prophet' (http://www.tgz-ilmenau.de/fhg-ast/german/EMS.html) to manage energy systems.

52. On Jesus regarded as a prophet in the Qur'an see Sura 19.30: 'Lo! I am the slave of Allah. He hath given me the Scripture and hath appointed me a Prophet.' On the Jewish perspective see D.A. Hagner, *The Jewish Reclamation of Jesus: An Analysis and Critique of the Modern Jewish Study of Jesus* (Grand Rapids: Zondervan, 1984), pp. 237-42.

Christianity in the specific sense in which we use it today in scholarly or popular usage. Today's theological scholarship will thus have to attach great importance to the faith of the early church, that is, the kerygma, if it proceeds in this direction.

To summarize: the quest for the historical Jesus made a number of great strides ahead during the last years; no one will deny this. I see future tasks for it in further applying perspectives of the religious, cultural and social sciences not only concerning antiquity, but also in view of today's language and terminology. Regarding the question of titles, I would propose that

1. there should be some effort to find common definitions, or if that is not possible
2. authors should provide their definitions of titles, and in either case,
3. one should ask if these titles still correspond with today's language.

On the other hand, if one wanted to save the effort, one could possibly refrain from giving any titles at all.[53]

---

53. See Sanders, *Figure*, pp. 239-40: 'We all think that if we know the right word for something we understand it better, but in this particular case such a view is probably incorrect. The quest for the right title—the word that encapsulates Jesus' view of himself, as well as the first disciples' view—supposes that titles had fixed definitions and that we need only discover the definition of each. If title *a* meant *x*, and if Jesus used *a* of himself, we know that he thought of himself as being *x*. I think that the basic assumption, that titles had standard definitions, is in error.'

THE JEWISHNESS OF JESUS IN THE 'THIRD QUEST'

Tom Holmén

1. *Introduction*

It has been stated that the 'new shape' of the quest for the historical Jesus 'comes from taking very seriously the Jewishness of Jesus and trying to understand him within the limits of first-century Judaism'.[1] 'Third Quest' is a phrase used for the new research on the historical Jesus that has surfaced during the past two decades.[2] As the phrase

1. D.J. Harrington, 'The Jewishness of Jesus: Facing Some Problems', in J.H. Charlesworth (ed.), *Jesus' Jewishness: Exploring the Place of Jesus within Early Judaism* (Shared Ground among Jews and Christians, 2; New York: Crossroad, 1996), pp. 123-36 (125).

2. For this new phase in Jesus-of-history research see, e.g., S. Neill and N.T. Wright, *The Interpretation of the New Testament 1861–1986* (Oxford: Oxford University Press, 2nd edn, 1988), p. 379; G. Stanton, 'Historical Jesus', *DBI* (1990), pp. 285-90 (289); C. Brown, 'Historical Jesus, Quest of', *DJG* (1992), pp. 326-41 (337-41); N.T. Wright, 'Quest for the Historical Jesus', *ABD*, III, pp. 796-802 (800); B. Holmberg, 'En historisk vändning i forskningen om Jesus', *STK* 69 (1993), pp. 69-76 (72); B. Witherington III, *The Jesus Quest: The Third Search for the Jew of Nazareth* (Downers Grove, IL: InterVarsity Press, 1995); G. Theissen and D. Winter, *Die Kriterienfrage in der Jesusforschung: Vom Differenzkriterium zum Plausibilitätskriterium* (NTOA, 34; Göttingen: Vandenhoeck & Ruprecht, 1997), pp. 145-46. Cf., however, the skepticism of W.R. Telford ('Major Trends and Interpretative Issues in the Study of Jesus', in B. Chilton and C.A. Evans [eds.], *Studying the Historical Jesus: Evaluations of the State of Current Research* [NTTS, 19; Leiden: E.J. Brill, 1994], pp. 33-74 [74]). J.H. Charlesworth (*Jesus within Judaism* [ABRL; Garden City, NY: Doubleday, 1988], p. 26) prefers to use the label 'Jesus Research' in order to distinguish this new phase from the previous ones that more or less, according to him, were grounded on dogmatic and theological interests (cf. here J.I.H. McDonald, 'New Quest—Dead End? So What about the Historical Jesus?', *Studia Biblica* 2 [1978], pp. 151-70 [160-61]). However, as to the theological interests (see also W.P. Weaver, 'Reflections on the Continuing Quest for Jesus', in J.H. Charlesworth and W.P. Weaver [eds.], *Images of Jesus*

implies, the era would be third in order.[3] The two previous phases have traditionally been named 'die Leben-Jesu-Forschung' (end of the nineteenth century) and 'die neue Frage' or 'the new quest' (from 1950 onwards). Unanimously keeping with the above quotation of D.J. Harrington, the estimate of today's Jesus scholars is that a constitutive factor clearly distinguishing the 'Third Quest' from the previous phases of Jesus research is precisely its laying a clear emphasis and stress on the Jewishness of Jesus.[4]

There have been plenty of thorough studies into what kind of Jew Jesus was.[5] Likewise, many reviews of these studies assessing whether

---

Today [Faith and Scholarship Colloquies, 3; Valley Forge, PA: Trinity Press International], pp. xiii-xxi, xiv; Theissen and Winter, *Kriterienfrage*, pp. 146-47), it is not altogether clear that the present quest would be any freer from them than the previous phases of Jesus-of-history research were (cf. the laudable criticism of Telford, 'Major Trends', pp. 34, 62-64; N.T. Wright, *Jesus and the Victory of God* [Christian Origins and the question of God, 2; Minneapolis: Fortress Press, 1996], pp. 117-21; see also H. Moxnes, 'Den Historiske Jesus: Mellom modernitet og postmodernitet', *NorTT* 96 [1995], pp. 139-56).

3.   That is, if the period from Reimarus to Schweitzer, called below in the text 'die Leben-Jesu-Forschung', is seen to constitute one phase; cf. here G. Theissen and A. Merz, *Der historische Jesus: Ein Lehrbuch* (Göttingen: Vandenhoeck & Ruprecht, 1996), pp. 22-24, who divide the period into three phases; however, they, too, sustain the label 'Third Quest' for the present phase (Theissen and Merz, *Der historische Jesus*, pp. 28-29).

4.   See, e.g., Brown, 'Historical Jesus', p. 337; J.H. Charlesworth, 'Jesus Research Expands with Chaotic Creativity', in J.H. Charlesworth and W.P. Weaver (eds.), *Images of Jesus Today* (Faith and Scholarship Colloquies, 3; Valley Forge, PA: Trinity Press International, 1994), pp. 1-41 (5, 7); E. Schweizer, 'Jesus—Made in Great Britain and U.S.A.', *TZ* 50 (1994), pp. 311-21 (311); Telford, 'Major Trends', pp. 49, 52; Weaver, 'Reflections', p. xvi; Theissen and Merz, *Der historische Jesus*, p. 28; see further the list of scholars in Charlesworth, 'Jesus Research Expands', p. 8.

5.   The list could be continued almost endlessly, but see, e.g., B.F. Meyer, *The Aims of Jesus* (London: SCM Press, 1979); J. Riches, *Jesus and the Transformation of Judaism* (London: Darton, Longman & Todd, 1980); G. Vermes, *Jesus and the World of Judaism* (Philadelphia: Fortress Press; London: SCM Press, 1983); E. Bammel and C.F.D. Moule (eds.), *Jesus and the Politics of his Day* (Cambridge: Cambridge University Press, 1984); B.D. Chilton, *A Galilean Rabbi and his Bible: Jesus' Use of the Interpreted Scripture of his Time* (GNS, 8; Wilmington, DE: M. Glazier, 1984); H. Falk, *Jesus the Pharisee: A New Look at the Jewishness of Jesus* (New York: Paulist Press, 1985); E.P. Sanders, *Jesus and Judaism* (Philadelphia: Fortress Press; London: SCM Press, 1985); B.J. Lee, *The Galilean Jewishness*

the Jewishness of Jesus has really been taken seriously in them have emerged.[6] However, the laying of an emphasis on the Jewishness of Jesus as a particularity of the 'Third Quest', a history of research question, has not been subjected to any more detailed analysis. It is merely being stated as a fact. As the quest now has reached maturity (at least in terms of the official age of adulthood), it is perhaps time to pursue some further inquiries about that particularity.

Thus, in this essay the object of scrutiny is the phenomenon of emphasizing the Jewishness of Jesus as making the 'Third Quest' stand out as a distinctive phase of Jesus-of-history research. Time imposes limits on the discussion. I shall seek to find out what there is new in the 'Third Quest's' way of understanding Jesus' Jewishness. Further, I shall try to unravel the designation 'Jewishness' as it is attached to Jesus by the

of Jesus: Retrieving the Jewish Origins of Christianity (New York: Paulist Press, 1988); I. Zeitlin, *Jesus and the Judaism of his Time* (Cambridge, MA: Polity Press, 1988); G. Baumbach, 'Randbemerkungen zu Jesu Judaizität', in K. Kertelge, T. Holtz and C.-P. März (eds.), *Christus bezeugen: Für W. Trilling* (Freiburg: Herder, 1990), pp. 74-83; Charlesworth, *Jesus within Judaism*; M. Reiser, *Die Gerichtspredigt Jesu: Eine Untersuchung zur eschatologischen Verkündigung Jesu und ihrem frühjüdischen Hintergrund* (NTAbh, NS 23; Münster: Aschendorff, 1990); J.P. Meier, *A Marginal Jew: Rethinking the Historical Jesus. I. The Roots of the Problem and the Person* (ABRL; New York: Doubleday, 1991) (and II. *Mentor, Message and Miracles* [ABRL; New York: Doubleday, 1994]); J.D. Crossan, *The Historical Jesus: The Life of a Mediterranean Jewish Peasant* (San Francisco: HarperSanFrancisco, 1991); B. Witherington III, *Jesus the Sage: The Pilgrimage of Wisdom* (Minneapolis: Fortress Press, 1994); K. Berger, *Wer war Jesus wirklich?* (Stuttgart: Kreuz, 1995); C.A. Evans, *Jesus and his Contemporaries: Comparative Studies* (AGJU, 25; Leiden: E.J. Brill, 1995); B.H. Young, *Jesus the Jewish Theologian* (Peabody, MA: Hendrickson, 1995); R.H. Stein, *Jesus the Messiah* (Downers Grove, IL: InterVarsity Press, 1996); B.D. Chilton and C.A. Evans, *Jesus in Context: Temple, Purity, and Restoration* (AGJU, 39; Leiden: E.J. Brill, 1997).

6. See, e.g., D. Novak, 'The Quest for the Jewish Jesus', *Modern Judaism* 8 (1988), pp. 119-38; Charlesworth, *Jesus within Judaism*, pp. 9-29; H.D. Betz, 'Wellhausen's Dictum "Jesus was not a Christian, but a Jew" in Light of Present Scholarship', *ST* 45 (1991), pp. 83-110; Charlesworth, 'Jesus Research Expands'; R.A. Horsley, 'Jesus, Itinerant Cynic or Israelite Prophet?', in J.H. Charlesworth and W.P. Weaver (eds.), *Images of Jesus Today* (Faith and Scholarship Colloquies, 3; Valley Forge, PA: Trinity Press International, 1994), pp. 68-97; Schweizer, 'Jesus'; Wright, *Jesus and the Victory of God*, pp. 28-82; B.D. Chilton, 'Jesus within Judaism', in B.D. Chilton and C.A. Evans (eds.), *Jesus in Context: Temple, Purity, and Restoration* (AGJU, 39; Leiden: E.J. Brill, 1997), pp. 179-201; Theissen and Winter, *Kriterienfrage*, pp. 148-57.

quest, to inquire what is actually meant with the designation, what is its import. The discussion ends with an evaluation.

2. *What Is There New in the 'Third Quest's' Way of Dealing with the Issue of the Jewishness of Jesus?*

The recognition of the fact that Jesus was a Jew is, of course, not an innovation of the 'Third Quest'. Leaving aside earlier times, we can mention for instance A. Schweitzer, at the beginning of the twentieth century, as one who stressed, in opposition to the liberal and modernized Jesuses, the Jewish background of Jesus (more exactly the context of apocalyptic Judaism) and the necessity of understanding Jesus as within the Judaism of his time.[7] Similarly, the scholars of the history of religions school emphasized understanding Jesus in his religious and cultural context.[8] Shortly following (and partly simultaneously with) Schweitzer there was a flux of Jewish scholars portraying a profoundly Jewish Jesus.[9] The New Quest,[10] again, explicitly acknowledged the

---

7. Cf. A. Schweitzer, *Geschichte der Paulinischen Forschung von der Reformation bis auf die Gegenwart* (Tübingen: Mohr Siebeck, 1911), p. vii: 'Ist die am Schlusse meiner Geschichte der Leben-Jesu-Forschung entwickelte Auffassung richtig, so ragt die Lehre des Herrn in keiner Anschauung aus der jüdischen in eine nichtjüdische Welt hinein, sondern stellt nur eine tief ethische und vollendete Fassung der zeitgenössischen Apokalyptik dar'.

8. I.H. Marshall, *I Believe in the Historical Jesus* (London: Hodder & Stoughton, 1977), pp. 117-18. See, e.g., J. Weiss, *Die Predigt Jesu vom Reiche Gottes* (Göttingen: Vandenhoeck & Ruprecht, 1892); W. Wrede, *Das Messiasgeheimnis in den Evangelien: Zugleich ein Beitrag zum verständnis des Markusevangeliums* (Göttingen: Vandenhoeck & Ruprecht, 1901); W. Bousset, *Kyrios Christos: Geschichte des Christusglaubens von den Anfängen des Christentums bis Irenäus*, (FRLANT, 21; Göttingen: Vandenhoeck & Ruprecht, 2nd edn, 1913). The early church had (hellenizingly), altered the simple Judaism of Jesus. Cf. J. Wellhausen (*Einleitung in die ersten drei Evangelien* [Berlin: Reimer, 2nd edn, 1911], p. 102): 'Jesus war kein Christ, sondern Jude'.

9. Cf., e.g., C.G. Montefiore, *The Synoptic Gospels* (London: Macmillan, 2nd edn, 1927); J. Klausner, *Jesus von Nazareth: Seine Zeit, sein Leben und seine Lehre* (Berlin: Jüdischer Verlag, 1930); L. Baeck, *Das Evangelium als Urkunde der jüdischen Glaubensgeschichte* (Berlin: Schocken Books, 1938). See further in G. Lindeskog, *Die Jesusfrage im neuzeitlichen Judentum: Ein Beitrag zur Geschichte der Leben-Jesu-Forschung* (Arbeiten und Mitteilungen aus dem neutestamentlichen Seminar zu Uppsala, 8; Leipzig: Almqvist & Wiksells, 1938); S. Ben-Chorin, *Jesus im Judentum* (Wuppertal: Theologischer Verlag Brockhaus, 1970); D.A.

Jewishness of Jesus. It maintained that a plausible picture of the historical Jesus 'should be "at home" within first-century Palestinian Judaism'.[11]

It is in the light of this notice that the question about the newness of the 'Third Quest's' understanding of the Jewishness of Jesus shows its pertinence. If the fact that Jesus was a Jew has indeed been acknowledged even earlier, and if the previous phase of the Jesus quest already set out from the very fact, how has the 'Third Quest' been dealing with the issue of the Jewishness of Jesus so that this actually lends the quest its 'new shape'? One certain novel aspect immediately comes to mind.

Hagner, *The Jewish Reclamation of Jesus: An Analysis and Critique of the Modern Jewish Study of Jesus* (Grand Rapids: Zondervan, 1988).

10. The beginning of this new phase is commonly connected with the Marburg lecture of E. Käsemann in the early 1950s (published in 'Das Problem des historischen Jesus', *ZTK* 51 [1954], pp. 125-53), chronicled by J.M. Robinson (*A New Quest of the Historical Jesus* [SBT, 25; London: SCM Press, 1959]) as *A New Quest of the Historical Jesus*. See also, e.g., H. Conzelmann, 'Jesus Christus', *RGG*, 3rd series, 3 (1959), pp. 619-53.

11. So precisely M.D. Hooker, 'Christology and Methodology', *NTS* 17 (1970–71), pp. 480-87, 482. Cf. also, e.g., E. Käsemann, *Exegetische Versuche und Besinnungen*, I (Göttingen: Vandenhoeck & Ruprecht, 2nd edn, 1960), p. 206: 'Er ist wohl Jude gewesen und setzt spätjüdische Frömmigkeit voraus'; N. Perrin, *Rediscovering the Teaching of Jesus* (New York: Harper, 1967), p. 51: 'In the first place, he [a Jesus scholar] should demand of himself that the understanding of the teaching of Jesus he reaches should do justice to the categories of first-century Judaism in terms of which that teaching was originally expressed'; J. Jeremias (*Neutestamentliche Theologie. I. Die Verkündigung Jesu* [Gütersloh: Gerd Mohn, 1971], p. 14) complains of the significant methodological failure of the criterion of dissimilarity in detaching Jesus from his true historical context, Judaism (this has also become a complaint of the 'Third Quest'; see, e.g., R.T Osborn, 'The Christian Blasphemy: A Non-Jewish Jesus', in J.H. Charlesworth [ed.], *Jews and Christians: Exploring the Past, Present, and Future* [Shared Ground among Jews and Christians, 1; New York: Crossroad, 1990], pp. 211-38 [218-21]; Harrington, 'The Jewishness of Jesus', pp. 132-33; Theissen and Winter, *Kriterienfrage*; T. Holmén, 'Doubts about Double Dissimilarity: Restructuring the Main Criterion of Jesus-of-History Research', in B.D. Chilton and C.A. Evans (eds.), *Authenticating the Words of Jesus* (NTTS, 28.1; Leiden: E.J. Brill), pp. 47-80 [esp. pp. 76-79]); similarly W.G. Kümmel, *Heilsgeschehen und Geschichte. II. Gesammelte Aufsätze 1965–1977* (Marburger theologische Studien, 16; Marburg: Elwert, 1978), p. 190. However, it cannot be denied that despite the recognition of the importance of history and the Jewish context of Jesus, the New Quest did not succeed in paying sufficient attention to this. See below in the text; see n. 16.

There was, as is well known, in between Schweitzer and the New
Quest the dreadful period when biblical scholarship was, in Nazi Germany, harnessed to serve anti-Semitic ends. In a key position in the
anti-Semitic understanding of Christianity lay the question of the Jewishness of Jesus; Jewishness was then more or less clearly denied. In
wildest explanations, Jesus was claimed to be both ideologically and
ethnically non-Jewish, and his Aryan ancestry was pleaded for.[12]
    The period of anti-Semitism necessarily affected all subsequent re-
search on Jesus. However, it is the 'Third Quest', not the previous
phase, the New Quest, which explicitly has wanted to emphasize the
Jewishness of Jesus in contrast with the earlier claims to the opposite.
An attempt to balance and to compensate the previous attitudes is
clearly discernible.[13] The emphasis on the Jewishness of Jesus functions
as a (delayed) reaction to the anti-Semitic picture of Jesus, as a kind of
healthy antidote.[14]

    12. For instance, W. Grundmann (*Jesus der Galiläer und das Judentum*
[Veröffentlichungen des Instituts zur Erforschung des jüdischen Einflusses auf dem
kirchlichen Leben; Leipzig: Wigand, 1940], pp. 165-200) argued that Jesus' teach-
ing is not Judaism at all. In Galilee Jesus had come into contact with Parsism and
Hellenism, which explains his independence from Judaism. In addition, since Galilee
had from 150 BCE onwards been practically free from Jews, it is well possible that
Joseph and Mary were not Jews. In fact, Aryan tribes had for long populated
Galilee. But, Grundmann is prepared to admit (with the words of E. Hirsch),
'irgendeinen äußeren Anhaltspunkt Jesu blutsmäßige Herkunft genauer als mit dem
Worte "nichtjüdisch" zu definieren, hat die Wissenschaft nicht'. Cf. also, e.g.,
G. Kittel, 'Neutestamentliche Gedanken zur Judenfrage', *AELKZ* 39 (1933), pp.
903-907. As forerunners, A. Harnack, R. Wagner and H.S. Chamberlain could be
mentioned. For investigations, see R.P. Ericksen, *Theologians under Hitler: Gerhard
Kittel, Paul Althaus amd Emmanuel Hirsch* (New Haven: Yale University Press,
1985); G. Friedrich and J. Friedrich, 'Kittel, Gerhard (1888–1948)', *TRE* 19 (1990),
pp. 221-25; L. Siegele-Wenschkewitz and C. Nicolaisen, *Theologische Fakultäten
im Nationalsozialismus* (Arbeiten zur kirchlichen Zeitgeschichte, B.18; Göttingen:
Vandenhoeck & Ruprecht, 1993).
    13. Wright, *Jesus and the Victory of God*, p. 119. Cf., e.g., in Sanders, *Jesus
and Judaism*, pp. 23-58; Osborn, 'The Christian Blasphemy'; J.H. Charlesworth,
'The Foreground of Christian Origins and the Commencement of Jesus Research',
in *idem* (ed.), *Jesus' Jewishness: Exploring the Place of Jesus in Early Judaism*
(Shared Ground among Jesus and Christians, 2; New York: Crossroad, 1996), pp.
63-83 (65-71); Chilton, 'Jesus within Judaism'.
    14. J.D.G. Dunn, *The Partings of the Ways: Between Christianity and Judaism
and their Significance for the Character of Christianity* (London: SCM Press;

Here is one fundamental difference or novelty of the 'Third Quest' in dealing with the issue of the Jewishness of Jesus. More time having passed from the explicitly un-Jewish picture of Jesus, the anti-Semitic Jesus 'research' and the related tendencies that long afterwards continued to be effective—the view of Judaism as inferior to Jesuanic and Christian teaching, the use of biblical exegesis for apologetic ends—can now more easily be fully denounced.

However, though the emphasis of the issue is thus well justified and important, it still remains a mere emphasis. The 'Third Quest' surely has something more substantial to add to understanding Jesus as a Jew. It would be interesting to inquire further into what is special about the 'Third Quest's' view of the Jewishness of Jesus. What else new is there besides the strong emphasis of the issue?

A substantial novelty would seem to be the fact that while the New Quest, despite having its starting point in Jesus the Jew, often resulted in viewing Jesus as significantly differing from the 'normative' or 'mainstream' Judaism (as it was then usual to speak), the 'Third Quest' has wanted to place Jesus *within* Judaism, to view him as properly integrated into the Judaism of his time.[15] The investigations of the New Quest mostly resulted in emphasizing the distance and difference of Jesus from Judaism.[16] The 'Third Quest' now wants to rectify this view:

Valley Forge, PA: Trinity Press International, 1996), p. 15; Theissen and Winter, *Kriterienfrage*, p. 148.

15. F. Mussner, *Traktat über die Juden* (Munich: Kösel, 1979), pp. 182-84; Charlesworth, 'Jesus Research Expands', p. 9; J.D.G. Dunn, 'Judaism in the Land of Israel in the First Century', in J. Neusner (ed.), *Judaism in late Antiquity*. II. *Historical Syntheses* (Handbuch der Orientalistik, 1.17; Leiden: E.J. Brill, 1995), pp. 229-61 (240); Harrington, 'The Jewishness of Jesus', pp. 124-25; Wright, *Jesus and the Victory of God*, p. 119.

16. Theissen and Merz, *Der historische Jesus*, p. 27. See the detailed analysis in Sanders, *Jesus and Judaism*, pp. 27-47. For example, the quote of Käsemann (*Exegetische Versuche und Besinnungen*, I, p. 206) in n. 11 above continues: '...aber er zerbricht gleichzeitig mit seinem Anspruch diese Sphäre [Judaism]'. G. Bornkamm (*Jesus von Nazareth* [Stuttgart: W. Kohlhammer, 4th/5th edn, 1960], p. 130, states: 'Im Gegensatz zu jüdischem Denken...löst ihn [the topic of reward as motivation for moral behavior] Jesus völlig auf dieser Verflechtung.' Similarly, it stands that the confidence in the election of the Jewish people '...in der Wurzel angegriffen und erschüttert ist' (Bornkamm, *Jesus von Nazareth*, p. 71). L. Goppelt, *Theologie des Neuen Testaments* (repr.; ed. F. Hahn; UTB, 850; Göttingen: Vandenhoeck & Ruprecht, 1981), p. 148, again, thinks 'daß Jesus tatsächlich das Judentum von der Wurzel her durch Neues aufhebt'.

Jesus was not such a 'different kind of Jew'.[17] We hear statements such as 'it is now widely recognized that Jesus stood foursquare within the Judaism of his day and that the movement which sprang from him initially was entirely Jewish in character',[18] or 'Jesus is now recognized to have been a devout Jew',[19] or, again, it is said that Jesus was 'a vigorous participant' of Judaism.[20] This probably is also what Harrington means by the statement that the new research has taken Jesus' Jewishness 'very seriously'.[21]

Thus, it would seem, the novelty of the 'Third Quest' in talking about the Jewishness of Jesus lies especially in having challenged the picture of Jesus as distanced or alienated from Judaism, the picture of Jesus as a 'different kind of Jew'. Though there have already been individual scholars and even theological schools that have acknowledged it as a fact that Jesus was a Jew, the 'Third Quest' is distinguished from them by viewing Jesus as profoundly Jewish, properly integrated into the Judaism of his time (which, again, makes his Jewishness an important factor for all scholarly undertakings to portray him). We could put this observation into words also by stating that the 'Third Quest' regards Jesus as more Jewish than what was recognized by the New Quest.[22]

This is all sound, clear and desirable. However, a closer examination into how the 'Third Quest' has arrived at this view reveals that there are some intricate difficulties involved here.

The Jewishness of Jesus in the 'Third Quest' (or the 'Third Quest' itself) cannot be considered without paying attention to the recent revision of the scholarly understanding of first-century Judaism.[23] The past two or three decades of research have marked a considerable change in the attitude that there was something that could be called 'normative Judaism'.[24] Concepts such as 'mainstream' or 'normative' have given

17. J.H. Charlesworth, 'Preface', in *idem* (ed.), *Jesus' Jewishness* 1, pp. 13-16 (16).

18. Dunn, 'Judaism', pp. 240-41.

19. Charlesworth, 'Jesus Research Expands', p. 9.

20. B. Chilton, *The Temple of Jesus: His Sacrificial Program within a Cultural History of Sacrifice* (University Park, PA: Pennsylvania State University, 1992), p. 190.

21. Harrington, 'The Jewishness of Jesus', p. 124.

22. So precisely Wright, *Jesus and the Victory of God*, p. 119.

23. See Holmberg, 'En historisk vändning', p. 72.

24. See here G.F. Moore, 'Christian Writers on Judaism', *HTR* 14 (1921), pp. 197-254 (244). The discussion in E.P. Sanders, *Paul and Palestinian Judaism: A*

way to understanding first-century Judaism as a more dynamic and heterogeneous religion:[25] there was no orthodox Judaism in those days;[26] there were many different groupings with diverging agendas, even competing with each other and trying to gain hegemony.[27] Early Judaism should be characterized as *formative* as to its nature:[28] new groupings were developing; agendas were in transition and change. Accordingly, it has been stated that 'early Judaism appears to encompass almost unlimited diversity and variety',[29] that 'there were only the infinitive and diverse Judaic systems'[30] and that radical pluralism was 'the order

Comparison of Patterns of Religion (London: SCM Press; Philadelphia: Fortress Press, 1977), p. 34, shows the circumstances in which the introduction of the term took place. On the change of attitude, cf., e.g., G.W.E. Nickelsburg and R.A. Kraft, 'The Modern Study of Early Judaism', in R.A. Kraft and G.W.E. Nickelsburg (eds.), *Early Judaism and its Modern Interpreters* (The Bible and its Modern Interpreters, 2; Philadelphia: Fortress Press, 1986), pp. 1-30 (9-21); W.S. Green, 'Introduction: The Scholarly Study of Judaism and its Sources', in J. Neusner (ed.), *Judaism in late Antiquity*. I. *The Literary and Archaeological Sources* (Handbuch der Orientalistik, 1.16 Bd.; Leiden: E.J. Brill), pp. 1-10 (1-5); J.J. Scott, Jr, *Customs and Controversies: Intertestamental Jewish Backgrounds of the New Testament* (Grand Rapids: Baker Book House, 1995), pp. 20-22.

25. See, e.g., G.G. Porton, 'Diversity in Post-biblical Judaism', in R.A. Kraft and G.W.E. Nickelsburg (eds.), *Early Judaism and its Modern Interpreters* (The Bible and its Modern Interpreters, 2, Philadelphia: Fortress Press, 1986), pp. 57-80; H. Maccoby, *Judaism in the First Century* (Issues in Religious Studies; London: Sheldon, 1989); A.I. Baumgarten, *The Flourishing of Jewish Sects in the Maccabean Era: An Interpretation* (JSJS, 55; Leiden: E.J. Brill, 1997). Porton ('Diversity in Post-biblical Judaism', p. 73) ascribes the demonstration of the heterogeneity of early Judaism to M. Smith, M.J. Cook, J. Murphy-O'Connor and J. Neusner.

26. See, e.g., N.J. McEleney, 'Orthodoxy in Judaism of the First Christian Century', *JSJ* 4 (1973), pp. 19-42; L.L. Grabbe, 'Orthodoxy in First Century Judaism: What are the Issues?', *JSJ* 8 (1977), pp. 149-53; cf. also A.F. Segal, *The Other Judaisms of Late Antiquity* (BJS, 127; Atlanta: Scholars Press, 1987).

27. J.K. Riches, *The World of Jesus: First-Century Judaism in Crisis* (Understanding Jesus Today; Cambridge: Cambridge University Press, 1990), pp. 30-48; Dunn, 'Judaism', pp. 246-51; Scott, *Customs and Controversies*. According to *y. Sanh*. 10.6.29c there were 24 sects at the time of the destruction of the Temple.

28. See, e.g., J. Neusner, *Formative Judaism: Religious, Historical, and Literary Studies. Series 2* (BJS, 41; Chico, CA: Scholars Press, 1983), pp. 1-6.

29. Nickelsburg and Kraft, 'Modern Study', p. 2.

30. J. Neusner, *The Judaism the Rabbis Take for Granted* (South Florida Studies in the History of Judaism, 102; Atlanta: Scholars Press, 1994), p. 18.

of the day'.[31] Correspondingly, again, it stands that one should realize 'the total impossibility of any type of closed, systematic, normative Judaism',[32] and that 'all these movements were in some way unique, controversial, contentious, and convinced of their "orthodoxy"'.[33]

Now, in a matrix like this, diversity and particularism become commonplace.[34] It becomes difficult, if not impossible, to isolate a person or a movement from the totality of all varying groups. Since it is now realized that there was no 'official' Judaism, there is nothing Jesus' views could be compared with any more so that they would appear as exceptional. Instead, there were many 'Judaisms' which were all, in a sense, exceptional.[35] Hence, the alleged exceptionality of Jesus still advocated by the New Quest has in the 'Third Quest' been subsumed into the diversity of first-century Judaism.

This, in my view, is the main factor that has led the 'Third Quest' to see Jesus as properly Jewish, to portray him as properly integrated into the Judaism of the time. The new picture of first-century Judaism has disclosed that the previously usual practice of comparison and contrasting of Jesus with something like a monolithic entity is not in keeping with reality.[36] It is more accurate to seek to find the place of Jesus *within* the variety of Judaism.

However, as noted, there are some difficulties involved here. As often, even here the coin has two halves. Now we come to the question about the meaning of the designation 'the Jewishness of Jesus'.

3. *What is Meant by the Jewishness of Jesus in the 'Third Quest'?*

What can be determined as 'Jewish' is, of course, dependent on how 'Judaism' is defined. To the contention of the 'Third Quest' that Jesus should be seen as profoundly Jewish, this simple recognition has quite radical corollaries. We can actually determine what is 'profoundly

---

31. Chilton, *The Temple of Jesus*, p. 181.
32. Charlesworth, 'The Foreground of Christian Origins', p. 72.
33. Betz, 'Wellhausen's Dictum', pp. 100-101.
34. Betz, 'Wellhausen's Dictum', pp. 100-101; Harrington, 'The Jewishness of Jesus', pp. 130, 136.
35. Betz, 'Wellhausen's Dictum', pp. 100-101.
36. Sanders, *Jesus and Judaism*, p. 29; Betz, 'Wellhausen's Dictum', p. 100; B. Chilton and J. Neusner, *Judaism in the New Testament: Practices and Beliefs* (London: Routledge, 1995), p. xv.

Jewish' only if we use some kind of 'normative Judaism' as a yardstick. However, on the basis of the modern view of first-century Judaism (as explicated above), it is impossible to find any justification to the claim that some form or type of that Judaism would be more Jewish than some other.[37] Consequently, we have no means to gauge Jesus' Judaism —whatever it was like—so that we could say that he was or was not profoundly Jewish. Even if Jesus were pictured as a teacher with no other agendas to match with his, we still could not say that this picture of him would not present him as Jewish—genuinely, profoundly, or properly Jewish.[38] Only if we posit a 'normative' or 'mainstream' Judaism to serve as a benchmark, may it then be possible for us to state the claim that some form of Judaism widely deviating from the norm we have set is not properly or profoundly Jewish.

Thus, somewhat paradoxically, the change in the understanding of first-century Judaism that triggered the 'Third Quest' to pursue a view of Jesus as properly integrated into Judaism, at the same time trivializes the pursuit.[39] We cannot actually reject the characterization of Jesus as a 'different kind of Jew' because we now realize that Judaism was heterogeneous, full of 'different' teachers and groupings. To portray Jesus as a 'different kind of Jew' in no way means to picture him as 'not particularly Jewish' because diversity and plurality of opinions and agendas so inherently belonged to the Judaism of his time. And conversely, we cannot actually propose that Jesus was profoundly Jewish, since, due to the lack of any 'normative' Judaism, we have no means of

---

37. If first-century Judaism is defined as a compound of highly diverse views on what is (true) Judaism with no clear leading or normative agenda, we have no justifiable means to tell (that is, to set the norm for) what 'profound Jewishness' is; S.J.D. Cohen, *From the Maccabees to the Mishnah* (Library of Early Christianity, 7; Philadelphia: Westminster Press, 1987), p. 135. Cf. also Chilton, *The Temple of Jesus*, p. 181: 'The adjective "faithful" cannot usefully or legitimately be limited to any one group'.

38. To be sure, there were many other figures, too, in early Judaism who created their own idiosyncratic theologies and who well merit the characterization 'a different kind of Jew' while at the same time displaying profound Jewishness. The Old Testament prophets were all quite interesting individuals. In later times we could mention the Teacher of Righteousness, Bannus, Jesus son of Ananias, and Bar Kokhba. Why could not we continue the list by stating that Jesus of Nazareth was also quite a character?

39. Cf. here Betz, 'Wellhausen's Dictum', pp. 100-101.

assessing this. There is no 'normative' or 'mainstream' Judaism Jesus could closely be integrated into so to make him very Jewish.

The crucial problem of the 'Third Quest' seems to be that it is not the least clear what 'Jewishness' means. Indeed, judged on the basis of different scholarly pictures of Jesus it can mean almost anything.

According to G. Vermes, Jesus smoothly integrates into the Judaism of his time.[40] Similarly, G. Theissen and A. Merz see Jesus' message as relying on the common Jewish belief in God and on the foundation of the Torah.[41] J. Riches, again, proposes that Jesus aimed at a transformation of Judaism.[42] But according to N.T. Wright, Jesus strived to reconstitute a new Israel.[43] And H. Merklein comes to the conclusion that the traditional ways of granting divine mercy did not suffice for Jesus but he thought that a totally new relationship with God was needed.[44]

These samples swiftly display Jesus the Jew as a proper representative of Judaism, as its transformer, and as a reconstituter of something totally new. In addition, the following characterizations can be mentioned: Jesus was an eschatological prophet;[45] he was a political revolutionary;[46] he was a magician;[47] a Hillelite Jew;[48] or he was someone with peculiarly non-eschatological views;[49] a Cynic philosopher;[50] a sage;[51] or a social prophet;[52] or then one with apocalyptic ideas.[53]

40. G. Vermes, *Jesus the Jew: A Historian's Reading of the Gospels* (New York: Macmillan; London: Collins, 1973); *idem, Jesus and the World of Judaism*; *idem, The Religion of Jesus the Jew* (Philadelphia: Fortress Press, 1993).

41. Theissen and Merz, *Der historische Jesus*.

42. Riches, *Jesus and the Transformation of Judaism*.

43. N.T. Wright, 'Jesus, Israel and the Cross', *SBLSP* 24 (1985), pp. 75-95.

44. H. Merklein, *Jesu Botschaft von der Gottesherrschaft: Eine Skizze* (SBS, 111; Stuttgart: Katholisches Bibelwerk, 3rd edn, 1989).

45. Sanders, *Jesus and Judaism*.

46. H. Maccoby, *Revolution in Judaea: Jesus and the Jewish Resistance* (London: Ocean Books, 1973).

47. M. Smith, *Jesus the Magician* (New York: Harper, 1978).

48. Falk, *Jesus the Pharisee*.

49. M.J. Borg, *Conflict, Holiness, and Politics in the Teachings of Jesus* (Harrisburg, PA: Trinity Press International, new edn, 1998 [1984]).

50. Crossan, *The Historical Jesus*.

51. Witherington III, *Jesus the Sage*.

52. R.A. Horsley, *Jesus and the Spiral of Violence: Popular Jewish Resistance in Roman Palestine* (San Francisco: HarperSanFrancisco, 1993).

53. C. Rowland, *The Open Heaven: A Study of Apocalyptic in Judaism and Early Christianity* (New York: Crossroad, 1982).

Notwithstanding the deviating views as to what kind of Jew Jesus was, the scholars behind the above characterizations would no doubt all subscribe to his Jewishness. And I think it is impossible also for us to say that one of them would have presented a Jesus who was not so Jewish—impossible unless we use some kind of 'normative' Judaism as a yardstick to indicate what a genuinely Jewish portrait should look like. But this we cannot do, can we?

So, what is meant when enouncing 'the Jewishness of Jesus'? What can the designation really propose about Jesus? What is gained by stressing that Jesus was Jewish, if this can mean so many different things? To talk about the Jewishness of Jesus has become a very sweeping issue, quite void of real meaning and easily attracting hidden agendas. We can ask, for instance, why B. Chilton regards J. Riches' *Jesus and the Transformation of Judaism* as 'an appeal to the old saw' and as an example of the 'apologetic tendency' (i.e. the book does not take seriously Jesus' Jewishness),[54] while G. Theissen and D. Winter hold the book as a 'brilliant beginning' for the 'Third Quest' (i.e. the book manages well to integrate Jesus into Judaism).[55] Obviously, these critics of Riches understand 'Jewishness' in different ways which, again, may depend on how they themselves wish to portray Jesus. In this particular example, that charge rests with Chilton. Chilton, whom we earlier hear talk about 'the radical pluralization of Judaism, of which Jesus was both symptom and a result',[56] now employs a conception of Judaism deradicalized in such a way that no room for Riches' Jesus the Jew is left. Theissen's and Winter's Judaism, however, subsumes this Jesus without any problems. And further examples could be presented.[57]

54. Chilton, 'Jesus within Judaism', pp. 186-87.
55. Theissen and Winter, *Kriterienfrage*, p. 152.
56. Chilton, *The Temple of Jesus*, p. 181.
57. Cf., e.g., Sanders (*Jewish Law from Jesus to the Mishnah: Five Studies* [London: SCM Press; Valley Forge, PA: Trinity Press International, 1990], p. 28) does not believe that Jesus would have expressed the idea in Mk 7.15 (according to the absolute understanding; cf. Holmén, 'Doubts about Double Dissimilarity', pp. 70-74), because this would suggest that he broke with Judaism. But again, Theissen and Winter (*Kriterienfrage*, p. 184) find nothing so un-Jewish in the very idea. J.H. Charlesworth wants to question the understanding of 'Judaism' 'in exclusively religious categories' and accordingly does not dare to 'assume that a Jew is a "religious" Jew' (Charlesworth, 'The Foreground of Christian Origins', pp. 69-70). When he comes to speak about Jesus, however, 'Judaism' suddenly attains a much narrower description, for Jesus, we learn, is precisely to be seen as a 'devoutly

'Jewishness' has become a fluid concept. Fluidity of concepts inevitably leads to confusion. Confusion, again, is a favorable soil for conclusions not based on coherent thinking but rather on preconceptions lurking in the mind of every scholar.

4. *Evaluation*

Considering all that has been said, I can but state that the 'Third Quest's' understanding of the Jewishness of Jesus appears to be in a state of turmoil.[58] To be sure, the understanding is clearly different from that, for instance, of the New Quest. However, the difference does not lie in the fact that while the New Quest detached Jesus from Judaism, the 'Third Quest' would have 'brought him home'.[59] Like before, scholars can today set out from the conviction that Jesus was a Jew. But unlike before, scholars may today result in completely deviating pictures of Jesus, none of which can be rejected merely by appealing to the fact that Jesus should be viewed as within Judaism. To top it all, claims that, for example, Jesus was profoundly Jewish or that he was, on the contrary, a 'different kind of Jew', can be presented without actually saying or meaning anything and without there being any possibility to counter.[60] Given such fluidity, the designation 'the Jewishness of Jesus' may hide more things than it reveals.

religious Jew' (Charlesworth, 'Preface', p. 16). Cf. also the statements of Chilton that to understand Jesus from within necessarily implies that 'he is to be apprehended as having a positive definition of purity' (Chilton, 'Jesus within Judaism', p. 200), or that the characterization of the Temple incident (Mk 11.15-17) as cleansing is a 'transparently ... apologetic designation' (Chilton, *The Temple of Jesus*, p. 100). What I am asking here is whether the simple recognition that Jesus was a Jew really can lead us to conclude that he cannot have said Mk 7.15 (according to the absolute understanding), that he could not have wanted to cleanse the Temple, or that he must have been devoutly religious, etc. Why cannot we allow Jesus to construe a Judaism of his own? Would not this be anything else but symptomatic of 'the radical pluralization of Judaism'? Many scholars, even if they would in principle sustain the highly pluralistic understanding of Judaism, when they come to talk about Jesus tend to lean back to a narrower view thereof, so being able to argue for or against some certain picture of Jesus.

58. Cf. Wright, *Jesus and the Victory of God*, p. 93.

59. Cf. Ben-Chorin, *Jesus im Judentum*, p. 7.

60. Let me illustrate this with an example. Many have regarded the Cynic picture of Jesus as a not so Jewish picture (Betz, 'Wellhausen's Dictum', pp. 93-94, 106 nn. 50-51, 100, 110 n. 83; P.R. Eddy, 'Jesus as Diogenes? Reflections on the

So, I fully subscribe to the ideas that Jesus was a Jew, that his Jewishness must be taken seriously, and that the emphasis on the Jewishness of Jesus is a central characteristic of the 'Third Quest'. But I find it very difficult to agree with the view that the 'Third Quest' really had taken the issue so seriously. Rather, it has made the designation 'the Jewishness of Jesus' into not much more than a slogan which leaves the impression of representing something good and enlightened but under the veil of which many things can happen.[61] Now, just one humble suggestion of how the situation could be improved.

Cynic Jesus Thesis', *JBL* 115 [1996], pp. 449-69 [463-67]; D.E. Aune, 'Jesus and Cynics in First-Century Palestine: Some Critical Considerations', in J.H. Charlesworth and L.L. Johns [eds.], *Hillel and Jesus: Comparative Studies of Two Major Religious Leaders* [Minneapolis: Fortress Press, 1997], pp. 176-92 [187-91]). Rather, it represents, if at all, a quite peripheral Judaism. Now, on the basis of the modern view of Judaism as a diverse and heterogeneous religion without any 'normative' or 'official' core, we have no means to tell what belongs, on the one hand, to the periphery, what, on the other, to the center. Accordingly, we have no means to argue that the Cynic Jesus would not be Jewish, not even can we claim that this Jesus would not be profoundly Jewish. The question whether the Cynic portrait is historically verifiable, that is, (a) whether Cynic ideas were indeed so prevalent in Galilee, (b) whether Jesus' teaching in fact can be aligned with them, is another issue (though I think that both [a] and [b] should be answered negatively). But as it comes to the question of how the Jewishness of Jesus is reflected in the Cynic picture of Jesus, we cannot, justifiably, complain.

61. In addition to what has been described above (see p. 155 and n. 57), patronizing *apologetics of Judaism* is to be mentioned. Christian scholars may sometimes find it difficult to accept some aspects of Judaism as genuine without noticing that this difficulty is due to their own Christian frame of references. One example could be the charge leveled against E.P. Sanders by J. Neusner (*Judaic Law from Jesus to the Mishnah: A Systematic Reply to Professor E.P. Sanders* [South Florida Studies in the History of Judaism, 84; Atlanta: Scholars Press, 1993], pp. 270-73). According to Neusner, Sanders has, in defense of Judaism, dismissed as trivial something (purity matters) that Neusner himself finds important and essential. 'Nor do I value a defense of my religion that implicitly throughout and explicitly at many points accepts at face value what another religion values and rejects what my religion deems authentic service to the living God' (*Judaic Law*, pp. 272-73.) But cf. E.P. Sanders, *The Historical Figure of Jesus* (Harmondsworth: Penguin Books, 1993), pp. 36-37. Another example (bringing the issue more into contact with Jesus-of-history research): the list of the Pharisee's careful observance of the law in Lk. 18.11-12 making him quite self-assured has often bothered scholars (cf. L. Schottroff, 'Die Erzählung vom Pharisäer und Zöllner als Beispiel für die theologische Kunst des Überredens', in H.D. Betz and L. Schottroff [eds.], *Neues Testament und*

As can be seen, the problematic situation is a result of the definition of Judaism as a highly diverse entity lacking any obvious center,[62] the definition also repeatedly stated in modern Jesus books as a part of the 'Third Quest's' new way of looking upon things. A more conceptual point of view could perhaps offer a solution here. The key insight is that it is possible to alternate between different kinds of *strategies or modes of defining Judaism* without actually altering the perception of the historical reality of Judaism.

J.D.G. Dunn has differentiated between the outsider's and the insider's view of Judaism in Israel in the first century. For him, the modern scholarly understanding of that Judaism as a highly diverse and heterogeneous religion is precisely such as is attained when viewed from without.[63] Interestingly, M. Hengel and R. Deines characterize E.P. Sanders's 'common Judaism', a concept seeking to focus on the joint elements of all 'Judaisms', as a description of Judaism as it is seen from outside.[64] For Hengel and Deines, people in Palestine itself (thus Dunn's from within), 'noticed much more acutely the considerable differences and tensions'.[65]

The important point in both Dunn's and Hengel's and Deines's notions is the recognition that it is possible to focus the analysis of the data on different elements: what is common and what unites, and what is different and what separates.[66] *Hanging on either of these alternative*

---

christliche Existenz: Festschrift für H. Braun [Tübingen: Mohr Siebeck], pp. 439-61; G. Petzke, *Das Sondergut des Evangeliums nach Lukas* [Zürcher Werkkommentare zur Bibel; Zürich: Theologischer Verlag, 1990], pp. 162-65). But on the basis of what values should we regard such a self-assurance as dubious? Further, the earlier unfortunate tendency to consider a difference discovered between Jesuanic and other Jewish teaching to testify to the superiority of the former, should not be compensated by a tendency to deny any difference; cf. here, e.g., G.M. Zerbe's (*Non-Retaliation in Early Jewish and New Testament Texts: Ethical Themes in Social Contexts* [JSPSup, 13; Sheffield: JSOTPress, 1993], pp. 19-20) critical remarks of W. Klassen (*Love of Enemies: The Way to Peace* [OBT, 15; Philadelphia: Fortress Press, 1984). After all, difference and uniqueness were commonplace in first-century Judaism.

62. Cf. Green, 'Introduction', pp. 5-6.

63. Dunn, 'Judaism', pp. 236-51.

64. M. Hengel and R. Deines, 'E.P. Sanders' "Common Judaism", Jesus, and the Pharisees', *JTS* 46 (1995), pp. 1-70 (68).

65. Hengel and Deines, 'E.P. Sanders' "Common Judaism" ', p. 68.

66. A (modern) spectator can, of course, both look for common features and analyze differences. I agree with W.S. Green ('Introduction', p. 8) in that 'insider'

features, we arrive at different definitions of Judaism not to be seen as mutually exclusive but as complementary and purpose-oriented.[67] There are, in other words, various strategies of defining Judaism that can be applied, strategies that by ending up with different kinds of definitions can serve different pursuits of investigation. The pursuit of the recent research of early Judaism to bring more light on the diversity aspect of Judaism has greatly benefited from a strategy that has been labeled 'nominalism'.[68] As explained by W.S. Green, 'nominalism' works well in attempts to account for differences in Judaism, to articulate diversity and heterogeneousness.[69] However, it does not provide analytic traits to permit classification or comparison. More apt for comparison, again, is the 'essentialist' strategy. 'Essentialism' understands Judaism in terms of core belief and foundational metaphor, such as monotheism, covenant, ethnic exclusivism, etc. It seeks common characteristics and similarity and is well suited to account for complex religious behaviors.[70]

Now, the definition of Judaism employed in the 'Third Quest' also approximates the 'nominalist' mode of defining. The focus is clearly on accounting for variety and heterogeneousness. Still, the pursuits of Jesus-of-history research are different from those of the current research of early Judaism. As noted, the 'Third Quest' has sought to understand Jesus within Judaism, to explore his place in Judaism, to compare him with his contemporaries.[71] It is a pursuit of locating one specific phe-

and 'outsider' are labile categories, as is also demonstrated by their contradictory application by Dunn and Hengel and Deines.

67. In addition to Dunn, Hengel and Deines, S.J.D. Cohen (*From the Maccabees to the Mishnah*, p. 135) and L.H. Schiffman (*From Text to Tradition: A History of Second Temple and Rabbinic Judaism* [Hoboken: Ktav, 1991], p. 4), *inter alia*, have pointed out this optionality.

68. Green, 'Introduction', pp. 6-9. Green discusses three strategies: 'essentialism', 'nominalism' and 'polythetic classification'. See even W.S. Green, 'Ancient Judaism: Contours and Complexity', in S.E. Balentine and J. Barton (eds.), *Language, Theology, and the Bible: Essays in Honour of J. Barr* (Oxford: Clarendon Press, 1994), pp. 293-310 (297-300, 306-310).

69. Green, 'Introduction', pp. 7-8. This would be Dunn's outsider's view, Hengel's and Deines's view from within.

70. See Green, 'Introduction', pp. 6-7. Dunn's from within, Hengel's and Deines's from outside.

71. See, e.g., the titles of Chilton, 'Jesus within Judaism', and Charlesworth, *Jesus within Judaism*; *idem* (ed.), *Jesus' Jewishness*; and Evans, *Jesus and his Contemporaries*.

nomenon among many others that are similar. Precisely here, 'nominalist' definitions are not particularly useful. The identity-centered strategy of 'nominalism' can result in definitions such as the following by S.J.D. Cohen: Judaism is '...the religious behavior of all people who call themselves and are known to others as Jews'.[72] According to such definitions, Jesus would always come up as simply Jewish (not profoundly Jewish [cf. Vermes, Theissen and Merz], differently Jewish [cf. Riches], nor marginally Jewish [cf. Merklein, Wright])[73], granted that he *himself* considered himself a Jew. Being Jewish—or rather, what we justifiably can call Jewish—becomes dependent solely on the self-estimation of the object of research: every phenomenon scrutinized, the representatives of which *themselves* regarded themselves as Jewish should be included in 'Judaism'. This perception is a conspicuous characteristic of 'nominalist' definitions.[74] And we see how impotent they are in determining the place of Jesus' Judaism among the other 'Judaisms'.

In order to bring the definition of Judaism better in line with the peculiar task of Jesus-of-history research, an alternative strategy is needed. This would in the first place be that of 'essentialism'.[75] As it happens, scholars such as E.P. Sanders, J.D.G. Dunn and N.T. Wright have each in their own way strived at determining guidelines for something like basic or common Judaism.[76] Such approaches have often been considered suspicious since they easily leave the impression of reverting back to painting the old picture of 'normative' or 'official' Judaism.

---

72. Cohen, *From the Maccabees to the Mishnah*, p. 135.

73. For the views of these scholars, see the short review on p. 154.

74. Green, 'Introduction', pp. 7-8. Besides Cohen's (*From the Maccabees to the Mishnah*, p. 135) definition quoted above, cf. Schiffman, *From Text to Tradition*, p. 1: 'By Judaism, we mean the collective religious, cultural and legal tradition and civilization of the Jewish people as developed and passed down from biblical times until today'. This makes of every Jew a creator of Judaism.

75. Cf. Green, 'Introduction', pp. 6-7. I do not find the terms altogether satisfying.

76. Sanders has advocated 'restoration eschatology' and 'covenantal nomism' (Sanders, *Jesus and Judaism*, pp. 61-119, 335-37); Dunn the four pillars: temple, God, election, and Torah (Dunn, 'Judaism', pp. 251-57; *idem*, *The Partings of the Ways*, pp. 18-36), and Wright talks about 'mainline' which is explained through the study of worldview, beliefs and hope (N.T. Wright, *The New Testament and the People of God* [Christian Origins and the Question of God, 1; Minneapolis: Fortress Press, 1992], pp. 215-338). See also Nickelsburg and Kraft, 'Modern Study', pp. 20-21.

But in reality, it is altering the strategy of defining, altering the focus in analyzing the data that is at issue here. As noted, one definition does not invalidate the other, but the strategies are complementary and serve different purposes.[77] The guidelines for basic or common Judaism would not question the diversity of first-century Judaism, neither would they question Jesus' Jewishness. But the guidelines would enable us meaningfully to evaluate just how he was Jewish by justifying the positing of pictures of Jesus varying from the commonly Jewish to the marginally Jewish.[78] We could again assess whether Jesus was, for example, profoundly Jewish or a 'different kind of Jew'. Characterizations like these would again mean something, thus giving the desired backbone to the 'Third Quest's' way of dealing with the issue of the Jewishness of Jesus.[79]

Thus, in my view, the 'Third Quest' has lacked sensitivity about the conceptual needs of its peculiar task. The 'nominalist' kind of strategy of defining Judaism, almost exclusively employed in the 'Third Quest', is not in line with the task of determining the place of Jesus within

77. So Dunn ('Judaism', pp. 236-51) and Hengel and Deines ('E.P. Sanders' "Common Judaism"', pp. 67-68) differentiate between various ways of observing the phenomenon of Judaism (for them, inside versus outside perspectives) and consider these to complement each other.

78. And everything between.

79. In reality, many scholars who otherwise openly engage themselves to the view to Judaism according to the 'nominalist' strategy and result in the all-inclusive picture and denying the existence of any core or center, must in some occasions silently take a precisely opposite kind of stand (cf., e.g., J.H. Charlesworth, 'From Jewish Messianology to Christian Christology: Some Caveats and Perspectives', in J. Neusner *et al.* [eds.], *Judaisms and their Messiahs at the Turn of the Christian Era* (Cambridge: Cambridge University Press), pp. 225-64 [227]; and *idem*, 'The Foreground of Christian Origins', p. 72 with *idem*, 'Jesus Research Expands', p. 22; Harrington, 'The Jewishness of Jesus', pp. 130-31 with p. 134). That is, they have to adopt the 'essentialist' approach and conceive limits for what can properly be called Jewish simply in order to be able—when the time comes—to tell what Jewishness in the case of Jesus actually implies (i.e. that it actually implies something). The problem here is the unnoticed shift from one definition to another which is allowed to do the work of an argument: From the perspective of a 'nominalist' definition of Judaism, the designation 'profound Jewishness' can mean almost anything; however, in an 'essentialist' definition it means some quite particular kind of Judaism. Cf. n. 57.

Judaism, though it serves well in articulating the diversity aspect in Judaism. Adopting another kind of strategy, as delineated above, we would still perhaps result in a great cluster of different pictures of Jesus. However, we would be able to arrange the pictures in a meaningful way and value them as expounding the Jewishness of Jesus.

THE NEW QUEST FOR JESUS AND THE NEW RESEARCH
ON THE DEAD SEA SCROLLS

Craig A. Evans

The publication of the last of the remaining materials from Qumran's fourth cave has aided the new revival of scholarly interest in the historical Jesus. This new phase of study, sometimes called the 'Third Quest', has freed itself from the Bultmannian hermeneutic that so heavily influenced the 'New Quest' of the 1950s and 1960s.[1] The Third Quest is less apologetically driven and theologically motivated, but more amenable to viewing Jesus in his Palestinian and Jewish context. The Dead Sea Scrolls have shed light on Jesus and his context, and at the same time provide a basis for criticisms of certain recent studies, notably those emanating from the North American Jesus Seminar, that neglect this important new source material and fail to place Jesus adequately in his Jewish context.[2] The Scrolls are helpful and very important, but they do not answer all of our questions, nor do they preclude other source materials.

My interest is not to cite strings of verbal parallels between the Dead Sea Scrolls and various sayings and activities attributed to Jesus. These kinds of parallels have some usefulness, to be sure. However, they may not indicate more than a common milieu and a common language. After all, Jesus was Jewish and grew up in Palestine, so we should hardly be surprised that he employed words and phrases that other Palestinian Jews utilized. Linguistic and dictional overlap alone does not shed much light on questions of aims, purpose and self-understanding. What

---

1. This is not entirely true of the Jesus Seminar, whose assumptions and dubious results reflect at points Bultmannian influence.

2. G. Theissen and A. Merz (*The Historical Jesus: A Comprehensive Guide* [Minneapolis: Fortress Press, 1998], p. 11) take a playful swipe at the Jesus Seminar, when they say that the '"non-eschatological Jesus" seems to have more Californian than Galilean local colouring'.

are more important than mere verbal parallels are patterns or collocations of themes and concepts. E.P. Sanders's preference for speaking of
'patterns of religion' is, in my opinion, the correct approach to take.[3]

With this methodological concern in mind, I would like to look at
three themes and emphases in Jesus' ministry and compare them to what
appear to be similar themes in the Dead Sea Scrolls, particularly those
Scrolls thought by many to have been produced by the sectarians themselves. I also hope to show that these three themes are closely related
and make up components of a larger theological construct. These three
themes are (1) the proclamation of the kingdom of God, (2) a jubilee
proclamation that entails healing, forgiveness and restoration, and (3)
severe criticism of the Temple establishment. Not only do these three
themes find significant parallels in the Dead Sea Scrolls, they appear to
constitute components of an eschatology whereby God is understood
to be *in the process* (in the case of Jesus), or *about to initiate the process* (in the case of the Qumran sectarians), of redeeming and restoring
Israel.[4]

Of course, to speak of the 'historical' Jesus inevitably entails the
question of authenticity and the criteria for determining it. I have elsewhere discussed my views on this difficult and complicated question
and have no intention here of going into much detail.[5] It will be sufficient to comment briefly that many of the elements that will be considered below enjoy the support of the criteria of dissimilarity and
embarrassment. By dissimilarity I mean, of course, dissimilarity from

---

3.   As in E.P. Sanders, *Paul and Palestinian Judaism: A Comparison of Patterns of Religion* (London: SCM Press; Philadelphia: Fortress Press, 1977); idem,
Jesus and Judaism (London: SCM Press; Philadelphia: Fortress Press, 1985).

4.   I probe other points of contact between Jesus and the Scrolls in C.A. Evans,
'Jesus and the Dead Sea Scrolls', in P.W. Flint and J.C. VanderKam (eds.), *The
Dead Sea Scrolls after Fifty Years: A Comprehensive Assessment*, II (Leiden: E.J.
Brill, 1999), pp. 573-98. These other points of contact include Jesus' use of Isa. 5.1-7
in his Parable of the Vineyard (Mk 12.1-12; cf. 4QBen 1.2-7), the idea of enthrone-
ment and exaltation (Mk 14.62; cf. 4QM^a 11.i.12-19), and the authority of the Torah
(Lk 10.25-28; cf. CD 3.12-20).

5.   C.A. Evans, 'Authenticity Criteria in Life of Jesus Research', *Christian
Scholar's Review* 19 (1989), pp. 6-31; *idem, Jesus and his Contemporaries: Com-
parative Studies* (AGJU, 25; Leiden: E.J. Brill, 1995), pp. 2-26. See the survey and
critical assessment of the criteria in J.P. Meier, *A Marginal Jew: Rethinking the
Historical Jesus.* I. *The Roots of the Problem and the Person* (ABRL, 3; New York:
Doubleday, 1991), pp. 167-95.

emphases in early Christianity.[6] I do not mean dissimilarity from Judaism.[7] However, it will be possible to highlight here and there features that are somewhat unusual or atypical in the Jewish setting. By embarrassment I mean tradition that resists being explained plausibly as that created by the early Church. The criterion of embarrassment is, of course, cognate to the criterion of dissimilarity, but it is not identical to it. Whereas the latter observes material that is unlike the emphases of the early Church, or lacks continuity with the emphases that emerged in the early Church, the former identifies material that the early Church tried to edit, even suppress, because of its potentially embarrassing content. Other supporting criteria include attestation in multiple sources and multiple forms. Another important criterion, frequently overlooked, is the criterion of result.[8] In other words, we must ask what sayings and activities of Jesus account for what happened to him and to his movement? Why was Jesus crucified as 'king of the Jews' and why did the Christian Church emerge in the aftermath? Also of some value is the criterion of Semitic and Palestinian features. Isolated words and phrases mean little, for they could owe their origin to the early, Aramaic-speaking Church as much as to Jesus. But complex exegeses and themes that are only fragmentarily preserved in the dominical tradition and which make sense in the light of later, more fully extant Jewish sources may be significant indicators of underlying authentic tradition. For if the early Church invented this material, why is it not more fully preserved in the dominical tradition; why is it incomplete? Moreover, if the early Church invented it, why is there not more evidence of its transformation from Aramaic/Hebrew to Greek language and conceptuality?

Without further introduction, let us consider the first theme.

---

6. This is not to say, of course, that there is no continuity between Jesus and the early Church; such a stance is improbable and illogical.

7. Here the criterion of *double* dissimilarity has been rightly criticized in recent years. In their recent treatment of the subject, with special attention given to the deficiencies of the criterion of dissimilarity, G. Theissen and D. Winter (*Die Kriterienfrage in der Jesusforschung: Vom Differenzkriterium zum Plausibilitätskriterium* (NTOA, 34; Freiburg: Universitätsverlag; Göttingen: Vandenhoeck & Ruprecht, 1997], pp. 183-91) have argued for a 'criterion of plausibility', a criterion that looks favorably upon tradition deeply rooted in the concrete Jewish context of Palestine and Galilee. See my review of this book in *JBL* 118 (1999), pp. 551-53.

8. This criterion is properly taken into account in Sanders, *Jesus and Judaism*, and is recommended in Meier, *A Marginal Jew*, I.

1. *The Kingdom of God*

It is widely accepted that Jesus proclaimed the 'kingdom of God' (ἡ βασιλεία τοῦ θεοῦ).[9] His proclamation is consistent with ideas about the kingdom expressed in the Scrolls and the Aramaic paraphrase of Isaiah. But Jesus' proclamation is also rooted in the Scriptures themselves, a point which in my opinion is not always sufficiently appreciated. In the Scriptures there is present a shift from the kingdom *of David* or the kingdom *of Israel* to kingdom *of God.* A superficial survey of the data bears this out: in 1 Sam. 28.17 God gives the kingdom to David. Elsewhere Israel's ancient story speaks of the kingdom as belonging to David (e.g. 2 Sam. 3.28: 'my kingdom'; 2 Sam. 5.12: 'his kingdom'; cf. 1 Kgs 2.12, where Solomon sits on David's throne and 'his kingdom' is firmly established). But this picture changes in the Chronicler, who speaks of the Lord's kingdom and the Lord's throne (cf. 1 Chron. 17.14 'my kingdom'; 1 Chron. 29.23 'the throne of the LORD'; 1 Chron. 28.5 and 2 Chron. 13.8 'the kingdom of the LORD'). In Daniel God himself is depicted as king over all of humanity, whose kingdom will displace all previous human kingdoms (cf. Dan. 4.3, 17, 34; 6.26). Elsewhere Scripture makes reference to God's kingdom using personal pronouns or equivalents (e.g. Pss. 22.28; 103.19; 145.11, 12, 13; Obad. 21; 1 Chron. 29.11). Accordingly, Dennis Duling comments that

> These passages indicate that God was imagined as the reigning king over Israel, all peoples, and, indeed, nature itself. Thus, other scholars have concluded that although the exact phrase [viz. kingdom of God] is missing, the *idea* of the kingdom of God is present, indeed even widespread, in the Hebrew Scriptures.[10]

In later literature the idea of the kingdom of God becomes more explicit. According to *Jub.* 1.28 God rules from Mount Zion, while in *Pss. Sol.* 17.3 we encounter the exact phrase 'kingdom of God' (ἡ βασιλεία τοῦ θεοῦ) and in *T. Benj.* 9.1 the synonymous phrase 'kingdom of the

---

9. The variation 'kingdom of heaven' (ἡ βασιλεία τῶν οὐρανῶν), mostly found in the Gospel of Matthew, is understood as a circumlocution introduced by the evangelist. For a current review of the topic, see B.D. Chilton, 'The Kingdom of God in Recent Discussion', in B.D. Chilton and C.A. Evans (eds.), *Studying the Historical Jesus: Evaluations of the State of Current Research* (NTTS, 19; Leiden: E.J. Brill, 1994), pp. 255-80.

10. D.C. Duling, 'Kingdom of God, Kingdom of Heaven', *ABD* IV, p. 50.

Lord' (ἡ βασιλεία κυρίου). In many passages in *1 Enoch* God is depicted as king and as ruling the world. The author of the *Testament of Moses* anticipates the appearance of the kingdom of God and the demise of the Devil (*T. Mos.* 10.1-3).

The Dead Sea Scrolls present ideas that are consistent with the ideas of the literature already surveyed.[11] The idea of a 'kingdom of God' is reflected in the War Scroll: 'And to the God of Israel shall be the kingdom, and by the saints of his people will he display might' (1QM 6.6); and 'You, O God, resplendent in the glory of your kingdom [מלכותכה]' (1QM 12.7). The reference to 'his kingdom' in 1QH 11.i.4-7 should probably be understood in the same way. 4QMª, which is related in some way to the War Scroll, says: 'And [the kingdo]m shall be for God and the salvatio[n] for His people...' (11.ii.17). This text appears to cohere with the eschatological dimension of Jesus' proclamation of the kingdom.

In the Rule of Blessing the following is said of the High Priest: 'May you serve in the Temple of the kingdom [בהיכל מלכות]' (1QSb 4.25-26). This is the prayer of blessing for the priest who will serve when Israel is restored and the Messiah takes his place. The last column of 1QSb blesses this figure as well. Part of the blessing says: 'And he shall renew for him the covenant of the community, so as to establish the kingdom of His people [מלכות עמו] forever' (1QSb 5.21). The passage goes on to quote parts of Isaiah 11 and apply them to the awaited Messiah. (See also 4QBerª 7.i.5, which speaks of God supporting 'your kingdom [מלכותכה] in the midst of...' (The singular suffix probably refers to the anticipated Messiah.)

No texts more than the Songs of the Sabbath have extolled the glory of the kingdom of heaven. We find more than 20 references to the celestial kingdom in these fragmentary scrolls. Although in no one instance do we have the exact phrase 'kingdom of God', it is nevertheless about the kingdom of God that these texts speak. The pronouns appear in the second and third persons: '[Your] lofty kingdom' (4QShirShabbª 1.ii.1); 'His lofty kingdom' (4QShirShabbᵈ 1.i.8; 1.i.14; 4QShirShabbᶠ 3.ii.4; MasŠŠ 2.20); 'the beauty of Your kingdom' (4QShirShabbª 1.ii.3); 'the praiseworthiness of Your kingdom among

---

11. See B. Viviano, 'The Kingdom of God in the Qumran Literature', in W. Willis (ed.), *The Kingdom of God in 20th-Century Interpretation* (Peabody, MA: Hendrickson, 1987), pp. 97-107; Evans, 'Jesus and the Dead Sea Scrolls', pp. 575-85.

the holiest of the h[oly ones]' (4QShirShabb[a] 1.ii.3; 2.1; 4QShirShabb[b] 14.i.7); 'and they declare His kingdom' (4QShirShabb[a] 2.3); 'the heavens of Your glor[ious] kingdom' (4QShirShabb[b] 14.i.6); '[in all] the heavens of His kingdom' (4QShirShabb[a] 2.3-4); '[who pr]aise His glorious kingdom' (4QShirShabb[d] 1.i.25); 'in the splendor of praise is the glory of His kingdom' (4QShirShabb[d] 1.i.32); 'the praises of all the gods together with the splendor of all His kingdom' (4QShirShabb[d] 1.i.32-33); 'And the tabernacle of highest loftiness, the glory of His kingdom' (4QShirShabb[d] 1.ii.10); 'a seat like the throne of His kingdom' (4QShirShabb[f] 20–22.ii.2); 'the kingdom...glorious seats of the chariot thrones' (4QShirShabb[f] 20–22.ii.4); 'the throne of His glorious kingdom' (4QShirShabb[f] 23.i.3); 'the chiefs of the realm of the holy ones of the King of holiness in all the heights of the sanctuaries of His glorious kingdom' (4QShirShabb[f] 23.ii.11-12); and 'the glorious kingdom of the King of all the g[ods]' (4QShirShabb[f] 24.3) are among the best preserved texts that speak of the divine kingdom.[12]

The upshot of all this is that Jesus' idea of God as king, or the kingdom of God in the sense of the sphere in which God rules, or in the sense that God rules over humanity and the cosmos, is hardly distinctive of Jesus and hardly need be explained by an appeal to Hellenism, as Burton Mack has recently done.[13] Jesus' proclamation of God's rule is consistent with the expressions found in the Dead Sea Scrolls. The precise diction, 'the time is fulfilled and the kingdom of God has come' (e.g. Mk 1.15) and 'the kingdom of God has come upon you', appears to reflect the diction of Daniel,[14] a popular work at Qumran. According to the Theodotian text, Dan. 7.22 reads (with verbal parallels in bold type):

---

12. For text, reconstructions, and criticial discussion, see C.A. Newsom, *Song of the Sabbath Sacrifice: A Critical Edition* (HSS, 27; Atlanta: Scholars Press, 1985).

13. B.L. Mack, 'The Kingdom Sayings in Mark', *Forum* 3.1 (1987), pp. 3-47. Mack claims that the exact Greek phrase, ἡ βασιλεία τοῦ θεοῦ, is only found in three Hellenistic texts (i.e. Philo, *Spec. Leg.* 4.164; Wis. 10.10; *Sentences of Sextus* 310-12). He has overlooked *Pss. Sol.* 17.3, which is a Palestinian Jewish text dating to the first century BCE. Mack doubts that it is necessary to understand Jesus' proclamation of the kingdom in terms of Jewish ideology. His position is odd and implausible on many counts and may even stand in tension with the fact that two of the three texts he cites are themselves Jewish.

14. For more on Daniel and Jesus' proclamation of the Kingdom of God, see D. Wenham, 'The Kingdom of God and Daniel', *ExpTim* 98 (1987), pp. 132-34.

Dan. 7.22 Θ	καὶ ὁ **καιρὸς ἔφθασεν** καὶ τὴν **βασιλείαν**
	κατέσχον οἱ ἅγιοι
Mk 1.15	πεπλήρωται ὁ **καιρὸς** καὶ ἤγγικεν ἡ **βασιλεία**
	τοῦ θεοῦ
Mt. 12.28 = Lk. 11.20	**ἔφθασεν** ἐφ᾿ ὑμᾶς ἡ **βασιλεία** τοῦ θεοῦ

Bruce Chilton has also shown that Jesus' words, 'the kingdom of God has come', cohere with the interpretive Aramaic paraphrase of Isaiah. Hebrew Isaiah's 'Behold your God' (40.9) and 'Your God reigns' (52.7) become in the Isaiah Targum 'The Kingdom of your God is revealed' (cf. Mic. 4.7-8; Zech. 14.9). Although this Aramaic tradition is preserved in Targums that post-date the time of Jesus by several centuries, there is good reason to believe that they contain primitive verbal, thematic and exegetical traditions. In the case of Jesus' proclamation of the kingdom of God it is probable that the Isaiah Targum retains language similar to what was in circulation in the synagogue of Jesus' day.[15] The significance of the fact that in the Isaiah Targum the kingdom of God is understood as something *to be proclaimed* should not be overlooked, for in no other Jewish literature of late antiquity do we find this association.[16]

Jesus' proclamation of the kingdom of God is thus coherent with certain Jewish traditions. These traditions envision God as king, as well as a kingdom of God that will supersede all of the human kingdoms. In this respect, Jesus' proclamation is no different. Yet Jesus' proclamation is somewhat distinctive. The author of Daniel, the Dead Sea Scrolls, and the Aramaic paraphrase of Isaiah anticipate *the coming* of the kingdom of God. Jesus proclaims it *as having come*. This sense of fulfillment, which Jesus apparently linked to his own ministry and to his own time, involves some interesting, perhaps unique features. To these features I now turn.

15. B.D. Chilton, *God in Strength: Jesus' Announcement of the Kingdom* (SNTU.B, 1; Freistadt: Plöchl, 1979; repr.; BibSem, 8; Sheffield: JSOT Press, 1987), pp. 86-90; cf. *idem, The Glory of Israel: The Theology and Provenience of the Isaiah Targum* (JSOTSup, 23; Sheffield: JSOT Press, 1983), pp. 77-81; C.A. Evans, 'From Gospel to Gospel: The Function of Isaiah in the New Testament', in C.C. Broyles and C.A. Evans (eds.), *Writing and Reading the Scroll of Isaiah: Studies of an Interpretive Tradition* (VTSup, 70.2; FIOTL, 1.2; Leiden: E.J. Brill, 1997), pp. 651-91, esp. pp. 664-74.

16. See P. Stuhlmacher, *Das paulinische Evangelium* (FRLANT, 95; Göttingen: Vandenhoeck & Ruprecht, 1968), pp. 147-49; *idem*, 'The Pauline Gospel', in *idem*

2. *Jubilee Proclamation*

One of the most important passages in the dominical tradition is the exchange between Jesus and the questioning, imprisoned John the Baptist. The tradition has been preserved in Q and is accepted by most as authentic.[17] The text reads:

> [John] sent word by his disciples and said to him, 'Are you he who is to come, or shall we look for another?' And Jesus answered them, 'Go and tell John what you hear and see: the blind receive their sight and the lame walk, lepers are cleansed and the deaf hear, and the dead are raised up, and the poor have good news preached to them. And blessed is he who takes no offense at me' (Mt. 11.2-6 = Lk. 7.19-23).

What does John's question tell us of the Baptist's expectations of Jesus? What does Jesus' reply to John tell us about the former's self-understanding? Is it messianic, or something else? What meaning have the numerous allusions to passages from Isaiah?[18]

(ed.), *The Gospel and the Gospels* (Grand Rapids: Eerdmans, 1991), pp. 149-72, (162-63). See the point made of this observation in Chilton, *God in Strength*, pp. 277-79, with n. 2.

17. See J.A. Fitzmyer, *The Gospel According to Luke I–IX* (AB, 28; Garden City, NY: Doubleday, 1981), p. 663. Not surprisingly, the Jesus Seminar gives the material a black rating, indicating that they think it is not authentic. Their reasoning for this decision is quite revealing: '[Jesus' reply] is ... taken from scripture, which means this response is a piece of Christian apologetic ...'; cf. R.W. Funk and R.W. Hoover (eds.), *The Five Gospels: The Search for the Authentic Words of Jesus* (Sonoma, CA: Polebridge Press; New York: Macmillan, 1993), pp. 177-78. One of the dubious assumptions of the Seminar, for which they have been sharply criticized, is that Jesus himself had little interest in Israel's Scriptures or their fulfillment. This is not to deny the presence of Christian interpretation, however. Matthean redaction is seen in the mention in 11.2 of 'the works of the Messiah'. Lukan redaction is seen in 7.21, where Jesus busily performs miracles in the very presence of John's messengers. But the core of the material surely goes back to the *Sitz im Leben Jesu*, for it is inconceivable that early Christians would invent a dialogue between John and Jesus where the former expresses doubts in the calling of the latter. The concluding saying, 'Blessed is he who takes no offense at me', is in all probability authentic; as a Church formulation it constitutes an odd Christian recommendation of Jesus. R. Bultmann (*The History of the Synoptic Tradition* [Oxford: Basil Blackwell, 1972], p. 126) accepts Mt. 11.5-6 = Lk. 7.22-23 as authentic because of its eschatological orientation.

18. On the presence of the words and phrases from Isaiah in this Q tradition, see F. Neirynck, 'Q 6,20b-21; 7,22 and Isaiah 61', in C.M. Tuckett (ed.), *The*

One of the more celebrated of the recently published Scrolls, 4Q521, may help us answer these questions. According to 4Q521 2 + 4.ii.1-13:

[1][...For the hea]vens and the earth shall listen to his Messiah [2][and all w]hich is in them shall not turn away from the commandments of the holy ones. [3]Strengthen yourselves, O you who seek the Lord, in his service. (*vacant*) [4]Will you not find the Lord in this, all those who hope in their heart? [5]For the Lord seeks the pious and calls the righteous by name. [6]Over the humble his spirit hovers, and he renews the faithful in his strength. [7]For he will honor the pious upon the th[ro]ne of the eternal kingdom, [8]setting prisoners free, opening the eyes of the blind, raising up those who are bo[wed down.] [9]And for [ev]er (?) I (?) shall hold fast [to]the [ho]peful and pious [...] [10]...[...]...shall not be delayed [...] [11]and the Lord shall do glorious things which have not been done, just as he said. [12]For he will heal the critically wounded, he shall revive the dead, he shall proclaim good news to the afflicted, [13]he shall...[...the...], he shall lead the [...], and the hungry he shall enrich (?).[19]

This text borrows words and phrases from Ps. 146.6-8 ('heaven and earth...and all that is in them ... YHWH opens the eyes of the blind'), Isa. 35.5 ('the eyes of the blind shall be opened') and 61.1 ('anointed ... to proclaim good news to the afflicted... liberty to prisoners ... opening of the eyes'). It is possible too that Isa. 53.5 ('he was critically wounded [מְחֹלָל] for our transgressions, he was bruised for our iniqui-ties... and with his stripes we are healed [4]') lies behind the anticipa-tion that God will 'heal the critically wounded' (רפא חללים). The hymn of the Suffering Servant goes on to speak of the servant's death (Isa. 53.9, 12), but says that he will see offspring and will have his days prolonged (53.10). Again, the fate of the Suffering Servant possibly

Scriptures in the Gospels (BETL, 131; Leuven: Leuven University Press, 1997), pp. 27-64.

19. Adapted from M.G. Abegg's translation, in M.O. Wise, M.G. Abegg, Jr and E.M. Cook, *The Dead Sea Scrolls: A New Translation* (San Francisco: HarperSan-Francisco, 1996), p. 421. For Hebrew text and critical discussion, see E. Puech, 'Une apocalypse messianique (4Q521)', *RevQ* 15 (1992), pp. 475-522; J.D. Tabor and M.O. Wise, '4Q521 "On Resurrection" and the Synoptic Gospel Tradition: A Pre-liminary Study', *JSP* 10 (1992), pp. 149-62; R. Bergmeier, 'Beobachtungen zu 4 Q 521.f.2, II, 1-13', *ZDMG* 145 (1995), pp. 38-48; J.J. Collins, 'The Works of the Messiah', *DSD* 1 (1994), pp. 98-112; *idem*, *The Scepter and the Star: The Messiahs of the Dead Sea Scrolls and Other Ancient Literature* (ABRL, 10; New York: Doubleday, 1995), pp. 117-22; K.-W. Niebuhr, 'Die Werke eschatologischen Freud-enboten (4Q521 und die Jesusüberlieferung)', in C.M. Tuckett (ed.), *The Scriptures in the Gospels* (BETL, 131; Leuven: Leuven University Press, 1997), pp. 637-46;

underlies 4Q521's 'he shall revive the dead' (ומתים יחיה). Another, and better, possibility is Isa. 26.19's 'your dead shall live, their bodies shall rise' (יחיו מתיך נבלתי יקומון).[20] The parallels between 4Q521 and Jesus' reply to John are remarkable:

Q (Mt. 11.5 = Lk. 7.22)	Isa. 35, 26, 61	4Q521
he cured many of diseases		heal the wounded
blind receive sight	blind receive sight	make blind see
lame walk	lame walk	
lepers are cleansed		
deaf hear	deaf hear	
dead are raised up	their dead bodies will rise	revive the dead
poor have good	poor have good	poor have good
news preached	news preached	news preached

John Collins has suggested that 4Q521 describes the expected activity of a prophetic Messiah, probably not a royal figure.[21] Collins could be correct, for there is a citation of part of Mal. 3.24 in 2.iii.2 ('the fathers will return to the sons'). Malachi may also be alluded to in the Baptist's question to Jesus: 'Are you he who is to come [ὁ ἐρχόμενος]?' (cf. Mal. 3.1 ἰδοὺ ἔρχεται). Another supporting point is the observation that Isaiah 61 concerns someone anointed to 'bring good news' and to 'proclaim liberty' and 'the year of the Lord's favor'. These are the responsibilities of a prophet. Indeed, the Targum renders Isa. 61.1: 'The

J. Zimmermann, *Messianische Texte aus Qumran: Königliche, priesterliche und prophetische Messiasvorstellungen in den Schriftfunden von Qumran* (WUNT, 2.104; Tübingen: Mohr Siebeck, 1998), p. 344. For photographs, see PAM 41.676 and 43.604.

20. For some differences in analysis, see Zimmermann, *Messianische Texte aus Qumran*, pp. 344-47, 377-78. Zimmermann is correct in seeing Ps. 146 and Isa. 61 as the most important texts underlying 4Q521. Zimmermann's phrase-by-phrase and word-by-word analysis of this portion of 4Q521 is the most detailed to appear since Puech's study in 1992.

21. Collins, 'The Works of the Messiah', pp. 99-106; *idem, The Scepter and the Star*, pp. 118-19, 205. Zimmermann (*Messianische Texte aus Qumran*, pp. 379-86, 388-89) agrees with Collins, though he is more open to other related possibilities. Niebuhr ('Die Werke eschatologischen Freudenboten', p. 638) asserts that 'identification of the Anointed of line 1 with the End-Time Davidic, prophetic or priestly Messiah is, in my opinion, questionable'. Niebuhr instead thinks this anointed personage is a priest who proclaims the interpretation of Torah. I think Niebuhr minimizes the eschatological thrust of this scroll.

Prophet said, "A spirit of prophecy ... is upon me ... to announce good news ...""

11QMelch explicitly links the jubilee legislation of Leviticus 25 with Isa. 61.1-3 and declares that it is to be fulfilled 'in the last days' (2.4). Scholars have rightly studied this text as a possible backdrop to Jesus' use of Isaiah 61 (as in Mt. 11.5 = Lk. 7.22; cf. Lk. 4.16-30) and his pronouncements of the forgiveness of debts/sins (cf. Mk 2.5; Lk. 7.36-50). The eschatological figure envisioned in 11QMelch is probably based on the expected prophet like Moses and/or the second coming of Elijah.[22]

Part of the jubilee is the announcement of liberation from Satan. The exorcisms were for Jesus evidence of the powerful presence of the kingdom of God and of the binding and defeat of Satan. Perhaps his most distinctive saying, Jesus is remembered to have said: 'If it is by the finger of God that I cast out demons, then the kingdom of God has come upon you' (Lk. 11.20).

Here again we have another important parallel with Qumran:

> [5]This shall be the sign that this shall come to pass: when the sources of evil are shut up and wickedness is banished in the presence of righteousness, as darkness in the presence of [6]light, or as smoke vanishes and is no more, in the same way wickedness will vanish forever and righteousness will be manifest like the sun. [7]The world will be made firm and all the adherents of the secrets of <sin> [MS: wonder] shall be no more. True knowledge shall fill the world and there will never be any more folly. [8]This is all ready to happen, it is a true oracle, and by this it shall be known to you that it cannot be averted (1QMyst 1.i.5-8).[23]

The 'sign' of the eschatological moment, according to this text, is 'when the sources of evil are shut up'. Now it is true that the 'evil' and 'wickedness' envisioned in this text are probably to be understood as human beings—wicked Gentiles and apostate Jews—but elsewhere Qumran teaches that Satan (or Belial) and his minions are the ultimate source of human evil. For Jesus, too, the sign of the eschatological moment is the shutting up of evil. But for Jesus this means the liberation of humans who are held in bondage to evil.

---

22. For critical discussion of this scroll, see Zimmermann, *Messianische Texte aus Qumran*, pp. 389-412. Zimmermann rightly concludes that 11QMelch envisions the coming of an anointed prophet, based on Deut. 18.15-18 or Mal. 3.23-24, who will proclaim the kingdom of God and the forgiveness of sins.

23. Translation from Wise, Abegg, Jr, and Cook, *The Dead Sea Scrolls*, p. 176.

According to *T. Mos.* 10.1, 'Then his [viz. God's] kingdom will appear throughout his whole creation. Then the devil will have an end.' The linkage between the appearance of the kingdom of God and the demise of Satan is presupposed in Jesus' teaching also. In Mk 3.23-27 Jesus counters the charge that he is casting out evil spirits through the power of Satan: 'If Satan has risen up against himself and is divided, he cannot stand, but is coming to an end'. The last part of this saying, 'is coming to an end' (τέλος ἔχει), is the equivalent of the Latin's 'will have an end' (*finem habebit*) of the *Testament of Moses*. This is a remarkable parallel. It should also be noted that some think the *Testament of Moses* is an Essene document, though not attested in the fragments of the region of the Dead Sea.

3. *Criticism of Temple Establishment*

Jesus' criticisms of the Jerusalem Temple establishment are again consistent with criticisms found in the Scrolls and in other sources. In the Qumran commentary on Habakkuk, Jerusalem's High Priest is called the 'Wicked Priest' (1QpHab 1.13; 8.9; 9.9; 11.4). In a few places he is accused of robbing the people, including the poor (1QpHab 8.12; 9.5; 10.1; 12.10; cf. CD 6.16), and of amassing wealth (1QpHab 8.8-12; 9.4-5; cf. CD 6.15). Similarly, 4QpNah 1.11 refers to 'riches that he [the Wicked Priest?] heaped up in the Temple of Jerusalem'. It is likely, however, that the Wicked Priest of these commentaries originally referred to one of the Hasmonean priest-kings (cf. 1QpHab 8.8-11). Therefore, one might assume that the Habakkuk commentary does not represent the views of the Qumran community, and the Essenes in general, in the time of Jesus. But I cannot agree with such an assumption. Admittedly, the Wicked Priest of this pesher originally had nothing to do with Caiaphas, or any other High Priest of the first century, but I suspect that Qumran's critical views of the high priesthood in Jesus' time were essentially the same as those of the earlier generation. One reason for this suspicion rests upon the eschatological orientation of the Qumran community in general and in the Habakkuk pesher in particular. According to 1QpHab 7.1-2 the events described were to happen in the 'last generation'. In light of the fact that every generation of the covenanters of Qumran believed that theirs was the final generation, it is probable that every Jersualem High Priest was identified, at least potentially, as the Wicked Priest.

Apparently Jesus also viewed the Temple establishment, particularly the ruling priests, as an oppressor of the poor. He regarded the qorban tradition as potentially contrary to the commandment that enjoins support and honor for one's parents (Mk 7.9-13; cf. Exod. 20.12). These vows usually had to do with goods dedicated to the Temple. Jesus warned of the scribes 'who devour widows' houses' (Mk 12.38-40). Economic oppression, evidently in the name of religion, is clearly in view. As is observed by the context, the Markan evangelist evidently thought that these (Sadducean?) scribes had something to do with the Temple establishment. In the next pericope (Mk 12.41-44) Jesus' comment concerning the widow who threw her penny into the Temple treasury was likely originally a word of lament, not of praise. That is, he lamented the fact that the Temple had become an economic burden to the poor and not the source of relief that it should have been (cf. CD 6.21, where the Temple establishment is criticized for not supporting 'the hand of the needy, the poor, and the stranger'). In many of Jesus' sayings there is clear evidence of a bias in favor of the poor and of warning for the rich (Mt. 5.3; 6.19-34; Mk 10.17-22, 23-31; Lk. 6.24-26; 12.15-21; 14.12-14, 15-24; 16.19-25; 19.1-9).

Qumran also questioned certain aspects of the pragmata of the Jerusalem Temple establishment (e.g. regarding the Temple tax, 4QOrd[a] 1.ii.6-8; cf. Mt. 17.24-27; regarding the calendar, 1QpHab 11.6-14; regarding clean and unclean, CD 11.18–12.2; regarding covenant, 4QpsMos[e]).[24] Jesus' demonstration in the Temple precincts (Mk 11.15-18), whatever its specific occasion, in all probability constituted a prophetic complaint against perceived corruption, improper halakah, or both.[25]

24. H. Ringgren, *The Faith of Qumran: Theology of the Dead Sea Scrolls* (Philadelphia: Fortress Press, 1963), pp. 214-29; C.A. Evans, 'Opposition to the Temple: Jesus and the Dead Sea Scrolls', in J.H. Charlesworth (ed.), *Jesus and the Dead Sea Scrolls* (ABRL, 4; New York: Doubleday, 1992), pp. 235-53; J.C. VanderKam, 'Calendrical Texts and the Origins of the Dead Sea Community', in M.O. Wise, N. Golb, J.J. Collins and D.G. Pardee (eds.), *Methods of Investigation of the Dead Sea Scrolls and the Khirbet Qumran Site: Present Realities and Future Prospects* (Annals of the New York Academy of Sciences, 722; New York: The New York Academy of Sciences, 1994), pp. 371-86; B.Z. Wacholder, 'The Historiography of Qumran: The Sons of Zadok and their Enemies', in F.H. Cryer and T.L. Thompson (eds.), *Qumran between the Old and New Testaments* (JSOTSup, 290; CIS, 6; Sheffield: Sheffield Academic Press, 1998), pp. 347-77.

25. B.D. Chilton, *The Temple of Jesus: His Sacrificial Program within a*

Just as Qumran predicted the destruction of the Temple establishment (1QpHab 9.2-7; 12.3-5), so Jesus predicted the demise of the ruling priests in his Parable of the Wicked Vineyard Tenants (Mk 12.1-12) and explicitly predicted the doom of the Temple (Mk 13.2).[26] Neither the Markan contextualizaton of the vineyard parable[27] or the authenticity of the prediction of the Temple's destruction should be rejected.[28] The doom of the Temple establishment is due to its alignment with the forces that oppose God and his redemptive, restorative purposes for Israel. In broad outline the eschatological expectations of Jesus and those expressed in the sectarian writings found among the Dead Sea Scrolls are in essential agreement.

4. *Conclusion*

The three themes that have been briefly considered are related and form an eschatological collocation, or paradigm, that strongly suggests that Jesus' proclamation and self-understanding may helpfully be viewed as in a broad sense parallel to ideas at Qumran. This is not to say that Jesus was a member of Qumran or that he even was acquainted with the Essenes. Jesus' very different style of ministry ('eating and drinking … a friend of tax collectors and sinners') strongly argues against such an hypothesis.

Cultural History of Sacrifice (University Park: Penn State Press, 1992), pp. 91-111; C.A. Evans, 'Jesus and the "Cave of Robbers": Toward a Jewish Context for the Temple Action', *BBR* 3 (1993), pp. 93-110.

26. The Scrolls anticipate the demise of the Temple establishment, but not necessarily the Temple buildings themselves.

27. 4QBen attests the Aramaic interpretation of Isa. 5.1-7 that some scholars recently have suggested underlies Jesus' Parable of the Wicked Vineyard Tenants. The complexity of the Hebrew/Aramaic exegesis presupposed by this parable argues against the parable's creation by the church and against the claim of some that the parable's contextualization in the Gospel of Mark is due to the evangelist, not to reliable tradition. On these points, see C.A. Evans, 'On the Vineyard Parables of Isaiah 5 and Mark 12', *BZ* 28 (1984), pp. 82-86; B.D. Chilton, *A Galilean Rabbi and his Bible: Jesus' Use of the Interpreted Scripture of his Time* (GNS, 8; Wilmington, DE: Michael Glazier, 1984), pp. 111-16; G.J. Brooke, '4Q500 1 and the Use of Scripture in the Parable of the Vineyard', *DSD* 2 (1995), pp. 268-94.

28. Anticipations of the destruction of the Second Temple are attested in many texts; cf. C.A. Evans, 'Predictions of the Destruction of the Herodian Temple in the Pseudepigrapha, Qumran Scrolls, and Related Texts', *JSP* 10 (1992), pp. 89-147;

Jesus' proclamation of the kingdom of God, informed by ideas of forgiveness of debts/sins, and criticisms of the Temple establishment for failing to meet the expectations of the prophetic tradition form a coherent and calculated agenda; these elements should not be viewed as ad hoc, spontaneous or unrelated. These integrated elements comprise the aims of Jesus, whose central goal was the restoration of Israel. The Covenanters of Qumran nurtured similar aims. These men also spoke of a celestial kingdom, anticipated the overthrow of the corrupt Temple establishment, and the inauguration of a restorative, rectifying jubilee.

The Dead Sea Scrolls assist researchers in clarifying significant themes and emphases in Jesus' teaching and public activities and at the same time encourage us to situate Jesus in a Jewish Palestine (more than a Hellenistic one) that fostered movements keenly interested in the divinely empowered restoration of Israel. The parallel patterns observed in the Scrolls stand in tension with some of the popular hypotheses put forward in some circles in recent years, namely that Jesus' teaching and ministry are significantly clarified against the backdrop of Hellenism, even Cynicism.[29]

5. Postscript: Reflections on the Panel Discussion

Several interesting topics were raised during the panel discussion, some of which I would like to address in the paragraphs below. The first concerns sources and criteria of authenticity. I am in essential agreement with James Robinson's paper and comments regarding the presence and usefulness of primitive clusters of dominical tradition in Q, regardless of one's position on the question of 'layers' in Q, speculations about the *Sitz im Leben* of each of these hypothetical layers, or whether or not Q was a unified literary unit or 'Gospel'. In my view, the hazard of Q research for investigation of the historical Jesus lies in the assumption that Q's contents perhaps represents virtually all of the authentic dominical tradition. In other words, what is not in Q is often viewed as late and secondary, including the narrative traditions provided by Mark. Although Robinson himself did not state or imply this in his paper or comments, some Q scholars apparently do operate on these assumptions.

repr. in J.H. Charlesworth (ed.), *Qumran Questions* (BibSem, 36; Sheffield: Sheffield Academic Press, 1995), pp. 92-150.

29. I criticize the 'Cynic hypothesis' in the Postscript that follows.

Two caveats are in order: (1) we cannot be certain that Matthew and
Luke preserve all of Q; Q may very well have been longer than what
has been preserved in the two evangelists;[30] (2) we cannot be certain of
Q's theological *Tendenz* or the extent of its access to dominical tradition. Accordingly, we must avoid arguments from silence. For example, what is not in Q (e.g. miracles or passion) is not necessarily
rejected by the Q 'community', nor is it necessarily late and inauthentic.
Leif Vaage's paper, read in the Q section of the meeting,[31] offers an
example of what I think is an inappropriate inference. Because the
function of Scripture in Q 7.22 (Jesus' reply to John's question) is
unlike the function of Scripture elsewhere in Q, Vaage suspects that this
saying is inauthentic. On the contrary, the observation that this tradition
stands in tension with Q tradition and its editorial tendency supports its
authenticity. Q 7.22 may not reflect the Q compiler's preferred use of
Jewish Scripture, but this in no way suggests that the tradition is
inauthentic. The further observation that John's question ('Are you the
one who is coming, or should we look for another?') surely occasioned
embarrassment for the early community also recommends authenticity,
for it is highly improbable that the early Church created such tradition.[32]
Furthermore, it strikes me as odd procedure to dismiss tradition as inauthentic because it fits awkwardly within the context of a hypothetical

30. C.A. Evans, 'Authenticating the Words of Jesus', in B. Chilton and C.A.
Evans (eds.), *Authenticating the Words of Jesus* (NTTS, 28.1; Leiden: E.J. Brill,
1998), pp. 3-14. In this study I show that a reconstructed Mark, based solely on
what is preserved by both Matthew and Luke, provides an insufficient basis for
modern redactional and literary theories of the Markan evangelist's purpose for
writing. I suggest that Matthew and Luke probably do not preserve all of Q, just as
they do not preserve all of Mark. On Q's being longer than scholars often assume,
see C.E. Carlston and D. Norlin, 'Once More—Statistics and Q', *HTR* 64 (1971),
pp. 59-78; *idem*, 'Statistics and Q—Some Further Observations', *NovT* 41 (1999),
pp. 108-123. Carlston and Norlin conclude that the Matthean and Lukan evangelists
follow the wording of Q somewhat more closely than that of Mark. From this and
other factors they conclude, rightly in my judgment, that Q was indeed written
tradition.

31. L. Vaage, 'Q and Jewish Scripture: Where, How, and Why' (read 19 July
1999).

32. On the authenticity criteria of 'tradition contrary to editorial tendency' and
'embarrassment', see D.G.A. Calvert, 'An Examination of the Criteria for Distinguishing the Authentic Words of Jesus', *NTS* 18 (1972), pp. 209-219; Meier, *A
Marginal Jew*, I, pp. 168-71; C.A. Evans, *Life of Jesus Research: An Annotated
Bibliography* (NTTS, 24; Leiden: E.J. Brill, 1996), pp. 134-36.

Sitz im Leben of a hypothetical source. The question of authenticity should be determined in the light of the full dominical tradition and its place in the context of Jesus and the broader context of Jewish Palestine. I agree with Robinson that there are primitive clusters of material in Q,[33] and these clusters do not necessarily fit smoothly, literarily or theologically, in their Q context.

Gerald Downing questions the general usefulness of the authenticity criteria. It is to be admitted that some criteria have been misused. Two come readily to mind: (1) Semitic and Palestinian features; and (2) double dissimilarity. The first criterion provides general support for authenticity, but scarcely provides certainty of the *ipsissima verba Jesu*, for the presence of Aramaic or Palestinian tradition just as easily points to the early Aramaic-speaking Church as it does to Jesus. The second criterion has been used to rule out sayings of Jesus, because they are not dissimilar to emphases in the early Church and to tendencies in early Judaism. The negative employment of this criterion is dubious (the criterion either supports or fails to support a given saying; it cannot rule it out), while insistence of dissimilarity to Jewish tendencies is illogical and unwarranted.[34]

Downing expressed reservations because the criteria are based on generalities. In my paper I appealed to dissimilarity and embarrassment. Implicit is the assumption that certain sayings and activities of Jesus would have been embarrassing to many, even most Christians, while others would not have reflected emphases of many Christians. Downing counters, saying that these traditions, embarrassing to some, even many, may not have been embarrassing to others. Therefore, what is embarrassing to most Christians may have been the invention of an individual or small group for whom the saying held no embarrassment.

Downing's hypothetical scenario is to some extent plausible. But does it realistically account for *all* sayings supported by these criteria? Study of ancient history involves probabilities, not certainties, and not even possibilties. Accordingly, we can never know for certain that Jesus really

---

33. J.M. Robinson, 'Early Collections of Jesus' Sayings', in J. Delobel (ed.), *Logia: Les paroles de Jesus* (BETL, 59; Leuven: Leuven University Press, 1982), pp. 389-94; *idem*, 'A Written Greek Sayings Cluster Older than Q: A Vestige', *HTR* 92 (1999), pp. 61-77.

34. For trenchant criticism of the dissimilarity criterion, see T. Holmén, 'Doubts about Double Dissimilarity: Restructuring the Main Criterion of Jesus-of-History Research', in Chilton and Evans (eds.), *Authenticating the Words of Jesus*, pp. 47-80.

said this and did that. The historian, however, is content with discovering what Jesus *probably said and probably did*. To discount the criteria of authenticity on the grounds that most of the sayings supported by these criteria may very well be products of fringe groups whose odd 'sayings' somehow slipped into the dominical tradition is in essence special pleading. If one believes that such a high degree of skepticism is called for, then pursuit of the historical Jesus becomes futile and pointless.

In his own presentation, Downing underscores the importance of the parallels between certain sayings of Jesus and sayings attributed to Cynics or to Cynic sources.[35] Again, we are faced with what is probable, not what is merely possible. Is it possible that Jesus encountered Cynics, perhaps at nearby Sepphoris, and adopted some of their teachings and lifestyle? Yes, it is possible, but the question should be: is it probable? Jesus grew up in Nazareth, only a stone's throw from a synagogue. Throughout the Gospel tradition we are presented with a Jesus who frequents the synagogue, debates aspects of Scripture and Israel's sacred tradition, and proclaims the kingdom of God. Given the context of Jewish Palestine in general and these pervasive tendencies in the Gospel tradition, is the Cynic hypothesis compelling? I don't think so.

Geza Vermes's holy man hypothesis was dismissed out of hand, as lacking sufficient evidence, but it has some supporting evidence (in Josephus, in reference to Honi the Circle-Drawer, and in rabbinic literature, in reference to Hanina ben Dosa and others, some of whom were Galilean contemporaries of Jesus) and, in any event, there is more evidence for the presence of Jewish holy men in early first-century Jewish Palestine than for a Cynic presence. Downing points to Jesus' repudiation of wealth as evidence of Cynicism. By this reasoning are the Essenes, whose members renounced private property, Cynics also? Downing notes that Jesus, like Cynics, made use of parables in his teaching. By this reasoning does this make the rabbis Cynics, because of their usage of parables? Downing points to several parallels between Jesus and Cynics, parallels found nowhere else. He finds this compelling evidence of Jesus' Cynic orientation. But how close are these

---

35. Besides his paper in the present volume, see his *Christ and the Cynics: Jesus and Other Radical Preachers in First-Century Tradition* (Manuals, 4; Sheffield: JSOT Press, 1988); *idem, Cynics and Christian Origins* (Edinburgh: T. & T. Clark, 1992); *idem*, 'Deeper Reflections on the Jewish Cynic Jesus', *CBQ* 117 (1998), pp. 97-104.

parallels? Are all of these parallels truly of Cynic origin?[36] Robinson, moreover, rightly commented that traditions that describe Cynic garb simply do not agree with the alleged parallel tradition in the Gospels. More significantly, Robinson pointed out that Jesus' attitude to food and clothing was fundamentally different from the Cynic attitude. Jesus believed in *God* for provision of life's necessities; this was not the rationale that lay behind the Cynic view of property and provisions.[37] Finally, with John Dominic Crossan, as well as Downing, in mind, nearby Sepphoris provides little support for the Cynic hypothesis, for recent archaeological work has revealed how pervasive the Jewish presence was in this city.[38] Indeed, as David Aune has remarked, there is 'no literary or archaeological evidence for a Cynic presence in first-century Galilee'.[39]

36. See the criticisms raised against the Cynic hypothesis, in C.M. Tuckett, 'A Cynic Q?', *Bib* 70 (1989), pp. 349-76; H.D. Betz, 'Jesus and the Cynics: Survey and Analysis of a Hypothesis', *JR* 74 (1994), pp. 453-75; D.E. Aune, 'Jesus and Cynics in First-Century Palestine: Some Critical Considerations', in J.H. Charlesworth (ed.), *Hillel and Jesus: Comparisons of Two Major Religious Leaders* (Minneapolis: Fortress Press, 1997), pp. 176-92.

37. Recently M.A. Powell (*Jesus as a Figure in History: How Modern Historians View the Man from Galilee* [Louisville, KY: Westminster/John Knox Press, 1998], p. 63) has summed up the contrasts between Jesus and the Cynics: 'Cynics were Greeks and lived in the cities; Jesus was Jewish and wandered the countryside. Cynics had a strong this-worldly attitude; Jesus is represented as preaching about a coming kingdom of God, about life after death and the final judgment. Cynics were noted for embracing asceticism; Jesus, for avoiding it (Mk 2.18-19; Lk. 7.33-34). Cynics advocated dependence on self; Jesus, dependence on God (Mt. 6.25-33)'. J.M. Robinson ('The History-of-Religions Taxonomy of Q: The Cynic Hypothesis', in H. Preissler and H. Seiwert [eds.], *Gnosisforschung und Religionsgeschichte: Festschrift für Kurt Rudolph zum 65. Geburtstag* [Marburg: Diagonal-Verlag, 1994], pp. 247-65; *idem*, '*Galilean Upstarts*: A Sot's Cynical Disciples?', in W.L. Petersen *et al.* [eds.], *Sayings of Jesus: Canonical and Non-Canonical: Essays in Honour of Tjitze Baarda* (NovTSup, 89; Leiden: E.J. Brill, 1997], pp. 223-49) has also weighed in against the Cynic hypothesis, particularly in the form advocated by L.E. Vaage, *Galilean Upstarts: Jesus' First Followers According to Q* (Valley Forge, PA: Trinity Press International, 1994).

38. By 'Jewish presence' I mean Torah-observant Judaism. This is seen not only in the presence of a synagogue and various Jewish inscriptions and symbols, but in the ubiquity of *miqvaot* and stone water pots. See M. Chancey and E.M. Meyers, 'How Jewish was Sepphoris in Jesus' Time?', *BARev* 26.4 (2000), pp. 18-33, 61.

39. Aune, 'Jesus and Cynics in First-Century Palestine', p. 188. Menippus and

Downing's parallels and proposals are helpful—and we are all in his debt for assembling such a useful collection—but I am very doubtful that Jesus' thinking and behavior were truly of a Cynic nature. This is not to say that Cynic sayings had not entered Jewish Palestinian parlance; they may have and Downing may very well have identified some that did. The problem has to do with worldview, mission, theology, and the 'result' of Jesus' teaching and activities. Are these elements consistent with Cynic teaching and behavior?[40] Had Jesus truly been a Cynic, would he have been crucified as 'king of the Jews'? Would the Church have emerged, with its universal confession of Jesus as God's Messiah?

As a brief footnote to the above discussion, I have a comment about François Vouga's (unpublished) paper in which Jesus' parables are compared with Aesop's fables. I am somewhat mystified by the conclusion that 'form-critically considered, Aesop's fables are the closest parallels to the parables of Jesus'. There is nothing 'fabulous' about the parables of Jesus; for example, never in his parables do animals and trees talk. The characters and events of Jesus' parables are realistic, even if the behavior of the characters is sometimes unexpected, even irrational. Jesus' parables function much as do the juridical parables of the Old Testament, in which the hearer is invited to pass judgment upon himself. The Parable of the Ewe Lamb (2 Sam. 12.1b-4), the Parable of the Two Brothers (2 Sam. 14.4-7), the Parable of the Escaped Prisoner (1 Kgs 20.38-43), and Isaiah's famous Parable of the Fruitless Vineyard (Isa. 5.1-7) are probably the clearest examples of the juridical parable. Formally, however, Jesus' parables resemble those of the rabbis. Phrases such as 'to what may this be compared', 'it is like' and 'thus it shall be' are common in the parables of Jesus and the rabbis. In my opinion, with reference to *function* Jesus' parables are closest to the parables of the Old Testament prophets, while with reference to *form* Jesus' parables are closest to the parables of the rabbis. Aesop's fables probably have little to contribute to our understanding of Jesus' parables.

Oenomaus, two Cynics who hailed from nearby Gadara and who are frequently cited as evidence for a Cynic presence in Palestine, in fact did not embrace the Cynic lifestyle until after departing from their native city.

40. The self-reference as 'prophet' in Mk 6.4, which is surely authentic tradition, does not square easily with the Cynic hypothesis. In my estimation Markus Öhler's investigation of Jesus as prophet, 'Jesus as Prophet: Remarks on Terminology' (in this volume, pp. 125-42) is asking the correct questions.

I conclude with a few comments on Jesus' self-understanding. Robinson remarked that Jesus had a 'shocking dependence on God', which if recognized should help us understand much of the Jesus tradition. This is a good point. Faith in God, confidence in the Scriptures, and the conviction that Israel was God's chosen people are the essential ingredients that underlie individuals (such as John the Baptist, Theudas, and the Jew from Egypt) and movements (covenanters of Qumran, Josephus's 'fourth philosophy', and early Christianity) committed to the restoration of Israel.

In my view, the messianism of Jesus should be a given. Two data warrant this position: (1) Jesus' crucifixion as 'king of the Jews'; and (2) among his following the universal post-Easter confession of him as ὁ Χριστός are most plausibly explained as due to a messianic self-understanding prior to Easter.[41] Here I invoke the criterion of result. Elements in the dominical tradition, such as Q 7.22 (supported by the criterion of embarrassment and, in reference to Q, the criterion of tradition contrary to editorial tendency), provide corroboration for this conclusion. What is at issue is the nature of Jesus' messianism. Was it royal, or was it more of a prophetic nature? More importantly, what does this messianic self-understanding tell us about Jesus' mission and aims? It is to these questions that Jesus scholars should attend.

41. By now it should be clear to scholars working in this field that the Easter proclamation alone does not provide an adequate explanation of the universal confession of Jesus as Israel's Messiah. Had no messianism been present in the pre-Easter ministry, then the resurrection would not have generated it. Jewish messianism of Jesus' day cannot account for a shift from a pre-Easter non-messianism to a post-Easter messianism in the dominical tradition. See M. Hengel, 'Jesus, der Messias Israels', in I. Gruenwald *et al.* (eds.), *Messiah and Christos: Studies in the Jewish Origins of Christianity* (Festschrift D. Flusser; TSAJ, 32; Tübingen: Mohr Siebeck, 1992), pp. 155-76; expanded ET 'Jesus, the Messiah of Israel', in M. Hengel, *Studies in Early Christology* (Edinburgh: T. & T. Clark, 1995), pp. 1-72.

THE JEWISH CYNIC JESUS

F. Gerald Downing

I wish to advance a number of theses. Theses 1-9 I simply list and briefly explain some prior conclusions. Even though they are not uncontroversial at least it may be recognized that more than I hold them to be arguable; and supporting references are given in the footnotes. My intention here is to elaborate and support some further theses related more directly to the title of this essay. Even here the grounds for a defence of these will only be sketched.

1. *General Theses*

1. *It is entirely possible though by no means certain that the Synoptic traditions include quite a lot of quite good information about the meaningful activities of Jesus of Nazareth*: that is to say, we may through these documents be quite close to a range of Jesus' own intentional actions, including verbal communication.

My own reconstruction includes arguments for Q; but the Cynic-seeming matter in the Synoptic tradition warrants attention however the relationships between the documents are analysed.

It is, of course, also possible that very little if any of what is recorded goes back at all closely to Jesus ('the Jesus Seminar'), and scholarly reconstructions of the traditions can be assembled which ascribe most if not all to later creativity in the Christian communities. In the nature of things these can no more be conclusively proved than can the former possibility. The trouble with this choice of attribution is, as I argued more than 30 years ago, '*We do not know enough about Jesus to allow us to construct a clear account of the primitive church because we do not know enough about the primitive church to allow us to construct a clear account of Jesus*'.[1] But (as I also then went on the argue), neither

1. F.G. Downing, *The Church and Jesus* (SBT, 2.10; London: SCM Press,

do we have a clear enough picture of the contexts of Jesus or the early communities to shed decisive light on either. We are left with rival reconstructions which compete in terms of coherence and inclusiveness.[2] There is nothing to tell us before we start drafting our reconstructions, where the best balance of attributions must lie; and, however the decisions go, the Cynic-seeming elements still warrant attention.

2. *None of the traditions is to be ruled out in advance in our reconstructions.* The 'criteria' we use, albeit often shared, are internal to our reconstructions. If I (for instance) rule out some item from my reconstructed sketch of Jesus by the 'criterion of dissimilarity', that does not mean it must be ruled out of yours. What is 'dissimilar' or is contextually validated in your reconstruction (of Galilaean Judaism and Jesus and the communities that nursed the traditions of Jesus) may not be so in hers.[3]

3. *In our reconstructions we do best to discuss intentional actions, with verbal communication as a major sub-group*, rather than divide 'sayings' from 'narratives' (even though many scholars do that). 'Speech-act' analysis (J.L. Austin) has been taken up quite widely, but it has to work both ways: actions communicate, words perform.[4]

1968), p. 51 (original italics). It was gratifying to have this conclusion quoted with approval recently by D.C. Allison, *Jesus of Nazareth: Millenarian Prophet* (Minneapolis: Fortress Press, 1998), p. 5 n.17.

2.   Cf. F.G. Downing, 'The Social Contexts of Jesus the Teacher: Construction or Reconstruction', *NTS* 33 (1987), pp. 439-51; *idem, Jesus and the Threat of Freedom* (London: SCM Press, 1987), pp. 147-60. For brevity I list where possible my own previous work, but these do regularly include extensive interaction with others' arguments and proposals.

3.   Cf. Downing, *The Church and Jesus*, pp. 93-131; and the references in n. 2 above, and F.G. Downing, 'Shifting Sands', in *idem, Doing Things with Words in the First Christian Century* (JSNTSup, 200; Sheffield: Sheffield Academic Press, 2000), pp. 218-33 (esp. pp. 220-24); and among other recent discussions of 'criteria' (or 'indices'), J.P. Meier, *A Marginal Jew*. I. *The Roots of the Problem and the Person. Rethinking the Historical Jesus* (2 vols.; ABRL; New York: Doubleday, 1991), chap. 6, 'Criteria', pp. 167-95; G. Theissen, 'Historical Criticism and the Criteria of Jesus Research', *SJT* 49 (1996), pp. 147-76; Allison, *Jesus of Nazareth*, pp. 1-57.

4.   Cf. F.G. Downing, 'Words as Deeds and Deeds as Words', *BibInt* 3.2 (1995), pp. 129-43; repr. in *idem, Doing Things with Words*, pp. 41-56. J.L. Austin, *How to Do Things with Words* (Oxford: Clarendon Press, 1962). Austin is taken up by, among others, J.R. Searle, *Speech Acts: An Essay in the Philosophy of Language* (Cambridge: Cambridge University Press, 1969) and by e.g., J. Habermas,

4. *Intentional actions (with speech as an important and varied sub-group) presuppose a community with a shared even if diverse culture*, a 'language' of behaviour, including verbal behaviour. For innovation (innovative non-verbal/part-verbal action included) to register, be noteworthy, it must still reflect convention ('langue-parole-idiolect').[5]

5. *Action (thus including verbal utterance) is thus 'intertextually' structured*, significance depends on much more than discerning momentary limb movements or recognizing the bits of sentences which we call individual 'words'.[6]

6. *So, for Jesus (or Paul) to do things (including say things, including innovative things) that were noteworthy, significant in any sense, we must assume communities where not just the individual movements (including phonemes) were in use, but where the complexes (activities including utterances) that were intentionally deployed would be perceivable as intentional, purposeful, meaningful.*

It is not simply a matter of shared Aramaic or Greek, but of shared practices, shared kinds of sequences of activity (including speech). We might use such terms as 'roles', 'ideas' or 'concepts', though I myself prefer to avoid these, as suggesting undue precision and set boundaries. Better is Wittgenstein's 'family resemblances' ('Familienähnlichkeiten').[7]

7. So (to come a little closer to my announced subject matter), Jesus *could* (for instance) have used parable form(s) quite spontaneously, and/or chosen his particular range of subject matter (labourers, land-owners, housewives, plants…) without precedent. *However, it is more/most likely that others had been doing and saying some things of similar kinds, for Jesus (or anyone else) to repeat and/or innovate on that basis—and be understood, and be taken seriously by some.* So we have studies on 'New Testament background' (*Hintergrund? arrière-plan?*) or 'environment' (*Umwelt, milieu*) or (better) 'context' or 'intertext' (*Zusammenhang? contexte/intertexte?*)

Communication and the Evolution of Society (ET; London: Heinemann, 1979); cf. G. Theissen and A. Merz, *The Historical Jesus: A Comprehensive Guide* (ET; London: SCM Press, 1998), p. 283 n. 2, allowing the point argued; (orig. *Der historische Jesu: Eine Lehrbuch* [Göttingen: Vandenhoeck & Ruprecht, 1996]).

5. Searle, *Speech Acts*, p. 17, with reference to F. de Saussure.

6. See in particular L. Wittgenstein, *Philosophische Untersuchungen/Philosophical Investigations* (Oxford: Basil Blackwell, 1963).

7. Wittgenstein, *Philosophical Investigations*, §67 (p. 32).

8. *Quite simply, any plausible reconstruction of the activity of Jesus (or followers or Paul, etc.) must involve a plausible context*—plausible in terms of wider information, plausible in terms of the supposed person, the movement as reconstructed, and so on.[8]

9. *Sociological/anthropological/economic models may have considerable heuristic value, but they do not provide us with historical 'laws'.* There are no such laws of a kind that may tell us that some events otherwise unevidenced 'must' have happened, nor that specific social pressures must have been exerted irrespective of the data available to us, nor that happenings apparently evidenced could not have occurred.[9] (Physical laws are in a different category; even those who accept 'miracle' rely on physical regularities in their accounts.)

2. *Specific and Elaborated Theses*

10. *We have very little if any independent information relating to Galilee during the supposed time of Jesus' narrated activity there.* By 'independent' here I mean 'independent of the four Gospels'. They are the only documents we have that *purport* to tell us something specific about what some people were noteworthily and apparently thoughtfully doing (including saying) then and there. (Of course, they may in fact to a greater or lesser extent misinform us, and, anyway, do not always agree on how things were.)[10]

10.1 Josephus, not a native of Galilee, and writing later than most would date 'Q' and Mark, tells us very briefly of the Galilaean, Judas, his 'Fourth Philosophy' ('a passion for liberty, convinced that God alone is their master', *War* 2.118; *Ant.* 18.23) and the revolt Judas led, crushed by Varus (*War* 2.56, 58; *Ant.* 17.288-89); of Augustus confirming Herod Antipas as tetrarch (*War* 2.95; *Ant.* 17.318) and the latter's rebuilding

---

8. 'Plausibility' is a preferred term of Gerd Theissen's, and I acknowledge the value of some of his detailed suggestions, while disagreeing with the main thrust of many of his conclusions. See G. Theissen and A. Merz, *The Historical Jesus*, pp. 116-18, 122, 297, 310, 338-39.

9. Downing, *The Church and Jesus*, pp. 150-59.

10. On which see most cogently J.S. Kloppenborg Verbin, 'A Dog among the Pigeons: The Cynic Hypothesis as a Theological Problem', in J.M.A. Asgeirsson *et al.* (eds.), *From Quest to Q: Festschrift J.M. Robinson* (BETL, 146; Leuven: Peeters, 2000), pp. 72-117; cf. *idem*, 'A Dog among the Pigeons: A Cynic Q?', in *idem*, *Excavating Q: The History and Setting of the Sayings Gospel* (Edinburgh: T. & T. Clark, 2000), pp. 420-46.

of Sepphoris (*Ant.* 18.27) and founding of Tiberias (*War* 2.168; *Ant.* 18.36-38); after that, nothing about Galilee until we are told of the failed attempt to persuade Gaius to grant Antipas royal status (*Ant.* 18.240-56), and, later still, of the crowd at Tiberias that dissuaded Petronius from complying with Gaius's command to install a statue of himself in the Jerusalem Temple (*War* 2.184-203). What little Josephus tells in *The Jewish War* and in his *Life* of Galilee in the late 60s has only the most general relevance for Galilee 35 years earlier. I think that is all the documentary evidence we have for Galilee around Jesus' (supposed) time, and it is very sparse, even though some have thought to construct quite a lot largely on this meagre basis.

10.2. Josephus tells us a little more about Judaea and Jerusalem, and we might feel justified in extrapolating from that information; but others would rather point to signs of divergence between Judaea and Galilee.

10.3. We have documents from the Dead Sea caves, some of which may be contemporary with Jesus, or at least reflect practices and beliefs that were current in his day; but we have no clear indication that those who wrote and/or collected them (Essenes, I take it) had any close contacts with Jesus' Galilee. For what Josephus's information is worth, he never, on my reading, mentions Essenes in Galilee. As is well known, the Gospels do not refer to them.[11]

10.4. There are many other apocryphal and pseudepigraphical Jewish documents, besides those figuring in the Dead Sea finds, documents which could have had Galilaean links; but none to my knowledge claims Galilaean provenance, nor do any Gospel passages seem to quote let alone cite any such (save, perhaps, an allusion to the *Lives of the Prophets*—Lk. 11.47-50//13.33-34).

10.5. The Mishnah and other rabbinic writings were produced very much later. We may, obviously, nonetheless argue for their relevance in some reconstruction that we offer, but there are also strong arguments for their ethos belonging to that much later age, and not to our period and circumstances. They have no *automatic* right of inclusion among our data for early first-century Galilee.[12]

---

11. Cf. G.J. Brook's carefully guarded comparison between literary procedures in Luke and in some Dead Sea Scrolls, in his 'Qumran: The Cradle of Christ?', in *idem* (ed.), *The Birth of Jesus: Biblical and Theological Reflections* (Edinburgh: T. & T. Clark, 2000), pp. 23-34.

12. See especially, e.g., J. Neusner, *Messiah in Context* (Philadelphia: Fortress Press, 1984), Preface, pp. ix-xxiii; *idem*, 'Mishnah and Messiah', in *idem et al.*,

10.6. Our non-Jewish (including non-Christian) Graeco-Roman sources have no directly relevant information specifically about Galilee in the first third of the first century to add, either.

10.7. Archaeological evidence to date offers some leads—for instance, on the range of lifestyles that may have obtained—but little on the available range of people's enacted or spoken appraisals of their lives and possibilities, apart from the briefest of tomb inscriptions.[13] The implications of this material are disputed.

3. *Theses on Jesus' Context: The Evidence is Inconclusive*

11. *Since* we do not know for sure *from other sources the range of practices including the kinds of patterns of words which were the currency available to Jesus and his first followers, and have no clear independent leads, then, if we decide to proceed at all (and we might not, we might decide it better to give up at this stage),* we have to rely for indications of the possible context of Jesus and his first followers almost entirely on the Synoptic Gospels themselves, *for positive information and for controls on our other chosen sources.*[14]

On this basis we are plausibly still at liberty to consider a wide range of potentially illustrative materials, and check for better or worse matches. And this is in effect what scholars do, though their conclusions differ.

11.1. Seán Freyne's 1988 *Galilee, Jesus and the Gospels (GJG)* refers us back to his 1980 *Galilee from Alexander the Great to Hadrian 323 B.C.E. to 135 C.E. (GAGH)*, which relies mostly on Josephus (11 pp. of references) with four pages of rabbinic references, half a page of Greco-Roman authors.[15] There is no other major source of evidence,

Judaisms and their Messiahs (Cambridge: Cambridge University Press, 1987), pp. 265-82.

13. E.g. J.F. Strange, 'Archaeology and the Religion of Judaism in Palestine', *ANRW*, II, pp. 646-85; L.I. Levine (ed.), *The Galilee in Late Antiquity* (Cambridge, MA: Harvard University Press, 1992), pt. VI, 'Archaeological Evidence in the Galilee', pp. 289-371; R.A. Horsley, *Archaeology, History and Society in the Bible: The Social Context of Jesus and the Rabbis (AHSB)*, (Valley Forge, PA: Trinity Press International, 1996); see further, below.

14. On this and what follows, see the very helpful discussion by J.S. Kloppenborg Verbin, 'A Dog among the Pigeons: A Cynic Q?'.

15. S. Freyne, *Galilee from Alexander the Great to Hadrian 323 B.C.E. to 135 C.E. (GAGH)* (Wilmington, DE: Michael Glazier; Notre Dame: University of Notre

and the relevance of the rabbinic material used is (so it seems) assumed without argument in the earlier book, but curtailed in the second in the light of Jacob Neusner's arguments. The Gospels themselves provide most of the illustrations for generalities about peasants, share-croppers and urban landlords (*GJG*, pp. 143-55, 159-61). Galilee in Antipas's reign is seen as politically 'stable' (*GAGH*, p. 69; *GJG*, pp. 154, 161-66), specifically disagreeing with R.A. Horsley's espousal of a theory of 'social banditry' (while using the same data).[16] The ideology of Galilean peasants can only be conjectured, as a discontent with poverty and resentment of urban wealth (*GJG*, p. 167). Greek cultural influence on the peasant population can neither be ruled in nor ruled out, though hostility to wealthy Greek townspeople might indicate the latter (*GJG*, 171). 'If the gospels do not give us a very full picture of Galilean religious loyalties, our other literary sources are often as tantalisingly vague' (*GJG*, p. 177). A possible conclusion—also based in the Gospels —is that there was devotion to the Temple combined with hostility towards its wealthy aristocratic resident priesthood (including those resident in Sepphoris [*GJG*, p. 190]); there was a loyalty to Torah (evidenced from a few asides in Josephus, and without our being told the ways in which Torah was locally interpreted); and a commitment to the land expressed by the faithful payment of the tithes of its produce (*GJG*, p. 219).

Freyne in fact quotes with approval Vermes's conclusion summarized as 'perhaps the N. T. itself is our best guide to Palestinian Judaism in the first century' (*GJG*, p. 208).[17]

11.2. No important new data appear in L.I. Levine's 1992 publication from a 1989 conference on 'The Galilee in Late Antiquity'.[18] H.C. Kee

---

Dame Press, 1980; I have not seen the recent 2nd edn); and *idem*, *Galilee, Jesus and the Gospels* (*GJG*) (Dublin: Gill & Macmillan, 1988). In the latter Freyne allows that rabbinic matter reflects a different social age, pp. 213-28 with 192, 199, 202. See now *idem*, *Galilee and Gospel* (WUNT, 125; Tübingen: Mohr Siebeck, 2000), affirming while refirming previous conclusions.

16. R.A. Horsley and J.S. Hanson, *Bandits, Prophets and Messiahs: Popular Movements at the Time of Jesus* (New York: Seabury, 1985); and see further, below.

17. The reference given is to G. Vermes, *Jesus and the World of Judaism* (London: SCM Press, 1983), pp. 74-88.

18. Levine (ed.), *The Galilee in Late Antiquity*; in what follows are noted H.C. Kee, 'Early Christianity in the Galilee: Reassessing the Evidence from the Gospels', pp. 3-22; D. Edwards, 'The Socio-Economic and Cultural Ethos of the Lower Galilee in the First Century: Implications for the Nascent Jesus Movement', pp. 23-38;

argues both for a vigorous but informal synagogue activity and for 'extensive economic and cultural contact by inhabitants of Nazareth' with Sepphoris, and for a Jesus free to associate with those 'whose values and perspectives were so strongly influenced by Greco-Roman culture, in a bilingual Lower Galilee.'[19] D. Edwards emphasizes buying and selling linking (Jewish) villages and (Greek) towns. There is no sound basis for a 'cultural split'—nor for a wholesale acceptance of Greco-Roman culture.[20] (This is rebutted—not refuted—by Horsley, *AHSG*, pp. 118-19 and n. 27). S. Freyne distinguishes 'orthogenetic' and 'heterogenetic' cities in relation to their hinterlands, with rural Galilaeans more sympathetic to 'orthogenetic' Jerusalem, (further supporting his earlier conclusions summarized above), though he notes the evidence for Greek culture among the aristocratic urban leadership. E.M. Meyers points to a Torah-based population in Sepphoris (extra-mural burials; many miqva'ot—the latter dated later, and their Jewish character queried by Horsley, *AHSG*, p. 63), with no theatre as yet in Jesus' time; Sepphoris itself would not in Jesus' day have been a particular focus of Greek culture; but Meyers does not retract his earlier conclusion that this locally dominant culture would have been hard to escape.[21]

11.3. R.A. Horsley, in his 1995 *Galilee: History, Politics, People* (*GHPP*), and then in his 1996 *Archaeology, History and Society in Galilee* (*ASHG*)[22] insists that much more attention be given to the 'class division between the [urban] ruling strata … and the indigenous peasantry … whose background and culture has yet to be determined very clearly' (*GHPP*, pp. 7-8), for 'we do not know very much directly about Galilee and Galileans' (*GHPP*, p. 13). His declared preference is to avoid the Synoptic Gospels as a main source, unless they provide 'the primary or only source for a particular matter, when they suggest a

---

S. Freyne, 'Urban-Rural Relations in First-Century Galilee: Some Suggestions from the Literary Sources', pp. 75-94; E.M. Meyers, 'Roman Sepphoris in Light of New Archaeological Evidence and Recent Research', pp. 321-38, all in Levine (ed.), *The Galilee in Late Antiquity*.

19. Kee, 'Early Christianity', pp. 15, 19, 20. For an earlier report, see Strange, 'Archaelogy and the Religion of Judaism'.

20. Edwards, 'Ethos of the Lower Galilee', p. 71.

21. E.M. Meyers, 'The Cultural Setting', p. 698.

22. R.A. Horsley, *Galilee: History, Politics, People* (Valley Forge, PA: Trinity Press International, 1995); *idem, Archaeology, History and Society in Galilee* (Valley Forge, PA: Trinity Press International, 1996).

general pattern, or when some Jesus-saying offers a commentary on some matter established by other evidence' (*GHPP*, p. 14). Instead we have (for instance) 'extrapolations' from Deuteronomy and the Mishnah, after a token acknowledgment of the problematic nature of the procedure (*GHPP*, pp. 198-99). The picture of a market relationship between villagers and towns proposed by Freyne and others is rejected in favour of a different theoretical model supported from the Mishnah. Neusner's argument that the Mishnah represents a purely theoretical economics and does not reflect real life even at the end of the second century is dismissed as itself theoretical, but with no further argument (*GHPP*, pp. 202-203 and n. 9).[23] The evidence from pottery finds suggesting wider trading relations is to be interpreted to suit the earlier conclusions from the Mishnah (*AHSG*, pp. 70-76). People whose descendants ransacked a town cannot have themselves traded there (*AHSG*, p. 119). I would suggest that this is as arbitrary a basis for reconstruction as any Horsley criticizes, one model simply preferred to another, even if the result is itself still no less plausible. The evidence is compatible with the conclusions, but in no way demands them.

References to debt in the Gospels is acceptable evidence (*GHPP*, p. 219); it will support Horsley's case for 'economic banditry'. So, too, are critical references to urban wealth (*AHSG*, p. 121). Horsley is more sceptical than others reviewed here as to synagogue buildings in Galilee in the first century, doubting the interpretation of even the few that have been claimed; but is more convinced of the reality of village assemblies for what we might see as a wide range of community purposes (*GHPP*, pp. 227-33; *AHSG*, pp. 145-53); and again the Gospels are allowed to corroborate the much later Mishnah and the much earlier Judith. The Mishnah, however, is said to be misleading in its exclusion of women from public life (*GHPP*, pp. 235-37).

Having determined the structure of peasant society on the basis of general theory and some ambiguous archaeological evidence, with eclectic illustrations from Mishnah and Gospels, Horsley is able to determine what could and what could not comprise the culture of those among whom Jesus may have carried out his programme (*GHPP*, pp. 238-55). Although 'much of the population of Lower Galilee must have been able to communicate a bit in Greek', most oral communication

---

23. Horsley's confidence in his models is criticized by J. Schwartz, in his review of *GHPP* and *AHSG*, *JJS* 49 (1998), pp. 155-58.

would have been in Aramaic (*AHSG*, pp. 162-71), and we should imagine cultural hostility, 'reaction and resistance' rather than any extensive 'assimilation and acculturation'. Sepphoris (in the light of the most recent excavations) and Tiberias would have had at most a 'Roman-Hellenistic-style' overlay and only a very tiny elite with Graeco-Roman cultural pretensions; for this latter conclusion there is no fresh evidence adduced. Such a Sepphoris would provide 'hardly the sort of cultural atmosphere in which Cynic philosophers would have flourished and somehow influenced or provided models for Galilaean villagers' (*AHSG*, pp. 53-60). We are expected to know what quite different contexts would and did encourage popular Cynicism.

As descendants of the northern tribes (earlier argued), most Galilaeans 'must have continued Israelite traditions' (*GHPP*, p. 249; *AHSG*, p. 122). And then (when it suits) the Gospel traditions are again allowed in, without any supporting evidence (for there is none available, as Horsley admits):

> There Jesus is implicitly and explicitly compared with Moses and Elijah (Mark 4–9), he declares the renewal of Israel under way (Luke/Q 13:28-29, 22:28-20), he presupposes and restates Mosaic covenantal teaching (Luke 6:20-49; cf. Matthew 5) and (apparently) stands opposed to specifically Jerusalem institutions such as the Temple and high priest on the basis of an alternative understanding of Israel (*GHPP*, p. 252; repeated *AHSG*, pp. 171, 181).

Horsley concludes by repeating his case for 'social banditry' in Galilee. Though Josephus's evidence indicates unrest only in the middle of the first century BCE and then the middle of the first century CE, 'it is likely that banditry was a recurrent social problem in Galilee', for that is what the informal models adopted suggest (*GHPP*, p. 258).[24]

There are, of course, a number of other reconstructions of socio-cultural-religious life in Galilee in the first century CE, based on the selections from the same limited available evidence. I choose just two to summarize more briefly.

11.4. R. Riesner, *Jesus als Lehrer*,[25] depending on the earlier work of Freyne and Meyers cited here, and of M. Hengel and others, accepts a

---

24. Be it said, I am in agreement with Horsley in opposing any theory of widespread and continuous Zealotry.

25. R. Riesner, *Jesus als Lehrer* (*JL*) (WUNT, 2.7; Tübingen: Mohr Siebeck, 2nd edn, 1984).

strong Hellenistic presence in Galilee, but posits a conservative Jewish populace, with lots of synagogue buildings, a Sabbath liturgy continuous with that evidenced much later, a high level of elementary education and so literacy, imparted weekdays in the synagogue buildings, involving Greek-style teaching matter (pp. 206-232 with pp. 136-99)—but no Cynicism (pp. 353-54).

11.5. In their guide for interested lay people G. Theissen and A. Merz note the proximity of Sepphoris and Nazareth, and raise without deciding the issue the possibility of influence, and the possibility of a synagogue building at least in Capernaum. The language of Jews was Aramaic, though some will have managed Greek; despite a lively economic exchange (contra Horsley), tension characterized relationships with Greeks and between country-dwellers and the towns where the wealthy lived, contra Freyne's view of comparative tranquillity. 'It is difficult to produce an adequate picture of the religious mentality in Galilee', but Jn 7.41-52 can be taken (contra both Freyne and Horsely) to authenticate rabbinic disparagement of Galilean religion, and that despite the Galileans' attachment to the Temple, the land and the Torah (pp. 176-78).[26] Theissen has some but far fewer expressed qualms in using the Gospels as evidence for conditions in Galilee than has Horsley but more than has Riesner, and has himself, of course, produced a number of illuminating studies of the 'local colour' that may be discerned in the Gospel narratives, but no new evidence that affects the overall picture.[27]

My hope is that this may suffice as a reminder of the variety of conclusions as to the socio-religio-cultural Galilean context of Jesus that can be reached on the basis of much the same potential evidence. *No one clear picture is demanded by the data, which (apart from the Gospels) is very sparse indeed.* Without Gospel matter at least as corroborative illustration, there is very little for our authors to offer, and in the event even in Horsley's work, Gospel matter seems itself to provide

---

26. Theissen and Merz, *The Historical Jesus*, pp. 162-75, 182-83 and 176-78. This is still the 'social rootlessness' which Theissen discerned 20 years ago, in *The First Followers of Jesus* (London: SCM Press, 1979); ET of *Soziologie der Jesusbewegung: Ein Beitrag zur Entstehungsgeschichte des Urchristentums* (Munich: Chr. Kaiser Verlag, 1977), pp. 33-37.

27. G. Theissen, *Lokalkolorit und Zeitgeschichte in den Evangelien: Ein Beitrag zur Geschichte der synoptischen Tradition* (NTOA, 8; Göttingen: Vandenhoeck & Ruprecht, 1989).

necessary evidence for its own context if that is to be presented with any concrete detail; and this is even more obviously the case for the other authors.[28]

We may well note that what is to count as evidence seems already—and inevitably—deeply affected by the reconstruction in mind.

I have chosen scholars whose reconstructions exclude any contribution—or any positive contribution (Theissen)—of Cynicism to the practice and teaching of Jesus. I shall of course argue that my reconstruction, which does allow for such a positive contribution of Cynicism to the practice and teaching of the Galilaean Jew (or Israelite) Jesus, has at least no less warrant than have those I have just summarized.

12. *But first, as I interpret the evidence, Jesus is presented in the Gospels as they stand, and in what seems to many as tradition before the current forms, as a Jew* (in our terms, perhaps we might agree 'Israelite' in first-century local terms; when precise locality is at stake he is not 'Judaean', Ἰουδαῖος).

12.1. He has a very real concern (at the least) for Jerusalem and the Temple, even if the latter needs drastic renewal (Lk./Q 13.34; the passion narratives, etc.) There is no very obvious reason for excluding this matter.

12.2. He is from time to time represented as attending congregational meetings ('synagogues', Gospels, but not Q).

12.3. He respects Torah; and even if he interprets it at times distinctively, so do other contemporaries (Lk./Q 16.16-17; Mk 7.1-13; 10.1-12).

12.4. He is from time to time represented as quoting scriptural traditions—very occasionally the text (most full quotations being editorial), more often allusively. Here I would reject out of hand Riesner's exaggerated list (*JL*, p. 225), and agree more readily with Horsley, that Jesus is represented as alluding to a selection of orally retold and transmitted traditions, even elements with an Israelite (northern) bias (e.g. Elijah and Elisha). It seems too readily assumed that every village (Nazareth included) will have had available for repeated reading most if not all the emergent canon of Scriptures. Cost, and the absence of a community

---

28. M.A. Powell, *Jesus as a Figure in History: How Modern Historians View the Man from Galilee* (Louisville, KY: Westminster/John Knox Press, 1998), celebrates 'the wealth of information' we now have to broaden our view of Jesus' world', without showing any signs of realizing the paucity of 'information' relating to Galilee, of the difficulty of turning a wealth of *data* into agreed 'information'.

building for storing so valuable a collection would seem to make it unlikely. The only evidence adduced seems to point in a different direction. The Roman soldier executed, so Josephus tells us, for desecrating a scroll of the law he found in one village (*War* 2.229) found only one scroll there to burn, not a library. It would hardly have been all five books in one scroll, for that would have been far too fragile; compare the Qumran finds. If a village had only one book, one might conjecture that it would be Deuteronomy, the most frequently found at Qumran; and one may compare the one 'copy of the laws of Moses' brandished by Jesus son of Sapphias in a confrontation at Tarichaeae (Josephus, *Life* 134-35). The other two books most frequently found at Qumran (Isaiah and the Psalter) also figure quite often in the tradition. But there seems no good reason to imagine Jesus immersed in reading and re-reading any extensive set of books. Even the traditions that portray him as literate (Mk 7.6; Lk./Q 7.27; Lk. 4.16-21; 10.26; Jn 8.6-8) do not suggest he was bookish.[29] His intellectual-religious-cultural food would be received for the most part orally, and he would not need to be torn away from books to engage with it, absorb it, digest it, talk it over, live it, interact with others living it, ruminate on it, interpret it, sort it, select within it, reinterpret it, recast it, elaborate it, expand it, add to it…

Since only quite a small proportion of the activity ascribed to Jesus finds a context clearly provided by Temple, synagogue, Torah and Scripture, we need to search more widely for what might have provided the 'langue' and the stimulus for the rest of what he seems to have tried to do and share, by reproducing, adapting, innovating, in interaction with others.

12.5. Jesus, according to the Gospels, experienced revelations of divine reality, and expected a universal divine judgment and a new beginning.[30] The language in which this is expressed seems to stem for the most part from the emergent canon of Scripture, rather than from

---

29. Contra, e.g., J. Jeremias, *New Testament Theology*, I (London: SCM Press, 1971); ET of *Neutestamentliche Theologie. I. Die Verkündigung Jesu* (Gütersloh: Gerd Mohn, 1971), p. 205, 'Jesus lived in the Old Testament'; cited with approval by Riesner, *Jesus als Lehrer*, p. 225; cf. W. Popkes, 'James and Scripture: An Exercise in Intertextuality', *NTS* 45 (1999), pp. 213-29—there was no ready access to texts.

30. I find myself often in qualified agreement on the latter two themes with Allison, *Jesus of Nazareth*; however, Allison does not sufficiently allow for revelatory experience.

the surviving eschatological apocalypses ('Apocrypha and Pseude-pigrapha'). 'Son of Man' becomes a title with eschatological signifi-cance only later. 'Kingdom of God' has few precise antecedents in surviving documents, but is anyway less frequent and so less significant than it is often made out to be. The Gospel traditions with their comparative lack of elaborate details (even in Mk 13, etc.) seem only distantly related to surviving eschatological documents.

Perhaps something like the traditions in the *Lives of the Prophets* was important to Jesus, but he does not use any of the most prominent pro-phetic forms; there is no 'thus says the Lord'.[31]

Geza Vermes' attempt to create a tradition of 'charismatic' Galilaean wonder-workers has no *compelling* evidence to support it, and what is adduced has little if anything in common with Jesus as narrated. We have no independent evidence of other healers, though in the Gospel traditions there are notes of other exorcists (Lk./Q11.19; Mk 9.38).[32]

12.6. Apart from an allusion to Solomon Jesus does not seem to quote the literary wisdom tradition and his ethos is quite different (see below). Furthermore, there is no clear evidence for a living Galilean wisdom tradition of wandering sages continuous with some or all the very diverse stand-points and forms of Sirach, Qoheleth, Proverbs, Wisdom of Solomon, *Pseudo-Phocylides*.[33]

12.7. We are not told of any first-century Galilean other than Jesus using the various figurative speech-forms termed 'parables' in the Gos-pel tradition. We may well imagine such forms were already in circu-lation, and that Jesus did not invent the forms nor introduce to the later (much later) rabbis those forms they also subsequently used; but we have no compelling reason to suppose such forms were used by con-temporary Pharisees or by Scribes whether Pharisaic or not. Pharisees do not seem to have set out to to teach as such, but simply to set an

31. Against, e.g., M. Sato, *Q und Prophetie: Studien zur Gattungs- und Tradi-tionsgeschichte der Quelle Q* (WUNT, 2.29; Tübingen: Mohr Siebeck, 1988).

32. G. Vermes, *Jesus the Jew: A Historian's Reading of the Gospels* (London: Collins, 1973), pp. 69-80. Onias/Honi is a pacific Judaean rain-maker, Hanina ben Dosa survives snake-bite and heals by prayer (not word and touch, etc.) and his link with Galilee is tenuous. Neither Honi nor Hanina teaches, collects disciples or wan-ders the countryside; cf. S. Freyne, 'Hanina Ben Dosa: A Galilean Charismatic', in *idem, Galilee and Gospel*, pp. 132-59.

33. Against, e.g., B. Witherington, III, *Jesus the Sage: The Pilgrimage of Wis-dom* (Minneapolis: Fortress Press, 1994); and, e.g., P.R. Eddy, 'Jesus as Diogenes? Reflections on the Cynic Jesus Thesis', *JBL* 115 (1996), pp. 449-69, esp. pp. 460-61.

example of strict adherence to traditional norms of behaviour. In the Gospels Pharisees appear in Galilee, but Josephus would lead us to suppose few if any lived there. Scribal lawyers helped to interpret law and apply it, perhaps on the staff of Jewish rulers and other wealthy landowners (especially the priests among them) and we may presume lawyers taught apprentice lawyers; but even the scribalism of the much later Mishnah does not deploy parable forms for its exposition.[34] If parabolic communication was in circulation, affording precedent for rabbis later, and for Jesus in the first century, it was circulating in other circles than those of the scribes or of the Pharisees.

4. Cynic Influences Could Provide Some of the Context

13. *For elements of the Jesus tradition lacking analogies in other available near-contemporary Jewish sources, popular contemporary Cynicism, with some roots in Palestine, affords some quite close analogies, and thus a possible context for those elements.*

But, note, if we do find in Jesus Cynic elements from the Greek tradition he remains no less a Jew than does Philo or Josephus or the author of Wisdom of Solomon, or the writer of *4 Maccabees*—or those responsible for the Mishnah, and the Talmuds, with the Greek influence discernible in them.

13.1. It has been quite often noted that itinerant Christians obeying some version of the Synoptic mission-charge (Mk 6.8-10; Mt. 10.9-10; Lk. 9.3-4, 10.4-5) might well have looked to spectators somewhat like

---

34. Some Sadducees respond to Jesus imaginatively (Mk 12.18-23); no one else does. On this (limited) account of Pharisees, see, e.g., M. Goodman, 'A Note on Josephus, the Pharisees, and Ancestral Tradition', *JJS* 50.1 (1999), pp. 17-20; B.B. Scott, 'Essaying the Rock', *Foundations and Facets Forum* 2 (1986), pp. 3-11 (5), 'as to such similitudes as master/servant, tower/war, lost sheep/lost coin, the faithful servant, children at play, leaven… we have nothing of the sort'; and *idem*, *Hear then the Parable: A Commentary on the Parables of Jesus* (Minneapolis: Fortress Press, 1989), p. 14, 'in those layers of the [rabbinic] tradition that can be isolated as belonging to the Pharisees there are no parables', citing J. Neusner, 'Types and Forms in Ancient Jewish Literature: Some Comparison', *History of Religions* 11 (1972), pp. 354-90. Paul, as a self-professed Pharisee, uses figurative language, but none at all close to the Synoptic 'parables'. See also A.J. Saldarini, *Pharisees, Scribes and Sadducees in Palestinian Society* (Wilmington, DE: Michael Glazier, 1988). For the scribes as 'bureaucrats… and experts on Jewish life', but nothing more, see Saldarini, *Pharisees*, p. 266, summarizing a detailed argument.

Cynics. The point was made by Gerd Theissen, for instance, in his 1973 article, 'Wanderradikalismus'. Theissen then went on to argue, however, that the specific prohibitions in Lk. 9.3 were 'probably intended to avoid the least shadow of an impression that the Christian missionaries were these [Cynic] beggars or were like them'.[35] This supposed difference in uniform has then been widely approved by others.[36]

The evidence for a supposed uniformity in Cynic dress is in fact derived from a small number of caricatures derived from outsiders. If one looks at the Cynic sources themselves in detail (rather than at today's or yesterday's generalizations—Theissen quotes a few secondary sources and Diogenes Laertius 6.13 only), there was even more variety in Cynic get-up (and in the terminology[37] for the various items of 'equipment' that might or might not be deployed) than we find among the sets of instructions in the Synoptic Gospels. Mark allows both sandals and staff, which many Cynics would carry; Matthew forbids the staff, as Luke does in one list, and Matthew forbids sandals, as Luke does in his other list. 'Barefoot' is how Dio describes Diogenes; on this sculptors vary in their depictions of Cynics. (Particularly significant in fact are the photographs of [acknowledged] statues of Cynics available in various published collections, but perhaps now especially those in Diskin Clay's recent essay.)[38] Some Cynics forgo a staff;

35. G. Theissen, 'Wanderradikalismus: Litertursoziologische Aspekte der Überlieferung von Worten Jesu im Urchristentum', *ZTK* 70 (1973), pp. 245-71, referring to pp. 255-59, 'Das Verbot von Tasche und Stab zielt wahrscheinlich darauf hin, auch den geringsten Anschein zu vermeiden, die christlichen Missionare seien solche oder ähnliche Bettler', as in the ET, 'The Wandering Radicals', in *Social Reality and the Early Christians: Theology, Ethics and the World of the New Testament* (Minneapolis: Augsburg, 1992), p. 47. This distinction is repeated without argument in Theissen and Merz, *The Historical Jesus*, p. 216.

36. E.g. by R.A. Horsley, *Jesus and the Spiral of Violence* (San Francisco: Harper & Row, 1987), p. 230; C.M. Tuckett, variously, including *Q and the History of Early Christianity* (Edinburgh: T. & T. Clark, 1996), pp. 385-89; Eddy, 'Reflections on the Cynic Jesus Thesis', pp. 461-62.

37. M.-O. Goulet-Cazé, 'Le cynisme à l'époque impériale', *ANRW*, II.36.4, pp. 2720-2823, referring to pp. 2738-46. I am grateful to Professor J.M. Robinson, for helping me, in conversation, clarify and strengthen (I hope) this and some of the following points.

38. D. Clay, 'Picturing Diogenes', in R.B. Branham and M.-O. Goulet-Cazé (eds.), *The Cynics* (HCS, 23; Berkeley: University California of Press, 1996), pp. 366-87; especially fig. 9, p. 381, naked with bowl; and fig. 10, p. 384, with no cup, staff or satchel, but here with sandals and cloak draped around his midriff.

for some the begging bag (or, for some, bowl) is a positive symbol, others would prefer to earn their keep. Though Jesus' followers do not beg (αἰτεῖν), they are expected to depend on others' hospitality, like some Cynics.[39] The critics of any Jewish Cynic Jesus thesis tend to ignore or dismiss such inconvenient data, preferring a clearly defined Cynic appearance with which to contrast a clearly defined early Christian self-presentation. Yet to appear poorly dressed, to draw attention to yourself with a message encouraging poverty while relying on others' support, is, in much of the first-century east Mediterranean world, certainly quite enough to risk being seen as a Cynic.[40] The variegated Cynic tradition could provide an intelligible context for the variations the early Christians allowed themselves in response to these injunctions from Jesus (cf. also 1 Cor. 9).

Would this hold, however, in Galilee? Negatively we have no evidence from outside the Gospels for *anyone* in Galilee around Jesus' day behaving in any closely similar way. Josephus's account of Essenes travelling light to visit other known or unknown members of their dispersed community affords no close analogy at all; nor, in ancient tradition, do Elijah or Elisha. But significant actions of this sort are only at all fully significant in if in some measure recognizable, they seem to presuppose a context in which people know how to interpret them (a commonplace of 'sociology of knowledge' so-called). We can of course always still posit coincidence—and that could be the correct assessment. Jesus could just have chanced on a method of approach with (apparently) no precedent in his own culture, but one that happened to have been adopted over the past few centuries by innumerable others travelling through the countryside among the Hellenistic towns of the Mediterranean world, not excluding Gadara, a few kilometers to the south-east of Nazareth, Gadara where two significant named Cynics, two famous sons, had originated (and at least one vigorous critic of Cynicism) and where another, Oenomaus, would emerge. Well, coincidences

39. F.G. Downing, *Cynics and Christian Origins* (Edinburgh: T. & T. Clark, 1992), pp. 10-11, 32-33, 133-34 for some long lists; but cf. Dio Chrysostom, *Discourses* 6.15 and 60; Musonius, *Discourses* 19 (Lutz 120-22); Pseudo-Lucian, *The Cynic* 3; Teles, Stobaeus IVA, Hense 44; Philostratus, *Lives of the Sophists* 488; Pseudo-Crates *Epistles* 2, 19; Pseudo-Diogenes *Epistles* 38.4; R.F. Hock, *The Social Context of Paul's Ministry* (Philadelphia: Fortress Press, 1980), pp. 37-42.

40. Jesus' followers do not beg ('ask'); but they expect support: Lk. 10.7, and cf. Pseudo-Crates *Epistles* 2, 22; Pseudo-Diogenes *Epistles* 38.4.

do occur. Jesus himself may have thought he was innovating. And still no one (no wider-travelled merchant, soldier, artisan, scribe, Pharisee, Herodian or Sadducee, no one acquainted with the Greek-speaking world) told him or his followers what sort of itinerants they might be mistaken for, even without staff or shoes or satchel. Or, if anyone did exclaim, 'Why get yourselves up like a Cynic? Get back to Gadara!' Jesus and his friends (or the later tradents at least) remained content with the image and the likely interpretation.

13.2. Freyne and Horsley (as leading examples) differ as to the extent and depth of poverty in Jesus' Galilee. We have no evidence in older or contemporary Jewish thought of poverty being commended as a condition for the good life. The dangers of wealth, of seeking it, placing too much reliance on it (Pss. 49.6; 62.10; Prov. 30.7-9), are noted; and there are scriptural references to 'the poor' who may be God's special concern, without our knowing the kind of poverty in question. But nowhere do we seem to find poverty as such commended, let alone commanded,[41] until we reach Philo in Alexandria, where T.E. Schmidt finds 'his expressions of teleological devaluation [of wealth], however, most clearly resemble Cynic ideals... in their radical extent of renunciation, as opposed to the mere detachment of the Stoics'.[42]

Jesus commended the blessedness of the poor, forbade the accumulation of wealth, and judged it incompatible with service to God, demanding dispossession (Lk./Q(?) 6.21-25; 12.22-31, 33-34; 16.13; Mk 10.17-26). So, again, we find Jesus, with no clear precedent in his own culture, hitting on poverty as constitutive of the good life, of blessedness: an approach that for centuries in the Hellenistic world had been exhibited and commended and talked about and related in lively Cynic anecdotes that could be part of the school curriculum for anyone learning to write Greek. But Jesus, we guess, reached this Cynic conclusion

---

41. C. Boerma, *Rich Man, Poor Man—and the Bible* (ET London: SCM Press, 1979); D.L. Mealand, *Poverty and Expectation in the Gospels* (London: SPCK, 1980); T.E. Schmidt, *Hostility to Wealth in the Synoptic Gospels* (JSNTSup, 15; Sheffield: JSOT Press, 1987), p. 49, concludes that no canonical passages listed 'puts poverty in a favourable light'; 'none can be said to laud poverty', p. 73. Cf. also R.J. Coggins, 'The Old Testament and the Poor', *ExpTim* 99 (1987–88), pp. 11-14; R.N. Whybray, 'Poverty, Wealth and the Point of View in Proberbs', *ExpTim* 100 (1989–90), pp. 332-36; N.T. Wright, *Jesus and the Victory of God* (London: SPCK, 1996), pp. 398-405.

42. Schmidt, *Hostility*, p. 82.

independently and expressed it in Cynic-like dress, also independently; and with no cultural precedent some Galilaeans accepted his lead, while no one with contacts in the world where Greek was the first language ever said, 'You're just another Cynic!' or put him off by telling him it wasn't just non-Jewish, it was foreign, it was Greek. Well, coincidences do occur.

13.3. It is not just the fact that Jesus adopted poverty and commended it (so we are told), but the way in which he commended it that is also striking:

> So, I tell you, don't be anxious about your living self/soul, or about what you are to eat, nor about your body, what you are to put on it. For your living self/soul is more than food and your body itself is more than its clothes. Consider the ravens—they don't sow or reap, they've neither store-houses nor barns; yet God feeds them. And which of you can add a cubit to his span of life by worrying about it? So, if you can't even do something as insignificant as that, why are you so anxious about the rest? Look at the lilies, see how they grow. They don't toil or spin. Yet I tell you, even Solomon in all his grandeur was not got up as splendidly as one of these. But if God dresses up the plants growing in the field like this, there today and tomorrow burnt in the stove, just think how much more he'll care about clothes for you, however little you trust him. Don't spend your time looking for things to eat or drink, just don't worry so. For all the world's people spend their time like that. But your Father knows your needs. Instead, give your time and attention to looking for his royal rule—and all this will be yours as well (Lk./Q 12.22-31, my translation).

It is widely admitted that this seems rather like a passage from Dio Chrysostom (*Discourses* 10.16) in Cynic vein:

> Why not consider the beasts and the birds, and see how much more painlessly they live than humans do, how much more pleasantly and healthily. They are stronger, each one lives the longest span for their kind—despite lacking hands or human intelligence... They have one enormous advantage to counter-balance any ills they may suffer—they are free of property (my translation).

However, a scholar such as C.M. Tuckett, allowing some initial similarity, then insists,

> there is a radical difference in the underlying ethos. With Cynics, the ethos is to give up one's possessions and live a life of austerity and physical deprivation in the belief that that life as such will provide true and lasting happiness and fulfilment. Moreover, the ideal for the Cynic is a life of self-sufficiency (αὐτάρκεια) and independence from the rest of

society. In Q the ethos is radically different: it is to encourage not independence, but dependence—upon God.[43]

It is worth pursuing the similarities and supposed differences a little further. Earlier in his collection on Q Tuckett discusses the above passage in some detail:

> It is widely acknowledged that Q 12:23 (the ψυχή is more than food, and the σῶμα more than clothing) does not fit well after the exhortation in v. 22 not to worry about food or clothing. The motives given in v. 23 on the one hand, and in vv. 22, 24, 26-28 on the other, for the general advice not to worry are different: in vv. 24, 26-28 there is no grading of concerns but simply an assurance that God will provide; v. 23, however introduces a contrast between the more important ψυχή-σῶμα and the less important food and clothing. It looks very much as if either v. 23 has been added secondarily to vv. 22, 24 and 26-28 or vice-versa… [This latter is judged less likely.] …So, too, v. 25, interrupting the twin appeals to examples from nature (ravens/birds and lilies) and introducing a quite different kind of argument appealing to human inability to solve the problems of anxiety, is almost universally regarded as a secondary addition to the early tradition.[44]

Tuckett does not think it necessary to tell us how he knows that the distinctions he and others discern would have been so striking that a first-century east Mediterranean speaker (Jesus or a follower) could not have combined them from the start; and that despite the fact that some supposed early redactor of the pericope (*ex hypothesi*) found them quite compatible and the sequence entirely coherent; as, obviously, also did both Matthew and Luke.

Sequences enjoining the avoidance of cares about food, clothing and property appear in ancient Greek and Latin works ascribed to Cynics and to Stoics with a Cynic cast to them. Among a score of passages I have assembled[45] two, three or four of the following strands occur in

---

43. Tuckett, *Q and the History of Early Christianity*, p. 389.

44. Tuckett, *Q and the History of Early Christianity*, pp. 149-50, citing D. Zeller, D. Catchpole, U. Luz, J.S. Kloppenborg and P. Hoffmann for v. 23, and R. Bultmann, J. Jeremias, D. Zeller, J.S. Kloppenborg, R.A. Piper and P. Hoffmann for v. 25. Possibly vv. 25-26 is intended.

45. F.G. Downing, *Christ and the Cynics* (JSOT Manuals, 4; Sheffield: JSOT Press, 1988), pp. 68-71, § 58. I am not convinced by J.M. Robinson, 'A Written Greek Sayings Cluster Older than Q: A Vestige', *HTR* 92 (1999), pp. 61-78. I do not see how OYΞAINEI could be changed into ΠΩΣAYΞANEI, though in the light of the canonical and other textual variants, a change the other way would seem

the more elaborate sequences in various combinations: (1) Most often we find the example of adequately fed and clothed animals (8×); (2) plants less often (2×); (3) their lack of property is noted four times; (4) that it is 'God' who provides is made explicit in seven cases; (5) a comparison of values occurs in six; (6) humans' limited powers are noted only three times, but are also implicit in the references to the divine care that obviates busy anxiety.

It is thus quite clear that there was a complex topos comprising a cluster of at least half a dozen strands on avoidance of cares, available for any wanting to urge this kind of conclusion in detail. Any smaller or larger selection of these themes can be brought in to make the overriding point: we should forgo anxious cares.

Jesus, by coincidence, and quite independently, chooses all six strands —including, of course, the theme of dependence on God (absent from Dio's passage, but quite frequent in others). And, as it happens, this complex sequence, though lacking Galilean cultural precedent is meaningful enough to have been remembered, recorded, repeated, in detail. Coincidences certainly do seem to be piling up.

(It has been argued that references in Proverbs to the behaviour of insects, for instance, provide a purely Jewish precedent for Jesus' words. The evidence is not usually quoted in full. It turns out to be about busy ants and bees, quite the opposite of Jesus' insouciant crows and anemones; and nowhere does *anything like* the full Q complex occur in wisdom or other older Jewish writings.)[46]

13.4. Although in one strand Jesus affirms respect for father and mother (Mk 7.10-13) and for marriage (Mk 10.4-9), elsewhere he enjoins the fracturing of families (Lk./Q 12.51-53; Mk 10.29-30) and even forbids the pious duty of burial for a parent (Lk./Q 9.59-60). As Tom Wright notes, this presents 'a shocking challenge to the Jewish world of Jesus' day'.[47] It is significant that while D.C. Allison places

---

plausible. However, even if Robinson were right it would have no effect on the argument above.

46. Prov. 6.6, 'Go to the ant, you sluggard', is cited but not quoted by Witherington III, of his *Jesus the Sage*, pp. 133-34. On this passage, cf. J.M. Robinson, 'Galiaean Upstarts: A Sot's Disciples?' in W.L. Petersen, J.S. Vos and H.J. de Jonge (eds.), *Sayings of Jesus, Canonical and Non-Canonical: Essays in Honor of Tjitze Baarda* (NovTSup, 89; Leiden: E.J. Brill, 1997), pp. 223-49 (224-25).

47. Wright, *Jesus and the Victory of God*, p. 402; Freyne, *Galilee and Gospel*,

considerable stress on voluntary celibacy as undertaken in the light of an imminent end, the only explicit passage he can cite in illustration is from 1 Cor. 7.26.[48] Allison's Jewish eschatological sources promote other kinds of renunciation, but not this. There is precedent for such radicalism, however, in Cynic teaching, where it is part of a considered and fairly coherent rejection of civic values, and this gives it sense.[49] We are again asked to imagine Jesus arriving at this apparently grace-less irresponsibility within no supporting context known to us, yet he is (or is presented as being) understood and followed by some.

13.5. To return to the issue of parables, we noted (see pp. 129-98) that we have no independent evidence for such communication being used in Jesus' Galilee. We are assured, however, by one critic that 'one of the most characteristic forms of Jesus' teaching style—the parable—has no real Cynic parallels'.[50] In fact, most of the short metaphors and similes in the synoptic tradition do have close parallels in Cynic and related sources; and that is most of the material.[51] In the Synoptic Gospels

pp. 205-206, allows for some of these 'radical' and distinctive aspects of Jesus' programme, but not for any Cynic resonances. Jesus is their sole source.

48. Allison, *Jesus of Nazareth*, pp. 188-97, referring to p. 190. It is a weakness of Allison's argument that he places so much stress on sexual renunciation (and elaborate arguments to enhance its importance in the tradition) and simply lists in passing other items, pp. 174-75. This emphasis fits Allison's own estimate of the importance in the tradition of 'intention' whereas that is a Matthaean theme, and the other Synoptic passages cited as instances of 'intention' are concerned with enacted commitment (p. 186 cf. p. 47 §12 and n. 151). The Jesus tradition as a whole (like those of many Cynics, and in this case, like some Jewish tradition) places its emphasis on what is done, not on intention on its own: Philo, *Mut. Nom.* 241-43; *4 Macc.* 3.3-5; cf. Mishnah, *Mak.* 3.15.

49. Cf. W. Deming, *Paul on Marriage and Celibacy: The Hellenistic Back-ground of 1 Corinthians 7* (SNTSMS, 83; Cambridge: Cambridge University Press, 1995), chap. 2, 'The Stoic-Cynic Marriage Debate', pp. 50-61; and Downing, *Christ and the Cynics*, pp. 44, 79 (To supplement the latter on the break with family: Diogenes Laertius, *Lives of Eminent Philosophers* 6.20-21; 54; 72; Pseudo-Dio-genes 21, 38.5, 47; cf. Epictetus, *Dissertations* 3.22.47, 67-82; 4.1.153); and Down-ing, *Cynics and Christian Origins*, pp. 133, 139. As in the Jesus tradition, one can find a counter-balance among Cynics, too: in favour of marriage, Diogenes Laertius 6.96-98; and respect for an abandoned parent, Pseudo-Diogenes 7, 30, 34.

50. Eddy, 'Reflections on the Cynic Jesus Thesis', p. 461.

51. See F.G. Downing, *Christ and the Cynics*.

we can also see longer and shorter versions (of, for instance, the Thief in the Night, the Sower, and the Mustard Seed; and different 'expansions' of the Pounds/Talents). Longer figurative constructions are admittedly not frequent in our Cynic materials (they are not frequent in the Gospels); but when we do find such in Cynic sources, we realize how readily the short forms may have been condensed from the longer ones or shorter ones expanded. We may instance Antisthenes on 'strongholds' in Diogenes Laertius compared with the preserved fragment of his Odysseus; or the brief example of 'athletic prizes' in Paul compared with the treatment of the same model in Dio; and in Dio in particular we find other 'expansions' of metaphors and similes found in brief elsewhere. The metaphor of 'fighting with wild beasts' used with reference to controlling the passions can be used in Cynic writing as briefly as by Paul (1 Cor. 15.32), or as expanded by Dio into his 'Libyan Myth'.[52] Dio's 'Good Euboean' has formal as well as substantial similarities with Luke's 'Good Samaritan'. Dio here writes at very much greater length, but uses an everyday rural setting and an unexpected generous 'hero' to challenge narrow-minded expectations (besides portraying a rural Cynic 'natural' simplicity).[53] Dio says that people come to men dressed as he was (as a Cynic) expecting such stories. To quote an earlier conclusion of my own, 'the sheer quantity of parable, metaphor and simile [in the Synoptic tradition] would strongly reinforce the impression that anyone repeating this material was some sort of Cynic'.[54]

---

52. Arguing that the metaphor is shared, A.J. Malherbe, 'The Beasts at Ephesus', *JBL* 87 (1968), pp. 71-80, repr. in his *Paul and the Popular Philosophers* (Minneapolis: Fortress Press, 1989), pp. 79-89. Q/Lk. 11.24-26 (the returning unclean spirit) also affords an interesting comparison with Dio's Libyan Myth, *Discourse* 5.

53. A.J. Malherbe discusses the Antisthenes passages in 'Antisthenes and Odysseus and Paul at War', *HTR* 76 (1983), pp. 143-73, repr. in his *Paul and the Popular Philosophers*, pp. 91-119; H. Funke discusses the prizes in 'Antisthenes bei Paulus', *Hermes* 98 (1970), pp. 459-71; the passages can be found in G. Giannantoni, *Socratis et Socraticorum Reliquiae*, II (Naples: Bibliopolis, 1990); the 'Good Euboean' is in Dio 7.1-80.

54. Dio Chrysostom 55.9, 11, 22; cf. 72.13; quoting Downing, *Cynics and Christian Origins*, p. 139; this entire present paragraph is drawn from F.G. Downing, 'Deeper Reflections on the Jewish Cynic Jesus', *JBL* 116.4 (1997), pp. 97-104 (100-101); repr. in *idem*, *Making Sense in (and of) the First Christian Century* (JSNTSup, 197; Sheffield: Sheffield Academic Press, 2000), pp. 122-33.

13.6. Mark, Matthew and Paul in 1 Corinthians, together with some longer texts of Luke and also Justin Martyr, supported allusively by John, indicate that Jesus encouraged his immediate entourage to share bread and wine designated as his body and his blood. There is no plausible Jewish context, no otherwise suggested Galilaean Jewish context in which this might seem acceptable. Of course food and drink could be consumed in a way we might term 'symbolic', and 'blood' might be used as a metaphor ('the blood of the grape', Deut. 32.14; cf. Prov. 5.15). But the idea of drinking blood simply horrifies (2 Sam. 23.17), as is often noted.[55] Although pagan mysteries as an alternative context have often been canvassed for such an apparently 'Thyestean' feast, I have shown elsewhere that when such charges are later levelled at Christians, it is always in combination with 'Oedipean intercourse'; and this combination (cannibalism and incest) is only ever proposed for Cynics in our most nearly contemporary sources. In theory Cynics could accept both such possibilities as 'natural' (without there being any record of their putting theory into practice).[56] Again, Jesus could quite independently have hit on an idea—body and blood shared—that only Cynics are known to have contemplated with serious equanimity. Just one more coincidence.

13.7. It has also been difficult to find earlier 'purely Jewish' antecedents for Jesus' teaching on love of enemies (Lk./Q 6.27-29, 35), and on not judging (Lk./Q 6.37-38, 41-42). Again there are plentiful Cynic or Cynic-influenced instances. As I have in the past noted, there are also inconsistencies: Diogenes in the tradition can be very vindictive; but, in the wider tradition at least, so, too, can Jesus.

13.8. Jesus speaks in his own name, and uses none of the canonical prophetic formulae ('the word of the Lord', etc.), and, as we noted above, rarely quotes and infrequently even alludes to Scripture. Similar forthrightness, readily interpretable as self-opinionated, was characteristic of many Cynics, who also eschewed references to authority or technical arguments. The tradition assumes that Jesus' hearers we unfazed

55. H. Maccoby, *Paul and Hellenism* (London: SCM Press, 1991), p. 99, citing Jn 6.60-66; M. Casey, 'No Cannibals at Passover,' *Theology* 96 (1993), pp. 199-208 (203).

56. F.G. Downing, 'Cynics and Christians, Oedipus and Thyestes', *JEH* 44 (1993), pp. 1-10, repr. in *idem, Making Sense*, pp. 134-47. Zeno and the earliest Stoics seem to have retained this twin motif, but by Jesus' day the Stoics had long abandoned it.

by his self-assurance; only once in the combined synoptic tradition is Jesus challenged on this score (Mk 11.27).

13.9. From strands I have discussed in more detail elsewhere[57] I have here picked out a number of very significant items and themes where activity including teaching ascribed to Jesus has no at all obvious known Jewish precedent to render it persuasive, let alone intelligible, even 'thinkable' for him and his Galilaean audiences (or his followers and their audiences), and even runs counter to otherwise evidenced varieties of Jewish ethos, but where an otherwise still Jewish Jesus is displayed exhibiting and articulating ideas, attitudes and practices resembling strands of Cynicism in recognizably Cynic ways: and being understood and persuasive.

13.10. There are many other issues on which known Jewish and Cynic sources together say similar things (as shown in my *Christ and the Cynics*). If these common strands were recognized in Jesus' Galilee, they could have made assimilation of some of the more distinctive Cynic themes much easier. In fact in these areas, where there are non-Cynic Jewish analogies, teaching ascribed to Jesus is still often closer in content to the Cynic than to the non-Cynic Jewish sources.

13.11. I have carefully noted in advance (see §12, pp. 195-96, above) areas where Jesus in the tradition *does* also recall for us close precedents in non-Cynic Judaism, for which I have only been able to argue elsewhere that even these are not without some analogies among some Cynics. So his eschatology is Jewish (but eschatological themes are widely shared). The rhetoric of his 'subversive' kingdom talk can strike a fairly detached observer (L.G. Bloomquist) as similar in its drive to the kingdom language of Cynics.[58] This Jesus can speak of himself or of attitudes to himself as significant for a coming judgment (but so can some Cynics). He heals and exorcises (or heals exorcistically). We have only a very general analogy in Cynic concern for physical well-being, and one very partial Cynic analogy in the apparent value of relics of the

57. F.G. Downing, *Jesus and the Threat of Freedom* (London: SCM Press, 1987); *idem*, *Christ and the Cynics*; *idem*, *Cynics and Christian Origins* and other work listed there and in other notes here.

58. L.G. Bloomquist, 'Methodological Considerations in the Determination of the Social Context of Cynic Rhetorical Practice: Implications for our Present Studies of the Jesus Traditions', in S.E. Porter and T.H. Olbricht (eds.), *The Rhetorical Analysis of Scripture: Essays from the 1995 London Conference* (JSNTSup, 146; Sheffield: Sheffield Academic Press, 1997), pp. 200-31, citing pp. 222-30.

self-immolated Cynic Peregrinus (but then we have no independent evidence for healers of any other kind in Jesus' Galilee). And so on.[59]

14. *No single interpretation of these data forces itself on us. how are we to proceed?*

14.1. We can stress (or invent by general redescription) dissimilarities between Christian and Cynic sources, stress or invent by general redescription, similarities between the Christian and non-Cynic Jewish sources. I prefer to try to allow for both similarities and differences on all sides. (I note gratefully John Kloppenborg Verbin drawing attention to the high standards imposed by critics on supposed Cynic analogies; assessed as severely, he justly notes, other commonly adduced analogies would also fail.)[60]

14.2. We can allow that there are real similarities, but argue that they are culturally simply coincidental, they are epiphenomenal, simply a function of similar economic and social conditions (Theissen, Horsley, Vaage, and others, in their various ways.)[61] This seems to me hard to credit. Similar attitudes may well be evinced in similar socio-economic circumstances in different cultures; but we have no evidence elsewhere for as closely similar significant actions-and-articulation as the ones discussed above simply arising spontaneously from parallel socio-economic conditions in distinct cultures. Why should we resort to such a 'marvellous' conclusion here?[62]

59. See Downing, *Cynics and Christian Origins*, pp. 140-41 (on eschatology; now adding *Socratic Letter* 25.1 and Lucian, *Downward Journey* 23, to Pseudo-Heraclitus, *Letters* 5, 9, Pseudo-Diogenes, *Letters* 39, Epictetus, *Encheiridion* 15 and F.G. Downing, 'Common Strands in Pagan, Jewish and Christian Eschatologies in the First Century', *TZ* 51 [1995], pp. 197-211); and *idem, Cynics and Christian Origins*, pp. 130-31 (on healing; for the miraculous relic of a Cynic, Lucian, *Peregrinus* 39).

60. Kloppenborg Verbin, ' "A Dog among the Pigeons": A Cynic Q?', 'The Sub-Text of Criticism'.

61. Theissen and Horsley as above; L.E. Vaage, *Galilaean Upstarts: Jesus' First Followers According to Q* (Valley Forge, PA: Trinity Press International, 1994); and his review of F.G. Downing, 'Cynics and Christian Origins', *CBQ* 56 (1994), pp. 587-89; and Vaage, 'Q and Cynicism: On Comparison and Social Identity', in R.A. Piper (ed.), *The Gospel behind the Gospels: Current Studies on Q* (NovTSup, 75; Leiden: E.J. Brill, 1995), pp. 199-29; J.D. Crossan, *Jesus, a Revolutionary Biography* (San Francisco: HarperSanFrancisco, 1994), p. 122, perhaps Jesus was 'just re-inventing the Cynic wheel all by himself', cited by Powell, *Jesus as a Figure in History*, p. 97.

62. So, when Allison, *Jesus of Nazareth*, argues that similar situations produce

We may, however, note that the general socio-economic situation that we are able to reconstruct from our archaeological and other sources for Galilee in Jesus' day would indicate that his attitude to wealth and security would at least be relevant, even if not necessarily popular, let alone inevitable.

14.3. Against any sketch of a Jewish Cynic Jesus we can insist that our Cynic sources are too far distant in time or place for any such contagion to have occurred. There are gaps in the sequence of highbrow Cynic writings, but these do not indicate an absence of popular Cynicism; as M.-O. Goulet-Cazé has concluded, 'la chaîne n'était point interrompue' ('the chain was never broken').[63] The amount of Cynic analogies and allusions that others as well as I have found in Philo and in Paul suggest that Cynicism is alive and well in the east Mediterranean, at least, in Jesus' day (see further, below). Cynic chreiai figure prominently in the surviving Progymnasmata, and so, it would seem, formed part of the education of anyone learning Greek in Palestine as much as elsewhere. That significant Cynic figures (Menippus, Meleagar and Oenomaus) emerged from time to time from Gadara in the Decapolis, a few kilometers south-east of the Sea of Galilee, is widely admitted. All this should show that Cynic influence in the area was *not impossible*. Whether or not it had actually occurred is the issue in question. The Gospel evidence (in the absence of conclusive evidence to the contrary) seems to indicate just such popular Cynic influence within Galilaean Israelite culture, to allow Jesus to make his own selection and synthesis, and be understood.[64]

5. *Paul Saw Strong Cynic Colouring in the Jesus Movement*

15. *It would seem that Paul perceived the young Jesus movement as a sort of Jewish Cynicism (or Cynic Judaism), and so quite naturally*

millennarian prophets with often very similar attitudes, but in instances quite independently of each other, we nonetheless note that the precise articulation argued is still culturally specific.

63. Goulet-Cazé, 'Une tradition vécue,' in 'Le cynisme à l'époque impériale', pp. 2722-724, citing p. 2724; cf. again the very useful contribution of Kloppenborg Verbin, '"A Dog among the Pigeons": A Cynic Q?'.

64. I note the interesting suggestion of D. Fiensy, 'Leaders of Mass Movements and the Leader of the Jesus Movement', *JSNT* 74 (1999), pp. 3-27, that if Jesus were a carpenter he would have been in a good position to 'network', encounter a variety of people—and so, of ideas.

deployed major strands of Cynic praxis and articulation in living, developing and propagating his new commitment.

15.1. I have argued all this at length recently, in my *Cynics, Paul and the Pauline Churches*.[65] In that work I have attempted to show, on the basis of others' researches, and fresh work of my own, that the Paul of the Thessalonian and Corinthian and Galatian letters depicts and articulates a lifestyle in terms that would so clearly look and sound Cynic to the ordinary townspeople he met that he must have been aware of that, and content with it. What he had to say on 'neither Jew nor Greek, neither bond nor free, no male and female' would sound Cynic, as would his disparagement of law, and much of the discussion of sexual and dietary taboos, along with the consuming of bread and wine as body and blood; but also his ostentatious poverty, half-naked, showing the scars of shameful beatings, in fact his entire self-presentation as a teacher working with his hands to gain a living, would look Cynic. A recognizably Cynic deviancy constituted much of the initial thrust of his invitation to a Christian deviancy. When Paul joined the Christians he seems to have supposed it appropriate to behave and talk in ways that must often have seemed Cynic.

15.2. Stepping back for a moment to Paul well before the letters: as a zealot for his people and their sacred traditions, Paul had originally persecuted some early Christian communities (Gal. 1.13-14; Phil. 3.6). Presumably he saw their lifestyle and their announced views as a threat to the security and integrity of both nation and inheritance. The insistence of these followers of Jesus that a man whom God had allowed to suffer crucifixion was nonetheless God's anointed leader, God's Messiah, on its own might well have disturbed Paul ('a stumbling-block', 1 Cor. 1.23);[66] but much more significant would have been the lifestyle these 'Messianic Jews' had adopted. As we are often reminded of Judaism over the ages, it is 'orthopraxis' that is central; ideas are secondary, important only if they threaten or actually disturb the faithful observance of the Torah as interpreted.[67]

---

65. F.G. Downing, *Cynics, Paul and the Pauline Churches* (London: Routledge, 1998); what follows summarizes chap. 10 of that book, pp. 287-95. Along with my own researches I rely particularly on work by A.J. Malherbe (without claiming his support for my conclusions).

66. Philo says, 'A merciful and forgiving God would never surrender an innocent man to be done to death', *Spec. Leg.* 3.121.

67. G.F. Moore, *Judaism in the First Centuries of the Christian Era* (Cam-

Yet Paul became convinced that he had been encountered by (and himself enlisted by) the Christians' crucified leader, now totally vindicated by God, glorified Messiah and Lord (as his disciples had been claiming). So what Jesus' followers had apparently been *doing* wrong would now be seen by Paul as pre-eminently right. The lifestyle Paul had tried to eradicate he would now himself adopt and propagate. The Christian-Cynic way of life we can see Paul enacting and articulating must, then, be presumed to have been his version (even if not a precise imitation) of what he had up to then seen and detested. He now propagated the πίστις, the faithful response to God, that he had tried to destroy (Gal. 1.23). At least in broad terms the conclusion seems irresistible; otherwise one would be imagining a Paul become convinced that what his erstwhile opponents had been doing was right, yet himself then in response still doing something quite different.

To live a life that matched his new convictions in a way that would also create the appropriate impression in the Greek towns where he was at home, he would seem to have had to adopt many facets of a fairly gentle but still rigorously self-disciplined Cynicism. If he were to live out and display his new convictions in action, this was (at the time) the most apposite manner. His praxis and its articulation obviously must be presumed to have mirrored quite closely, if not precisely, that of those he had been opposing, but with whom he now had allied himself. To draw people away from their ancestral gods (neither Jew nor Greek), and to proclaim an end to linked basic social conventions (neither bond nor free, no male and female) could only be seen as a Cynic deviancy; and this is what Paul espoused as the appropriate way to be a Christian missionary in Greek towns.

15.3. It is clear from 1 Corinthians 9 that Paul is responding to the Jesus tradition represented by the synoptic 'mission charge'.[68] Paul parading himself 'hungry and thirsty, [half-]naked and homeless' is also displaying an image and deploying slogans from Cynic stock; but he does all this precisely because it is the appropriate working out of the

---

bridge, MA: Harvard University Press, 1927), pp. 110-11; though in our period there was clearly less uniformity of practice than Moore supposed before the Qumran library had been discovered; cf., e.g., J. Neusner, *Judaisms and their Messiahs at the Turn of the Christian Era* (Cambridge: Cambridge University Press, 1987), pp. ix-xiii.

68. D. Wenham, *Paul: Follower of Jesus or Founder of Christianity?* (Grand Rapids: Eerdmans, 1995), pp. 190-200.

new life he has been drawn into. It provides the appropriate 'spectacle', it is to imitate Christ so others may too, it is to allow Christ's power (his characteristic power) to be effective. It may well be that it is by living so that Paul is 'crucified with Christ' and thus able to portray him publicly (Gal. 2.20; 3.1);[69] certainly it is by accepting tribulations in a Christian-Cynic way, he tells us, that he 'carries round in his body the death of Jesus' (2 Cor. 4.8-11). Paul himself, of course, maintains a Cynic freedom to adopt a variant method of obtaining a livelihood (one that puts him in effective touch with people (1 Thess. 2.1-12); but it is still 'in poverty' that he makes others rich (2 Cor. 6.10; as in his own way his Lord has done, 2 Cor. 8.9). Though quite obviously it is the match between his lifestyle and his understanding of Jesus Christ his Lord that is most important to Paul, he is fully aware that this Cynic-seeming way of living is rooted in a part of the wider church's Jesus tradition.

15.4. What we should conclude from this is that on many fundamental programmatic issues Paul is at one both with Cynic-seeming strands in the Jesus tradition but also with such strands among the wider Christian communities.

He has for now adopted the common deviant programmatic Christian-Cynic baptismal slogan, whose enactment not long before had aroused his principled and zealous hostility.

15.5. Obviously these findings (if in fact found at all persuasive) are important for our understanding of Paul's perception of nascent Christianity but they are also highly significant for our understanding of other Christians' reaction to Paul's Cynic Christian Judaism. Paul tells us that 'after fourteen years' he checked out the message he'd been sharing with leading Christians in Jerusalem 'lest somehow I should be running or had been running in vain' (Gal. 2.2). It was apparently agreed that in essentials he was on the right lines. The implications for legal matters (circumcision, diet and Sabbath, in particular) of the 'neither Jew nor Greek' in the baptismal formula did become controversial. On no other point where Paul appears Cynic in his behaviour and his articulation of it does he have to defend himself: in fact, quite the opposite. His Cynic-seeming practice and Cynic-sounding accounts of it are deployed as having considerable apologetic value in controversy, and

---

69. Cf. B.S. Davis, 'The Meaning of προεγράφη in the Context of Galatians 3.1', *NTS* 45 (1999), pp. 194-212.

especially in 2 Corinthians, in response to those who (even if not original apostles) represent a rival 'conservative' strand among the early communities. Paul can match their claims both to Jewish inheritance and to Cynic lifestyle: 'Hebrews ... Israelites ... descendents of Abraham ... ministers of Christ...in laborious hard work, going without sleep, hungry, thirsty, fasting, cold, [half-]naked' (2 Cor. 11.22, 27). For his response to have seemed to Paul himself to have worthwhile force, he must have seen the Cynic presentation of these central strands in his practice as affording quite uncontrovertibly important and agreed common ground.

15.6. *Already before Paul joined them around 33 CE, within a year or within at most three of the crucifixion of Jesus, the early Christian communities in many significant ways looked and sounded Cynic, to Paul (who responded in the light of this perception), and to others, and to themselves; and they went on doing so. This Cynic Judaism (or Jewish Cynicism) must seem to have been part of the earliest origins of the movement, in the life, activity and shared thoughts of Jesus himself.*

6. Concluding Thesis

A Jewish–Cynic strand in Christian origins seems to be asked to meet much higher standards than scholars use in support of their own alternatives or in discussion of others' cases, as John Kloppenborg Verbin has recently forcefully noted.[70] Deploying much the same standards with much the same rigour as serve other competing hypotheses, no easier, no harsher, Jewish–Cynic elements in the early Christian movement seem clearly arguable, along the lines sketched above, and to deserve open-minded appraisal.

---

70. J.S. Kloppenborg Verbin, '"A Dog among the Pigeons": A Cynic Q?', suggesting that the disparity seems ideological.

B

THEOLOGICAL AND HERMENEUTICAL INVESTIGATIONS
INTO THE PROCLAMATION OF JESUS

ESCHATOLOGY IN THE PROCLAMATION OF JESUS[*]

Marius Reiser

In the Foreword to the sixth edition of his *Geschichte der Leben-Jesu-Forschung*, published in 1950, Albert Schweitzer once again emphasized his principal thesis: 'Thus the oldest tradition of Jesus' proclamation and attitude can only be truly understood, as a whole and in detail, from the standpoint of eschatology, and it is only in this way that its authenticity can be genuinely demonstrated against any possible doubt'.[1] This opinion achieved consensus in the field of exegesis. For Ben F. Meyer, writing in 1979, it was a 'definitively settled fact that the proclamation and ministry of Jesus were totally eschatological'.[2] He also saw eschatology as the key to the Wisdom traditions: 'There is no sign in the gospel tradition that Jesus wished to offer sapiential principles applicable to all time'.[3] In the *Dictionary of Jesus and the Gospels*, Dale C. Allison writes: 'Perhaps the pre-eminent contribution of modern New Testament scholarship has been the demonstration that eschatology lies at the heart of Jesus' message and indeed at the heart of all the New Testament'.[4]

Beginning in the 1980s, however, the consensus on this point seems to be crumbling a little. Jesus the teacher of Wisdom has been carefully separated from Jesus the 'apocalypticist', and some scholars have absolutely denied that he made any sort of eschatological proclamation. This development began in America,[5] but it seems to be extending to Germany as well. Here Martin [5]Ebner has recently depicted Jesus as the

*   I thank Linda M. Maloney for the translation of my German manuscript.

1.   A. Schweitzer, *Geschichte der Leben-Jesu-Forschung* (Tübingen: Mohr Siebeck, 9th edn, 1984), p. 36.

2.   B.F. Meyer, *The Aims of Jesus* (London: SCM Press, 1979), p. 58. Cf. p. 211: 'Jesus' mission was eschatological through and through'.

3.   Meyer, *The Aims of Jesus*, p. 165.

4.   D.C. Allison, Jr, 'Eschatology', *DJG*, pp. 206-209 (206).

5.   Cf. M.J. Borg, *Jesus in Contemporary Scholarship* (Valley Forge, PA:

teacher of popular wisdom that can be 'assigned neither to Torah wisdom nor to apocalyptic wisdom teaching'.[6] According to Ebner his sayings served primarily as defense against vulnerable behaviors such as table fellowship with toll collectors; they were thus situationally conditioned and hence indeed not considered to be 'sapiential principles applicable to all time'. Jesus abandoned the apocalyptic convictions he had learned from the Baptizer after his vision of the fall of Satan (Lk. 10.18); from then on he viewed the reign of God as a purely present reality; 'according to Jesus it was visible and effective in his street parties with toll collectors and in his successful exorcisms',[7] 'in the midst of the old world', as 'the reign of God in fragmentary form'.[8]

Such a Jesus and a Jesus-proclamation thus interpreted is, in my opinion, a fantastic construction that can lay no claim to historical probability. The same is true in principle of every picture of a non-eschatological Jesus. In what follows I want to give my reasons for this position. In doing so, I understand 'eschatology' to mean the notion or teaching about the ἔσχατα, the Last Things, which finds twofold attestation in early Judaism: as the 'before' and 'after' surrounding the Last Day (historical eschatology), and as the 'before' and 'after' of the day of death (eschatology of the hereafter). In the first concept the cardinal point is the great judgment on the Last Day; only in the course of the

Trinity Press International, 1994), pp. 3-96. A helpful critical review of scholarship is given by B. Witherington, III, *The Jesus Quest: The Third Search for the Jew of Nazareth* (Downers Grove, IL: InterVarsity Press, 1995). Sharper in tone, but spirited, is the survey by N.T. Wright, *Jesus and the Victory of God* (Minneapolis: Fortress Press, 1996), pp. 28-124.

6. M. Ebner, *Jesus—ein Weisheitslehrer? Synoptische Weisheitslogien im Traditionsprozess* (HBS, 15; Freiburg: Herder, 1998), p. 393. See B. Witherington, III, *Jesus the Sage* (Minneapolis: Fortress Press, 1994), p. 385: 'Jesus should be viewed in the main as a prophetic sage offering primarily counter-order wisdom'. He shows that 'sapiential, prophetical, and eschatological material cross-fertilized long before Jesus' day' (*Jesus the Sage*, p. 385).

7. Ebner, *Jesus—ein Weisheitslehrer?*, p. 414. Where did Ebner find the street parties?

8. Ebner, *Jesus—ein Weisheitslehrer?*, p. 417. Here he speaks of Jesus' 'banquets'. Where is the evidence for these? Mk 2.13-17 par. and Mt. 11.19 par. cannot be so regarded. Only at the multiplication of loaves (Mk 6.35-44; 8.1-8 par.) and at the Last Supper (Mk 14.22-24 par.) does Jesus appear as organizer and host at a meal. Moreover, Heinz Schürmann has already described Jesus' 'meals organized with sinners' as a 'scholarly legend' (*Gottes Reich: Jesu Geschick* [Freiburg: Herder, 1983], p. 37 n. 58, p. 206 n. 85).

second to the fifth centuries CE did the idea of a personal judgment immediately after death arise (and with it the difficulty of relating the two judgments to one another). I understand 'apocalyptic' as a particular form or way of presenting eschatology, namely by means of the elements typical of apocalyptic description: accounts of visions, cryptic language, historical overviews, etc.[9] In my opinion there is little sense in talking about Jesus 'the apocalypticist', since we know of apocalypticists only as literary authors. However, to the extent that we encounter elements of apocalyptic literature in Jesus' eschatology we can call it apocalyptically colored eschatology.

1. *History as Puzzle*

The acceptance of an uneschatological Jesus involves historical and tradition-historical difficulties that make the historical phenomena both of Jesus and of early Christianity a single incomprehensible puzzle. This can be demonstrated from two angles.

First, after the exile that followed the conquest of Jerusalem in 587 BCE we can observe a growing eschatological and apocalyptic coloring in Jewish faith convictions. At the center of those convictions is the expectation of a great day of judgment that will bring with it a definitive turn in Israel's history and that of the world, for on that day God would establish divine rule throughout the world. This conviction was associated with prophetic traditions such as 'the day of YHWH', and it dominates apocalyptic literature from the earliest Enoch writings and the book of Daniel through *4 Ezra*, which is a compendium of widely varied manifestations of such beliefs.[10] A considerable part of the Essene literature fits within this context as well.[11] That these were not simply the convictions of small groups is evident from the Jewish prayer tradition with its eschatological petitions, especially in the Kaddish and the Tefillah. It is further demonstrated by the general inclination to an

---

9. I offer a more detailed basis for these distinctions in my *Jesus and Judgment: The Eschatological Proclamation in its Jewish Context* (trans. Linda M. Maloney; Minneapolis: Fortress Press, 1997), pp. 1-25, 144-63.

10. See Reiser, *Jesus and Judgment*, pp. 19-163.

11. There is a fine summary in J.J. Collins, *Apocalypticism in the Dead Sea Scrolls* (London: Routledge, 1997). Cf. *idem*, *Jewish Wisdom in the Hellenistic Age* (Louisville, KY: Westminster/John Knox Press, 1997), pp. 226-29 ('Wisdom and Apocalypticism').

eschatological interpretation of passages from the Old Testament that we can observe in the Septuagint, the scriptural commentaries from Qumran, and the rabbinic writings.[12] Finally, we should not forget that both the great Jewish rebellions in Palestine in 66–70 and 132–135 CE, as well as the rebellion in Egypt in 115–117 CE, were sustained by eschatological expectations. This deeply rooted eschatological orientation of early Judaism was maintained in early Christianity. 'Thus, in the age of Hillel and Jesus, apocalyptic beliefs influenced and even precipitated key political events, generated a vast popular literature, reflected the love of the folk, informed popular piety, and motivated several of the major sects, including infant Christianity.'[13]

Against this background a non-eschatological Jesus is highly unlikely. In addition, nothing suggests that the saying about the fall of Satan in Lk. 10.18 was associated with a turning point in the life of Jesus or with any kind of rejection of the Baptizer's eschatology on his part.[14] Finally, why would the Sanhedrin have instigated the death of a harmless itinerant preacher, and on what grounds would a Roman governor have had him crucified?

Secondly, supposing a Jesus without an eschatological proclamation, where did the eschatological logia and parables in the synoptic tradition come from?[15] The thesis of a non-eschatological proclamation of Jesus implies that at least a third of the logia and parables in the Synoptic Gospels are post-Easter constructions. Who is supposed to have been responsible for these ingenious ideas? Why did the person to whom they appealed have to be first remodeled, in fact almost reinvented? Who was in charge of this deliberate process of transformation—the post-Easter 'community'? Who is that? Where did it come from if it cannot be traced historically to Jesus? Again Albert Schweitzer had a correct

12. Cf. Reiser, *Jesus and Judgment*, pp. 24-25, 32-38, 142-43.

13. S.E. Robinson, 'Apocalypticism in the Time of Hillel and Jesus', in J.H. Charlesworth and L.L. Johns (eds.), *Hillel and Jesus* (Minneapolis: Fortress Press, 1997), pp. 121-36 (126).

14. U.B. Müller has attempted to demonstrate such a connection in his article, 'Vision und Botschaft: Erwägungen zur prophetischen Struktur der Verkündigung Jesu', *ZTK* 74 (1977), pp. 416-48.

15. Cf. E. Rau, 'Wie entstehen unechte Jesusworte?', in E. Brandt, P.S. Fiddes and J. Molthagen (eds.), *Gemeinschaft am Evangelium: Festschrift für Wiard Popkes zum 60. Geburtstag* (Leipzig: Evangelische Verlagsanstalt, 1996), pp. 159-86. According to Rau, 'new constructions of entire sayings as well as additions are based entirely on traditional logia' ('Wie entstehen unechte Jesusworte?', p. 177).

insight when he wrote: 'Scholarship that wants to set aside eschatology must cut out major parts of the accounts in the two oldest gospels as later additions, and in the end retains only a text cut to ribbons, which is of no good use for anything'.[16]

2. *On the Wrong Track*

The Fellows of the Jesus Seminar have rendered decisions about the authenticity or non-authenticity of every saying and parable of Jesus by voting on them.[17] John Dominic Crossan organizes the sources, as would an archaeologist, according to age strata, adds up the independent witnesses to a tradition, and then assigns each one a plus (for genuine) or a minus (for non-genuine).[18] This analysis of strata, like every attempt to distinguish authentic from non-authentic Jesus traditions by whatever method, is based on an idea that has accompanied research on the historical Jesus from the very beginning: the idea of a portrait that has been painted over. Many historical Jesus researchers see themselves as some sort of restorers who will remove the layers of overpainting from the original picture of Jesus in order to bring out the first, unfalsified image. 'Whoever wants to get through to the historical Jesus must clear away the *Christian* reworkings.'[19] But what in fact emerges from beneath the layers that are removed is a set of lines and dots of color that at best indicate some vague outlines and sketches. The restorers have to add quite a bit in order to produce a clear, colorful picture from these indications. But then the result is anything but the original picture. Those who think they can arrive at the historical Jesus through some kind of process of making distinctions among the sources are suffering from an illusion.[20] The historian Henri-Irénée Marrou saw that quite

16. Schweitzer, *Geschichte*, p. 33.

17. R.W. Funk, R.W. Hoover and the Jesus Seminar, *The Five Gospels: The Search for the Authentic Words of Jesus. New Translation and Commentary* (New York: Macmillan, 1993).

18. J.D. Crossan, *The Historical Jesus: The Life of a Mediterranean Jewish Peasant* (San Francisco: HarperSanFrancisco, 1991). German translation: *Der historische Jesus. Aus dem Englishen vou P. Hahlbrock* (Munich: C.H. Beck, 1994).

19. Ebner, *Jesus—ein Weisheitslehrer?*, pp. 49-50 (emphasis in original). Ebner cherishes a deep distrust of the Christian tradition about Jesus, as is abundantly clear from the conclusion of his book.

20. Cf. T. Söding, *Wege der Schriftauslegung: Methodenbuch zum Neuen Testament* (Freiburg: Herder, 1998), pp. 287-88.

clearly as early as 1954: he called 'naïve' the notion that one could 'take apart' the witness of the Gospels 'and by separating the wheat from the chaff shell out a kernel of authentic "facts"'. He concludes that 'we reach Jesus only through the picture his disciples made of him'.[21] It follows from this that 'If we cannot trust the Church to have understood Jesus, then we have lost Jesus: and the resources of modern scholarship will not help us to find him'.[22]

However, the enterprise of separating the wheat from the chaff in the Jesus traditions is subject not only to this fundamental reservation; in its concrete execution it is also often more than merely unsatisfying. This is true not least with regard to the eschatological sayings and especially Jesus' sayings and parables about judgment. In *The Five Gospels* from the Jesus Seminar they are all printed in black, thus counting as ungenuine. The reason given is: 'The vindictive tone of these sayings is uncharacteristic of Jesus'.[23] Apparently the Fellows of the Jesus Seminar know even *before* separating the wheat from the chaff what is characteristic of Jesus. They do not wait until the overpainting has been removed to see what kind of picture emerges; instead, they already know what the picture will be.[24] This is the kind of *petitio principii* that we encounter again and again in this field. John Dominic Crossan also sets a minus against all the sayings complexes that speak of eschatological judgment, without regard to the stratum of tradition to which they belong and the number of independent witnesses that contain them. One searches his book in vain for any reason for this.[25]

In this connection I must say a word also about the tiresome question of the burden of proof: what is to be proved—the authenticity or the non-authenticity of a tradition?[26] Among exegetes one repeatedly encounters the opinion that anything that cannot be shown positively to be

---

21. H.-I. Marrou, *De la connaissance historique* (Paris: Editions du Seuil, 1954), p. 108.

22. A. Louth, *Discerning the Mystery: An Essay on the Nature of Theology* (New York: Oxford University Press, 1983), p. 93.

23. Funk, Hoover and the Jesus Seminar, *The Five Gospels*, p. 188.

24. Cf. N.T. Wright, 'Five Gospels but no Gospel: Jesus and the Seminar', in B. Chilton and C.A. Evans (eds.), *Authenticating the Activities of Jesus* (NTTS, 28.1; Leiden: E.J. Brill, 1999), pp. 83-120 (101-103).

25. For more detail see Reiser, *Jesus and Judgment*, pp. 3-4. See also my review of Crossan's book, *Der historische Jesus*, in *TTZ* 104 (1995), pp. 78-80.

26. See my remarks in *Jesus and Judgment*, pp. 4-5, 204-205.

authentic must be regarded as inauthentic.[27] Writing Greek or Roman
history under the restrictions of this principle would be a hopeless task.
The method thus demanded recalls a satiric episode in G.K. Chesterton's novel, *The Ball and the Cross*, in which the master of a mental
hospital seeks a change in the laws about lunacy. He explains 'the real
scientific objection to all existing legislation about lunacy':

> [T]he mistake was supposing insanity to be merely an exception or an
> extreme. Insanity, like forgetfulness, is simply a quality which enters
> more or less into all human beings; and for practical purposes it is more
> necessary to know whose mind is really trustworthy than whose has
> some accidental taint. We have therefore reversed the existing method,
> and people now have to prove that they are sane.[28]

The analogy is hard to dismiss. In the case of the question of the
authenticity of Jesus traditions it is just as absurd to presume that it is
more necessary to know which of them is really trustworthy than which
of them has 'some accidental taint', and therefore to demand the reversal of sound methodical principles.

Moreover, the principle of methodical doubt and the hermeneutics of
suspicion that this kind of scholarship has prescribed for itself, a scholarship, that likes to call itself 'critical',[29] does not do justice to the
sources. Henri Marrou demonstrated that in a brilliant chapter of his
book.[30] The historian 'should not adopt a sullen, nit-picking, belligerent
attitude toward the witnesses of the past, like a bad policeman for
whom every person called to appear is suspect *a priori* and considered

27. Thus the Fellows of the Jesus Seminar, or W. Zager, *Gottesherrschaft und
Endgericht in der Verkündigung Jesu: Eine Untersuchung zur markinischen
Jesusüberlieferung einschliesslich der Q-Parallelen* (BZNW, 82; Berlin: W. de
Gruyter, 1996), p. 47. He, too, cannot manage without the *petitio principii*
described above. See my review in *BZ* NS 42 (1998), pp. 135-36.

28. G.K. Chesterton, *The Ball and the Cross* (Woodbridge: Boydell, 1984), pp.
156-57. The novel was originally published in installments in 1905–1906 and as a
book by J. Lane Co. (New York) in 1909.

29. For the concept of the 'critical' in connection with historical research see the
enlightening remarks of B.L. Martin, 'Reflections on Historical Criticism and Self-
Understanding', in D.J. Hawkin and T. Robinson (eds.), *Self-Definition and Self-
Discovery in Early Christianity: A Study in Changing Horizons. Essays in
Appreciation of Ben F. Meyer from Former Students* (SBEC, 26; Lewiston, NY:
Edwin Mellen Press, 1990), pp. 55-77.

30. Marrou, *De la connaissance historique*, pp. 97-121: 'Conditions et moyens
de la comprehension'.

guilty until the contrary is proven', because this attitude renders one incapable 'of recognizing the real significance, the import, and the value of the documents one is studying'.[31] The right attitude is instead one of sympathy, even friendship, which does not exclude a critical spirit, but includes it. The goal of historical research is not criticism, but an understanding of the past and its documents. Marrou therefore desires to see 'the positive notion of *understanding* a document' substituted for 'the fundamentally negative notion of 'critical' inquiry'.[32]

Under these circumstances, is discovering the early traditions and authentic words of Jesus entirely hopeless and without meaning? Surely not. But we have to be clear about the restricted nature of the question. It is neither possible nor necessary to reconstruct the authentic image of Jesus and his proclamation from a selected number of traditions drawn from a supposedly 'oldest' stratum, no matter by what method the selection is made. As a rule, literary strata do not lie one above the other in such a way that they can be cleanly separated, as happens in archaeology. Correct information and accurate interpretations can also be found in later traditions. Revised and even newly created logia can reproduce the sense of what was really said. A great deal always depends on the genre and manner of presentation of a document and its components, as well as on the ways by which its authors obtained their information. We may not, from the viewpoint of the twentieth or twenty-first centuries, place utopian demands on the New Testament traditions. In addition, inconsistencies and contradictions in these traditions are by no means signs that they are untrustworthy as a whole; on the contrary:

> [T]he very abundance of historical inconsistencies speaks in favor of an … untidy, but certainly developed oral tradition whose honest basic effort at the beginnings of the formation of tradition was apparently to preserve as precise as possible a memory of Jesus, his teaching and proclamation, that is, to give a true and historical witness. And precisely this unique, unfalsifiable overall impression has undoubtedly been preserved in the canonical gospels—and for critical observers the effect is scarcely different than for the naïve—no matter how many details in the accounts may still, and perhaps forever, remain disputable.[33]

31. Marrou, *De la connaissance historique*, pp. 97-98.
32. Marrou, *De la connaissance historique*, p. 107.
33. H. Strasburger, 'Die Bibel in der Sicht eines Althistorikers', in *idem*, *Studien zur Alten Geschichte* (Collectanea, 42.3; Hildesheim: Georg Olms, 1990), pp. 317-39 (336-37).

This honest judgment of a renowned historian of the ancient world is worthy of note and may help us to keep inappropriate skepticism within its limits.

3. Fundamental Rules of Historical Reconstruction

> Nor is it a slight benefit to know what is probable, and what is not so, what is needed for the proof of a point, what is wanting in a theory, how a theory hangs together, and what will follow, if it be admitted.[34]

Before I attempt a sketch of Jesus' eschatological preaching I want to describe the principles that guide me. They arise in part out of the preceding considerations.

1. In the case of logia, parables and anecdotes we should start with the oldest version that can be reconstructed. However, this basic principle may not lead us to regard secondary versions that are shown by tradition criticism to be secondary as *eo ipso* without value. Redactions can also work with historically accurate information or offer historically accurate interpretations. No complete picture of Jesus and his preaching can be derived from an earlier, but fragmentary, stratum of source material such as the Sayings Source.[35]

2. A tradition may be regarded as authentic as long as there are no serious reasons for not doing so. In some cases, of course, it is advisable or even necessary to leave the question undecided.[36] That will be the case here as regards all the Son of Man sayings, because they present special difficulties both as to their tradition history and to their interpretation.

---

34. J.H. Newman, *An Essay in Aid of a Grammar of Assent* (New York: Oxford University Press, 1985 [orig. London: Burns & Oates, 1870]), p. 186.

35. Cf. D. Kosch, 'Q und Jesus', *BZ* 36 (1992), pp. 30-58. I simply cannot understand how one can treat the preaching of judgment in Q separately from the historical question of Jesus, as does, e.g., C.-P. März, 'Zum Verständnis der Gerichtspredigt in Q', in H.-J. Klauck (ed.), *Weltgericht und Weltvollendung* (QD, 150; Freiburg: Herder, 1994), pp. 128-48. He thinks that the strong accent on judgment preaching in Q is 'a reflection of the negative missionary experiences of the Q community' ('Zum Verständnis der Gerichtspredigt', p. 145). But what do we know of the Q community? Was there even such a thing? Is it not the case that here the historically certain figure of Jesus of Nazareth is being replaced by the hypothetical entity of a Q community?

36. B.F. Meyer pointed this out repeatedly: see *The Aims of Jesus*, pp. 83-84; *idem*, 'Jesus Christ', *ABD*, III, pp. 773-96 (776).

3. A variety of criteria may be used for a positive assessment of authenticity. The strongest is the so-called 'criterion of dissimilarity' or 'non-derivability'. It seeks discrepancies with the Jewish tradition on the one hand and the Christian tradition on the other hand. But the weight and scope of this criterion are under constant discussion.[37] There is certainly agreement that no claim to exclusivity may be raised, because with the aid of this criterion we can detect only what is absolutely unique and original with Jesus. We must, however, presume that Jesus stood in a relationship both of continuity *and* discontinuity to early Judaism and early Christianity. The demands of the double criterion of dissimilarity in regard to a single tradition are, in any case, exaggerated, for 'that the community should gratuitously adopt from Judaism elements in discontinuity with its own concerns, practices, and tendencies simply does not make sense. Discontinuity with the post-paschal church is sufficient by itself to establish historicity.'[38] I see no reason to dispense entirely with this criterion, as has recently been demanded.[39]

4. The proposal of a purely inductive method for reconstructing Jesus' authentic proclamation is unsustainable and illusory.[40] It overlooks the different hermeneutical circles to which every historical interpretation is subject. Thus in the case of textual interpretation the hermeneutical circle of the part and the whole is unavoidable.[41] The interpretation of

37. See most recently T. Holmén, 'Doubts about Double Dissimilarity: Reconstructing the Main Criterion of Jesus-of-History Research', in B. Chilton and C.A. Evans (eds.), *Authenticating the Words of Jesus* (NTTS, 28.2; Leiden: E.J. Brill, 1999), pp. 47-80.

38. Meyer, *The Aims of Jesus*, p. 86.

39. Cf. G. Theissen and D. Winter, *Die Kriterienfrage in der Jesusforschung: Vom Differenzkriterium zum Plausibilitätskriterium* (NTOA, 34; Fribourg: Universitätsverlag; Göttingen: Vandenhoeck & Ruprecht, 1997). In regard to the criterion of dissimilarity it is also a question of plausibility!

40. This can be found, e.g., in Ebner, *Jesus—ein Weisheitslehrer?*, p. 53.

41. Cf. H.-G. Gadamer, *Wahrheit und Methode* (Tübingen: Mohr Siebeck, 4th edn, 1975), pp. 275-83; R. Bultmann, 'Das Problem der Hermeneutik', in *idem*, *Glauben und Verstehen*, II (Tübingen: Mohr Siebeck, 1961), pp. 211-35. To my knowledge B.F. Meyer was the exegete who devoted the most fundamental attention to historical hermeneutics. The whole first section of his book, *The Aims of Jesus* (pp. 23-110), is devoted to that question. Especially pertinent to our theme here is his book, *Reality and Illusion in New Testament Scholarship: A Primer in Critical Realist Hermeneutics* (Collegeville, MN: Liturgical Press, 1994), pp. 87-113. Still scarcely noticed are J.H. Newman's acute observations on the role of the 'illative sense' in historical studies, in his *Grammar of Assent*, pp. 234-47.

individual passages is always governed in part by a previous understanding, that is, a more or less clear overall picture in the mind of the
interpreter; in turn, a carefully investigated individual passage can (and
should) alter and correct the prior understanding.[42] The dynamic of this
hermeneutical circle, which is certainly not a vicious circle, ought to
leave to a well-founded overall picture in which every individual element seems to be meaningfully integrated and ordered. What ultimately
persuades is the overall picture, and in the end it determines the acceptance enjoyed by the interpretation of an individual passage or aspect of
the matter.

5. 'A new conjecture should only be presented in the awareness that,
if it doesn't solve its next problem by its own evidence and thereby
cease to be a mere conjecture, it can nevertheless serve to shed light on
other series of facts in its field and within that field to narrow what
is problematic, incomprehensible, and opaque. Otherwise conjectures,
hypotheses, suggestions are not aids to historical scholarship, but
plagues.'[43]

4. *Jesus' Eschatological Proclamation*

For we which now behold these present days,
Have eyes to wonder, but lack tongues to praise.[44]

According to the Synoptic Gospels Jesus summarized the main idea of
his proclamation in the phrase βασιλεία τοῦ θεοῦ.[45] With this expression he described that to which his whole activity and all that he said
were directed. Semantically, what we have here is a concept or cipher
whose concrete meaning must be derived from its common usage and

42. Cf. F. Hahn, 'Methodologische Überlegungen zur Rückfrage nach Jesus', in
K. Kertelge (ed.), *Rückfrage nach Jesus* (QD, 63; Freiburg: Herder, 1974), pp. 11-
77 (37-40).

43. F. Overbeck, *Werke und Nachlaß*. IV. *Kirchenlexicon* (ed. B. von Reibnitz;
Stuttgart: Metzler, 1995), p. 398.

44. W. Shakespeare, Sonnet 106, ll. 13-14.

45. A good overview of its use by Jesus and in Jewish tradition is found in D.C.
Duling, 'Kingdom of God, Kingdom of Heaven', *ABD*, IV, pp. 49-69. Cf. also J.P.
Meier, *A Marginal Jew: Rethinking the Historical Jesus*. II. *Mentor, Message and
Miracles* (ABRL; 2 vols.; New York: Doubleday, 1994), pp. 237-506. There are
important contributions in M. Hengel and A.M. Schwemer (eds.), *Königsherrschaft
Gottes und himmlischer Kult im Judentum, Urchristentum und in der hellenis-
tischen Welt* (WUNT, 55; Tübingen: Mohr Siebeck, 1991).

its application by Jesus himself. The Greek word βασιλεία means both 'kingdom' and 'kingly power' or 'kingly rule'. Corresponding abstract concepts derived from the root מלך are also found in Hebrew and Aramaic in a number of variant forms. It is true that the Old Testament literature, as well as that of early Judaism and the rabbis, seldom speak of God's rule in abstract terms, but we do find them at important points in prayer literature and in the Targums.[46]

Thus in Psalm 145 three successive verses (11-13) speak of the 'glory' and 'everlasting' nature of God's reign (מַלְכוּת),[47] and Ps. 103.19 says: 'The LORD has established his throne in the heavens, And his kingdom [מַלְכוּתוֹ] rules over all.' The Psalm closes with a call to praise the Lord 'in all places of his dominion' (מֶמְשַׁלְתּוֹ).[48]

Thus the devout knew that God's kingly power rules the universe; all the more painful, then, was it to find that there were people and powers who resisted that rule, even in Israel. And God apparently allowed these people and powers to do as they pleased. The consequence was that God's rule for the most part had only a nominal character. Hence the devout set their hopes more and more on the future, when God would cease to have patience with these opponents and 'his kingly rule over all creation' would really 'appear'.[49] Joined to this was the expectation that God would 'establish' (קוּם) this indestructible rule *for God's people* and thus put an end to all foreign rule (Dan. 2.44).[50] Probably the most famous expression of this is in Daniel 7.

46. B.D. Chilton has repeatedly pointed to the Targums: 'Regnum Dei Deus Est', *SJT* 31 (1978), pp. 261-70; *idem, The Glory of Israel: The Theology and Provenience of the Isaiah Targum* (JSOTSup, 23; Sheffield: JSOT Press, 1983), pp. 77-81; *idem, A Galilean Rabbi and his Bible: Jesus' Own Interpretation of Isaiah* (GNS, 8; London: SPCK, 1984), pp. 58-63. Cf. also his translation of the *Targum of Isaiah*, *The Isaiah Targum* (The Aramaic Bible, 11; Wilmington, DE: Michael Glazier, 1987).

47. Dan. 3.33; 4.31; 6.27 also speak of God's eternal reign.

48. Cf. also Ps. 22.28 (29).

49. *Ass. Mos.* 10.1: 'Et tunc parebit regnum illius in omni creatura illius.' We also read of the 'appearing' (φαίνεσθαι) of God's βασιλεία in *Sib. Or.* 3.46-47. The eight instances in the Targums of the prophetic books also all speak of the 'appearing' (גלי) of God's royal rule: *Targ. Isa.* 24.23; 31.4; 40.9; 52.7; *Targ. Ezek.* 7.7, 10; *Targ. Obad.* 21; *Targ. Mic.* 4.7, 8; *Targ. Zech.* 14.9.

50. Cf. *Sib. Or.* 3.767-68: ἐξεγερεῖ βασιλήιον εἰς αἰῶνας/πάντας ἐπ' ἀνθρώπους: 'He [God] will establish an eternal kingdom over all people'.

The tension, and indeed the paradox, expressed here remained characteristic of the conception of the reign of God in the rabbinic period as well. This is impressively shown by *Mekhilta de Rabbi Ishmael*,[51] according to which God made his kingly rule visible through his victory over the Egyptians at the Exodus. But Israel neglected to proclaim that rule and thus delayed its true realization until the eschatological future, when Israel's enemies will finally be conquered (with reference to Zech. 14.9: 'And the LORD will become king over all the earth; on that day the LORD will be one and his name one'). This interpretation is connected to a certain understanding of the imperfect יִמְלֹךְ in Exod. 15.18, which is read as future.[52] Nevertheless, God's kingly rule is not fully banished from the present; Israel remains God's beloved people and at Sinai it had accepted God as its ruler. (This is derived from Exod. 20.2: 'I am the LORD your God'.) This reign is realized in every place where God's will, revealed at that time, is lived up to.

We find a tension similar to the one expressed in this rabbinic conception in Jesus' concept of the reign of God. But here, significantly, the past plays no part; the tension is created instead by a new notion of the present aspect of this reign. Jesus was convinced of the present realization and ever possible realization of the royal reign of God in a way that is unknown to the tradition before him. He did not refer to scriptural passages such as Exod. 15.18, the Sinai tradition, or Zech. 14.9; instead, he derived his inspiration from Isa. 52.7:

> How beautiful upon the mountains
>   are the feet of the messenger who announces peace,
> who brings good news,
>   who announces salvation,
>   who says to Zion, 'Your God reigns'.[53]

51. In what follows I am relying on the careful study by B. Ego, 'Gottes Weltherrschaft und die Einzigkeit seines Namens: Eine Untersuchung zur Rezeption der Königsmetapher in der Mekhilta de R. Yishma'el', in M. Hengel and A.M. Schwemer (eds.), *Königsherrschaft Gottes und himmlischer Kult im Judentum, Urchristentum und in der hellenistischen Welt* (WUNT, 55; Tübingen: Mohr Siebeck, 1991), pp. 257-83.

52. Cf. Ego, 'Gottes Weltherrschaft', pp. 267-68; Reiser, *Jesus and Judgment*, p. 143. In the latter there is unfortunately a mistake: in l.24 it should of course read מֶלֶךְ.

53. Cf. Isa. 24.23; Ezek. 20.33; Mic. 4.7; *T. Dan.* 4.13.

The Targum paraphrases the proclamation of the 'messenger who announces peace' (מְבַשֵּׂר) with the aid of an abstraction: 'The reign of your God has been made manifest' (אתגליאת מלכותא דאלהיך).[54] It is not impossible that this version was in common use even before 70 CE. Isaiah 52.7 is cited in a clearly eschatological context in 11QMelch;[55] the 'messenger of peace' is there interpreted as the Messiah.[56] In addition, the whole fragment is marked by allusions to Isa. 61.1-2. The connection of these two prophetic passages is not accidental, for both contain the keyword בשׂר (pi), which the Septuagint translates with εὐαγγελίζεσθαι.

The two prophetic passages connected in 11QMelch seem to have been especially important for Jesus' proclamation and his self-understanding. Only in Isa. 52.7 (and the corresponding Isa. 40.9-11) do we find within the Old Testament the message of God's assumption of rule over God's people connected with an express mention of the messenger who brings this news. The inclination to interpret this messenger as an eschatological messenger and to make the identification with the Messiah is evident from 11QMelch and *Lev. R.* 9.9. Since Jesus made the message of God's assumption of rule over God's people the center of his proclamation, he must have seen himself as the eschatological messenger announced by Isaiah. That is also how the Synoptics present it.[57]

In the Nazareth pericope (Lk. 4.16-21) Luke made Isa. 61.1-2 Jesus' programmatic manifesto; however, there can scarcely be any doubt, that this stylization reflected Jesus' own self-understanding. This is shown especially by the anecdote of the Baptizer's question, transmitted in Q (Mt. 11.2-6//Lk. 7.18-23). There Jesus responds to the question whether he is the one expected in the end-time by pointing to the success of his activity, especially his miracles, and he does so by echoing the foretelling by the prophet Isaiah, which he depicts as being fulfilled; this includes the good news for the poor in Isa. 61.1.[58] This good news also

---

54. Chilton (see n. 46, *Isaiah Targum*) translates: 'The Kingdom of your God is revealed'.

55. Cf. Reiser, *Jesus and Judgment*, pp. 82–83; B.D. Chilton and C.A. Evans, 'Jesus and Israel's Scriptures', in B.D. Chilton and C.A. Evans (eds.), *Studying the Historical Jesus: Evaluations of the State of Current Research* (NTTS, 19; Leiden: E.J. Brill, 1994), pp. 281-335 (322-26).

56. This interpretation is also found in *Lev. R.* 9.9.

57. Cf. Mt. 4.23; 9.35; Mk 1.14-15; Lk. 4.43; 16.16.

58. For the interpretation cf. H. Kvalbein, 'Die Wunder der Endzeit: Beobachtun-

forms the content of the first beatitude (Mt. 5.3//Lk. 6.20). From all this
it follows that we may regard Isa. 52.7 in connection with Isa. 61.1-2
'as not only a plausible but a probable source' for Jesus' proclamation.[59]

These two passages from the prophets also summarily indicate what
is new and distinctive about Jesus in contrast to John the Baptizer. The
latter also associated his self-understanding with two prophetic passages, but these are drawn not from Isaiah, but from Malachi: Mal. 3.1,
23-24.[60] The first verse speaks of the messenger (מַלְאָךְ) who will prepare for God's eschatological coming as judge; the second identifies
that messenger as the prophet Elijah. Both the Baptizer and Jesus thus
see themselves, on the basis of prophetic words in Scripture, as messengers, the one as Malachi's messenger of judgment, the other as Isaiah's
bringer of good news.

What was Jesus' concrete conception of the meaning of the message
he, as the bringer of good news, had to deliver? What was involved, for
him, in the symbol called in Greek βασιλεία τοῦ θεοῦ? That symbol
appears in many texts as a 'place' or 'realm' into which one may enter,
where there is eating and drinking (Mt. 8.11-12 par.; Mk 14.25), but
that is inaccessible to the rich (Mk 10.25 par.). In those cases the translation 'kingdom of God' is appropriate. That kind of spatial conception
also dominates the Parables of the Great Feast (Lk. 14.16-24) and the
Mustard Seed (Mk 4.30-32 par.). Other logia and parables are based
more on the idea of ruling *power* and the *exercise of authority,* as when
the text speaks of 'proclaiming' the βασιλεία (Lk. 9.2) or of its 'coming', as in the second petition of the Lord's Prayer (Mt. 6.10//Lk. 11.2).
In those cases a translation such as 'reign' is more accurate. The special
way in which God exercises ruling authority is illustrated in parables
such as those of the Unmerciful Servant (Mt. 18.23-34) or of the Work-
ers in the Vineyard (Mt. 20.1-15). Both aspects are united in the logion:

gen zu 4Q521 und Matth 11,5p', *ZNW* 88 (1997), pp. 111-25. Cf. C.M. Tuckett
(ed.), *The Scriptures in the Gospels* (BETL, 131; Leuven: Leuven University Press,
1997). A number of essays in this volume are concerned with the influence of Isa.
61.1-2 on the Jesus tradition (C.M. Tuckett, F. Neirynck, K.-W. Niebuhr, P.J.
Tomson). Unfortunately, the question of Jesus' understanding plays only a very
marginal role in these studies.

   59. Meyer, 'Jesus Christ', p. 780. Cf. idem, *The Aims of Jesus*, pp. 133-34.
   60. Cf. Lk. 1.16-17, 76. On this see Reiser, *Jesus and Judgment*, p. 183. In both
places the Baptizer is designated, contrary to the usual Christian view, as the pre-
cursor of God, not of Jesus.

'Truly I tell you, whoever does not receive the βασιλεία of God as a little child will never enter it' (Mk 10.15). The first part of the logion sees the βασιλεία as a rule that one accepts, the second as a realm into which one enters. Both the German and English languages are somewhat at a loss for an adequate translation here.

The sense of the petition 'Your βασιλεία come!' is: Come to rule as king.[61] It points to the historical *future*, as does the saying about being companions at table in the reign of God (Mt. 8.11-12//Lk. 13.28-29). Jesus' announcement at the Last Supper that he will drink wine anew in the kingdom of God (Mk 14.25), in contrast, points to *something after death*. This conception, at first surprising, that the salvation of the final and complete realization of God's rule is, on the one hand, transferred to the historical future and on the other hand to some kind of existence after death may appear contradictory, yet the combination of historical eschatology and eschatology of the hereafter had a long tradition in early Judaism.[62] Jesus places himself within that tradition.

But Jesus does not simply take up a variant form of Jewish eschatology; he brings a new element into it, and one that fundamentally alters its conception. This unheard-of new element is the claim that the βασιλεία of God is being given its final and definitive manifestation or even actualization in his own work. Jesus was convinced that the reign of God becomes present everywhere he appears and is accepted as Isaiah's messenger of good news. He justifies this claim by pointing to his miracles: '…if it is by the finger of God that I cast out the demons, then the kingdom of God has come to you' (Lk. 11.20; cf. Mt. 12.28).[63] That seals the fall of Satan, of which the saying in Lk. 10.18 speaks: Jesus, the 'stronger', has overcome the 'strong one' (= Satan) (Mk 3.27). In his answer to the Baptizer's question (Mt. 11.2-6//Lk. 7.18-23) Jesus refers to his miracles of healing, his raising the dead, and the good news preached to the poor. He thus sees the presence of God's rule demon-

---

61. Cf. Meier, *A Marginal Jew*, II, p. 299.

62. Cf. Reiser, *Jesus and Judgment*, pp. 150-52. We find this combination, for example, in *1 En.* 22, in the *Wisdom of Solomon*, in the *Liber Antiquitatum Biblicarum* of Pseudo-Philo, in *4 Ezra* 7, and in the *Paralipomena Jeremiae*.

63. The word φθάνω here, as throughout the New Testament, has its usual *koine* meaning, 'come'. For the interpretation of the logion see now M. Hengel, 'Der Finger und die Herrschaft Gottes in Lk 11,20', in R. Kieffer and J. Bergman (eds.), *La main de Dieu, Die Hand Gottes* (WUNT, 94; Tübingen: Mohr Siebeck, 1997), pp. 87-106.

strated especially in these miracles; he regards them as real symbols of the βασιλεία τοῦ θεοῦ.[64] The blessing of the eye- and ear-witnesses in Lk. 10.23-24 par. also belongs in this context:

> Blessed are the eyes that see what you see!
> For I tell you that many prophets and kings desired to see what you see,
>> but did not see it, and to hear what you hear, but did not hear it.

Jesus' words and deeds are the things to be seen and heard. The contrast to the otherwise usual conception becomes clear when we compare this beatitude of Jesus with the analogous beatitudes in the *Psalms of Solomon* (17.44; 18.6):

> Blessed are they who will live in those days
>> and see the goodness of Israel,
>> which God will create in the union of the tribes!

> Blessed are they who will live in those days
>> and see the goodness of the Lord,
>> which he will create for the generation to come...!

In both cases, for Jesus as in the *Psalms of Solomon*, the visible goods of the end-time are an occasion for blessing. For the psalmists those goods are reserved for a 'generation to come'; the happiness they convey is music for the future. For Jesus, in contrast, the longed-for goods are present: for all eyes that see and all ears that hear; the music of the future is already sounding; the 'coming generation' of the end time is that of his contemporaries.

The double parable of the treasure and the pearl (Mt. 13.44-46) also presumes the presence of the eschatological goods. Until they are found, this present is, however, hidden. Thus this parable can explain the paradoxical reality of the eschatological goods: they are invisibly there until a finder comes, one who has eyes to see.

The relationship between present and future in the reign of God is usually defined in such a way that the present is characterized as proleptic and incomplete, while the future is the perfection of the things now begun, which until then remain fragmentary.[65] Gerhard Lohfink

---

64. Cf. M. Reiser, 'Die Wunder Jesu–eine Peinlichkeit?', *EuA* 73 (1997), pp. 425-37 (434-37).

65. Thus also Meier, *A Marginal Jew*, II, p. 453. M. Hengel sees a continuity between the 'punctual arrival' of the reign of God 'now' and its future completion 'then'. It consists 'in the activity of Jesus', which leads toward perfection ('Der Finger und die Herrschaft Gottes', p. 105).

has correctly described such definitions as inappropriate and inadequate reductions of the real presence of the reign of God, by means of which 'the reign of God is, in fact, forced back into the future'.[66] In truth it is only possible to avoid diminishing the present aspect of the reign of God (or of any Christian eschatology!) by regarding the two aspects as a paradoxical unity.[67] It is one of the fundamental paradoxes that permeate human life and all reality. If we are unaware of the full presence of the eschatological goods, the fault is only with us. We must again and again confess to God, with Augustine: *Mecum eras, et tecum non eram.*[68]

The summary of Jesus' message as formulated in Mk 1.15 speaks of the closeness of the reign of God and gives that closeness as the reason for the call to repent and believe in the gospel. But in the logia and parables of the βασιλεία of God that can claim authenticity there is no sign of the motif of proximity.[69] Jesus apparently links the idea of urgency and nearness more directly with a proclamation of judgment. The same is true of the call for repentance.[70] The latter appears in three logia that may be regarded as authentic: in the double saying about the slain Galileans and those killed by the falling tower (Lk. 13.1-5); in the woes over Chorazin and Bethsaida (Mt. 11.21//Lk. 10.13); and in the saying about the Ninevites (Mt. 12.41//Lk. 11.32). In this context Jesus no longer interprets 'repentance' as a return to the Torah, as does the

66. G. Lohfink, 'Die Not der Exegese mit der Reich-Gottes-Verkündigung Jesu', *TQ* 168 (1988), pp. 1-15; reprinted in *idem*, *Studien zum Neuen Testament* (SBA, 5; Stuttgart: Katholisches Bibelwerk, 1989), pp. 383-402 (386). His ideas are expanded in his book: *Does God Need the Church? Toward a Theology of the People of God* (Collegeville, MN: Liturgical Press, 2001).

67. In this regard G. Lohfink himself has pointed to Christology: we cannot say: 'Jesus is truly God, but only proleptically', or 'God became human in him, but only partially'. (See 'Die Not der Exegese' [1989], p. 395.) Of course there are many people today who do say just that...

68. 'You were present to me, but I was not present to you'. Augustine, *Conf.* 10.27. The analogy is all the more apt since we must say, with Chilton, '*regnum dei deus est*' (the reign of God is God). See 'Regnum Dei Deus Est', p. 268. Cf. also Meyer, *The Aims of Jesus*, p. 137: 'The "reign of God" signifies "God" and signifies God precisely as Jesus knows him'.

69. One exception could be Mt. 10.7//Lk. 10.9, perhaps Mark 9.1 as well, but I join the *communis opinio* in regarding these logia as more probably formulations by the evangelists themselves.

70. For the motif of repentance in early Judaism, with John the Baptizer, and with Jesus cf. the excursus in Reiser, *Jesus and Judgment*, pp. 249-55.

tradition before him, including the Baptizer, but turning to himself and his message. Jesus' call for repentance and renewal thus no longer takes its concrete content from the Torah, but from his own paraenesis, which is therefore fundamentally eschatological.[71] The motif of urgency, which is a consequence of the nearness of judgment, is several times expressed,[72] for example in the parable-like warning about reconciliation with the opponent in Mt. 5.25//Lk. 12.57-59, in the double saying about the Galileans and the tower (Lk. 13.1-5), and in the saying about the Flood (Mt. 24.37//Lk. 17.26-27).[73]

I thus conclude that the summary in Mk 1.15 was entirely the work of the evangelist. It represents a fully accurate characterization of Jesus' preaching, and its succinctness deserves our highest admiration. It places the ultimate arrival of the reign of God and thus the fulfillment of all eschatological expectations at the center, echoes in the word εὐαγγέλιον what is probably the most important source of Jesus' preaching, namely Isa. 52.7 and 61.1-2, and regards the new direction of one's life that is thus demanded as a logical consequence of the eschatological situation.[74]

Obviously it was clear to the evangelist, as to Jesus, that judgment was inextricably bound up with the coming and establishment of the reign of God. The rejection of that reign brings with it a self-chosen exclusion from salvation. But for Jesus, in contrast to the Baptizer, it was less a question of how one may escape damnation than of how one may win salvation. Hence he places in the foreground not the dark side of the matter, but the bright. His whole activity was directed to showing the fascination and inspiring power of God's βασιλεία. That in doing

71. Cf. H. Merklein, *Jesu Botschaft von der Gottesherrschaft: Eine Skizze* (SBS, 111; Stuttgart: Katholisches Bibelwerk, 3rd edn, 1989). M. Ebner's critique of Merklein in his *Jesus—ein Weisheitslehrer?*, pp. 5-8, rests on the hermeneutical premise that whatever is not part of the oldest layer is 'dogmatic superstructure' (p. 8).

72. See the overview in R. Schnackenburg, *Gottes Herrschaft und Reich* (Freiburg: Herder, 4th edn, 1965), pp. 137-38. There is now a broadly conceived study by K. Erlemann, *Naherwartung und Parusieverzögerung im Neuen Testament: Ein Beitrag zur Frage religiöser Zeiterfahrung* (TANZ, 17; Tübingen: Francke, 1995).

73. For these logia cf. Reiser, *Jesus and Judgment*, pp. 245-49, 281-90, 318.

74. This last is expressed in the syntax: a statement is followed by an asyndetically attached imperative. In Greek this structure regularly denotes a consecutive parataxis. Cf. M. Reiser, *Syntax und Stil des Markusevangeliums* (WUNT, 2.11; Tübingen: Mohr Siebeck, 1984), pp. 144-45.

so he did not deny the judgment aspect is evident from a whole series of undoubtedly authentic sayings and parables concerning judgment.[75] Some of these we have already mentioned. Let me now refer only to two sayings from the Q tradition and a parable from Matthew's special material.

In the double saying about the queen of the South and the Ninevites, with its strictly symmetrical structure (Mt. 12.41-42//Lk. 11.31-32), Jesus proclaims to 'this generation', that is, the whole nation of his contemporaries, the sentence that will be theirs at the last judgment if they do not repent and listen to his message. The logion appears to presume a rejection of his preaching, and as an answer to that rejection formulates the reverse of the blessing of the eye- and ear-witnesses (Mt. 13.16-17//Lk. 10.23-24). In the judgment scene here intimated Jesus envisions traditional elements of early Jewish conceptions of judgment: it is conceived as a forensic trial; it presumes the general resurrection of the dead; witnesses arise and give testimony. We find corresponding depictions of the last judgment, for example, in Dan. 7.9-10, in the vision of the animals in *1 En.* 90.20-26, and in the visionary discourses in *1 En.* 47.3-4 and Wis. 4.20–5.14.[76] The logion, with its provocative contrasting of 'this generation' with 'good' Gentiles, clearly functions as a warning; the strophic parallelism further gives it 'an effect of singular intensity and dramatic power'.[77] There is scarcely any other logion in the Jesus tradition that has so many positive indices of its authenticity: the Semitic diction and 'rabbinic' argumentation (the conclusion a minori ad maius); the application of a biblical passage independent of the Septuagint;[78] the form of strophic parallelism, which should be regarded as a distinctive characteristic of Jesus' poetry and 'his special contribution to the forms of poetry in general';[79] the provocative apostrophizing of the whole nation as 'this generation'; and finally the open formulation of Jesus' claim, which at the same time is unsurpassable:

75. Cf. C. Riniker, *Die Gerichtsverkündigung Jesu* (EHS, 23.653; Bern: Peter Lang, 1999).

76. For the fragmentary and inconsistent character of this image of judgment see Reiser, *Jesus and Judgment*, pp. 154-56.

77. T.W. Manson, *The Teaching of Jesus* (Cambridge: Cambridge University Press, 2nd edn, 1963 [1935]), p. 55.

78. The phrase ἦλθεν...ἀκοῦσαι τὴν σοφίαν Σολομῶνος is from 1 Kgs 5.14, where the LXX has παρεγίνοντο...ἀκοῦσαι τῆς σοφίας Σαλωμων.

79. Manson, *The Teaching of Jesus*, p. 56.

'something greater than Solomon is here! ... something greater than Jonah is here!'[80] Only an *a priori* decision can deny this saying to Jesus.

While this judgment saying probably belongs to the last phase of Jesus' public activity, when it was becoming apparent that his message would be rejected, the Parable of the Unforgiving Servant (Mt. 18.23-34) seems to be without any specific *Sitz im Leben*. It illustrates some fundamental things about the connection between salvation and damnation: the grace that God bountifully gives, like a munificent king, is meant to extend its influence; otherwise it has been received in vain (cf. 2 Cor. 6.1). This is illustrated with an example of forgiveness. (The metaphor of monetary debt is evident in the double meaning of the Semitic חוֹב/חוֹבָה, 'monetary debt', 'debt of sin'.) Thus there is again confirmed what we have now seen more than once: ethics and eschatology are closely connected. Of course there is nothing new about that connection;[81] but inasmuch as Jesus claims to bring the royal graciousness of God in its ultimate, unsurpassable form, the corresponding ethic acquires an ultimate urgency. The stringency of the parable action is faultless: first the forgiveness of the enormous debt, then the scandalous inability of the one forgiven to show forgiveness in turn to a small debtor, and finally the wrathful reaction of the king, who withdraws his offer of pardon and hands the uncomprehending slave over to the torturers. It would take a *petitio principii* to call the conclusion of the story illogical and try to excise the judicial sentence by literary-critical means. The fact that Jesus, in this parable, was alluding to the eschatological judgment is shown in the motif of royal wrath, which makes us think of the eschatological wrath of God and God's wrathful judgment, and in the motif of torture, which was a common way of referring to the sufferings in hell.[82] However, the principal idea in this parable is not the threatening *judgment* of God in the case of wrong behavior, but the anticipatory *grace* of God that should become the source of our own mercy.

The close connection Jesus saw between the message of the reign of God and the proclamation of judgment is illustrated by what is probably

---

80. For details see Reiser, *Jesus and Judgment*, pp. 206-21; Riniker, *Gerichtsverkündigung*, pp. 296-300.

81. Cf. C. Münchow, *Ethik und Eschatologie: Ein Beitrag zum Verständnis der frühjüdischen Apokalyptik* (Göttingen: Vandenhoeck & Ruprecht, 1981).

82. Demonstration and details in Reiser, *Jesus and Judgment*, pp. 273-81.

the most severe of Jesus' sayings about judgment that have come down to us, again preserved in the Sayings Source: the woes over Chorazin and Bethsaida, with the succeeding judgment on Capernaum (Mt. 11.21-24//Lk. 10.13-15).[83] These words of judgment are hard to interpret as warnings; they sound more like final judgments, anticipating the sentence of the last judgment (ἐν τῇ κρίσει as in Mt. 12.41-42//Lk. 11.31-34). The reason for the condemnation is: '... if the deeds of power done in you had been done in Tyre and Sidon, they would have repented long ago in sackcloth and ashes'. Here Jesus' miracles are viewed as eschatological proofs and real symbols of the present βασιλεία, as we have found to be the case in other logia as well. Jesus does not want to have his miracles evaluated as sensational things that people can see and then go on living as they had before; instead, they should serve as signals calling for repentance. That also makes it clear that for Jesus the motif of repentance is not intrinsically associated with the idea of judgment, even when the repentance motif appears in the framework of a saying about judgment; actually it belongs, instead, in the context of the βασιλεία. This shows that the corresponding connection in the summary in Mk 1.15 is appropriate. The example of Mk 1.15 shows a radical suspicion in Christian tradition and its depiction of Jesus as unfounded. The key the Synoptic authors present for understanding Jesus and his message cannot be replaced by any other: and that key is eschatology.

5. *'What Josephus Did Not See'*

Under this title Arnaldo Momigliano writes of 'Josephus's twofold blindness...about the synagogue and the widespread Jewish and Christian apocalyptic trends of his time'.[84] But the fact that Josephus failed to recognize the significance of these two factors, so that they almost disappear in his work, is not really to be attributed to his blindness, but, as Momigliano himself shows, to his having deliberately closed his eyes to them. This is evident especially when Josephus, in paraphrasing the book of Daniel, silently skips over ch. 7.[85] 'In the description of

83. See Reiser, *Jesus and Judgment*, pp. 221-30; Riniker, *Gerichtsverkündigung*, pp. 301-333.

84. A. Momigliano, 'What Josephus Did Not See', in *idem, On Pagans, Jews, and Christians* (Middletown, CN: Wesleyan University Press, 1987), pp. 108-119 (115).

85. Josephus, *Ant.* 10.186-281. Cf. Momigliano, 'What Josephus Did Not See',

Judaism as found in the *Apology* hope has no significance other than that it promises "the better life" to the pious individual.'[86] Thus eschatology appears only as an individual salvation for souls after death. Experts in Josephus studies are in agreement about the principal reason for this one-sided depiction and for Josephus's closing his eyes to important historical realities: apart from a certain alienation on his part from the Jewish community of faith, Josephus's reason was concern for the audience for which he was writing, 'his upper-class Greco-Roman readers' and 'his Jewish readers who could understand Greek'.[87] 'As a result, Josephus's Judaism was colorless, not false and not trivial, but rhetorical, generic, and rather unreal.'[88]

The analogy to a certain trend in current Jesus research is obvious. Again it is eschatology, especially historical and apocalyptic eschatology, that is the eyesore and that is to be eliminated out of regard for a certain upper- or middle-class public. And the Jesus who thereby emerges in a great variety of versions is colorless, perhaps not entirely false or trivial, but rhetorical, generic and rather unreal.

The concrete form and function that Albert Schweitzer gave to the eschatology in Jesus' preaching could not stand up to criticism, for many reasons. But on the main point Schweitzer was right: 'Thus the oldest tradition of Jesus' proclamation and attitude can only be truly understood, as a whole and in detail, from the standpoint of eschatology, and it is only in this way that its authenticity can be genuinely demonstrated against any possible doubt'.

pp. 116-19; Collins, *Apocalypticism in the Dead Sea Scrolls*, p. 155; L.H. Feldman, *Studies in Josephus' Rewritten Bible* (JSJS, 58; Leiden: E.J. Brill, 1998), pp. 554-68.

86. A. Schlatter, *Die Theologie des Judentums nach dem Bericht des Josephus* (Gütersloh: Gerd Mohn, 1932; repr. Hildesheim: Georg Olms, 1979), p. 259. The passage to which Schlatter is referring is Josephus, *Apion* 2.218. Cf. his whole section on 'what is to come' (pp. 252-63).

87. Momigliano, 'What Josephus Did Not See', p. 116.

88. Momigliano, 'What Josephus Did Not See', p. 119.

WHAT DID JESUS THINK ABOUT HIS APPROACHING DEATH?[*]

Peter Balla

1. *Introduction*

At first sight, this question looks out of place in a seminar on 'The Historical Jesus in New Research'. There are two reasons for this.

The first is that recent research is reluctant to think that we can know anything reliable concerning what Jesus thought about his possible death. The second reason is that, if we could find reliable evidence about what Jesus thought, this evidence would have a practical effect on Christian belief. If Jesus did not think that his death would have a saving role for his followers, then Christian belief about Jesus' salvific death would not coincide with the beliefs of the historical Jesus. Christians might continue to hold this belief, but they could not claim to do what Jesus expected his followers to do. We do not expect our historical work to have such direct effects on Christian belief. But why not?

As to the second reason, the organizers of this volume do not share this misgiving; they have encouraged the contributors to address the issue of the significance of the historical-Jesus Research for the Christian faith.

As to the first reason, the scholars of the Third Quest are not averse to asking what Jesus thought about his possible violent death. However, as they focus on the humanity of Jesus and try to understand him as a member of his human society, they often deny that Jesus had any particular religious notion of the meaning of his death. By now we are far from, for example, even Albert Schweitzer's view around the turn of the century: he at least saw that Jesus must have intended some

*   I thank the Alexander von Humboldt Foundation for enabling me to carry out research at the University of Heidelberg (1999–2000), in the course of which I was able to revise this paper for publication. I also thank Professor Dr Gerd Theissen and Dr Michael Labahn for their helpful comments on the manuscript.

momentous outcome from his death, an act of God answering to the event.[1]

Most of the present-day writers emphasize the humanity of Jesus to such an extent that they cannot say anything concerning Jesus' claim of a special relation to God as his father, especially in connection with his own death. In this regard, even a silence such as that of John Dominic Crossan's book on the historical Jesus is telling. He does not address our question.[2] This phenomenon seems to apply to most of the Third Questers, as represented, for example, by the Jesus Seminar.[3] Where the theme of the death of Jesus emerges in the Third Quest, it is most often discussed from the point of view of two questions: who was responsible for Jesus' execution? And, how did the early Church interpret Jesus' death?[4]

Historical-Jesus Research in recent years is not limited to the circle of the Third Questers. There are many scholars who write about matters related to the historical Jesus and/or exegete relevant passages, without being identified as Third Questers. In this essay, I shall refer to the works of scholars regardless of whether they explicitly say that they view their work as part of the Third Quest.[5] For example, the negative

1.   A. Schweitzer, *Geschichte der Leben-Jesu-Forschung* (UTB, 1302; Tübingen: Mohr Siebeck, 9th edn, 1984 [1906]), pp. 440-46. It is worth noting that in Schweitzer's view Jesus was prepared to die in order to fulfill the suffering necessary before the Kingdom comes. In Schweitzer's words (pp. 441-42): 'In dem Leidensgeheimnis, das Jesus zu Cäsarea Philippi ausspricht, ist die vormessianische Drangsal für die anderen außer Kraft gesetzt, aufgehoben, auf ihn allein konzentriert, und zwar so, daß sie sich in seinem Leiden und Sterben zu Jerusalem auswirkt. Das ist die neue Erkenntnis, die ihm aufgegangen. Er muß für die anderen leiden …damit das Reich komme.'

2.   J.D. Crossan, *The Historical Jesus: The Life of a Mediterranean Jewish Peasant* (New York: HarperCollins, 1992), see especially chap. 14, entitled 'Death and Burial', where we look in vain for a discussion of passion predictions, expectation of death—or its explanation—on Jesus' side.

3.   See, e.g., R.W. Funk, R.W. Hoover and the Jesus Seminar, *The Five Gospels: The Search for the Authentic Words of Jesus* (Sonoma, CA: Polebridge Press, 1993).

4.   See, e.g., C.A. Evans, *Life of Jesus Research: An Annotated Bibliography* (NTTS, 24; Leiden: E.J. Brill, rev. edn, 1996), esp. pp. 219-34 on the death of Jesus. The section on the self-understanding of Jesus (pp. 195-210) includes mainly works devoted to the Messianic consciousness of Jesus and the problem of his 'titles', and only few of them relate to our present topic.

5.   For such a self-reference see, e.g., Evans, *Life of Jesus Research*, p. 3. See

result mentioned above is confirmed by an article in a significant reference work published in 1990. In his *TRE* article on the suffering of Jesus, Wolfgang Schenk can only reaffirm what Conzelmann and Bultmann had said decades earlier concerning the historical 'substratum': 'The core-fact is that Jesus was crucified... All other aspects related to the events are controversial [*strittig*]' (Conzelmann); 'It is difficult to understand Jesus' execution as the inherently necessary consequence of his activity...' (Bultmann). Schenk summarizes his own view in this way: 'Jesus was executed on the basis of suspicion, perhaps denunciation, amidst a highly explosive situation of a Jewish pilgrims' feast, the Passover, that commemorated how they were liberated from foreign rule'.[6]

E.P. Sanders emphasizes that 'Jesus was a *charismatic and autonomous prophet*'.[7] Sanders acknowledges that Jesus 'regarded himself as having full authority to speak and act on behalf of God', and that he was 'viceroy: at the head of the judges of Israel, subordinate only to God himself'.[8] Nevertheless, when addressing the issue of Jesus' approaching death, Sanders sees Jesus of Nazareth as only a more dangerous version of Jesus son of Ananias who was flogged after he uttered words against the Temple at a feast:

> If we use this case as a guide, we can understand why Jesus of Nazareth was executed rather than merely flogged. Our Jesus' offence was worse than that of Jesus son of Ananias. Jesus of Nazareth had a following ... He had taught about the Kingdom for some time. He had taken physical action in the Temple. He was not a madman. Thus he was potentially dangerous.[9]

Sanders is reluctant to go any further than to say that Jesus taught about the Kingdom and taught his disciples that he himself would play the principal role in the Kingdom.[10] He holds that his historical analysis

further the following collection of studies by 'Third Questers': B. Chilton and C.A. Evans (eds.), *Studying the Historical Jesus: Evaluations of the State of Current Research* (NTTS, 19; Leiden: E.J. Brill, 1994). One essay in this volume is a good summary of issues related to the social and political context of Jesus' crucifixion: R.A. Horsley, 'The Death of Jesus', pp. 395-422.

6. W. Schenk, 'Leidensgeschichte Jesu', *TRE* 23 (1990), pp. 714-21.

7. E.P. Sanders, *The Historical Figure of Jesus* (Harmondsworth: Penguin Books, 1993), p. 238 (emphasis his).

8. Sanders, *Historical Figure*, pp. 238, 239.

9. Sanders, *Historical Figure*, p. 267.

10. E.P. Sanders, *Jesus and Judaism* (London: SCM Press, 1985), pp. 307-308.

corresponds to what a first-century Jew could have thought about the Messiah. In the following, I shall look afresh at some of the words and deeds of Jesus, which he claimed to carry out with full authority on behalf of God, as Sanders himself has put it. My question is whether we can say something more about this authority, even as historians, when exegeting those biblical passages. I shall not discuss the still unsolved problem of the Messianic consciousness of Jesus; rather, I shall ask the question as a historian: what did Jesus think about his approaching death?

In a short essay like this, I cannot aim to cover all the relevant passages. Even in the case of the chosen passages a full exegesis cannot be achieved. At best some aspects can be highlighted. However, a brief discussion of some of the key passages may serve as a call for the re-opening an issue that has often been regarded as closed. In dealing with the Gospel material, I have decided to focus on the Synoptics, although I hold, together with the authors of some more recent works, that the Fourth Gospel contains many historical insights that are yet to be discovered.[11]

2. *The Passion Predictions*

From the point of view of methodology, the two-document hypothesis imposes on us a major restriction. In order to satisfy the criterion of multiple attestation, we have only two possibilities: we can only turn to Mark or to the hypothetical Q source. Schenk adds a fresh restriction by his observation that the prediction/fulfilment structure, as well as the condemnation/rehabilitation structure, are already there in Mark's Gospel on the redactional level. Schenk summarizes his view in this way: 'The historical questioning has a narrow boundary because of its being necessarily limited to Mark and because of Mark's schematic character.'[12]

This essay cannot re-open the discussion of the problems of the two-document hypothesis. However, I have to indicate that I hold with an increasing number of scholars that every individual pericope or saying

11. See, e.g., R.E. Brown, *The Death of the Messiah: From Gethsemane to the Grave. A Commentary on the Passion Narratives in the Four Gospels* (2 vols.; ABRL; New York: Doubleday, 1994). With regard to the passion prediction sayings, see especially the relevant section of Appendix 8, II, pp. 1482-89.

12. Schenk, 'Leidensgeschichte', p. 719.

has to be examined afresh as regards the question of authenticity, original wording and possible dependence. On occasion a Matthaean version of a saying in the triple tradition may be older than Mark, or a Lukan version may be independent of both Mark and Matthew.

It is also beyond the scope of this essay to discuss the question of criteria in searching for authentic sayings of Jesus. I confine my discussion here to two questions. (1) Can we find arguments that counter the thesis that the passion predictions are redactional or a post-Easter creation of the early Church? (2) Can we argue that we have multiple attestation for the passion predictions? The thesis will be argued that we can find older traditions in these passages and that we have multiple attestation for them. It is acknowledged that our answers cannot prove that these are sayings of Jesus; it is argued, however, that this possibility can be maintained.

The majority view in recent exegetical works seems to be that the passion predictions cannot be authentic. They are regarded as post-Easter formulations of the early Church. The Jesus Seminar arrived at this conclusion on the basis of their 'rules' or 'axioms' set out in the Introduction of the work that summarizes the result of their votes. One such rule states that: 'Sayings and parables expressed in "Christian" language are the creation of the evangelists or their Christian predecessors.'[13] This axiom is reinforced by the statement in the immediate context: 'The language of Jesus was distinctive, as was his style and perspective...' Since 'Mark betrays his knowledge of the oral gospel' in the passion predictions, from this follows that he attributed his version of that oral gospel to Jesus.[14] It may suffice here to say that in the opinion of some contributors to the Third Quest the axiom underlying this decision needs correction.[15]

However, if the 'similarity' of a saying to early Christian statements in itself does not exclude the possibility that the saying originates with Jesus, another reason may still exist for viewing it as non-authentic. One might find a *Sitz im Leben* in the experience of suffering of the

13. Funk, Hoover and the Jesus Seminar, *The Five Gospels*, p. 24.

14. Funk, Hoover and the Jesus Seminar, *The Five Gospels*, p. 25.

15. In this regard, I agree with Theissen and Merz who affirm: 'Das Differenzkriterium ist durch das *historische Plausibilitätskriterium* zu ersetzen, das mit *Wirkungen* Jesu auf das Urchristentum und seiner Einbindung in einen jüdischen *Kontext* rechnet'. G. Theissen and A. Merz, *Der historische Jesus: Ein Lehrbuch* (Göttingen: Vandenhoeck & Ruprecht, 2nd edn, 1997), p. 117 (emphasis theirs).

early Christians. In their suffering they sought and found comfort and strength in the conviction that Jesus also had to suffer. Their interest resulted in the formulation of more and more sayings on suffering and possible martyrdom. These sayings were then attributed to the earthly Jesus. Another possibility is to give a reason why sayings attributed to Jesus should be seen as post-Easter creations.[16] Let us, however, turn to observations that might point in another direction.

My first observation is that those sayings belong to the Son of Man sayings. Ulrich Luz has affirmed concerning the Son of Man sayings in Matthew that they are usually taken from the sources of Matthew, that is, from Mark, Q and the *Sondergut*, or special source of the Gospel.[17] They all appear in the words of Jesus, and in no case do they appear in narrative texts or in confessions (*Bekenntnis*) or even in words of address (*Anrede*). The sayings about the suffering and rising Son of Man are not uttered in the presence of enemies or even before the crowds (*nie in der Öffentlichkeit*)—with the exception of the sign of Jonah (Mt. 12.40). Luz further affirms that the readers of Matthew knew who the Son of Man was from the Christian tradition.[18] This tradition is characterized by a relatively constant word- and motif-field, for example, the term παραδίδωμι occurs five times, ἐγείρω three times, and χείρ twice in the relevant Matthaean sayings. Thus we may add that there might be an argument for the case that these sayings were not a creation, but they were well remembered by the early guardians of

---

16. As, for example, represented by Theissen and Merz: 'Das Skandalon seiner entehrenden Hinrichtung provozierte nachösterliche Sinndeutungen (wie Mk 10,45) und Leidensweissagungen (wie Mk 8,31 u.ö.)', *Der historische Jesus*, p. 104. May I note here that Mk 10.45 would also deserve discussion in the context of our present theme. However, within the limits of this essay it is not possible to focus on more than a few passages. The authenticity of Mk 10.45 is doubted by the majority of present-day scholars. For arguments in favour of the view that it originates with Jesus, see P. Stuhlmacher, *Biblische Theologie des Neuen Testaments. I. Grundlegung: Von Jesus zu Paulus* (Göttingen: Vandenhoeck & Ruprecht, 1992), pp. 120-22 and 128-30; J.C. O'Neill, 'Did Jesus Teach that his Death would Be Vicarious as well as Typical?', in W. Horbury and B. McNeil (eds.), *Suffering and Martyrdom in the New Testament* (Cambridge: Cambridge University Press, 1981), pp. 9-27, esp. pp. 24-26.

17. U. Luz, *Das Evangelium nach Matthäus* (EKKNT, 1.2; Braunschweig: Benziger Verlag; Neukirchen–Vluyn: Neukirchener Verlag, 1990), p. 498.

18. Luz, *Matthäus*, p. 499.

the tradition. We can find other arguments that count against the theory that these sayings were created by the evangelists.

My further observations concern the variations among the Synoptic parallels of the passion predictions and the differences among the predictions themselves. I shall present my remarks in the order as found in Mark's Gospel, with the differences in the other two Synoptic Gospels.

Mark 8.31 is the first passion prediction of that Gospel: 'And he began to teach them that the Son of man must suffer many things, and be rejected by the elders and the chief priests and the scribes, and be killed, and after three days rise again'.[19] Joachim Gnilka affirms that it is easily separable from its present context: it is a self-contained tradition.[20] Whereas Lk. 9.22 is an exact parallel, in Matthew's parallel version (16.21) we find some differences: a direct reference to Jesus is substituted for the expression 'Son of Man'; one of the two main verbs, 'reject', ἀποδοκιμασθῆναι, is replaced by 'going to Jerusalem', εἰς Ἱεροσόλυμα ἀπελθεῖν: 'From that time Jesus began to show his disciples that he must go to Jerusalem and suffer many things from the elders and chief priests and scribes, and be killed, and on the third day be raised'. However, Albright and Mann have pointed to a significant agreement among the three versions in, what they call, 'a very odd order' of the expressions: elders, chief priests, and scribes.[21] We may further note the minor agreement of Matthew and Luke, 'on the third day', over against Mark's 'after three days'.[22] Taking all these little remarks together, we may raise the possibility that we have here an early Christian tradition with some variation rather than a saying formed by the evangelists.

19. Throughout this essay I refer to the RSV text when quoting the English Bible.

20. J. Gnilka, *Das Evangelium nach Markus* (EKKNT, 2.2; Zürich: Benziger Verlag; Neukirchen–Vluyn: Neukirchener Verlag, 1979), p. 10.

21. W.F. Albright and C.S. Mann, *Matthew: Introduction, Translation, and Notes* (AB, 26; Garden City, NY: Doubleday, 1979), p. 200. In other occurrences of similar lists of participants the 'chief priests' are mentioned first in the Gospels.

22. Georg Strecker observed that perhaps Matthew and Luke adjusted this expression to the passion narrative; or they may even have been influenced by the kerygmatic formula found also in 1 Cor. 15.4 (G. Strecker, 'Die Leidens- und Auferstehungsvoraussagen im Markusevangelium [Mk 8,31; 9,31; 10,32-34]', *ZTK* 64 [1967], pp. 16-39 [24]). At the same place he also noted that the Markan expression, 'after three days', stands in contradiction with Mark's own passion narrative: Mk 14.58; 15.29.

Mark 9.12 (par Mt. 17.12 with some differences; Luke has no parallel) is a saying about the suffering of the Son of Man, but there is no reference to death in this verse. However, before I move on to the second passion prediction in Mark, it may be relevant to note that this saying is applied by Jesus to John the Baptist, with a reference to Elijah: 'And he said to them, "Elijah does come first to restore all things; and how is it written of the Son of man, that he should suffer many things and be treated with contempt? But I tell you that Elijah has come, and they did to him whatever they pleased, as it is written of him"' (Mk 9.12, 13). As Jesus knew the fate of the Baptist, this must have been a sign to him that controversies around Jesus himself might lead to similar results. Schenk rightly affirms that the death of John the Baptist can be seen as a consequence of his activities,[23] and we may add that Jesus might have counted on that possibility for himself as well. This point is acknowledged by many scholars who do not accept the passion predictions as authentic sayings of Jesus.[24]

Mark 9.31, the second passion prediction, is seen by some scholars, for example, Strecker, as a Markan redactional work based on 8.31,[25] but Gnilka argues that beside the similarities, 9.31 has significant differences as well: for example, the Son of Man being delivered into the hands of men.[26] 'For he was teaching his disciples, saying to them, "The Son of man will be delivered into the hands of men, and they will kill him; and when he is killed, after three days he will rise".' Thus Gnilka thinks that although the context is Markan, the very saying about the Son is Man is not. Luz holds that the Matthaean parallel (Mt. 17.22-23) has Mark as its source, but Luz himself points to some peculiarities

---

23. Schenk, *Leidensgeschichte*, p. 715.

24. So, e.g., H. Schürmann, *Jesu ureigener Tod: Exegetische Besinnungen und Ausblick* (Freiburg: Herder, 1975), pp. 29-30. I note that Lorenz Oberlinner has argued against this view; in his opinion the death of John the Baptist did not necessarily lead Jesus to envisage the same fate for himself. See L. Oberlinner, *Todeserwartung und Todesgewißheit Jesu: Zum Problem einer historischen Begründung* (SBB, 10; Stuttgart: Katholisches Bibelwerk, 1980), pp. 38-58. Oberlinner's thesis is that Jesus did not have a certainty as regards his approaching death, but he has counted on its possibility in the very final days of his life.

25. Strecker, 'Die Leidens- und Auferstehungsvoraussagen', pp. 30-31. I note that Strecker argues that there is pre-Markan material in Mk 8.31 (see pp. 24-30), although he holds that the passion predictions are post-Easter creations (p. 33).

26. Gnilka, *Markus*, p. 53.

as well.[27] Matthew has an introductory expression that is difficult to explain, 'As they were gathering in Galilee'. The disciples are already with Jesus in v. 19, so there is no need for them to gather.[28] As in Matthew the following pericope is a Matthaean *Sondergut* (concerning the Temple tax), the passion prediction is isolated in Matthew's Gospel.[29] Albright and Mann have also observed this, and they went even further by affirming that the second passion prediction is not original to Matthew's version, but a later 'editorial addition to the original text'.[30] Luke's parallel to this pericope (Lk. 9.43b-45) does not have a reference to death, only to the Son of Man being delivered into the hands of men.[31] This verse, then, may reflect a tradition that is not dependent on Mk 8.31. It is also possible to maintain that the 'Synoptic parallels' are not in a literary dependence in this case, but can be seen as multiple witnesses to a tradition.

Mark 10.33-34, the third passion prediction, has considerable differences when compared with the first two. On the one hand, the list of those to whom the Son of Man is delivered is shorter, but on the other the fate of the Son of Man is depicted with more words and in greater detail: 'Behold, we are going up to Jerusalem; and the Son of man will be delivered to the chief priests and the scribes, and they will condemn him to death, and deliver him to the Gentiles; and they will mock him, and spit upon him, and scourge him, and kill him; and after three days

27. Luz, *Matthäus*, p. 526.

28. Is it not possible that Matthew knew a tradition that did not restrict the passion prediction to the circle of the disciples? This would fit with Mt. 27.63, a verse that may imply that Jesus openly spoke about his resurrection 'after three days'. I owe this remark to Professor Gerd Theissen.

29. Luz, *Matthäus*, p. 527.

30. Albright and Mann, *Matthew*, p. 210. I note that they hold the same about Mt. 17.12b, see p. 205.

31. There is a difference in the disciples' reaction to Jesus' second prediction in Matthew's and Luke's version: according to Matthew (17.23b), the disciples 'were greatly distressed', while Luke affirms that the disciples 'did not understand this saying' (9.45a). Mark also has this motif of non-understanding, but Luke is more emphatic when he also gives a reason by using a *divinum passivum*: 'it was concealed from them, that they should not perceive it'. It has to be noted that some of the differences among the Synoptics may be accounted for by the evangelists' editorial work. However, the personal involvement of the one who hands on the tradition does not necessarily exclude the possibility that he transmits earlier material.

he will rise.' Although Gnilka thinks that this third prediction is formulated by Mark,[32] he himself notes that it does not correspond fully
with the passion narrative of the same Gospel.[33] Matthew has a shorter
parallel (Mt. 20.17-19), but he is even more precise in naming the kind
of death that awaits the Son of Man: he will be crucified. As the prediction does not fit its context in Matthew, Albright and Mann think that
we have a later 'editorial insertion' also in this case.[34] Luke is closer to
Mark than to Matthew in the details concerning what will happen to the
Son of Man, but there are numerous differences as well: Luke adds a
reference to scriptural proof (Lk. 18.31);[35] Luke only speaks of the Son
of Man here, whereas in Mark the previous verse (10.32) makes clear
that Jesus speaks about his own fate; Luke also differs from Mark in a
few words in describing what is done to the Son of Man (ὑβρισθήσεται
in Luke; κατακρινοῦσιν αὐτὸν θανάτῳ in Mark); they also differ in
grammatical forms, for example, passive forms in Luke, a participle in
Luke (μαστιγώσαντες) instead of Mark's future indicative (μαστιγώσ-
ουσιν), and in word order (the reference to 'mocking' comes earlier in
Luke); Luke omits the reference to the Jewish leaders. Once again we
note the minor agreement of Matthew and Luke, 'on the third day', over
against Mark's 'after three days'. The passage can be seen as a tradition
not depending on the first two passion predictions.[36] The Synoptics may
be regarded as independent witnesses to that tradition.

Without entering the debate on the two-document hypothesis, I do

32. Gnilka, *Markus*, p. 96.

33. Gnilka, *Markus*, p. 95.

34. Albright and Mann, *Matthew*, p. 239.

35. I accept R.E. Brown's argument that it is a better methodological presupposition to hold that 'Jesus did use the Scriptures' (*Death of the Messiah*, II,
p. 1479), than to affirm that 'if a concept or pattern is traceable to ... a scriptural
background, it cannot have come from Jesus' (II, p. 1478).

36. I note that R.E. Brown has argued on the basis of Johannine 'predictions',
three Son of Man sayings (3.14; 8.28; 12.32-34), that 'already on a preGospel level
there was a collection of three sayings predicting the death and resurrection of the
Son of Man, and that the Marcan and Johannine traditions and/or evangelists
developed those sayings and used them independently' (*Death of the Messiah*, II,
p. 1485). Brown has also discussed other Synoptic texts which he calls 'less precise
or more allusive predictions' (II, pp. 1470-73). He argues that because their wording does not reflect exactly what happened in the passion of the respective Gospel,
'it is not possible to dismiss them simply as retrojections of what happened' (II,
p. 1473).

claim on the basis of these remarks that a simple literary dependence is not the only possible solution to the Synoptic problem in our case. I argue that the passion predictions can be seen as traditions that were not created by the evangelists. Although they may be creations of the early church from a pre-Gospel period, they may also be regarded as—at least in some parts—authentic sayings of Jesus. R.E. Brown has rightly observed that only a 'small portion' of the language of the texts speaking of this foresight of Jesus is 'clearly derivable' from the Gospels' passion narratives.[37] I agree with his conclusion that the thesis is very unlikely 'that none of these sayings anticipating a violent death stems from Jesus'.[38] With E.P. Sanders I hold that in these passages the expression 'the Son of Man' is a self-reference; it means 'I'.[39] If this is true, then they point to the awareness with which Jesus looked at his coming confrontations with the authorities. They would lead to a violent death.

If Jesus did foresee that a violent death awaited him, then it is relevant to ask what significance he attached to that death. The passion predictions are addressed to Jesus' disciples, in order to prepare them for the future. They are met with disapproval (e.g. Mk 10.32), or with lack of understanding (e.g. Mk 9.32) on the side of the disciples.[40] However, they do show that Jesus thought he had to die in obedience to the will of God, which is expressed in the term δεῖ (e.g. in Mk 8.31). As the passion predictions also include a reference to the resurrection, this—if authentic—would imply that Jesus expected that God would vindicate him.[41] In the following sections, I shall inquire concerning the meaning

37. Brown, *Death of the Messiah*, II, pp. 1486-87.

38. Brown, *Death of the Messiah*, II, p. 1487.

39. Sanders, *Historical Figure*, p. 246.

40. I do not discuss here whether the motif of the disciples' non-ability to understand is only a literary device or whether it has a historical background. Even in the latter case, I do not think that Jesus' predictions are to be seen as inauthentic because the disciples understood only after Easter what had happened. I think that the tragic character of the events is enough reason why the disciples were surprised at the death of Jesus even though he had warned them previously.

41. I note that this result of the discussion of the passion predictions does not mean that Jesus approached his death with some kind of suicide thoughts. For a good discussion of the difference between suicide and between someone being prepared to sacrifice oneself in martyrdom, see A.J. Blasi, 'Marginalization and Martyrdom: Social Context of Ignatius of Antioch', *Listening: Journal of Religion and Culture* 32 (1997), pp. 68-74. Blasi examines the letters of Ignatius, whose

of Jesus' necessary death (as vindicated by God) in two texts only, one related to a symbolic act, and the other related to the sayings on the occasion of the last supper.

3. *The Reported Act of Jesus Entering Jerusalem*

The majority of scholars working in the context of the Third Quest have seen some connection between the violent end of Jesus' life and his attack on the Jerusalem Temple. Before I turn to some observations in this regard, I note an exception: although J.D. Crossan holds that 'an action and equal saying involving the Temple's symbolic destruction goes back to the historical Jesus himself', he says he is nevertheless 'much less secure about whether that action/saying led directly to Jesus' arrest and execution', especially because of the symbolic character of the 'destruction'.[42]

In this essay, I confine my references to some works whose contribution can stand here as an example of many others. I argue that some of the arguments they bring forward have not been given their full strength. My aim is to highlight the significance of the relevant passages for our present subject.

Marcus Borg has summarized the recent majority scholarly opinion when he warned that although many Gospel texts 'are filled with a foreboding' that the likely result of Jesus' journey to Jerusalem would be death, nevertheless 'the *outcome* was not the *purpose* of the journey'.[43] We have already seen E.P. Sanders's view that the main reason for Jesus' execution was his attack on the Temple, combined with the danger implied in the fact that Jesus had a following. Sanders affirms: 'I conclude that Jesus' symbolic action of overthrowing tables in the Temple was understood in connection with a saying about destruction,

---

'social condition' differed from that of Jesus. However, I think Blasi's thesis is applicable also to Jesus' case: 'a martyrdom complex ... is not so much a psychological condition of an individual as a social condition in which an individual may be found' (p. 68). The 'social condition' for Jesus was also influenced by Jewish martyrdom ideas. For a the discussion of the main sources, see J. Downing, 'Jesus and Martyrdom', *JTS* 14 (1963), pp. 279-23.

42. Crossan, *The Historical Jesus*, p. 359.

43. M.J. Borg, *Jesus, A New Vision: Spirit, Culture, and the Life of Discipleship* (San Francisco: Harper & Row, 1987), p. 172 (emphasis his).

and that the action and the saying, in the view of the authorities, constituted a prophetic threat'.[44] However, Sanders himself acknowledges
that Jesus also carried out a symbolic action that implied high claims on
his side: 'he rode into Jerusalem on an ass'.[45] Concerning the significance of the prophecy in Zech. 9.9, Sanders rightly points to the two
historical possibilities: 'It is possible to think either that the prophecy
created the event or that the prophecy created the story and that the
event never occurred'. Sanders inclines 'to the view that it was Jesus
himself who read the prophecy and decided to fulfil it: that here he
implicitly declared himself to be "king"'. However, at this highly explosive time of the feast of the Passover, such a claim would be so dangerous that it would have led to Jesus' death almost immediately, so
Sanders goes on to affirm that 'Jesus' demonstration was quite modest:
he performed a symbolic gesture for insiders, for those who had eyes
to see'.

Unfortunately, Sanders leaves this point as it stands and does not draw
the possible consequences. He does not go on along the line of his own
observations in the direction where it leads. Marcus Borg rightly points
to the Gospels' presentations which make it clear that Jesus 'deliberately made arrangements to enter the city on a donkey's colt' (Mk 11.2-
6; Mt. 21.2-3; Lk. 19.29-32; I note that Jn 12.14 differs from the Synoptics: Jesus 'found a young ass', but it is also worth noting that the
very act of the riding on the donkey as well as the Zechariah prophecy
is also attested by the Fourth Gospel).[46] Borg even raises the possibility
that Jesus and his followers—forming a procession—may have arrived
at Jerusalem from the east on the same day the Roman troops arrived
from the west 'to cope with the throngs of Jewish pilgrims' at the season
of Passover.[47] We remember that Sanders emphasized that the authorities did not think that Jesus was mad; that is why they thought he
was dangerous. In my opinion, Theissen and Merz rightly argue that
Jesus' criticism of the Temple may have caused worry not only among
the Temple aristocracy, but also among the inhabitants of the city of
Jerusalem.[48]

---

44. Sanders, *Historical Figure*, p. 260.

45. Sanders, *Historical Figure*, p. 254. The following quotations are all from the
same page.

46. Borg, *Jesus*, p. 174.

47. Borg, *Jesus*, pp. 173-74.

48. 'Ihre wirtschaftliche Existenz hing zu eng mit dem Tempel zusammen:

From all these observations it seems to me more likely—what Sanders and Borg do not want to accept—that Jesus went up to Jerusalem at the time of Passover clearly counting on the possibility of his violent death.[49] If this is true, then Jesus must have attached a significance to his approaching death. What significance might it have been? If we think the timing is also significant, then the feast of Passover points to the realm of sacrifice. For example, John O'Neill has answered his own question, 'Why did Jesus go up to Jerusalem?', with the following affirmation.

> He [i.e. Jesus] went to Jerusalem not to bring in the Kingdom...not to make a complete abandonment of his will without any specific and understandable purpose. He went to Jerusalem as God's Son, sent by his Father to sacrifice himself for mankind. He went to give men time and opportunity to repent.[50]

Similarly, Maurice Casey, after a discussion of the predictions of the passion, the cleansing of the Temple, and the words of Jesus at the Last Supper concludes:

> We should deduce that Jesus' mind was working on the same basic lines as those who meditated on the deaths of the innocent Maccabean martyrs, and who concluded that their deaths were an expiatory sacrifice which assuaged the wrath of God and enabled him to deliver Israel

Kritik an ihm mußte sie als Kritik an ihrer Lebensgrundlage verstehen'. Theissen and Merz, *Der historische Jesus*, p. 170. The argument is based on an earlier detailed study of G. Theissen, 'Die Tempelweissagung Jesu: Prophetie im Spannungsfeld von Stadt und Land', in *idem, Studien zur Soziologie des Urchristentums* (WUNT, 19; Tübingen: Mohr Siebeck, 3rd edn, 1989), pp. 142-59.

49.   Another passage that would deserve attention in connection with our present theme is the passage on Jesus praying in the Garden of Gethsemane (Mk 14.32-42 par.). It might allow an insight into Jesus' understanding of his near future: he is ready to die—if that be the will of the Father for the sake of the Kingdom. Theissen and Merz contend that even if the story is not historical, it can rightly describe the feelings of Jesus in his last days (*Der historische Jesus*, p. 379): 'Er rechnet mit seinem Tod (dem Kelch), hofft aber noch immer auf das wunderbare und rettende Eingreifen Gottes, auf den Beginn der Gottesherrschaft'.

50.   J.C. O'Neill, *Messiah: Six Lectures on the Ministry of Jesus* (Cambridge: Cochrane Press, 1980), p. 58. I note that Jesus' consciousness of being the Son of God is controversial among scholars. Without entering this debate, I call attention to O'Neill's argument for the possibility that Jesus 'knew that he was [the Son of God], but did not know beyond the possibility of error'. See his more recent book: *Who Did Jesus Think He Was?* (BIS, 11; Leiden: E.J. Brill, 1995), p. 117.

(cf. 2 Macc 7.37-38; 4 Macc 17.20-22). Jesus' death likewise was to be
an expiatory sacrifice which assuaged the wrath of God and enabled him
to redeem Israel despite her faults.[51]

From the reported sayings of Jesus that are relevant for the search of
the meaning of Jesus' death, I have chosen the words uttered at the Last
Supper. Before I turn to them, may I close this section by pointing to
the fact, acknowledged by Sanders, that Jesus' followers understood
Jesus' action of entering Jerusalem on an ass: 'they hailed the coming
Kingdom (Mark 11.10) or even Jesus himself as king (Matt. 21.9; Luke
19.38)'.[52] To be sure, Sanders does not think that the followers of Jesus
understood Jesus' intention as the sacrifice of God's Son for all humanity. Sanders also doubts the Synoptics' reference to the 'crowds', or at
least many people, who witnessed and understood Jesus' symbolic
action. However, we may repeat that he does stop short of taking the
steps that are a logical consequence of his own observations. One wonders why his discussion of this passage ends so abruptly. In my opinion,
here we can see an example of exegeting certain passages in a different
way on the basis of assumptions about what one thinks was possible or
not possible for a first-century Jew to hold.[53]

4. *Jesus' Words at the Last Supper*

In a recent monograph on the table fellowships of Jesus, János Bolyki
argues that the story of the 'institution' of the Lord's Supper probably
originates very early, because its version in Paul (1 Cor. 11.23b-25) was
committed to writing in the 50s CE, and the oral tradition contained in it
probably goes back even to the 40s.[54] Bolyki also rightly adds that the

51. P.M. Casey, *From Jewish Prophet to Gentile God* (Cambridge: James Clarke,
1991), p. 65. He refers to C.K. Barrett, 'The Background of Mark 10.45', in A.J.B.
Higgins (ed.), *New Testament Essays: Studies in Memory of Thomas Walter Manson* (Manchester: Manchester University Press, 1959), pp. 1-18.

52. Sanders, *Historical Figure*, p. 254.

53. For a recent argument for the thesis that Jesus was conscious of the likely
outcome of the events his last week, see E.J. Schnabel, 'The Silence of Jesus: The
Galilean Rabbi Who was More than a Prophet', in B. Chilton and C.A. Evans (eds.),
Authenticating the Words of Jesus (NTTS, 28.1; Leiden: E.J. Brill, 1999), pp. 203-
257. Schnabel concludes that: 'Jesus went up to Jerusalem not just to preach, but to
die, so that the promised new covenant could become a reality' (p. 256).

54. J. Bolyki, *Jesu Tischgemeinschaften* (WUNT, 2.96; Tübingen: Mohr
Siebeck, 1998), p. 139.

search for the oldest form of the tradition has to be preceded by the question as regards historicity.

The majority of scholars accept the historicity of an occasion of a 'last supper' in the life of Jesus, yet not everybody is prepared to use it as a source for answering the question in this essay. For example, J.D. Crossan argues that the lack of any reference to the Last Supper in the passages dealing with the Eucharist in the *Didache* must mean that we have at least one group of Christians for whom elements of a Passover meal, the Last Supper, or 'passion symbolism' were not part of the origins of the Eucharist.[55] Crossan therefore concludes that these elements did not originate in the life of Jesus.[56] However, the argument from silence is not convincing. Bolyki has rightly pointed out that although the words of institution of the Lord's Supper are not reported by the Fourth Evangelist, this sacrament serves as a background to John 6.[57] In an analogical way, the lack of a reference to the Last Supper in the *Didache* does not prove that its community was not aware of those elements of the origins of the Eucharist.

Jesus' words at the Last Supper do not only include what the church has later called the 'words of institution', but also a reference to Jesus' drinking anew in the Kingdom to come. In an article entitled 'Bread and Wine', John O'Neill has subjected all the existing texts, including the variants, to an investigation as regards their authenticity, and their likely original form, with the aim of finding what significance Jesus attributed to his approaching death.[58] In the following, I am only interested in those observations which help to find an answer to our original question.

On the basis of the variants, O'Neill argues that the 'shorter text' of Luke in the Codex Bezae, which does not have Lk. 22.19b-20, is not to

---

55. Crossan, *The Historical Jesus*, p. 364.

56. It has to be noted that the discussion here does not include an attempt to answer the question whether or not the Last Supper was a Passover meal. For a good presentation of the arguments pro and contra, see Theissen and Merz, *Der historische Jesus*, pp. 373-76. They themselves argue against the thesis of a Passover meal. If the Fourth Gospel is right in its dating of the Last Supper as one day earlier than the day of Passover, then this could be used as an argument for the view that Jesus thought there might not be another occasion for him to have a meal with his disciples.

57. Bolyki, *Jesu Tischgemeinschaften*, pp. 132-38.

58. O'Neill, *Messiah*, pp. 59-76.

be preferred, because it was due to a scribal error.[59] However, in his opinion in Luke's Gospel 'a scribe added an account of the saying "I will not drink until the Kingdom come" to a version of the saying about the nature of the cup, "This cup is the new covenant in my blood which is shed for you" (Luke 22.19, 20)'.[60] This is the opposite process from the process in Mark, argued by Loisy long ago. O'Neill describes the Markan text history as follows: 'In Mark an editor or scribe added words about the wine to an account of how Jesus said he would drink the cup no longer until he drank it anew in the Kingdom'. However, since Paul also knows the word concerning the cup, it is possible to argue that it is an old tradition, because it is attested independently by Mark and Paul.

O'Neill argues that 'we possess four different versions of a tradition that Jesus declared at the last supper that he would not partake of any other such meal until the Kingdom come'.[61] Two of them may be results of translation differences from a common semitic original: Mt. 26.29 and Mk 14.25. The third version, Lk. 22.17-18, is distinct in as much as it stresses the coming of the Kingdom rather than the drinking anew in the Kingdom. Apart from the term 'coming', it is close to the first two. The fourth version, Lk. 22.15-16, is rather different from the previous ones: 'These verses speak of eating the passover and of the fulfilment in the Kingdom'. Marion Soards has argued that we do not only have to emphasize that this latter passage has no parallel in Mark, but we also have to see that in its present form in Luke—just as v. 18—it is an integral part of a balanced structure, because 'vv. 15-18 are a polished unit'.[62]

> And he said to them, 'I have earnestly desired to eat this passover with you before I suffer; for I tell you I shall not eat it until it is fulfilled in the Kingdom of God'. And he took a cup, and when he had given thanks he

59. O'Neill, *Messiah*, pp. 61-62. For an argument in favour of the thesis that the longer version is to be preferred, see H.F. Bayer, *Jesus' Predictions of Vindication and Resurrection: The Provenance, Meaning and Correlation of the Synoptic Predictions* (WUNT, 2.20; Tübingen: Mohr Siebeck, 1986), pp. 30-34.

60. O'Neill, *Messiah*, p. 61.

61. O'Neill, *Messiah*, p. 62.

62. M.L. Soards, *The Passion According to Luke: The Special Material of Luke 22* (JSNTSup, 14; Sheffield: Sheffield Academic Press, 1987), pp. 27-28 (28). This can be seen as a confirmation of the results of an earlier detailed study by H. Schürmann, *Der Paschamahlbericht: Lk 22,(7-14.)15-18*, I (NTAbh, NS 19.5; Münster: Aschendorff, 1953), p. 52.

said, 'Take this, and divide it among yourselves; for I tell you that from
now on I shall not drink of the fruit of the vine until the Kingdom of God
comes.'

Because of the Lukan redactional character of the unit, Bayer has
formulated his conclusion of the analysis of the parallel passages in this
way.[63] 'It is indeed most likely, on the basis of literary and material analyses, that Luke constitutes the original context for the eschatological
prospect while Mark transmits the more primitive form'. On the basis
of 'the fact that the form of eschatological sayings such as Mk 14:25/Lk
22:(16):18 is found in Q, Mark and Matthew'—as well as on the basis
of some earlier arguments of M. Black and J. Jeremias—Bayer also
argues that 'the eschatological prospect has its provenance with Jesus
himself'.[64]

It is worth noting that some scholars who are not willing to accept
that Jesus might have reckoned with the possibility of his violent death
earlier during his life, for example, at the time when the first passion
predictions are set in the framework of the Gospels, nevertheless hold
that he must have reckoned with it at the time of the Last Supper.[65] In
my opinion, O'Neill thus rightly argues that the only possible meaning
of Jesus' not drinking the wine can be that he 'expected an immediate
violent death'.[66]

63. Bayer, *Jesus' Predictions*, p. 41.

64. Bayer, *Jesus' Predictions*, pp. 41-42. Bayer lists the following passages that
have a similar form: Mt. 23.39 par. Lk. 13.35; Mt. 5.26 par. Lk. 12.59; Mk 9.1;
9.41; 10.15; 13.30; Mt. 5.18; 10.23. I note that the wide attestation for the form is a
good argument for its provenance with Jesus; however, not all of these examples
have an eschatological content.

65. Thus, for example, Lorenz Oberlinner has summarized his exegetical analyses in the thesis that 'Jesus in der Situation des letzten Mahles schon um die Pläne
seiner Gegner, ihn zu beseitigen, wußte und dieses sein Wissen im eschatologischen
Ausblick, einem "Trostwort" an die Jünger, zugleich als Ausdruck der Bereitschaft,
den Tod auf sich zu nehmen, mitteilte.' Oberlinner, *Todeserwartung*, p. 134. So
also Schürmann, *Jesu ureigener Tod*, pp. 56-59. For arguments in favour of the
thesis that reasons that led to Jesus' death can be found also in his ministry prior to
the last week of his life, see C.A. Evans, 'From Public Ministry to the Passion: Can
a Link Be Found between the (Galilean) Life and the (Judean) Death of Jesus?', in
idem, Jesus and his Contemporaries: Comparative Studies (AGJU, 25; Leiden: E.J.
Brill, 1995), pp. 301-318.

66. O'Neill, *Messiah*, p. 63.

The main question in relation to these traditions is, what role did Jesus envisage for himself at the messianic banquet to come? I think that Jesus' reference to the Kingdom as his Father's Kingdom in Mt. 26.29 points to the likelihood that Jesus thought he himself would be the host (together with his father), and not simply one participating member among many. Rather, he would receive his disciples anew. As Bayer has put it: 'the analogy between the fellowship of Jesus and his disciples during the Last Supper and Jesus' hope of a future meal celebration suggests that then again Jesus would perform the function of a "host" as the head of the household (*pater familias*)'.[67]

Bayer has argued for an 'implied *Zwischenzeit*' in some Gospel texts including Mk 14.25.[68] 'Truly, I say to you, I shall not drink again of the fruit of the vine until that day when I drink it new in the Kingdom of God'. If he is right, then Mk 14.25 also implies that there will be many occasions of such a meal fellowship until 'that day', but Jesus will not partake of them. Therefore, it may be argued that one message of the traditions I have discussed in this section is that Jesus' followers have to repent and believe that, for the sake of Jesus' sacrifice, they have forgiveness of their sins. As O'Neill affirms: 'The Kingdom's coming is dependent on men's repentance and God's forebearance; Jesus' death is the most powerful call to repentance ever made, and the signal sign of God's forebearance'.[69]

As a final observation, I may add that the reference to 'blood' is regarded by most exegetes as secondary.[70] However, Otto Betz has argued that the significance of the reference to 'blood' can be understood against the Old Testament background. As it was forbidden for Jewish people to drink blood, such a challenging thought is to be attributed to Jesus rather than the early Church.[71] O'Neill holds that the reference to blood is secondary in the sense that it did not occur at the Last Supper, but it may originate in another saying of Jesus that did have a reference

---

67. Bayer, *Jesus' Predictions*, p. 52.

68. Bayer, *Jesus' Predictions*, pp. 44-49.

69. O'Neill, *Messiah*, p. 64.

70. See, e.g., W. Schrage, *Der erste Brief an die Korinther (1Kor 11,17-14,40)* (EKKNT, 7.3, Zürich: Benziger Verlag; Neukirchen–Vluyn: Neukirchener Verlag, 1999), pp. 11-12.

71. O. Betz, 'Das Mahl des Herrn bei Paulus', in *idem, Jesus, der Herr der Kirche: Aufsätze zur biblischen Theologie*, II (WUNT, 52; Tübingen: Mohr Siebeck, 1990), pp. 217-51 (220).

to blood. This saying was added to our text (in Mk 14.24) by a scribe.[72]
Even if this saying originated with Jesus on some earlier occasion, 'the
words actually said about the cup at the last meal would have been all
the more transparent to his disciples'. O'Neill gives an excellent example of how unthinkable it was for Jewish people to drink blood.[73] David
poured out even the water that was brought to him from the well of
Bethlehem, then occupied by the Philistines, because he saw that his
men had brought him water by risking their lives (1 Chron. 11.19):
' "Far be it from me before my God that I should do this. Shall I drink
the lifeblood of these men? For at the risk of their lives they brought
it".' Therefore he would not drink it.' If the reference to blood in Jesus'
words is authentic, then it must refer to the life sacrificed for others.
The disciples of Jesus can drink the cup, because he would die for them.

I hope I have been able to show that there is still room for discussion
concerning the significance Jesus' attached to his own death. I am aware
that many more passages are to be exegeted afresh, and I do expect that
the discussion will continue. My aim has been to show that the exegesis
of some crucial passages is still not a finally settled issue. We have also
seen that one's view of first-century Judaism influences one's exegetical
results.

The understanding of the passages discussed in this essay bears a
strong influence on our Christian faith today. If Jesus did not think his
death was effective for sinners, it would be hard for his followers to
continue so to think. The evidence I have brought forward suggests that
Christians today can hold that they look upon Jesus' death as Jesus
intended his followers to look on it: as bringing forgiveness of sins; in
other words, as bringing reconciliation and salvation.

72. O'Neill, *Messiah*, p. 68.
73. O'Neill, *Messiah*, p. 65.

THE RHETORICS AND POLITICS OF JESUS RESEARCH:
A CRITICAL FEMINIST PERSPECTIVE[*]

Elisabeth Schüssler Fiorenza

As Marc Bloch said in *The Historian's Craft*, history is not animated by the love of the past—that is antiquarianism—but by a passion for the present. In the words of this most distinguished historian, 'This faculty of understanding the living is, in very truth, the master quality of the historian', it is a proper task of theoretical clarification to explore the political implications of historians' texts not to erase them in the futile endeavor of objectivity but to understand how this aspect enables and restricts the scope of the question.[1]

While I do not believe that to strive for objectivity is a futile endeavor, I agree with Mark Poster that it is important to explore the political implications of historians' texts and historiography. In the past decade a host of historical Jesus books has appeared, which range from the very scholarly to the very popular.[2] The newest or 'Third Quest' for the Jesus of history seems to bring many different fruits. Although Jesus in particular and Christology in general are widely discussed in Christian feminist theology[3] and books and articles on 'Jesus and Women'

[*]   For a more elaborate discussion see my book *Jesus and the Politics of Interpretation* (New York: Continuum, 2000).

1.   Mark Poster, *Cultural History and Postmodernity: Disciplinary Readings and Challenges* (New York: Columbia University Press, 1997), p. 158.

2.   It would be too much to list them here. For the discussion of the literature see my book *Jesus: Miriam's Child, Sophia's Prophet* (New York: Continuum, 1994).

3.   For instance, Jaqueline Grant, *White Women's Christ and Black Women's Jesus* (Atlanta: Scholars Press, 1989); Maryanne Stevens (ed.), *Reconstructing the Christ Symbol Essays in Feminist Christology* (New York: Paulist Press, 1993); Kelly Brown Douglas, *The Black Christ* (Maryknoll, NY: Orbis Books, 1994). See also the works by Chung Hyun Kyung, R. Nakashima Brock, Rosemary Radford Ruether, Susan Brooks Thistleswaite, Elizabeth Johnson, Verena Wodtke *et al.*

continue to proliferate, it is noteworthy that no fully fledged feminist study on the historical Jesus has been published.

While at first glance my book *Jesus: Miriam's Child, Sophia's Prophet* could be mistaken for such a historical Jesus project, a closer look will show that it is not at all a study of the historical Jesus but a critical investigation of different feminist discourses on Jesus, the Christ. Noticing feminist dis-ease with historical Jesus research, John Dominic Crossan has berated feminist scholars for their lack of interest in the most recent quest for the Jesus of history.

> But there is a special problem with 'feminist sources' on the historical Jesus? [*sic*] Where are they? Why are so few women interested in that area of research? ... Why are so few Christian feminists focusing on the historical Jesus or on questions of inventory, stratigraphy, and attestation, on, that is, the precise cartography of Christianity's *earliest* re-oppression of women?[4]

These rhetorical questions are a sweeping gesture to declare critical feminist historical work on Jesus and early Christian beginnings as non-existent because it has neither adopted Crossan's frame of analysis with its scientific method of inventory, stratigraphy and attestation, nor the liberal framework of Jesus, the great individual and popular hero. Since Crossan still operates out of the liberal positivist paradigm of historical Jesus research, which believes that adequate method produces historical 'fact',[5] he is not able to explore differences and affinities between his own model of historical reconstruction and feminist ones.[6]

---

4. In Jeffrey Carlson and Robert A. Ludwig (eds.), *Jesus and Faith: A Conversation on the Work of John Dominic Crossan, Author of the Historical Jesus* (Maryknoll, NY: Orbis Books, 1994), p. 151.

5. See also the positivist rhetoric of the Jesus Seminar, which was founded in 1985 and led by Robert Funk and John Dominic Crossan. Since the Jesus Seminar wants to intervene in public discourses, it has described its work from the beginning in positivist terms. According to Mark Allan Powell, *Jesus: As a Future in History. How Modern Historians View the Man from Galilee* (Louisville, KY: Westminster/ John Knox Press, 1998), p. 80, it is 'claiming to offer "the assured results of historical-critical scholarship". To some this conveys a false impression of "objective" scholarship, according to which evidence is impartially weighed by academics who had no vested interest in the outcome. This was not the case.'

6. Although the historical Jesus reconstruction of Crossan, Borg and Horsley characterizes certain aspects of the Jesus movement (e.g. equality, comensuality, marginals, prophet, eschatology and political death) in a similar fashion as I had done in *In Memory of Her: A Feminist Theological Reconstruction of Christian*

Jane Schaberg in turn has pointed to the 'ignoring, censoring, dismissing, silencing and trivializing of feminist scholarship, as well as its appropriation without attribution, which is a form of silencing' in male-stream biblical studies.[7] She argues that one would have expected that my work, particularly *In Memory of Her*, would have made a difference or been a serious dialogue partner for most of the historical Jesus studies of the past decade but that it is not mentioned in most of them. She then goes on

> to raise the question of the effect this studied ignorance or dismissal of her work—that of the most eminent feminist New Testament critic—has on the field, especially what impact it has on other feminist critics. State of the art discussions in other fields such as psychology, literature and history usually feature analyses of how feminist studies have changed them. Why have they not changed this field?[8]

In what follows I would like to explore more fully this last question raised by Schaberg: why has feminist work not been able to change the field of historical Jesus studies? It is interesting to note that even after Schaberg raised this question in a talk given to the Canadian Society of Biblical Studies in 1993, the taxonomies and surveys of the field[9]— with the exception of that of Edith Humphrey[10]—which were presented

Origins (New York: Crossroad, 1983; 10th anniversary edn with a new introduction, 1994), such dependency is generally not recognized. However, whereas I sought to depict the movement to which Jesus belonged and its expansion and modification in the cities of the Roman Empire, Jesus books generally seek to reconstruct Jesus as unequaled individual.

7. Jane Schaberg, 'A Feminist Experience of Historical-Jesus Scholarship', in William Arnal and Michel Desjardins (eds.), *Whose Historical Jesus?* (Studies in Christianity and Judaism, 7; Waterloo, ON: Wilfried Laurier University Press, 1997), p. 146.

8. 'A Feminist Experience of Historical-Jesus Scholarship', p. 147.

9. E.g. Halvor Moxnes, 'The Theological Importance of the "Third Quest" for the Historical Jesus', in *Whose Historical Jesus?*, pp. 118-31; Larry W. Hurtado, 'A Taxonomy of Recent Historical-Jesus Work', pp. 272-95 and Peter Richardson, 'Enduring Concerns: Desiderata for Future Historical-Jesus Research', pp. 296-307, all in William Arnal and Michael Desjardines (eds.), *Whose Historical Jesus?* (Studies in Christianity and Judaism, 7; Waterloo, ON: Wilfried Laurier University Press, 1997).

10. Edith M. Humphrey, 'Will the Reader Understand? Apocalypse as Veil or Vision in Recent Historical-Jesus Research', in William Arnal and Michael Desjardines (eds.), *Whose Historical Jesus?* (Studies in Christianity and Judaism, 7; Waterloo, ON: Wilfried Laurier University Press, 1997), pp. 215-37.

at the meeting in 1994 still did not mention feminist work in general and *In Memory of Her* in particular. This blatant disregard for feminist work, I will argue, is engendered not only by the social location and rhetorical situation of historical Jesus research and its positivist and empiricist discursive construction, which is not able to intervene in the public androcentric, or better, kyriocentric, discourses on Jesus. It is also due to the continuing refusal of the discipline to reflect critically on and take responsibility for the public political implications of its research program.[11]

By raising once more the question of theory, hermeneutics and epistemology in the face of an adamantly positivist and empiricist scholarly ethos in biblical studies, I will approach historical Jesus research as a scholarly discourse that constructs and constitutes as its subject the historical Jesus, while at the same time claiming to derive this 'reality' from the extant sources. It does so by re-arranging the extant information in a reconstructive model that, consciously or not, is determined by the experience and interests of the scholar at work. Yet, 'Texts do more and less than represent: they configure what they point to, and they are configured by it. To the extent that discourse configures what it indicates, it is a fiction as much as a representation.'[12]

As a scholarly discourse historical Jesus research, I therefore suggest, can be investigated as 'the study of the construction of the subject, the extent to which and the mechanisms through which individuals are attached to identities', and the investigation of the role the process of identity construction 'plays in the disruption or stabilization of political formations and the relation of all these processes to distinctions of gender, ethnicity, and class'.[13] In other words, I investigate historical Jesus research as a historical discourse that like historiography on the whole seeks to constitute identity in terms of historical positivism.[14] Hence the

11. See my book *Rhetoric and Ethic: The Politics of Biblical Studies* (Minneapolis: Fortress Press, 1999).

12. Poster, *Cultural History*, p. 9.

13. Poster, *Cultural History,* p. 10.

14. See, e.g., Robert W. Funk, Roy W. Hoover and the Jesus Seminar, *The Five Gospels: The Search for the Authentic Words of Jesus* (New York: Macmillan, 1993), pp. 34-35: 'the Fellows of the Seminar are critical scholars. To be a critical scholar means to make empirical, factual evidence—evidence open to confirmation by independent, neutral observers- the controlling factor in historical judgments... Critical scholars adopt the principle of methodological skepticism: accept only what passes the rigorous tests of the rules of evidence...'

challenge of feminist and other scholarship from the margins to the discipline is epistemic and political rather than thematic.

1. *The Sociopolitical Location of the Quest for the Historical Jesus*

Scholarship generally has come to distinguish four periods of Jesus research and three quests for the historical Jesus. Whereas the three quests doggedly pursue the historical Jesus in various ways and with differing methods in positivist terms, the period between the First and the Second Quests which began with the work of Martin Kähler in 1896[15] and ended with Ernst Käsemann's revival of historical Jesus research in 1953,[16] was actually a declaration against liberal 'life of Jesus scholarship'[17] that claimed to represent the 'real' historical Jesus free from all dogmatic overlay. This interlude lasted for about 60 years in which the quest for the historical Jesus was virtually abandoned.

In his article 'The Interest in Life of Jesus Theology as a Paradigm for the Social History of Biblical Criticism', Dieter Georgi has constructed a trajectory of bourgeois historical Jesus theology throughout Christian history, beginning with the early Christian 'divine man' theology and continuing to the New Quest for the historical Jesus.[18] According to Georgi, historical Jesus research understands Jesus as the great exceptional individual, genius and hero.

> This view that Jesus had been a genius of some sort became the dominant view in the late eighteenth, nineteenth, and twentieth centuries, not only in Germany but also in Western Europe and North America, among both Protestants and Catholics.[19]

Georgi observes that the First Quest's interest in Jesus, the exceptional man, is continued and reformulated in the New Quest, which

15. Martin Kähler, *The So-Called Historical Jesus and the Historic Biblical Christ* (trans. and ed. Carl Braaten; Philadelphia: Fortress Press, 1988).

16. This paper was published by Ernst Käsemann, 'The Problem of the Historical Jesus', in his *Essays on New Testament Themes* (trans. W.J. Montague; London: SCM Press, 1964).

17. See Barry W. Henaut, 'Is the "Historical Jesus" a Christological Construct?', in William Arnal and Michael Desjardines (eds.), *Whose Historical Jesus?* (Studies in Christianity and Judaism, 7; Waterloo, ON: Wilfried Laurier University Press, 1997), pp. 241-68.

18. Dieter Georgi, 'The Interest in Life of Jesus Theology as a Paradigm for the Social History of Biblical Criticism', *HTR* 85 (1992), pp. 51-83.

19. Georgi, 'The Interest in Life of Jesus Theology, p. 76.

stressed Jesus as active subject of history and focused on individual consciousness, intention and decision. Jesus' unique claim to extraordinary consciousness presupposes a peerless relationship to G*d in whose place he stood and acted. His essentially eschatological outlook and stress on G*d's sovereignty brought him according to Georgi into conflict not only with the Romans but also with his own people and leadership.

This emphasis of both the Old and New Quests on the exemplary or unique historical figure of Jesus and his radical ethics required a negative portrayal of Judaism as its foil. Since Jesus is said to have been conscious that his preaching radically undermined the fundamental beliefs of Judaism he is understood as having gone to Jerusalem in the full awareness that he risked death. In this interpretation Jesus' conflict with the Roman authorities is the result of his basic conflict with ritualistic or legalistic Judaism.

Georgi concludes that the New Quest, like the quest for the historical Jesus on the whole, has its

> social location within the evolution of bourgeois consciousness, not just as an ideal but as an expression of a socioeconomic and political momentum. The contemporaneity of the New Quest with the end of the New Deal and the restoration of the bourgeoisie in the United States and Germany after World War II and within the confines of a burgeoning market-oriented Atlantic community is not accidental.[20]

Although Georgi does not point out the racist, Eurocentric identity formation of historical Jesus research, he concludes with the assertion that the modern quests for the historical Jesus are revived whenever a revolutionary situation abates. Historical Jesus research, therefore, has always had a conservative, Eurocentric, kyriarchal (i.e. Lord/Father/Master/Husband domination) function.

Moreover, the Chinese theologian Kwok Pui-Lan has pointed out that most surveys of biblical scholarship neglect to reflect on the fact that the 'quest for the historical Jesus flourished in 19th century Europe at the height of Western colonization'. She argues that there were in fact not one but two quests taking place at the same time:

> The quest for the historical Jesus was an obsession of the West. It first took place at a time when the power of Europe was at its zenith—the quest for Jesus went hand in hand with the quest for land and people to

20. Georgi, 'The Interest in Life of Jesus Theology, p. 83.

conquer. From a postcolonial perspective we must plot the quest for the *authentic* Jesus against the search for knowledge of *authentic* 'natives' for the purpose of control and domination.[21]

The Eurocentrism of historical Jesus research is confirmed by a look at Two-Thirds-World biblical scholarship. Just as feminist, so also Two-Thirds-World scholars are not engaged in the (heroic) quests for the Jesus of history. Among others, Grant LeMarquand[22] has pointed to the ignorance of the Western academy about African biblical scholarship. Whereas African and postcolonial biblical scholars are well aware of the issues raised by Western historical Jesus scholarship, they frame and shape their own discourses on Jesus differently. Their major concern is to deconstruct colonialist readings of the Bible and to establish the common ground between their own cultures and the Bible. They focus on this issue not only because biblical cultures often come very close to their own but also because their own cultures were constructed by missionaries with the help of the Bible as inferior and even 'satanic'.

Finally, I myself have pointed to the conservative political contextualizations of the Third Quest which emerged in the USA during the Reagan/Thatcher years, and in a period where the USA had become the only superpower in the world after the demise of the Soviet Union and the failure of socialist state capitalism.[23] Moreover, the Third Quest continues to produce Jesus, the Lord or *kyrios*, as a naturalized historical fact in order to assert the importance of Western hegemonic identity formations as Christian and as elite male.[24] It does so in the face of a widespread liberal whitemale anxiety that feels threatened by feminists, immigrants, Two-Thirds-World persons and everybody else who seeks

21. Kwok Pui-Lan, 'Jesus/the Native: Biblical Studies from a Postcolonial Perspective', in Fernando Segovia and Mary Ann Tolbert (eds.), *Teaching the Bible: The Discourses and Politics of Biblical Pedagogy* (Maryknoll, NY: Orbis Books, 1998), p. 76.

22. Grant LeMarquand, 'The Historical Jesus and African New Testament Scholarship', in William Arnal and Michel Desjardins (eds.), *Whose Historical Jesus?* (Studies in Christianity and Judaism, 7; Waterloo, ON: Wilfried Laurier University Press, 1997), pp. 161-80.

23. See my *Jesus: Miriam's Child, Sophia's Prophet*, p. 5-12.

24. See the self-interview of Kwok Pui-Lan, 'On Color-Coding Jesus: An Interview with Kwok Pui-Lan', in R.S. Sugirtharajah (ed.), *The Postcolonial Bible* (The Bible and Postcolonialism, 1; Sheffield: Sheffield Academic Press, 1998), pp. 176-89.

to decenter academy and society in general and biblical studies in particular.

2. 'Historical Jesus and Women' Research

If the studies about Jesus and wo/men[25] subscribe to the methodological positivism of the Third Quest or take the grammatically androcentric language of our sources at face value, they reinscribe the wo/men-marginalizing and wo/men-erasing tendencies of such language into the history that they tell about biblical wo/men and about wo/men today.[26] They do so, not only because of the marginalizing and silencing tendencies of our androcentric sources written in grammatically masculine languages but also because of the marginalizing and silencing tendencies of hegemonic biblical scholarship and its kyriocentric frameworks of interpretation and models of historical reconstruction.

Although in my *In Memory of Her* I had argued that a feminist reconstruction of Christian beginnings must cease to conceptualize the field as the study *about* wo/men making wo/men the object of the scholarly gaze, in the context of the Third Quest articles and books about 'Wo/men in the Bible' or 'Wo/men in the Gospels' have proliferated. Instead of re-inscribing wo/men as peripheral, I argued, a pragmatic rhetorical

25. For the problematic meaning of the term woman/women see Denise Riley, *'Am I That Name?': Feminism and the Category of Women in History* (Minneapolis: University of Minnesota Press, 1988); Judith Butler, *Gender Trouble Feminism and the Subversion of Identity* (New York: Routledge, 1990). My way of spelling wo/men seeks to underscore not only the ambiguous character of the term 'wo/man or wo/men' but also to retain the expression 'wo/men' as a political category. Since this designation is often read as referring to white women only, my unorthodox writing of the term seeks to draw to the attention of readers that those kyriarchal structures which determine women's lives and status also impact that of men of subordinated race, classes, countries and religions, albeit in different ways. The expression wo/men must therefore be understood as inclusive rather than as an exclusive universalized gender term.

26. See, e.g., Ross Shepard Kraemer and Mary Rose D'Angelo (eds.), *Women and Christian Origins* (New York: Oxford University Press, 1999) for such an approach. They rework most of the materials in *In Memory of Her* in terms of the study of women, gender and religion. Since they know the broad influence of the book, it is unfathomable how they can go on to state: 'To date, no one has written a comprehensive treatment of wo/men and Christian origins appropriate for a wide audience ranging from undergraduate to general readers to scholars previously unacquainted with this literature' (p. 3).

understanding of language and a radical egalitarian model of historical reconstruction is able not only to tell the story of Jesus as belonging to a Jewish emancipatory movement but also to place Jewish wo/men as agents at the center of its historiography. Yet, while I was concerned to reconstruct the Jesus movement as an egalitarian Jewish movement, biblical wo/men's or gender studies has continued to make wo/men the object of historical Jesus study and to frame its research in terms of the cultural model of patriarchal romance[27] between the great man Jesus and his wo/men followers.

Since the first phase of the 'life of Jesus' research in the nineteenth century sought to write a biography of Jesus, the great individual and heroic man, women's studies research on the historical Jesus and Christian origins has adopted an 'add and stir' approach which adds wo/men to the subject historical Jesus and continues to make 'Jesus and women' rather than patri-kyriarchal structures of domination the object of its research. This approach overlooks the fact that the understanding of Jesus as a powerful religious genius who transgressed all normal boundaries is the product of an elite masculinist Eurocentric liberal ethos. Jesus, the extraordinary and heroic man, becomes the paradigm of true (Western male) humanity and individuality, which can be approximated only by those who are like him.

Many popular studies on the relationship of Jesus to wo/men still remain in the context of this first phase of 'life of Jesus' research when they seek to write biographies of Jesus, stress his close relationship with wo/men, or argue that he developed psychologically in the interaction with wo/men. Whereas Jesus is seen as the great (male) individual and hero who suffers conflicts and survives suffering and death, the wo/men around him, especially Mary of Magdala, are pictured in typically feminine fashion as romantically involved with him or as his loving support staff. Insofar as Jesus' behavior is imagined as always generous, friendly, helpful, kind and loving, he appears as a human being who successfully combined masculine and feminine qualities.

The *second* phase of Jesus research began after World War I and was dubbed by Marcus Borg as the 'no Quest' period.[28] This period distin-

---

27. For the impact of such reading see Janice A. Radway, *Reading the Romance: Women, Patriarchy, and Popular Literature* (Chapel Hill: University of North Carolina Press, 1991).

28. Marcus J. Borg, *Jesus in Contemporary Scholarship* (Valley Forge, PA: Trinity Press International, 1994), p. 4.

guishes between the historical Jesus of modern scholarship and the resurrected Christ of kerygmatic theology. Such kerygmatic theology insisted that it is no longer possible to distill a liberal historical Jesus freed from early Christian interpretation and apostolic tradition. The Gospels are to be studied as documents of faith and theological arguments of the evangelists and the communities they address.

But whereas many studies of the First Quest on 'Jesus and wo/men' see him in a gendered framework, many of the studies which follow in the footsteps of the No Quest utilize not only redaction criticism and literary criticism but also feminist analysis for investigating the evangelists' portrayal of wo/men and the traditions they incorporated. Exemplary here is the Jesus book of Elaine Wainwright, *Shall We Look for Another?*,[29] which uses feminist theory to reread Matthew's story about Jesus.

In general, feminist studies of the Gospels seek to analyze the androcentric narrative constructions of the evangelists and to trace their gendered traditions and sources in order to show how androcentric texts and traditions restrict discipleship to the male characters and thereby marginalize wo/men and their traditions. I mention here only the feminist works of Joanna Dewey, Hisako Kinukawa and Monika Fander on Mark, of Jane Schaberg and Turid Karlsen Seim on Luke, of Elaine Wainwright on Matthew, of Sandra Schneiders and Adele Reinhartz on John, and of Karen King on the Gospel of Mary and the *Gospel of Thomas*. All these studies were written after the 60-year interval in historical Jesus research but notwithstanding continue the No Quest approach in feminist terms.

Nevertheless, it must also be noted that most popularizing studies about 'Jesus and women' in the Gospels are not feminist. Often they uncritically assume linguistic determinism, and hence cannot but 'naturalize' the grammatically masculine androcentric language representation as well as the anti-Jewish tendencies of the Gospels and their traditions. Such studies are especially prone to re-inscribe the anti-Jewish polemic of the Gospels into their own historical narrative.

The *third* period of historical Jesus research, which was dubbed the 'New Quest' by James Robinson, owes its existence to the reaction against kerygmatic Jesus theology. It flourished in the 1950s and 1960s and insisted that it is possible to extract or distill the historical Jesus

---

29. Elaine M. Wainwright, *Shall We Look for Another? A Feminist Rereading of the Matthean Jesus* (Maryknoll, NY: Orbis Books, 1998).

from the early Christian sources like a kernel from the husk. To that end, the New Quest articulated criteria of historical authenticity. In order to be regarded as authentic, words and deeds must, first, be documented in more than one source (the criterion of multiple attestation). Secondly they must not be found in the Jewish culture of the time or be explainable as stemming from the interests of the early church (the dissimilarity or exclusivity—not difference—criterion). And thirdly they must cohere with the material judged previously as authentic (the coherence criterion).[30] In other words: the New Quest adopts a reductionist historical method that does not take into account that historiography must evaluate and place texts and artifacts in a coherent frame of meaning or reconstructive model in order to tell a story that makes sense. Moreover, this reductionist method assumes that Jesus is totally separable from both Judaism and his followers, the early Church. He is the totally Other.

In order to establish the historical singularity of Jesus and his ethics the New Quest, like the Old, needs a negative depiction of Judaism. Jesus supposedly knew that his teaching undermined the fundaments of Jewish belief. The Roman imperial authority executed him allegedly because of his conflict with a ritualistic and legalistic Judaism. This anti-Jewish framework has also determined many studies on 'Jesus and Women'.

It was a male[31] and not a female scholar who early on articulated the thesis that Jesus was a feminist because he broke the purity laws and in distinction to Jewish rabbis spoke to wo/men and had wo/men as his disciples. However, because of the challenge of Jewish feminists such as Judith Plaskow, Christian feminist scholarship much earlier than malestream historical Jesus scholarship has recognized and discussed the anti-Jewish prejudice resulting from attempts to depatriarchalize Jesus without challenging the scholarly construction and popular understanding of Judaism as patriarchal.[32] It must not be overlooked,

---

30. Norman Perrin, *Rediscovering the Teaching of Jesus* (New York: Harper & Row, 1967), pp. 39-40, who has labeled the criterion of exclusivity as criterion of dissimilarity.

31. L. Swidler, 'Jesus Was a Feminist', *SEAJT* 13 (1971), pp. 102-110; *idem*, *Women in Judaism: The Status of Women in Formative Judaism* (Metuchen: Scarecrow Press, 1976).

32. Although our knowledge of Jewish wo/men has increased considerably since *In Memory of Her* appeared, unfortunately until today no *feminist* recon-

moreover, that popular studies on 'Jesus and Women' have taken over their interpretive frameworks and materials from malestream Christian scholarship. They often do not intend to be anti-Jewish but seek to picture Jesus as a critic of his patriarchal religion and culture in order to indict their own church polity and hegemonic Christian practices.

Insofar as one of the most fertile grounds for Christian anti-Jewish articulations has been historical Jesus research, assertions of the uniqueness of Jesus, the feminist, and his atypical relations to women adopt the arguments of historical Jesus scholarship permeated with anti-Judaism. Since such feminist assertions about Jesus are formulated within a historical and theological discourse produced by predominantly malestream scholarship and theology, it becomes necessary to examine what kind of historical Jesus discourses engender feminist collusion in the reproduction of Christian anti-Judaism.

This collusion also seems to be at work in the Third Quest for the historical Jesus. The beginning of this Quest is generally dated in the early 1980s and its initiation is attributed to North American scholarship. In difference to the Old and the New Quests, the newest or Third Quest does not seek to reconstruct the historical Jesus over and against first-century Judaism but sees him as totally integrated in his time and culture. Even among the advocates of the Cynic hypothesis the debate is not about whether Jesus was a Jew but what kind of Jew Jesus was.

This Third Quest was prepared through studies of early Jewish writings, research of the Qumran scrolls and archaeological discoveries. Whereas these studies have amply documented that Judaism in the first century was variegated and pluralistic, the arguments on Jesus' Jewishness seem often to presuppose a unitary patriarchal form of Judaism. Insofar as scholars do not use a sociological conflict but an integrationist model for their reconstruction, they cannot picture Jesus as part of a variegated Jewish basileia movement that stood in conflict with the hegemonic patriarchal and kyriarchal structures of the Roman Empire, of which hegemonic Judaism also was a part. In short, they are not able to articulate a reconstructive frame of reference that can conceptualize the emergent Jesus movement and its diverse articulations as participating in popular Jewish and Greco-Roman movements of cultural, political and religious survival, resistance and change.

struction of early Judaism has been written. One wonders whether this is the case because leading Jewish wo/men scholars such as Ross Kraemer and Amy-Jill Levine favor the women's or gender studies approach.

One wonders whether it is historical accident that the Third Quest for the historical Jesus exploded not only during the resurgence of the political right and the revival of religious fundamentalism but also in a time when the wo/men's movement in the churches and the academy gained ground and developed rhetorical power. Yet, whereas the Second Quest stressed the difference of the 'feminist' Jesus to Judaism, the Third Quest argues for his integration into the patriarchal Jewish society and religion of his time. Jesus was a devout Jewish man who did not question the dominant structures of his society but fully subscribed to them. If the dissimilarity criterion is replaced with that of plausibility within a kyriarchal frame of reference, one cannot but reconstitute Jesus Jewishness in terms of the dominant patriarchal ethos of the first century. At this point the entrapping character of this new criterion of historical Jesus research becomes obvious.

Since the Third Quest justifiably rejected the Second Quest's reductionistic criteria of authenticity, it needed to develop new methods and criteria of evaluation. To that end the Jesus Seminar, whose members are mostly whitemale and Christian,[33] has adopted forms of opinion research and voting practices in order to stratify the traditions about Jesus. In addition, scholars have developed the plausibility criterion that judges materials on the grounds as to whether their content can be made plausible historically and be understood as fitting into the time and culture of Jesus.[34]

However, this criterion overlooks that what is regarded as 'common sense' or plausible in a culture depends on the hegemonic ideological understandings of 'how the world is'. For instance, the assumption that wo/men were marginal or second-class citizens in all forms of first century Judaism makes it impossible to assert plausibly that they were

---

33. For the intent of the Jesus Seminar and the controversy surrounding it see Mark Allan Powell, *Jesus: as A Future in History: How Modern Historians View the Man from Galilee* (Louisville, KY: Westminster/John Knox Press, 1998), pp. 65-82.

34. This hermeneutical circle between a preconstructed image of Jesus and evaluations of individual texts is recognized by Gerd Theissen and Dagmar Winter, *Die Kriterienfrage in der Jesusforschung: Vom Differenzkriterium zum Plausibilitätskriterium* (NTOA, 34; Göttingen: Vandenhoeck & Ruprecht, 1997), p. 206: 'Ein zutreffendes historisches Gesamtbild ist eine Idealvorstellung, ein Grenzwert, dem wir uns immer nur in Form von Plausibilität annähern können'. However, they do not critically question the plausibility criterion on the basis of this insight.

equal members in the Jesus movement if one understands it as a Jewish movement.

Some scholars in biblical wo/men's studies, who seek to avoid such Christian anti-Judaism in their research on 'Jesus and women', also argue that it is not plausible that Jesus and his followers challenged the dominant patriarchal institutions of his time. To the contrary, they insist, he was completely in line with Jewish and Greco-Roman patri-archalism.[35] Such scholars, however, do not realize that they also fall prey to negative stereotypical assumptions about Judaism insofar as they cannot imagine that the Jesus movement like other Jewish movements of the time could possibly have questioned the second-class citizenship of wo/men and disenfranchised men and have done so on Jewish theological grounds.[36]

---

35. See, e.g., the dissertation of Helga Melzer Keller, *Jesus und die Frauen: Eine Verhältnisbestimmung nach den synoptischen Evangelien* (HBS, 14, Freiburg: Herder, 1997), pp. 440-41: 'Auch sonst nahm Jesus in seinen Reden die patriarchale Gesellschaftsordnung als das Normale hin… Die traditionellen Verhaltensmuster und Schablonen wurden von ihm in keiner Weise hinterfragt oder gar aufgesprengt. Für wen Jesus sich vor allem einsetzte, waren die Notleidenden, die religiös Marginalisierten und die sozial Benachteiligten—auch wenn er kein Reform-programm oder sozialrevolutionäre Aktionen verfolgte… Wir müssen vielmehr das Fazit ziehen, dass er überhaupt kein Problembewusstsein hinsichtlich der in einem patriarchalen Gesellschaftssystem ungleichen Verteilung von Rechten und Möglich-keiten zwischen den Geschlechtern hatte, kein Gespür für eine sowohl rechtliche als auch lebenspraktische Benachteiligung von Frauen, kein Interesse an einer disbezüg-lichen Veränderung des Status quo.' The ideological interests of this text are obvious. A Roman Catholic wo/man student who claims to be a feminist has to prove that she is a 'good student' of her Doktorvater and that she is not interested in changing the status quo.

36. See, e.g., Amy-Jill Levine, 'Second Temple Judaism, Jesus, and Women: Yeast of Eden', *BibInt* 2 (1994), pp. 8-33, who concedes a 'feminist impulse' in Judaism but then in her argument against Luise Schottroff, 'Itinerant Prophetesses: A Feminist Analysis of the Sayings Source Q', *Institute for Antiquity and Christianity, Claremont Graduate School Occasional Papers* 21 (1991), and *eadem*, 'Wanderprophetinnen: Eine feministische Analyse der Logienquelle', *EvT* 51 (1991), pp. 332-44, retreats from it. Instead of researching the emancipatory tendencies in first-century Judaism, she ends up trivializing the textual information and justifying patriarchal religion: 'To the outsider, the life of women in an ultra-orthodox Jewish community is restricted. To many insiders and especially to the convert, life in Williamsburg, just as life under Islamic Law or life in a Carmelite convent, is lib-erating. Such regulated societies provide all their members order, meaning and sanctification of daily existence; a distance from the outside (profane) world that

3. *The Socio-Rhetorical Situation of Jesus Research*

I have attempted here to show that research on 'Jesus and Women' complements but does not radically question the hegemonic framework of historical Jesus research. Hence, some have argued that historical Jesus research should be abandoned because it is part of the problem rather than part of the solution. However, in my view historical Jesus research cannot be simply abandoned but must be critiqued.[37] It is necessary to engage in research of the historical Jesus traditions, if one seeks to dislodge the exclusionist tendencies inscribed in the Gospel portrait of Jesus that marginalize Christian wo/men and vilify Jewish wo/men.

In addition, Jesus research must be critically assessed because in Western societies it is a discourse that affects a larger public. For Jesus discourses are intertwined with hegemonic cultural and societal ideologies. A politics of meaning contends that Bible, history and theology are not just important for religious communities. Rather, as master narratives of Western cultures they are always implicated in and collude with the production and maintenance of systems of knowledge that foster either exploitation and oppression or contribute to a praxis and vision of emancipation and liberation.

Hence historical Jesus research as a rhetorical practice must critically explore and assess its own impregnation with hegemonic knowledges and discursive kyriocentric frameworks that make 'sense' of the world and produce what counts as 'reality' or 'commonsense'. Consequently, it must make visible the contesting interests and theoretical frameworks that determine historical Jesus articulations of both malestream and feminist biblical studies.

The political context and rhetorical situation in which feminist as well as malestream historical Jesus research takes place, I submit, is constituted by the resurgence of the religious Right around the world

distracts and detracts from the sanctified life; strong women-based groups (i.e. sisterhoods); and the developed traditions that overcome or at least counterbalance the patriarchalism involved in the communities' institutions and maintenance. Regulation of clothing, action, relationships is even found by some to counteract the far too frequent abuse and violence against women' ('Second Temple Judaism'), p. 32).

37. See Elisabeth Schüssler Fiorenza, 'Jesus and the Politics of Interpretation', *HTR* 90 (1997), pp. 343-58.

claiming the power to name and to define the true nature of religion.[38] Right-wing, well-financed thinktanks are supported by reactionary political and financial institutions that seek to defend kyriarchal capitalism.[39] The interconnection between religious antidemocratic arguments and the debate with regard to wo/men's proper place and role is not accidental or just of intra-religious significance. In the past decade or so, right-wing movements around the globe have insisted on the figuration of emancipated wo/men as signifiers of Western decadence or of modern atheistic secularism, and have presented masculine power as the expression of divine power.[40]

In the article quoted above Jane Schaberg has detailed her experience

38. See the variegated contributions in Hans Küng and Jürgen Moltmann (eds.), *Fundamentalism as an Ecumenical Challenge* (Concilium; London: SCM Press, 1992).

39. For an excellent critical analysis of the involvement of religion in this global struggle see especially the work of the late Penny Lernoux, *Cry of the People* (New York: Penguin Books, 1982); *eadem, In Banks We Trust* (New York: Penguin Books, 1986) and her last book before her untimely death *People of God: The Struggle for World Catholicism* (New York: Penguin Books, 1989); Robert B. Reich, *The Work of Nations* (New York: Vintage Books, 1992); Joan Smith, 'The Creation of the World We Know: The World-Economy and the Re-Creation of Gendered Identities', in Valentine M. Moghadam (ed.), *Identity Politics and Wo/men: Cultural Reassertions and Feminisms in International Perspective* (Boulder: Westview Press, 1994), pp. 27-41; see also Diana L. Eck, *Encountering God: A Spiritual Journey from Bozeman to Banaras* (Boston: Beacon Press, 1993), p. 176, who writes: 'A new wave of exclusivism is cresting around the world today. Expressed in social and political life, exclusivism becomes ethnic or religious chauvinism, described in South Asia as communalism... As we have observed, identity-based politics is on the rise because it is found to be a successful way of arousing political energy.'

40. See especially the declaration of the Division for the Advancement of Women on 'International Standards of Equality and Religious Freedom: Implications for the Status of Women', pp. 425-38; and Rebecca E. Klatch, 'Women of the New Right in the United States: Family, Feminism, and Politics', both in Valentine M. Moghadam (ed.), *Identity Politics and Wo/men: Cultural Reassertions and Feminisms in International Perspective* (Boulder: Westview Press, 1994), pp. 367-88. Most of the contributions in Moghadam (ed.), *Identity Politics* are on women and Islam in different parts of the world. However, see Sucheta Mazumdar, 'Moving Away from a Secular Vision? Women, Nation, and the Cultural Construction of Hindu India', pp. 243-73 and Radha Kumar, 'Identity Politics and the Contemporary Indian Feminist Movement', pp. 274-92 in that volume; see also the three-part award-winning PBS series *God and Politics* in which Bill Moyers explores the connections between state and church and its impact on US foreign policy.

of verbal and physical violence that was unleashed with the publication of her book *The Illegitimacy of Jesus*[41] and an article on Mary of Magdala in the *Bible Review*. The Associated Press and many newspapers informing the public that 'Mary Magdalene was not a whore' picked up this article. Since Schaberg was happy to receive the same publicity for her work as the Jesus Seminar,[42] she was not prepared for the vitriolic attacks that almost cost her her teaching position. Whereas Jesus Seminar scholars boost the sale of their books when they are celebrated as Jesus experts on radio and television, feminist work that uses the same historical-critical methods but questions the status quo is vilified and leads to threats of violence. A subsequent profile of Schaberg in the Detroit Free Press unleashed hundreds of letters to the administration threatening loss of financial support for the University and demanding that she be fired and even threatening her life. Schaberg sums up her personal experience as political:

> These letters...tell us what we already knew: that the general public is ignorant of the basics of historical criticism, and proud of it; that it serves the interest of the clergy and hierarchy to keep the general public in such ignorance and unable to think for themselves...that fundamentalism is a powerful and often cruel force; that feminist concerns and perspectives are not studied, but reduced to slogans, and perceived by many as immoral; and that... Sexism and misogyny are deeply rationalized, theologized, and spiritualized...[43]

In this context of struggle, it becomes apparent that the publication and proliferation of historical Jesus books for popular consumption on the one hand and on the other hand the trivializing or non-recognition of feminist work by malestream biblical scholars go hand in hand. Historical-Jesus books feed into literalist fundamentalism by reasserting disinterested scientific positivism in order to shore up the scholarly authority and universal truth of their research portrayal of Jesus.

They do not reflect upon the fact that the proliferation of 'new' scientific historical Jesus books does not undermine but sustains the literalist desire of biblical fundamentalism for an 'accurate' reliable biography of Jesus as firm foundation of Western culture and biblical

---

41. Jane Schaberg, *The Illegitimacy of Jesus: A Feminist Theological Interpretation of the Infancy Narratives* (San Francisco: Harper & Row, 1987; New York: Crossroad, 1990).

42. See Powell, *Jesus*, p. 73.

43. Schaberg, 'A Feminist Experience of Historical-Jesus Scholarship', p. 156.

religion. Hence, 'scientific' objectivist scholarship that does not threaten the status quo seems to function politically as the reverse side of the fundamentalist literalist coin. In a literalist dogmatic reading, fundamentalist interpretations seek to 'fix' the pluriform expressions of Christian Scriptures and traditions, variegated texts and ambiguous metaphors of Jesus the Christ, and to consolidate them into a definite, univocal and unambiguous malestream discourse of meaning.

In response to such literalist readings, 'liberal' biblical scholarship insists on its scientific character, value-neutrality and detachment from all theological and contemporary interests. If one asks what is it about feminist, postcolonial or other scholarship from the margins that it is not taken seriously by biblical studies and evokes violent public reactions, one is justified to suggest that it is the refusal of such emancipatory scholarship to shroud its work in the cloak of disinterestedness. Such scholarship is no less objective and critical than hegemonic malestream scholarship. Rather one could argue it is more so because it is self-consciously and openly biased in favor of an emancipatory reading and historical reconstruction.

In a very perceptive conclusion to *Whose Historical Jesus?* William Arnal points out that the reaction to feminist or postcolonial scholarship reveals

> What is ultimately at stake in the *desire* for objectivity: a desire to view the object of one's inquiry through the lens of things-as-they-are. The distinction between a fact and a value is itself not based on fact, but on a dichotomy between things as they are and things as one wishes them to be; the removal of so-called value from scholarship is really the removal of hope, something which is not central or necessary to the daily ideological work of the privileged.[44]

The refusal of the Third Quest to problematize its own methodological assumptions and ideological interests as well as its sophisticated restoration of historical positivism corresponds to political conservatism. Its emphasis on the 'realia' and 'facts' of history and the reliability of its methods serves to promote scientific fundamentalism. This is the case if Jesus discourses do not underscore methodologically that historians select and interpret archaeological artifacts and textual

44. William Arnal, 'Making and Re-Making the Jesus-Sign: Contemporary Markings on the Body of Christ', in William Arnal and Michel Desjardins (eds.), *Whose Historical Jesus?* (Studies in Christianity and Judaism, 7; Waterloo, ON: Wilfried Laurier University Press, 1997), p. 317.

evidence as well as incorporate them into a scientific model and narra-tive framework of meaning. The inability of such discourses to discuss plausibly the possibility of understanding the Jesus movement as an alternative Jewish movement that sought to abolish kyriarchal domina-tion and believed in the basic equality of all the children of G*d, not only bespeaks antifeminist tendencies, but also bespeaks a lack of feminist self-affirmation on the part of wo/men scholars who subscribe to the positivist methods of the Third Quest, as Judith Plaskow has recognized:

> I read this book excited and resisting every word. I made furious notes in the margins asking, 'How do you know women participated? Isn't it a large assumption, indeed an *a priori* commitment?' Forced to sort out my feelings for an American Academy of Religion symposium on *In Memory of Her*, I realized that I found the book deeply disturbing because it thrusts women into an unaccustomed position of power. To take seriously the notion that religious history is the history of women and men imposes an enormous responsibility on women: It forces us to take on the intellectual task of rewriting all of history… It does these things, moreover, without allowing us the luxury of nursing our anger and waiting for the patriarchs to create change, for it reminds us that we are part of a long line of women who were simultaneously victims of the tradition and historical agents struggling within and against it.[45]

If feminist self-affirmation is the *sine qua non* of writing history *otherwise*, it is not surprising that biblical Women's Studies have not always been able to resist the lure of malestream historical Jesus research and the reconstruction of early Christian origins in positivist terms. As long as the Third Quest tacitly assumes that Christian (male) identity must be bound up with a positivist 'scientific' reconstruction of the historical 'Jesus', the heroic patriarchal man, it cannot but produce the historical "fact" of Jesus' maleness as an objectified historical given that is constitutive for hegemonic Christian western (male) identity.

4. *The Epistemic Challenge of Feminist Scholarship*

It is not surprising, then, that feminist work on the Jesus movement and Christian beginnings has not had any palpable impact on the public discussion of the Third Quest. Since *In Memory of Her* appeared in the

---

45. Judith Plaskow, 'Critique and Transformation: A Jewish Feminist History', in Deborah Orenstein and Jane Rachel Litman (eds.), *Lifecycles*, II (Woodstock: Jewish Light Publishing House, 1997), p. 99.

early 1980s it belongs to the beginning stage of the fourth period of historical Jesus research. In discussion with social world studies and feminist historiography, the book sought to articulate a critical feminist theoretical model of early Christian history including that of the Jesus movement that is not pejorative of Jewish or Christian feminist identity. However, with the exception of a short discussion by Marcus Borg[46] and its selective reception by Richard Horsley,[47] my methodological proposals and critical historiographical explorations[48] have been virtually overlooked in recent historical Jesus research. One wonders whether this is the case because my work makes its feminist interests explicit and thereby challenges the positivist and empiricist ethos of the discipline.

The present proliferation of historical Jesus books and articles prove that the judgment of Albert Schweitzer is correct after all: scholars and writers inescapably fashion Jesus in their own image and likeness. At best we can glimpse a historical shadow but how we develop 'this picture' will always depend on the lens we use and the re-constructive model we adopt. This holds true also for the earliest portrayals of Jesus in the canonical and extra-canonical early Christian literature.

Any presentation of Jesus—scientific or otherwise—must therefore own that it is a disciplined but imaginative 're-construction' and open up its historical imagination and reconstructive models to public reflection and critical inquiry. Reconstructive historical models must be scrutinized not only for how much they can account for our present textual and archaeological information on the Jesus of history and his sociopolitical contexts but also for the rhetorical interests and theological functions of scholarly historical knowledge productions. Moreover, an ethics of interpretation would require that such reconstructive models must not re-inscribe mindsets of discrimination and exclusion.

When I set out to develop the reconstructive model shaping the narrative of *In Memory of Her* I did not start with the goal of producing an objectivist empiricist description of what actually happened in early Christian beginnings, nor did I want to prove that Jesus himself was totally egalitarian and without bias. Rather I wanted to show that the

46. Marcus Borg, 'Portraits of Jesus in Contemporary North American Scholarship', *HTR* 84 (1991), pp. 1-22.

47. Richard A. Horsley, *Sociology and the Jesus Movement* (New York: Crossroad, 1989).

48. See especially chaps. 2 and 3 of *In Memory of Her*.

historiography of early Christian beginnings was a theoretical-historical discourse of domination that was imagined and produced by contemporary scholarship. Consequently, I did not set out to prove that the hegemonic early Christian historiography was factually wrong but rather that it was *wrong-headed* and incomplete because of its kyriocentric frameworks and positivist empiricist rhetoric.

After I had become fully familiar with the feminist critique of language and historiography I set out to show that the early Christian story could be told—and must be told—*otherwise*. My question was not 'did it actually happen?' but 'do we still have sufficient information and source texts to tell the story of Jesus and the movements carrying his name *otherwise* envisioning it as that of a "discipleship of equals?"' The task, I argued, involves not so much rediscovering new sources as rereading the available sources in a different key.[49] Not only was there plenty of material that could be read in an egalitarian frame of interpretation but such an egalitarian reading, I argued, also could do more justice to our sources[50] that speak about wo/men's leadership which traditional scholarship always felt compelled to explain away, to overlook or to interpret in terms of cultural femininity.

In short, I did not want to write another book about 'Women and Jesus' or wo/men in the Bible but rather I wanted to see whether it was possible to write a feminist history of the Jesus movements in Palestine and in the Greco-Roman cities by placing wo/men in the center of inquiry. Since feminists are not concerned with conserving the world 'as it is' but rather want to change it to fit their own experience of being in the world as wo/men, they are not interested so much in the historical Jesus as in the historical people—Jewish wo/men and men- who joined a socioreligious Jewish movement which I understood as an emancipatory basileia-movement. It was obvious to me that I was able to imagine the beginnings of early Christianity differently because I was fortunate to belong to a social movement for change today.

49. *In Memory of Her*, p. xx.

50. I thereby anticipated in a somewhat different form the criterion for the adjudication of historical Jesus research, which Larry Hurtado has formulated in analogy to that used in textual criticism, 'where the aim in weighing "internal evidence" is to reconstruct the reading that best explains all the variants' (Larry W. Hurtado, 'A Taxonomy of Recent Historical-Jesus Work', in William Arnal and Michel Desjardins [eds.], *Whose Historical Jesus?* [Studies in Christianity and Judaism, 7; Waterloo, ON: Wilfried Laurier University Press, 1997], p. 294).

Hence, I suggest that the reductionist criterion of dissimilarity or better exclusivity and the conservative criterion of plausibility be replaced with the criterion of 'possibility'. What is 'thinkable' or 'possible' historically must be adjudicated in terms of an emancipatory reconstructive model of early Christian beginnings and how it utilizes its source-information and materials. Such a change of theoretical framework from one that uncritically reinscribes 'what is' to one that imagines 'what is possible' makes it plausible to understand the Jesus traditions and early Christian beginnings as shaped by the agency and leadership of Jewish, Greco-Roman, Asian, African, free and enslaved, rich and poor, and elite and marginal wo/men. Those who hold the opposite view, for instance that slave wo/men or Jewish wo/men were not active shapers of early Christian life, would have to argue their point.

If one shifts from a kyriarchal preconstructed frame of reference to that of the 'discipleship of equals' one no longer can hold, for example, that wo/men might or might not have been members of the communities that produced the hypothetical Sayings Source Q and the earliest Jesus traditions. If one cannot prove that wo/men were not members of this group and did not participate in shaping the earliest Jesus traditions, one needs to give the benefit of the doubt to the textual traces suggesting that they did. Rather than taking the androcentric text at face value, one must unravel its politics of meaning.

The objection that this is a circular argument applies to all hermeneutical and historiographical practices. For instance, social scientific studies which produce the preconstructed dualistic frame of the opposition between 'honor and shame' as a given 'fact' of Mediterranean cultures will read early Christian texts 'about women' within this theoretically 'constructed' kyriocentric frame of reference, and thereby reproduce the cultural 'commonsense' that wo/men are marginal people. So-called social scientific narratives, therefore, appear to be more 'realistic' and 'objective' than feminist ones because kyriocentric discourses function as ideologies that 'naturalize' the structures of domination as 'what is'. That is, they mystify the 'constructedness' of their account of historical reality in terms of their own understanding and experience of reality. Therefore malestream narratives of 'how the world of Jesus really was' are easily accepted as 'commonsense', objective, scientific historical accounts although they are as much a 'construction' as feminist ones are.

A *possible* reconstruction of early Christian beginnings as egalitarian does not mean that the extant early Christian sources do not also allow for a hegemonic kyriarchal reconstruction of the Jesus movements. The opposite is the case, since our sources are all written in grammatically androcentric/kyriocentric language that functions as generic language. It only means that one needs to show that a feminist egalitarian reconstruction is 'possible' in terms of a critical reading of the extant sources with a hermeneutics of suspicion and preferable in terms of the Christian identity construction that the writing of history engenders. In other words, scholars no longer can justify their reconstructive models in a positivist scientist fashion but need to stand accountable for them and their political functions in light of the values and visions they promote for today.

A feminist reconstructive historical model of egalitarian possibility, I submit, is able to place the beginnings of the Galilean prophetic-wisdom-basileia movement within a broader cultural-religious historical frame of reference that allows one to trace the tensions and struggles between emancipatory understandings and movements inspired by the radical democratic logic of equality on the one hand and the dominant kyriarchal structures of society and religion in antiquity on the other.

Since *In Memory of Her* and its reconstruction of the Jesus movement is often read in terms of the liberal Protestant historiographical model of pristine egalitarian origins and rapid decline into patriarchy,[51] its underlying historical model of struggle between egalitarian vision and kyriarchal reality is not understood.[52] To read early Christian history in terms of this model of rapid decline from the heights of radical equality to patriarchal institution is to overlook the struggles which are ongoing throughout Christian history between those who understand Christian identity as radically inclusive and egalitarian and those who advocate kyriarchal domination and submission.

51. See *In Memory of Her*, p. 92: 'The sociological-theological model for the reconstruction of the early Christian movement suggested here should, therefore, not be misread as that of a search for true, pristine, orthodox beginnings which have been corrupted either by early Catholicism or by "heresy", nor should it be seen as an argument for an institutional patriarchalization absolutely necessary for the historical survival of Christianity. The model used here is that of social interaction and religious transformation, of Christian "vision" and historical realization, of struggle for equality and against patriarchal domination.'

52. See, e.g., Powell, *Jesus*, p. 2, who not only mistakes my hermeneutics of suspicion 'as reading between the lines' but also misapprehends my reconstructive model of ongoing struggle: 'By the second century the Christian church had

Egalitarian social movements striving to change unjust relations of domination are not just a product of modernity but are found throughout history. Ancient social movements and emancipatory struggles against kyriarchal relations of exploitation do not begin with the Jesus movements. Rather they have a long history in Greek, Roman, Asian and Jewish cultures. The emancipatory struggles of biblical wo/men must be seen within this wider context of cultural-political-religious struggles. Such a historical model of emancipatory struggles sees the Jesus of history and the movement that has kept alive his memory not over and against Judaism but over and against kyriarchal structures of domination in antiquity and today. The history of these struggles in antiquity and throughout Western history still needs to be written.

become an extremely patriarchal institution, dominated by an all-male clergy'. He perceives the paradigm shift which I advocate ('Nevertheless she has been extremely successful in sensitizing modern scholars to an awareness of the social and political contexts in which the Gospels were produced and to consideration of ways in which this might have influenced the stories they relate'), but then does not explore this paradigm shift further.

INDEXES

INDEX OF REFERENCES

OLD TESTAMENT

NEW TESTAMENT

OTHER ANCIENT REFERENCES

INDEX OF AUTHORS